Reprints of Economic Classics

POLITICAL ECONOMY

AN INQUIRY INTO THE NATURAL GROUNDS OF RIGHT TO VENDIBLE PROPERTY OR WEALTH

POLITICAL ECONOMY

AN

INQUIRY

INTO THE

NATURAL GROUNDS OF RIGHT

TO

VENDIBLE PROPERTY

OR

WEALTH

BY

SAMUEL READ

WITH THE ADDITION OF

GENERAL STATEMENT OF AN ARGUMENT
ON THE SUBJECT OF POPULATION

AUGUSTUS M. KELLEY • PUBLISHERS
FAIRFIELD 1976

First Edition 1829
(*Edinburgh: Printed for the Author*;
and sold by Oliver & Boyd, *Edinburgh*; and Simpkin
& Marshall, *London*, 1829)

Reprinted 1976 by

AUGUSTUS M. KELLEY • PUBLISHERS

Fairfield, New Jersey 07006

Library of Congress Cataloging in Publication Data

Read, Samuel, fl. 1829.
Political economy.

Reprint of 2 works, the first of which was printed in 1829 for the author, Edinburgh; the second, printed in 1821 for T. & G. Underwood, London.
1. Economics. 2. Property. I. Read, Samuel, fl. 1829. General statement of an argument on the subject of population. 1974. II. Title.
HB161.R28 1974 330.1'6 68-56570
ISBN 0-678-00959-7

PRINTED IN THE UNITED STATES OF AMERICA
by SENTRY PRESS, NEW YORK, N. Y. 10013
Bound by A. HOROWITZ & SON, CLIFTON, N. J.

POLITICAL ECONOMY.

AN

INQUIRY

INTO

THE NATURAL GROUNDS OF RIGHT

TO

VENDIBLE PROPERTY,

OR

WEALTH.

BY SAMUEL READ.

EDINBURGH:
PRINTED FOR THE AUTHOR;
AND SOLD BY
OLIVER & BOYD, EDINBURGH, AND SIMPKIN & MARSHALL,
LONDON.

1829.

PREFACE.

By all who are acquainted with the most recent and most noted works on Political Economy, it will be readily admitted that the science is at present in a very unsettled and unsatisfactory state. There is indeed scarcely a single doctrine—if we except that of *commercial freedom*, as explained long since by the French economists—upon which there is a perfect and uniform, or even a *general* agreement, among the numerous sects and schools into which this science is now divided.

Almost all Dr Smith's doctrines have been controverted and rejected separately by one or another, whilst every one still assents and adheres to the greater part of them, and whilst all still continue to bestow on their author the highest eulogiums. For although every different school and sect finds a fault, and picks out a feature to condemn, in the "Wealth of Nations," it so happens that where one finds a deformity, another finds a beauty; so that the greater part of that work is still approved of by the majority, and still it is deemed worthy of the highest commendations.

Such notoriously is the present condition of this science;* and it is now at length beginning to be pretty generally felt and acknowledged, that it has been chiefly owing to the admixture and addition of the dogmas and paradoxes of Mr Ricardo and his followers with the plain and luminous doctrines of Dr Smith that the result described has been brought about. Even the Edinburgh Review, which has long lent its sanction and its powerful aid to propagate those dogmas, seems at length inclined to look about upon them with suspicion, and to show palpable symptoms of a disposition to retrace its steps, and to repudiate the misshapen and unsightly brood it has been induced to foster. On the subject of *poor-laws* it has recanted downright,† and in the last number‡ it says, "There are so many crude and mischievous theories afloat which are dignified with the name of Political Economy, that the science is in no small danger of falling into disrepute with a large portion of the world."§

When I began the following work, although I was chiefly stimulated to undertake it from observing those numerous new, and, as it appeared to me, false theories, which were then first broached, it was my intention not to have

* If indeed that can deserve the name of *science* in which so many discordant opinions and doctrines are so pertinaciously maintained.

† See No 94, article 2.

‡ No 95, p. 170.

§ What crude theory is it that the Edinburgh Review has not borne afloat and propagated, in reference to the subject alluded to, during the last ten years?

noticed or controverted them directly, but simply to have expounded and set forth what appeared to me to be the truth on the subjects to be treated, and so to have undermined and overturned them in the easiest manner. In the progress of my work, however, I found it impossible to adhere to this resolution, or to avoid all contact or collision with the authors and promulgators of those theories; and the reader will therefore find a considerable portion—I believe about one third of the book—of a controversial nature.

In thus departing from the plan I had originally chalked out for my guidance, it was a great satisfaction, and a pleasure to me to find myself encouraged and supported, and my apology on this head anticipated, by a very able writer on Political Economy, whose work was published while I was in the midst of these investigations.

"In the present state of Political Economy," says the writer I allude to, "a critical reference to the doctrines of preceding and contemporary economists cannot be avoided, and ought not to be avoided if it could. A mere direct expository treatise would be of far inferior utility. However true a doctrine may be, it is of little service until its relation to other doctrines, and its connexion with knowledge already extant, has been shown. Embarrassed as the science is with difficulties on which opinion is divided, it is of the utmost importance for its further progress, not only to explain and establish correct principles, but to expose the delusion which has formerly misled, to trace the process of error, to mark the particular point where inquiry departed from the right path, or where the unperceived fallacy, which has vitiated a train of reasoning, first insinuated itself into the argument. The science cannot yet be exhibited as a regular and perfect structure. The rubbish must be removed, the ground cleared, the scaffolding taken down, and all unnecessary and cumbrous appendages must be discarded, before the building can rise upon the eye in that simple beauty in which it is destined hereafter to appear."*

And further, the same author observes in the same place,—"From the defects here imputed to the science, it is evident that in any work, which professes to examine and remove them, the points discussed must be questions as to

---

* See the preface to "A Critical Dissertation on the Nature, Measures, and Causes of Value," by the author of "Essays on the Formation and Publication of Opinions."

Notwithstanding the very high respect I entertain for this author, it will be seen in the course of the following pages, that I find occasion to differ from him very widely in his main positions in the "Critical Dissertation." It appears to me that the fundamental error in that work, and that from which all the others to be found in it flow, consists in his treating of value as if it were *a mere relation of commodities between themselves*; whereas it appears to me that the idea of value in commodities *cannot even be conceived* without being mingled with the idea of their relation to mankind and to human labour, of which *some portion* must always be employed in producing or procuring them originally.

Lord Lauderdale is quoted as an authority for saying, "We cannot express value, or a variation of value, without a comparison of two commodities," (see the work referred to, p. 4.) Now this is a mistake, for we can express it by a comparison with labour, which is *not a commodity*.

the use of terms, the distinction of ideas, the logical dependence of arguments, rather than questions of fact or evidence, and that its character will be essentially critical, and even polemic."

But, although it may be true perhaps that this science "cannot yet be exhibited as a regular and perfect structure," and although in its present state the mere removal of "the rubbish" would be a service of no mean importance, still it is hoped that something more than this is accomplished in the following performance.

Political Economy has been hitherto designated as the science which treats of the production and distribution of wealth, and it has been totally overlooked that this includes the demonstration of the right to wealth. It is here therefore, for the first time, treated as an investigation concerning the right to wealth, (or property;) and this innovation, while it gives a more important and a more definite object to the science, presents it under a new and totally different aspect from that in which it has hitherto appeared, and causes it to assume an entirely new shape. Whether this be an improvement, or the contrary, it will be for the readers, and for those impartial persons who are acquainted with the subject, to decide.

ROSLIN, October, 1829.

To obviate an objection that may be taken to our *Title*, and to the way in which the word *Natural* is used in it, I adduce the following explanation of the meaning of that word, whence the sense will appear in which it is here employed:—

"NATURAL may be opposed either to what is *unusual, miraculous*, or *artificial*. In the two former senses, justice and property are undoubtedly natural."—*Hume; Inquiry concerning the Principles of Morals, Appendix 3,—note.*

"If self-love, if benevolence be natural to man; if reason and forethought be also natural; then may the epithet be applied to justice, order, fidelity, property, society. Men's inclination, their necessities, lead them to combine; their understanding and experience tell them that this combination is impossible, where each governs himself by no rule, and pays no regard to the possessions of others: and from these passions and reflections conjoined, as soon as we observe like passions and reflections in others, the sentiment of justice, throughout all ages, has infallibly and certainly had place, to some degree or other, in every individual of the human species. In so sagacious an animal, what necessarily arises from the exertion of his intellectual faculties, may justly be esteemed natural."—*Hume; Inquiry concerning the Principles of Morals, Appendix 3.*

A sense of justice and property is found, as will be shown in the following work, even among savages; and shall we deny that to be natural to man which "has infallibly and certainly had place" in his bosom, and influenced his conduct "throughout all ages?"

ERRATA.

P. 374, line 1, for *keep*, read *help*.
— 46, last line but one, in note, for *and* read *or*.

CONTENTS.

Page

INTRODUCTION, ... xvii

BOOK I.

ON THE NATURAL GROUNDS OF RIGHT TO VENDIBLE PROPERTY OR WEALTH, AS ARISING FROM THE MANNER IN WHICH IT IS PRODUCED OR ACQUIRED ORIGINALLY, AND FROM THE CONDITIONS NECESSARY TO ITS EXISTENCE IN ANY CONSIDERABLE QUANTITY OR ABUNDANCE.

CHAPTER I.

Of Wealth, Property, and Value.—Wealth defined, ... 1

CHAPTER II.

Of the Matter and Forms of Wealth.—Nature of Production, ... 12

SECT. I.—The Nature of Production explained, ... ib.

II.—The Matter and Forms of Wealth reviewed, ... 18

CHAPTER III.

Analysis and Classification of Wealth in reference to its different Uses and Employments, ... 22

CHAPTER IV.

Of Productive and Unproductive Labour, ... 35

CHAPTER V.

Of the Class of *Non-labourers*; or of those Persons who do not labour at all, or need to labour, ... 42

Page

SECT. I.—That the only Persons entitled to exemption from Labour, are the Proprietors of Land and the Proprietors of Capital,.....42

II.—Of the Manner in which Capital improves the Condition of the Labouring Class,.....48

III.—Conclusion of the Chapter,.....56

CHAPTER VI.

Of the material Means or Instruments of Production, and that these are the only original Sources of Wealth, ...61

CHAPTER VII.

Of the Manner in which Capital contributes to Production,.....65

SECT. I.—Capital defined—Its potent Agency in Production—Distinction of fixed and circulating Capitals—The Acquisition or Existence of both those Sorts of Capitals, or of Capital in general, a Condition necessary to the Existence or Attainment of the System of the Division of Labour, ...ib.

II.—Of the Mode in which the Division of Labour produces its Effect of assisting and improving the Powers of Production,...71

III.—That the Acquisition or Existence of Capital is a Condition necessary to the Establishment or Existence of the Division of Labour, ...80

IV.—Conclusion of the Chapter.—That all Wealth is *not* produced by Labour alone, but by Labour and Capital together,......83

CHAPTER VIII.

The natural Grounds of Right to Property defined and enumerated,.......89

CHAPTER IX.

The Three original Grounds of Right to Property traced to their Foundation in the Principles of Human Nature, ...94

SECT. I.—Of the Right to Property founded on Labour,.....ib.

II.—Of the Right to Land,.....100

III.—Of the Right to Capital in general,.....118

CHAPTER X.

Of the Moral Causes of Production,.....140

SECT. I.—The Two grand Moral Causes of Production delineated, and a highly-important concurrent Effect of these Causes pointed out,.....140

II.—Of the First Moral Cause of Production,.....143

Page

SECT. III.—Of the Second Moral Cause of Production,..................146

IV.—Of the Effects of good Government,..........................154

BOOK II.

ON THE CAUSES WHICH, UNDER THE SYSTEM OF THE DIVISION OF LABOUR, NATURALLY REGULATE THE DISTRIBUTION OF WEALTH, AND WHICH UNDER GOOD GOVERNMENT NECESSARILY DETERMINE THE EXACT SHARE THAT EVERY DIFFERENT INDIVIDUAL IS ENTITLED TO CONSUME, OR TO POSSESS AND COMMAND, IN STRICT ACCORDANCE WITH THE NATURAL GROUNDS OF RIGHT TO IT, AS THESE HAVE BEEN EXPLAINED IN THE PRECEDING BOOK.

CHAPTER I.

General Exposition of the Causes which naturally regulate the Distribution of Wealth under the System of the Division of Labour, and of the Principle on which these Causes depend,..........................177

SECT. I.—Demonstration of the Principle which naturally regulates the Distribution of Wealth under the System of the Division of Labour,.. ib.

II.—General Statement of the Effects in regard to Distribution, which the Principle explained in the foregoing Section is naturally calculated to produce,.............................183

CHAPTER II.

Of the Instrument of Distribution,—Money,.................................192

CHAPTER III.

That Labour is the only certain Measure of Value,........................199

APPENDIX TO CHAPTER III.

On the Nature of Value,..219

SECT. I.—Introduction,.. ib.

II.—Of the *Puzzle* founded on the Nature of Exchangeable Value, and on the Notion of its being a mere Relation of Commodities between themselves,.......................................220

III.—Of Absolute Value,..227

Page

CHAPTER IV.

Of the Causes which regulate the Price of Commodities; what constitutes Cost of Production, and what the constituent Parts of Price really are, ...231

SECT. I.—Of Natural and Market Price.—Price defined,.... ib.

II.—That the Labour expended in Production regulates the Natural Price of Commodities in the early Period of Society, before the Labourer and Capitalist become distinct Persons, and that the Capital expended regulates it after that Period,....236

CHAPTER V.

The distinct Nature of the three different Denominations of Income or Revenue, namely, Rent, Wages, and Profit or Interest, explained and discriminated, ...243

CHAPTER VI.

Of the Profit or Interest of Stock or Capital,....262

SECT. I.—Profit of Stock defined,.... ib.

II.—Of the Circumstances which regulate and determine the ordinary and average, or natural Rate of Profit, at any particular Time and Place,....273

CHAPTER VII.

Of the Rent of Land,....292

SECT. I.—Rent defined,.... ib.

II.—Of the Circumstances which regulate the Amount of Rent at any particular Time or Place,....297

III.—Corollary from the preceding View of the Nature and Causes of Rent—That the Interest of the Land-Proprietors is inseparably connected with the Interest of the Community, ...302

CHAPTER VIII.

Of the Wages of Labour,....307

SECT. I.—Of the Right to Wages—Limits of that Right defined—Wages defined, ... ib.

II.—Of the Circumstances which give occasion to a difference of Wages in different Employments,....314

III.—Of the Causes which regulate the natural Rate of Wages,....325

Page

CHAPTER IX.

Of Poor-Laws,..342

Sect. I.—Introduction to the Chapter,.................................... ib.

II.—The Poor-Laws of England ill-contrived and imperfect, considered as a System calculated for all Times and Circumstances—Still worse administered.—Possibility of a Legal and Compulsory Provision for the Poor, without thereby increasing their Numbers,....................................344

III.—Right of the Poor to Support,....................................363

CHAPTER X.

Of Taxes and Public Debts,..376

Sect. I.—Taxes defined—That all three distinct Sorts of Revenue afford Taxes, Wages as well as Profit and Rent,.................376

II.—Of Taxes and Public Debts as they affect the Condition of the Labouring Classes of People,.................................383

Appendix to the last Chapter, ...392

INTRODUCTION.

PART I.

The rights and duties of men in society have reference to three distinct objects;—to *persons*, to *property*, and to the whole society or *state*; and the science of politics,—which is the science of *all that is right and wrong, and that should, or should not, be established as compulsatory law*, in regard to those rights and duties,—naturally divides itself into three several parts, or branches, every one of which grows, in time, to be treated and regarded as a separate and distinct science by itself.

The peculiar object of each of these three several parts, or branches, of political science may be stated as follows:—

I. The first branch is that which is confined to the investigation and demonstration of all that is right and wrong, and that should, or should not, be established as compulsatory law, or "positive institution,"* in regard to those rights and duties of men in society, which relate chiefly or exclu-

* If I might be allowed to *coin* a word, which seems to me very necessary here, I would say *institutional*, in the sense of established and compulsatory law, and as opposed to, or distinct from, natural law or right. Established or institutional law may be right or wrong; but natural law is the same thing with natural or real right itself.

sively to the *person*, its safety and liberty; and which, although it has not yet been distinguished (in so far at least as I am aware) by any very appropriate, or generally recognized appellation, has nevertheless been very amply and ably treated, in all its details, by a numerous class of writers.

II. The second branch of political science is that which comprises the investigation and demonstration of all that is right and wrong, and that should, or should not, be established as compulsatory or institutional law, in regard to those rights and duties of men in society which relate chiefly or exclusively to property,—i. e. *transferable property* or *wealth*,—and which has lately grown up into an extensive and important separate science, under the name of "Political Economy."*

---

* It might have been called, perhaps with greater propriety, the science of Political Justice; seeing that its chief object is to demonstrate what is just or unjust, in all the most important and difficult points relating to the production and distribution of property or wealth; property (*i. e.* vendible or transferable property) being the chief, if not the only, subject of the virtue of justice. The terms *just* and *unjust* are nearly, if not altogether, synonymous with those of *honest* and *dishonest;* and are applied chiefly, if not exclusively, to conduct or actions which have property for their subject; and it will be found that all the discussions in Political Economy are directly or indirectly connected with the illustration of justice:—as, for example, those concerning free trade, monopolies, or restrictions, and other regulations of commerce, go to show their justice or injustice, as interfering, properly or improperly, with the production and distribution, and consequently with the *possession* or enjoyment, and consequently with the right, to wealth or property.

I may add, that those discussions, and the science itself of Political Economy, are chiefly, if not exclusively, valuable in proportion as they tend to illustrate the subject of right or justice in regard to the distribution, or acquisition and possession, of property.

III. The third and last division of the science of politics is that which includes all questions as to the rights and duties of independent states, or as to all that is right and wrong in their intercourse and treatment of one another, and which is well enough designated and understood by the title of "International Law."

These three divisions comprise the whole body of the science of politics; which is manifestly therefore the science of *natural* or *real right* in regard to property, and to personal as well as national security and liberty:—by natural or real right being understood, such *modes of conduct* and *relations* to persons and property as can be demonstrated to be consistent with the general good of mankind, and the best form of civil society, or with "those general principles which," as has been observed by a writer of the highest class and authority,* "ought to run through and be the foundation of the laws of all nations."†

It will be observed from what has been now stated, that political science takes cognizance of that class of rights and duties only which fall to be guaranteed or regulated by institutional law and force,—that is to say, the observance of which must be *compelled*, when necessary, by the whole force of the society—excluding altogether from its view or jurisdiction that other and perhaps still more numerous class which are discretionary; or which, although they may be not less imperative than the former in point of moral obligation, must yet be left to the free will and judgment, or conscience, of the obligant, as not being of that peculiar and determinate character which should render them fit to be enforced by compulsatory law.

---

* Dr Smith.

† Theory of Moral Sentiments, part 7, sec. 4, at the end.

With regard to the *first* and *third* branches of Political Science, (taking them in the order in which they are set down above,) we are to have nothing to do with *them* in the following treatise; and I have only mentioned them here for the purpose of laying them expressly and distinctly aside, and of circumscribing, by that means, the more perfectly our field of inquiry,* which is to be entirely and strictly confined to the second division above-mentioned, viz. Political Economy or Political Justice.

Political Economy has, by most late writers, been described as the science which investigates the "Laws"† which regulate the production and distribution (to which

---

* It appears to me to be essential to the improvement and perfection of the different branches of Political and Moral Science, to know their precise nature, extent, and limits,—their *genealogy* or *affinities*, so to speak,—and the place which they occupy in the field of human knowledge; and always to treat them after this manner, and to keep in view those affinities, might greatly facilitate the work of one day combining and exhibiting them as one connected, consentaneous, and complete whole.

There is another rule which I will here notice as of the utmost importance, and indeed altogether indispensable to any improvement in the moral sciences, and that is to treat them always with a reference to that great end for which alone all human science is or ought to be cultivated, namely, the furthering of the happiness of the world, or of mankind. Nothing is so well calculated to keep us from falling into errors, or to bring us back into the right path, when we have wandered from it, as to have this great end constantly in sight, and to make constant reference to it when difficulties occur. This is the golden rule for philosophizing, in this department, above all others.

† Meaning, of course, the *natural laws*, which are observed to regulate the production and distribution of wealth under the system of the division of labour, and of barter, or exchange, and where the right to accumulate as well as to freely produce and exchange property (which is an essential part of the system of the division of labour) is guaranteed and maintained to every individual by the united force of the whole society or government.

some persons have added, very needlessly in my opinion, the *consumption*) of wealth. But there is another and a far more important and more interesting subject, upon which the investigation of the laws which regulate the production and distribution of wealth is calculated to throw a new and clear light, and which it is now full time should be introduced and shown forth as one of the chief objects of the science of Political Economy,—namely, upon the natural grounds of right to it. For as the right to wealth or transferable property is acquired solely from the manner in which it is produced and exchanged, or distributed, under the system of the division of labour; that system does in fact consign it, as it were, to its proper owners; or what comes to the same thing, the natural laws which regulate barter or exchange under that system, (where men are allowed to act freely under them, without any undue or unnecessary constraint or restrictions,) cause it to fall *necessarily* into the hands of those who have the proper or natural right to it. Yet this most interesting and most important object of Political Economy has been entirely overlooked by preceding writers; and although it has necessarily happened that the whole drift of their reasonings, and all the arguments employed by them, (where they have not deviated altogether into paradox and absurdity,) have always had a tendency, more or less apparent, to illustrate the question of right to property,* they have never once mentioned that question

* It may indeed seem very obvious that the science of the production and distribution of wealth or property—the common definition of Political Economy—can be nothing else but the science of what has been called the rights of property. If you explain correctly how property is produced, and how it is properly or justly distributed, you must of necessity show the natural grounds of right to it; that is, you must show who it is that, according to the natural and equitable laws of distribution, should possess and enjoy it—that is, in other words, who has the right to it.

as forming any part of their subject, and far less have they ever thought of treating it, directly or expressly, as a leading point in their inquiries.

Nor ought this perhaps to be considered as altogether so surprising a circumstance as at first sight it may appear to be; for it often happens in the infancy of the different sciences, that all their usefulness, and all the subjects on which they are destined to throw light, do not discover themselves at once, and frequently not until a considerable progress has been made in them. Still, however, it will be admitted that the want of a distinct perception of the chief and ultimate object of our inquiries must form a serious obstruction to our successful prosecution of them; and it is probably much owing to this circumstance, that so little advance or improvement has been made in the science of Political Economy since the time of Dr Smith, notwithstanding the greatly increased attention which the subject has attracted of late years, and the immense volume of disquisition that has been published upon it.*

* It is true, that many of the questions in Political Economy have received a more ample discussion, and some of its soundest doctrines a fuller and more complete demonstration and development; but no real or considerable advance or improvement, or any thing deserving the name of *discovery*, has been made in the science since the period mentioned in the text. On the contrary, the new theories which are so much in vogue at present, appear to me to rest on a far too slender and insufficient foundation of fact and argument to be accounted such; instead of advancing the science, they seem rather to have thrown it back, and have given to the present inquiries respecting it a totally erroneous and unprofitable bent; and of this perhaps it may be deemed no unequivocal indication or evidence, that the late supposed improvements, instead of reconciling contrary opinions, and throwing a clear light upon its more abstruse questions, have totally overclouded and involved them in a thicker darkness, and have introduced many new points of difference which did not before exist.

If, indeed, we go back to the period when Dr Smith wrote, and to the state in which he found the science, it will not appear at all extraordinary that the view of it here explained should not have been taken, or rather should not have been brought conspicuously or expressly forward by him; for, having the cue now given, it will not be difficult to discover that all his disquisitions, and the whole drift and tendency of his arguments, as has been already hinted, point more or less obviously and unequivocally to this object. But it was not then necessary to extend the view so far, or perhaps even *possible* to treat the subject with advantage, in the manner here proposed, until many preliminary topics and extensive questions were previously discussed and settled. After the publication of the "Wealth of Nations," however, this view of the subject was brought comparatively near; and had Dr Smith lived to proceed farther in that great work, the design of which he has recorded at the conclusion of his "Theory of Moral Sentiments,"* or rather, had he *found* the science of political economy in the advanced state in which he *left* it, and come to the farther consideration of the subject with unexhausted vigour, it is not to be doubted but that the view here given would have opened upon him, and that he would have carried his inquiries to a degree of perfection which would have left little now to wish for or to add. But be this as it may, it seems to me now to be absolutely necessary to the further progress of the science, that it should be treated in this manner; that it should be well understood, and explicitly set down in the front of the discussion, that the great object of political economy is to point out and demonstrate the natural grounds of right upon which the great laws of property are or ought

* See likewise the *advertisement* prefixed to that work.

to be founded, and upon which they must ultimately rest for their justification and stability.

As to what the institutional or established law *actually is* or *has been*, at any period of time, or in any particular country, we shall have nothing to do with that question in the following investigations,—*that* is a subject of inquiry which belongs properly to the lawyers and judges of the time and place, whose business and office it is to propound, declare, and administer the laws whatever they may be. Our subject, on the contrary, is to demonstrate and determine what the established law *should be* in all matters relating to wealth or property, at all times and in all countries, without knowing or caring what it is in any.

The established laws, indeed, in countries which have a code approaching in any reasonable degree to common sense or justice, will of course coincide generally with the natural law, and consequently legal with natural right. But in no country will this coincidence be found universal or complete, since all the world knows that, even in countries where the institutions are the least imperfect, what is called a *legal right* is not unfrequently a natural and moral *wrong.**

---

* It is not, of course, insinuated that absolute perfection is to be attained in the laws or government of any state, any more than in the human character itself, or affairs in general; but if there is any one department of law which, more than any other, may be expected to approach perfection, it is that which relates to property and justice; and if absolute perfection should be unattainable even here, still it is allowable (I hope laudable) to endeavour to advance as near to it as we can. And it will not now, I trust, be considered as any improbable or unwarranted position to hold, that, by investigation, discussion, and reasoning, the laws may be improved in all countries, and legal and moral rights be made to approximate more nearly to one another than they yet do in any country, or under any government, even the best that exists; for the case with regard to improvement (it can never be

And yet it has been asserted by an author of no mean consideration or authority, that the only foundation of our right to property is "the law of the land,"* as if just grounds in reason could not be shown why certain *rules* or *relations*, and *modes of conduct*, in regard to property, *should be* "the law of the land;" or as if one set of such rules, or relations, and modes of conduct, could not be shown to be *better*, or more consistent with the general good of mankind, than another; which to assert would be to contend, that there was no such thing as right or wrong antecedent to "positive institution," and consequently no

---

too frequently repeated) is essentially altered now from what it was in times past, in consequence of that important event, *the invention of printing*, by means of which the experience and discoveries of every passing age are preserved, treasured up, and diffused so effectually, that right becomes ultimately so plain and obvious that it must be acted upon.

* Dr Paley, Moral and Political Philosophy, book iii. part i. chap 4. It is in reference to property in land more especially that this author has applied the assertion alluded to in the text, viz. that "the real foundation of our right is the law of the land;" but what is most extraordinary is, that Dr Paley had no sooner pronounced this "extraordinary aphorism," than, as if altogether forgetful of what he had just said, he proceeds *immediately* to adduce *reasons why* the institution of which he speaks *should be* "the law of the land;" and elsewhere he states many reasons to account for the institution of property in general, endeavouring to deduce from them the important fact, that, "with a few exceptions, even the poorest and the worst provided, in countries where property and the consequences of property prevail, are in a better situation with respect to food, raiment, houses, and what are called the necessaries of life, than *any* are in places where most things remain in common," (p. 82,)—a fact which, it is hoped, will be made fully apparent in the course of the following work; and which should be sufficient to justify the institution of property on better and more enduring grounds than the mere fact that such institution exists.

such thing as good or evil, happiness or misery, pain or pleasure, in the world.

But there is no law or institution relating to property, (especially the more important or fundamental laws,) whose effects will not be either good or bad, useful or detrimental, and consistent or inconsistent with the general good of mankind, and which may not therefore be shown to be so; that is, be shown to be right or wrong, and consequently proper or improper to be established. And although this may appear somewhat difficult whilst we are unused to such investigations, it can only be really so in very unimportant instances; for we need not by any means despair of discovering moral as well as physical truth, if the same freedom be allowed, the same methods pursued, and the same ardour and perseverance exhibited in the investigation of the one as of the other.

In their notions concerning right to property, the great bulk of mankind seldom give place to any idea beyond the legal rights, or actual tenures, by which it is held. Nor ought this to call forth any surprise, seeing that these are the only effectual rights for the time being, and those alone which immediately affect men's interests,—a consideration which necessity too often compels the greater number to be so much concerned about, as to leave them but little either of leisure or inclination to attend to matters so remotely affecting them, and so far removed out of the beaten track, as the grounds on which they have been instituted. But what is indeed to be wondered at is, that we so very frequently observe a like ignorance or inattention where it has no proper excuse;—that we observe every day men, and even legislators, pretending to reason concerning political justice and the general principles of law, as if there were no such distinction as that which has been here pointed out, and who seem to have scarcely the most distant comprehension that there is a *natural code* discoverable by the light of reason, to which alone reference ought to be had when any law, or project of law, is brought into question either for the purpose of enactment or repeal. Instead of *reasoning like legislators*, such persons merely *contend as lawyers*; they but inquire *what is*, or *what has been*, not *what ought to be*; and, provided they can find a *precedent*, think they have no need to trouble themselves with any farther investigation as to right or wrong. They pronounce the two cabalistic words, "vested right," and think themselves at once intrenched behind an impregnable fortress, without considering it as at all incumbent upon them to show that the investiture is consistent with real and natural right.

But the actual tenures, or legal rights, whereby property is held, may be "vested" either according to or contrary to real right; that is to say, either, *first*, under authority of established law founded upon and coinciding with real right or justice, when they will, of course, be perfectly unexceptionable; or, *secondly*, under authority of established law alone, in opposition to real right and justice; in which case it will be not *right* but *wrong* that they should continue to be "vested" or established law.* And this is the

---

* When, however, we would repeal or alter any established law affecting property which is found to be wrong, it is, I trust, almost unnecessary to observe, that it must be done with a due regard to the interests of present incumbents, or those who repose under the immediate sanction of legal rights. The laws must of course be obeyed while they continue to be laws, (so long at least as they are not altogether oppressive and intolerable,) and the happiness or misery of human creatures must not be wantonly sported with; only we must not on this pretence endeavour to perpetuate abuses, or to consecrate wrong, as if we could convert it into right. Our denunciation is against the claim of *perpetuity* for error; and all we would desire is, that right should be gradually and deliberately introduced, when it is

sole question as respects the lawgiver, or those inquirers who would investigate the principles of natural right with a view to the improvement of established law.

If those persons, therefore, who advocate the authority of "vested rights," would say any thing to the purpose in their favour, they must show, not only that they *are*, but that they *should be* "vested;" they must be able to advance reasons why they should be vested; they must, in a word, show that they are *right* in the proper sense of the term; namely, that they are calculated to promote the general interest and advantage or happiness of mankind.

I shall conclude this part of the introductory observations I have to advance with affirming, that what has been established by human authority may be altered by human authority, if found to be wrong; but what is sanctioned by reason, and established in the nature of things, is right at all times, and in every region, and cannot be justly, nor, in enlightened times, safely or permanently contravened or contradicted by human institutions.

PART II.

If we examine with attention the questions and disputes which so much divide and agitate the different classes of men in society, and in this country at present, in reference to property, it will be easy to discover that the most serious of all is the conflicting claims and pretensions of labour and

---

made undeniably apparent and familiar to the eyes and understandings of mankind.

capital to the wealth which is produced by the *use* of the one and the *exertion* of the other. This question, however it may be disguised, is really at the bottom of most others *of a general kind* relating to property; and it will never be ended or settled until the subject be thoroughly investigated and probed to the bottom, and until either party be convinced, on grounds of argument and reason, that full justice is done to them.

Although it seems to be one of the most obvious things imaginable, that, in all advanced periods of society, *capital* is at least as potent in its effects as *labour* in the production of wealth; yet the labourers have been flattered and persuaded that they produce all;* whilst the capitalists, on the other hand, not contented with their proper and just advantages, as being the possessors and proprietors of capital, and with the profit *naturally* and *fairly* arising from it, have combined and established laws of preference and favour—laws of restriction, monopoly, and exclusion—which increase that profit beyond its legitimate bounds, and really trench upon the rights of the labourers, not only as limiting unnecessarily and partially, and consequently *unjustly*, the

---

* The Ricardo economists maintain that "labour is the *only* source of wealth!"—(See Macculloch's Principles of Political Economy.) "The labour of the country," says Mr Ricardo himself, in his pamphlet on Protection to Agriculture, "constitutes its only real source of wealth;"—and the whole of the first chapter of his Principles of Political Economy consists of an elaborate, though indirect attempt to prove that labour produces all, as if capital produced nothing, and was not a "real" source of wealth also! It is truly astonishing that this doctrine should have been maintained till this time of day in a country where the effects of capital are so remarkably conspicuous. This most mischievous and fundamental error will, it is hoped, be found fully refuted in the following work. See in particular upon this subject chap. v. sec. 2, chap. vii. sec. 4, and chap. ix. sec. 3, of the First Book.

field for their exertions, but in various other ways preventing those exertions from being crowned with that ample and adequate remuneration which would naturally and necessarily reward them under a different and juster system.

Practical politicians are accustomed to treat this question with much contempt, and think they do enough when they "put down" its overt results. But it is not in this manner it will ever be finally or satisfactorily settled. The labourers are too numerous and powerful a body to be dealt unjustly by when they are made fully aware of their rights; and their means of information, and consequently their power, are increasing much too rapidly to give room for any hopes that they will allow the question to rest unresolved, or that they will be satisfied without full and complete justice.

"The improved education of the labouring classes," says a very able writer* and advocate of the labourers, "ought, in the present question, to have great weight with statesmen, and with the community at large. The schools, which are everywhere established, or are establishing, for their instruction, make it impossible for the greatest visionary to suppose that any class of men can much longer be kept in ignorance of the PRINCIPLES on which societies are formed and governed. Mechanics' Institutions will teach men the moral as well as the physical sciences. They excite a disposition to probe all things to the bottom, and supply the means of carrying research into every branch of knowledge. He must be a very blind statesman who does not see, in this, indications of a more extensive change in the frame of society than has ever yet been made. This change will not be effected by violence, and cannot be counteracted by force. No Holy Alliance can put down the quiet insurrection by which know-

---

* A writer, however, whom we shall have occasion strongly to controvert in the following work, (see chap. ix. sect. 3, of Book i.) but whom, nevertheless, we perfectly agree with here.

ledge will subvert whatever is not founded in justice and truth. The interest of the different classes of labourers who are now first beginning to think and act as a body, in opposition to the other classes among whom, with themselves, the produce of the earth is distributed, and who are now only for the first time beginning to acquire as extensive a knowledge of the principles of government as those who rule, is too deeply implicated by these principles to allow them to stop short in their career of inquiry. They may care nothing about the curious researches of the geologist, or the elaborate classification of the botanist, but they will assuredly ascertain WHY they only, of all the classes of society, have always been involved in poverty and distress. They will not stop short of any ultimate truth; and they have experienced too few of the advantages of society to make them feel satisfied with the present order of things. The mind is rather invigorated than enfeebled by the labour of the hands; and they will carry forward their investigations undelayed by the pedantry of learning, and undiverted by the fastidiousness of taste. By casting aside the prejudices which fetter the minds of those who have benefited by their degradation, they have every thing to hope. On the other hand, they are the sufferers by these prejudices, and have every thing to dread from their continuance. Having no reason to love those institutions which limit the reward of labour, whatever may be its produce, to a bare subsistence, they will not spare them, whenever they see the hollowness of the claims made on their respect. As the labourers acquire knowledge, the foundations of the social edifice will be dug up from the deep beds into which they were laid in times past, they will be curiously handled and closely examined, and they will not be restored unless they were originally laid in justice, and unless justice commands their preservation."*

---

* Labour defended against the Claims of Capital, &c., by a Labourer, pp. 30, 31. (London, 1825)

Dr Smith himself was not, it must be admitted, wholly free from error in his treatment of the question between the labourers and capitalists. He does not indeed treat that question directly, but, speaking of "the circumstances of the lower ranks of the people,"—of "servants, labourers, and workmen of different kinds,"—he says incidentally, "it is but equity that they who feed, clothe, and lodge the whole body of the people should have such a share of the produce of their own labour as to be themselves tolerably well fed, clothed, and lodged;*" meaning evidently, from the context, that the labourers alone feed, clothe, and lodge "the whole body of the people,"—an error which, though incidental, (and the position maintained therefore not probably deliberately or well considered,) is not the less likely, if unnoticed, to be attended with bad effects, and is by far the most important oversight that is to be discovered in the Wealth of Nations. For this position would seem to imply that capital is of no use, and affords no assistance in the work of feeding, clothing, and lodging the people!—a position which, if put in this shape, would at once have shown the importance of the fallacy which lurked in that apparently harmless sentence; and Dr Smith would at once have granted that the present generation of labourers could *not* FEED the people as well as they are now fed, if no *capital* had been expended and accumulated upon the land, or no farm-buildings, no fences, no drains, or other improvements, calculated to assist the labourer and increase the produce, had been made upon it previously to the present day. He would have granted that the existing generation of labourers could *not* CLOTHE the people as well as they are now clothed, if there were no cotton-mills, weaving-looms, or other machinery of any kind in existence:—and, lastly, he would have granted

* Wealth of Nations, book i. chap. 8.

that the existing generation of labourers could *not* LODGE the people as well as they are now lodged, if no houses had been built in former times, and left to the present proprietors and occupiers, or if, just when the present labourers came to be able to work, all the towns, villages, and houses throughout the country had been swept into ruins! And yet to admit these obvious truths is wholly to give up the portentous doctrine that the labourers alone feed, clothe, and lodge the whole body of the people, and at once to destroy the inference which must otherwise have been founded upon it, to the prejudice of the capitalists. To talk of equity as demanding that the labourers should receive a "*share* of the produce of their own labour" will never be satisfactory; why should they not receive the whole of its produce? The error lies in supposing that labour produces all,—that the whole of the produce of labour and capital arises from the exertions of the labourers, independently of the capital with which they work, and are assisted.

The capitalists have indeed always appeared to decline looking into the bottom of this question, as if afraid they should discover in it nothing to their advantage; but there are, in truth, no real grounds for any apprehensions on this head; and they will never enjoy their wealth in confidence and quiet till they discard this slavish and groundless fear, and meet their adversaries, as they may very safely do, on the fair field of argument and reason.

The labourers must be informed, and made to understand, that they *do not* produce all wherever they take the assistance of capital; and the capitalists lending that assistance must be equally instructed that whilst each should be free to demand what he pleases for his particular contribution or portion of capital, no individual, or body of men, can have right to exclude or interdict others from coming forward with their portions or capitals also, in open and equal competition, or to attempt to enhance their gains by means which are unjust and injurious to their neighbours.

In the following work an attempt is made to elucidate this question with the views that have been stated, and with an equal and impartial regard to the rights and just interests of the parties concerned; and if it is not discussed in its utmost extent, or with all that minuteness and fulness of detail which its importance demands, still it is hoped that such hints are given, and such a train laid, as may serve for the groundwork of a full discussion of it, and as may lead to a permanent and satisfactory adjustment of all the claims and interests involved in that discussion, upon the only principles that can be either satisfactory or permanent—those of equity and justice.

AN INQUIRY, &c.

BOOK I.

ON THE NATURAL GROUNDS OF RIGHT TO VENDIBLE PROPERTY OR WEALTH, AS ARISING FROM THE MANNER IN WHICH IT IS PRODUCED OR ACQUIRED ORIGINALLY, AND FROM THE CONDITIONS NECESSARY TO ITS EXISTENCE IN ANY CONSIDERABLE QUANTITY OR ABUNDANCE.

CHAPTER I.

OF WEALTH, PROPERTY, AND VALUE.—WEALTH DEFINED.

THAT sort of *property* or *wealth*, the protection and security of which forms the *second* grand object of law and government, and consequently of political science,—the protection and security of *persons* forming the *first*,—may be defined in two words,—*vendible property*. More particularly wealth may be defined as follows:—*Those external material objects, necessary, useful, or agreeable to mankind, which it costs some considerable exertion of human labour or industry to produce or acquire originally, and which, when once acquired, can be transferred from one to another—appropriated or alienated.*

1. Those things which nature provides in such abundance

as to exceed the desires or wants of mankind, as common air, the light and heat of the sun, &c., as they cannot be exclusively appropriated, and require not to be purchased by labour or industry, are not wealth; at least they are not that sort of wealth which requires to be protected or guaranteed to the possessor or proprietor by law and force, and consequently not that sort which can form any object of political science. Such things no person needs to buy, or will buy, and such things no person can sell. They are not vendible property.

2. Again, those things which are inherent and inalienable, however valuable they may be, and however limited in quantity, as the organs and members of our bodies, as well as our natural and acquired talents or abilities, though necessary, useful, and indispensable as the means or instruments of acquiring wealth, are not wealth themselves. Such things cannot be transferred from one to another, and they are therefore not wealth or vendible property. Vigorous and robust limbs and organs, or corporeal powers, as well as art or skill in professions and employments, with many other natural and acquired talents or abilities,—may increase the quantity or improve the quality of our labour; but labour is not wealth, but a part of the means only of producing or procuring it. For although wealth may arise from labour when it is employed in particular ways, none can arise from it till it be exerted; and man himself, unless where he is a slave and the property of another, is not actual wealth, but one of the instruments by which it is produced.

3. But those things necessary, useful, or agreeable to mankind, which can be appropriated or alienated, and which are only to be procured by the assistance and industry of man himself, as corn, cloth, houses, &c., as they require to be protected and guaranteed to the possessor or proprietor by law and force, so they are necessarily the objects of political science in general, and they constitute exclusively that

sort of wealth which is the peculiar subject of justice and of political economy.

The foregoing definition admits of being divided into two separate and distinct affirmative propositions, each of which may be illustrated by itself as follows:—

I. *That sort of wealth which is the object of political science, or of political economy, must require some considerable exertion of human labour to produce or procure it originally, and must be capable of being exclusively appropriated.*

1. There are some things which never are, or can be, wealth or vendible property, under any circumstances; because under no circumstances can they ever be exclusively appropriated, nor can they ever require any portion of labour or industry to produce or procure them. Such are those things first mentioned above, namely, the air, which surrounds us at all times, and the light and heat of the sun, which are rayed out upon us gratuitously. Such things never can become the objects of political science; because the interposition or assistance of society, or of law and force, can never be required to guarantee the possession of them; all men being at full liberty to use and enjoy as much as they please of those first and most indispensable of all necessaries, at all times, without price, and without challenge or charge.

2. Again, there are some things which are wealth in one situation and not in another, because it requires labour or industry to procure them in the one and not in the other. Such things are common sand and water.

Thus, sand upon the seashore, and water in a great river, are not wealth, because in those situations they can be procured with small and inconsiderable labour, viz. with so much merely as is necessary to lift them from the place where they lie; but let them be carried to a distance where the are wanted, and where they cannot be brought without considerable labour, and immediately they become wealth and vendible property. Let the sand, for example, be carried to any considerable distance, where it is wanted to be mixed with lime for building, and it then becomes wealth. Here it is brought with considerable exertion of labour or industry; and this circumstance it is, combined with the demand for it, that is, with the desire of mankind to possess it under such circumstances, which at once confers upon it the character of wealth. In like manner, water in a great river, where it can be had at will in unlimited quantity, and with no more labour than is merely required to lift it from the stream, is not wealth; at least it is not that sort of wealth which falls to be treated or considered in the science of Political Economy. But let the same element be brought to a distance,—let a part of the same river be carried, either by the labour of men directly, or by means of a canal or aqueduct, (in the construction and maintenance of which human labour is necessarily required,) to a neighbouring city, and then and there it instantly becomes wealth. It is not wealth at the river-side, where it can be had with small and inconsiderable exertion; but when by labour and industry it is brought where it is wanted, and where it is not otherwise to be had, then, and not before, it becomes wealth. If you could take the city, and place it by the river-side, or if it had been originally seated there, water, being in abundance, would never have become wealth, unless the extension of streets and houses were such as to require considerable labour and industry to bring an article so indispensable to its farthest parts.

But perhaps it may be said and objected, that even sand upon the seashore, and water in a great river, are wealth and property, as belonging to the proprietor of the adjoining land, who is not obliged to part with them, and might not choose to do so but for some equivalent price or knowledgment. In general, however, he does part with them under such circumstances without exacting any price; but if he should demand a price for such articles, and should succeed in obtaining any other vendible commodity in exchange for them, they would immediately acquire the character of wealth.

It may perhaps be thought and advanced as a farther objection to this part of our definition, that land was acquired at first without either labour or industry; but then, being free to all as air and water, and exceeding the desires or wants of mankind, it was not at that time wealth any more than air or water is now. Land was not then wealth, although its produce, which required labour and industry to gather and secure it, must still have retained that character. A tribe of shepherds who traversed the breadth of Tartary neither bought nor sold the land, nor considered it any part of their wealth; but their cattle, and the fodder which they gathered and stored up for them against winter, as well as the other articles of food or clothing for themselves, which they gathered from the land, must always have constituted a part of their wealth. Land may indeed, even now, be gotten in the uninhabited and unappropriated parts of the earth for nothing, or *for the taking;* but there it is hardly worth the taking, and its produce only where this is the case can be accounted wealth; but the moment the land is appropriated, and is not to be gotten for nothing, it acquires this character: and this is necessarily the state and condition of the land in all civilized and populous countries; because individual possession or appropriation of the land is a condition necessary to its being fully or highly cultivated and improved,—a condition without which neither population nor wealth could ever increase to any extent worth mentioning. In such countries therefore, and in such condition of the land, it must always be purchased by labour and industry, or, what comes to the same thing, by what has been procured or produced originally by labour and industry.

It is true, that in this condition of the land it may happen, and indeed often does happen, that particular parts of it increase in value without any labour at all being bestowed upon them, from the increase of wealth and population, and the expenditure of labour and capital on the parts adjacent; and if this should be thought an exception to the universality of the proposition above stated, or an objection of sufficient weight, our definition might easily be modified so as to obviate this objection, by the addition of the words, "land under particular conditions and circumstances." But the truth appears to be, that this seeming exception, even if it were more than seeming, is at all events so slight and inconsiderable, as hardly to deserve or require more particular notice.*

This, then, it appears, we may set down as one distinguishing characteristic of wealth, that those objects whereof it consists, are only to be produced or procured originally by the help of human labour.

In its most enlarged sense, the term wealth may perhaps be understood to signify abundance of every good thing, and may thus be allowed to include the free bounties of nature; but, as it is the object of political science, and of political justice, or of law and government, it must be confined to those good things which are bought with a price, which price must consist, either wholly or *in part*, of the labour and sweat of mankind themselves.

II. *That sort of wealth which is the object of political science, must be capable of being alienated or transferred from one to another.*

---

* It will not, however, be lost sight of hereafter, when occasion may require our attention to it.

The word *property*, it may be remarked, is commonly used by men of business and of the world to designate those things precisely which are meant to be understood by the term wealth, as explained by political economists. In the law courts, for example, we always hear the word property, never wealth; and in common discourse it is much the same:—we hear the one word ten times for once the other. But what sort of property is it we are to understand when we hear the word in our courts of law, or observe it used in the reports of law-proceedings? Or in common discourse when we hear such expressions as the following:—*A man of large property—much property was destroyed by that fire, or lost in that shipwreck*, or the like? What sort of property is it, I say, we are here to understand? Vendible property undoubtedly, and vendible property only.

Property is a word of very extensive signification;—as explained in our dictionaries, it denotes quality, disposition, or attribute, right of possession, as well as things possessed.

In reference to things possessed, property may be divided into two kinds, the alienable and inalienable; the former of which only can be wealth.

My eyes, my ears, and my limbs, are my property, but they are not wealth,—I cannot part with them. All the members and organs of my body, as well as my natural and acquired talents or abilities, are properties belonging to me; but I cannot call them wealth, because they are inalienable. These things are more exclusively and unequivocally my property than any external or foreign object can be; but they are not wealth. They cannot be sold, they cannot be appreciated. They are not so abundant either as to be in excess, and they are in the very highest degree useful, desirable, and necessary, and yet they are not wealth, because they are inalienable.

Could he eye be sold to the blind, or a limb to him who wants it, what price might they not command? Or rather I might say, what price should be sufficient to purchase them?

Again, the air I breathe, the light which glads my sight, and the heat which nourishes me, these things also are my property, at least so much of them as I actually consume. And nothing can be conceived more useful or more necessary; but they are not wealth, because they can neither be exclusively appropriated, nor do they require to be purchased by labour or industry. Of these things every man may consume, as was said before, as much as he pleases, without challenge and without charge. What he does consume of them he cannot alienate, and what is over his consumption he cannot appropriate. These things, therefore, are not, and never can be, vendible commodities.

This then, it appears, also, may be set down as another distinguishing characteristic of wealth, that it must be capable of being transferred from one to another, appropriated and alienated.

Dr Smith, indeed, in describing the *fixed capital* of a country, states as a part of it, "the acquired and useful abilities of all the inhabitants or members of the society."* But in this he is inconsistent with himself, and at variance with his own uniform idea of wealth, which he constantly designates as "the produce of land and labour;" according to which brief but comprehensive description of it, it is the produce only of those acquired and useful abilities that must be held to be wealth, not the qualities or capacities themselves. It is true, indeed, that a country which con-

* Wealth of Nations, book ii. chap. i.

tains an intelligent and industrious population, and multitudes of skilled or instructed labourers, having "acquired and useful abilities,"—possesses a great power of producing wealth, because, as was before observed, such abilities increase the quantity or improve the quality of our labour. But neither the persons nor qualities of a people, though the objects by which and for which all wealth exists, make any part of that wealth themselves; and all laws directly affecting them belong to a perfectly distinct department of political science, viz. to that branch of politics which relates to the protection and security of *persons*, and which we have already alluded to as forming the first grand object of law and government.

Before concluding the chapter, it will be proper to advert, though but shortly in this place, to the subject of *value*,* and to consider the two different meanings of that term, as resting upon the same grounds with those of the words already explained.

The word *value*, like the words property and wealth, has an enlarged and a limited signification. In its most extensive sense, it regards solely the utility of objects, or their necessity and subservience to human existence or well-being. Absolute value in any object is unquestionably in proportion to its utility or necessity, first to the existence, and secondly to the happiness of human creatures. Those things, however, which are furnished by nature in exhaustless profusion, however valuable they may be, and however necessary and indispensable to human existence, as air, water, &c., men trouble not themselves about; nor is there any reason why they should, when without trouble they have them.

---

* See this subject discussed more fully in appendix to chapter 3d of the second book.

Value in this sense forms no object of political science, or of political regulation,—government or law.

In its more confined sense, value relates entirely to the intensity of vendible quality in objects which fall short of the desires and necessities of mankind; in other words, to the quantity of one article which can be procured in exchange for another, or for labour, by voluntary consent of the proprietors, by treaty and agreement in the open market, that is, wherever commodities are bought and sold. Value in this sense is the same thing with price, which consists in the relative vendible power of commodities, and is generally proportioned to the quantity of labour and commodities, or capital expended in producing them; that is, to the cost of their production, which constitutes their *real price*, or, in other words, that price which is the indispensable condition or cause of their existence, and to which (though they may occasionally or temporarily depart from it,) they must always again return, and must continually gravitate towards it as to the "centre of repose and continuance."*

This twofold sense of the term value, here explained, is thus briefly and distinctly stated by Dr Smith:—"The word *value*," says he, "it is to be observed, has two different meanings, and sometimes expresses the utility of some particular object, and sometimes the power of purchasing other goods which the possession of that object conveys. The one may be called 'value in use,' the other 'value in exchange. The things which have the greatest value in use have frequently little or no value in exchange; and, on the contrary, those which have the greatest value in exchange have frequently little or no value in use. Nothing is more useful than water; but it will purchase scarce any thing, scarce any thing can be had in exchange for it. A diamond, on the con-

* Words of Dr Smith: Wealth of Nations, book i. chap. 7.

trary, has scarce any value in use; but a very great quantity of other goods may frequently be had in exchange for it."*

Thus, then, we perceive, that the words *wealth*, *property*, *value*, have all a more general and a limited signification, the confused and indiscriminate use of which must necessarily occasion endless misunderstandings, contradiction, and error, in the doctrines and reasonings of political economists, until they are properly defined and settled, and restricted to one sense. In the dictionary of our language, the sense of these words must of course continue to be retained and expounded in its full extent; but, as admitted into the vocabulary of Political Economy, they must be rigidly confined to their more limited signification, as defined and explained in the preceding pages. The word *value* must always be restricted to the meaning of *exchangeable value*; and the words *property* and *wealth*, whilst they are to be uniformly understood as synonymous between themselves, are at the same time equally to be understood as equivalent to the expression or definition given of the latter term—vendible property.†

---

* Wealth of Nations, book i. chap. 4.

† This chapter was written immediately after the publication of Mr Malthus's volume (in 1819) on the Principles of Political Economy, and long before Colonel Torrens's publication (in 1821) on the Production of Wealth, in which he defines wealth as follows:—"Wealth," he says, "considered as the object of economical science, consists of those material articles which are useful or desirable to man, and which it requires some portion of voluntary exertion to procure or preserve;" (page 1;) which essentially agrees in its main particulars with that which we have here endeavoured to establish. But this very able economist endeavours to lay down a distinction between wealth and exchangeable value, and even maintains that it would be inaccurate to define wealth "to consist in articles possessing exchangeable value," (Essay on the Production of Wealth, chap. i. p. 41.,) which is nearly equivalent to our "vendible property." His

CHAPTER II.

OF THE MATTER AND FORMS OF WEALTH.—NATURE OF PRODUCTION.

SECTION I.

THE NATURE OF PRODUCTION EXPLAINED.

EXCEPTING the land and its natural productions, all wealth is the produce of human labour and capital; and stock or

---

reasons are shortly as follow:—(1.) Because two savages returning from the chase, both being successful, and having acquired food and other things necessary to supply their wants, would possess wealth without the desire to exchange it. (2.) Because a single family shut out from all intercourse with the rest of mankind, cultivating the ground, and preparing its produce for use, would possess wealth which would not be exchanged. (3.) Because, in a country where the divisions of labour were unestablished, and every man combined in his own person a variety of employments, and produced for his family whatever articles they consumed, or in a society where a community of goods were established, "there would be neither buyers nor sellers, neither exchanges nor value in exchange." (Essay on the Production of Wealth, chap. i. p. 14.)

To these arguments I answer, *first*, that it is perhaps overlooked that things may be vendible which are not actually sold or exchanged. The produce consumed by a farmer in his family and on his farm, the corn he gives to his horses, and the potatoes he uses at his table, are vendible commodities as much as those he carries to market, although they are neither sold nor exchanged; and probably in the case of the two savages above mentioned, if one of them offered the whole or the greater part of the spoils he had brought home for a single arrow, or something of comparatively insignificant value, the other might agree to the exchange with the view of supplying himself, and pampering his appetite with the rarer and preferable pieces of flesh.

But, *secondly*, if there were a community of goods, and no such thing as barter, sale, or exchanges, or private property; or if wealth

capital which is saved and stored, or accumulated wealth, is simply *the effects* of antecedent *labour*, or of antecedent *la-*

---

existed under any of the circumstances supposed by Colonel Torrens in the above cases,—which are indeed partly unusual, and of little consequence, and partly improbable or imaginary,—I say, in such event, and under such circumstances, there being no coercive laws or regular government, there could hardly be any occasion for a definition of wealth at all, or for the cultivation of the science of Political Economy, the chief use of which is to improve the laws, and to show what is right and what is wrong in every circumstance which influences the distribution of wealth under the system of the division of labour and of private property. All the arts of production might be very well known without reducing them to the shape of science, if indeed they could assume that shape at all, under the supposed circumstances.

Colonel Torrens adds, that exchangeable value is not an essential quality of wealth, "inhering" in the articles whereof it consists, "but an accident belonging to it only, under those particular circumstances in which the divisions of labour and private property exist." (Essay on the Production of Wealth, chap. i., p. 16.) But it is believed that, without the existence of private property in wealth, it never can be accumulated to any considerable extent or abundance, and that this accident must attend it therefore wherever it can become the object of political science. Although, therefore, under rare and unusual circumstances, wealth should neither be exchanged nor exchangeable, this does not appear a good reason for rejecting a convenient and useful definition, founded on an accident attending the thing defined, in every situation where a definition of it can be required, and one which is equally correct under such circumstances, and perhaps more concise and convenient than any other which could be founded on an essential quality "inhering in it."

There is another circumstance or "accident" attending wealth, which has been noticed all along in the chapter just concluded, and on which I may here observe, that still another correct definition might probably be founded, namely, that it requires to be protected and guaranteed to the possessor or proprietor by law and force. I give the following:—*Those external material objects, necessary, useful,*

bour and capital, fixed and realized in certain material objects or vendible commodities.

Stock or capital has been described and considered as *accumulated labour*. But this is incorrect; and although the expression is of course to be taken in a metaphorical sense, still it conveys a very false idea, and leads to most erroneous and contradictory conclusions. For, besides that labour *cannot* be accumulated, it is to be observed, that, except in the very origin of society, capital comes in for a distinct and separate share, both of the effects produced and of the wealth or profits accruing; and in every advanced period it will be found, that the accumulations which exist have all been made with the assistance of previous accumulations or capital. These previous accumulations were not labour, nor even the effects of labour, after the first employment of capital; and to call them so is to sink the

---

or agreeable to mankind, of which the possession or enjoyment requires to be guaranteed and secured to the possessor or proprietor by law and force; and this, if I mistake not, denotes those objects, precisely and exclusively, which can be made the ground of an action at law *in civil cases*. For it may be observed, that when those objects appear, at first sight, the farthest removed from any connexion with the idea of wealth, as in cases of defamation, crim. con., &c., the satisfaction sought must still take the form of wealth, or *pecuniary damages*, without which the action could not be maintained. As to this particular, however, I offer it with some hesitation and diffidence for the consideration and under correction of the lawyers.

I will take the present opportunity of adding, that there are *four* other forms of words or expressions hitherto unnoticed, which are nearly synonymous with the definition *vendible property;* these are (1.) *Transferable Property;* (2.) *Exchangeable Property;* (3.) *Alienable Property;* (4.) *Vendible Commodities.* These expressions are all evidently much to the same purpose, and may be all used indiscriminately and indifferently when occasion requires; but *vendible property* I consider upon the whole as generally preferable to any of these, and as more universally and unexceptionably applicable and convenient.

effect of capital altogether, and to involve ourselves in contradiction and absurdity, when we come to treat of distribution and the different grounds of right to wealth; for then we must allow a share to be due to the capitalist, while we deny the efficacy of his contribution to the process of production; and while, at the same time, nothing can be more absurd in itself or more false than such denial.

Accumulated wealth, then, we say, is *not* accumulated labour, but the effects of labour sometimes alone, but more generally of labour and capital together, fixed and realized or impressed upon matter; and the process of production consists of certain effects, or changes of form, combination, or position, made upon material objects, by means either of labour* singly, or of labour and capital united, which endure for some time after the labour itself is past, and which make some addition to the exchangeable value of those objects. But labour itself, which is simply a movement or exertion of the human body and faculties, cannot be accumulated or retained in existence one moment beyond that in which the exertion is made. All labour perishes in the very instant of its performance; but the objects on which labour is bestowed may be preserved, and its effects be made to endure for a longer or shorter period in the forms and modifications which it impresses upon them.

Thus, when a house is built, the labour employed passes into non-existence as the work proceeds, and when the building is completed the labour exists no more; but its effects continue to exist in the fabric it has raised, fixed and realized in the new form it has given to the stones and other materials of which the structure is composed, and which

---

* When we use the word labour, we always of course mean human labour; for the labour of other animals belongs to the head of capital, —as do likewise the animals themselves, however employed by man for his purposes.

may endure for many years, and sometimes for many generations.

When labour is employed in sowing and tilling the ground, its effects appear in due time in the crop which follows; but the labour itself remains not in existence one moment beyond that in which it was performed.

When labour is employed in fabricating a web, or in fashioning a coat or a shirt, it still becomes extinct the very moment succeeding to that which gave it birth; but it also still leaves behind it effects which are more or less permanent and perceptible, in the new forms and properties with which it invests the *cotton*, or *wool*, or *flax*, or other materials on which it is bestowed. Those materials have all themselves been procured by means of labour, or of labour and capital, either immediately from the earth, or from the animals the earth sustains; and these and all other materials are formed and prepared in the same manner into commodities fit for use, by means of many capitals (necessarily accumulated by saving and privation) as well as by many efforts and operations of labour and painful industry,—every one of which, while it gives a new form or modification to the material substance, increases its value, and brings it still nearer, through every step of the process, to the end and object aimed at, until it issues at length in a perfect production fit for human use,—and thus it is that wealth is produced.

It is perfectly true, as has been remarked by M. Say and others, that in this process of production *there is no creation of matter*. But there is a modification of it; and always either a change and new arrangement of particles and of parts, or a new form, or new position, given to the mass; and there is generally an augmentation or diminution of the quantity under operation, though not certainly of matter in the universe. But there is a *creation* of modes and forms, though not of matter. Nothing indeed can be more certain or undoubted, than that matter can neither be created nor annihilated by man; but its forms may be varied by him, and portions of it under his hands may be varied in quantity, —increased or diminished.

Still in every variation of quantity which any portion of matter under the hands of the workman is made to undergo, whatever is added to it or abstracted from it, is all taken from or given back to the ultimate receptacle of all organized and all factitious forms—the boundless and all-containing "ocean of matter." The parings of a shoe, or refuse materials of a manufactory, are thrown all back to augment the source whence they were at first derived; and even the perfect products themselves, after being used and worn till they are no longer serviceable for their temporary purpose, are returned to the dunghill, and equally consigned to the same common destiny. By decomposition, the different particles of which they consist are set free, and either enter immediately into new combinations fit for human use, or fly to augment the vast and illimitable reservoirs of their homogeneous and kindred substances.

The particles which compose the present crop existed all, it is probable, in the earth, and in the atmosphere or heavens, before they took the present form of wheat, oats, &c. It is merely a change of combination or position they have undergone; to the effecting of which (if we consider narrowly) the industry of man has been but in a small degree subservient. He threw the seed into the ground perhaps, and prepared its bed, but nature did all the mysterious work of causing it to grow and to produce, "some thirty, some sixty, and some an hundred fold." In the gathering of the fruits of the earth, and in the preparing and disposing of them for use, the effects of human labour are more distinctly seen; still, however, it does nothing but move, form, new-model, and arrange, those material products which nature bestows. Labour creates them not; although it must be confessed, that in producing wealth it varies and determines their modes of existence. Yet still labour is an indispensable ingredient in the production or procuration even of the fruits of the earth, and of the matter of wealth, or what is called *rude* or *raw* produce generally; which cannot be obtained without it, at least in any considerable quantity, or in such abundance as to supply liberally the wants and necessities of human existence,—scarcely even those of a single savage or family in the state of nature, and far less of a numerous people in the civilised state.

SECTION II.

THE MATTER AND FORMS OF WEALTH REVIEWED.

Having thus briefly explained the meaning of the term production, and unfolded the nature of wealth in its elements, I shall now proceed to consider the whole wealth of a country in the mass, as it is found to exist in an extensive civilized and opulent community, by a summary statement or review of the principal objects or items of which it consists.

This, it is hoped, will serve to confirm our foregoing reasonings, as well as to elucidate those which are to follow. It will also serve to assist the student in endeavouring to acquire a distinct and definite conception of the aggregate quantity of vendible property at any time existing within a country; what that aggregate entirely and exclusively consists of; and the comparative amount of its different parts.

It is not our object, it may be observed here, to inquire into the actual state of wealth at any particular time or in any one country, but to present the reader with a general sketch or outline of its principal features, or of those objects it will always be found to consist of at all times and in all countries, wherever it has increased to any considerable magnitude.

In this statement, also, it is to be observed, that we pay no attention to classification as regards the employment of wealth, but endeavour to take a general and comprehensive view of it in the most natural order. Having done this, we shall in the following chapter apply ourselves to classify and analyze it in reference to its various uses and employments.

The following then I would set down as a general

SUMMARY OF WEALTH.

THE wealth of a country, or of any separate portion of mankind or community, consists, in the first place, of the country itself, that is, of the land or territory possessed by them, and all that is naturally borne upon its surface, or contained in its bowels within the reach of man; or in the waters and other elements bordering upon it, or enclosed within its boundaries; which form and comprise the first great division, or items of wealth, and the subject upon which the art and industry and labour of mankind fall to be exerted, in order to produce every other article of wealth besides. This head includes mines, the natural productions of the land and of the waters, fisheries, corn, and cattle, except in so far as any of these inferior items are improved or augmented by human industry, art, or labour.

Secondly, in connexion with the land must be stated as a part of wealth, those improvements made upon it, which either facilitate and abridge, or render more effective the operations of agriculture, as enclosures, drains, and all meliorations of the soil, the effect of culture and human labour, which make its produce permanently more abundant, or more easily obtained.

Thirdly, I enumerate, as having an inseparable connexion with the land, the houses, and other immoveable structures built or formed upon it for the use of man, whether they be calculated for accommodation and enjoyment merely, or for business and production; as roads, canals, harbours, docks, water-works, or arcs for water-wheels, dam-heads, &c.; all houses of every description, as dwelling-houses, public buildings for national or for local purposes, churches, chapels, theatres, arsenals, and all works and buildings necessary for manufactories, as founderies, potteries, glass-works, salt works, coal-works or mines, corn-mills, cotton-mills, &c.; or for mercantile purposes, as warehouses, granaries, &c.; or for agricultural purposes, as barns, storehouses, &c. These, it may be observed, and the two foregoing classes of wealth, except the natural productions of the land and waters, are all *fixed property*, stock or capital immoveable and inseparable from the land or territory.

Fourthly, I shall state, as a distinct portion of wealth, all useful machines and engines, or instruments of trade, together with all implements and utensils of every description, and for whatever purpose wanted or used, as water-wheels, steam-engines, cranes, wind-mills, thrashing-mills, ploughs, weaving-looms, washing-mills, beetling-engines, fulling-mills, paper-mills, printing-presses, types, anvils, hammers, planes, saws, augers, axes, *tools*; as also tables, chairs, beds, pokers, tongs, *fire-irons*, pots and pans. These, again, we observe, are all *moveable property*, except, perhaps, water-wheels,* which cannot, in general, be taken down and *removed* without almost their entire destruction, or at least without such expense, injury, and diminution of value, as would amount to the resolution of them into the original materials; that is, into the value of the wood and iron whereof they were made, or of such parts of those materials as should remain applicable to any new purpose.

* A singular exception perhaps it may be thought.

Fifthly and lastly, I state generally, that wealth consists of the productions of agriculture, manufactures, and commerce, that is, of rude produce and wrought goods, whether adapted for the purposes of trade or for immediate use or enjoyment; as corn, cattle, sugar, wine, tobacco, coffee, tea, beef, bread, meal, flour, wool, cotton, silk, leather, cloth, household furniture, musical instruments, paintings, maps, books, wood, iron, silver, gold, pots and pans; money, goods, wares, and merchandises of all sorts; ships, carriages, waggons, carts, and coaches. These also, it is evident, are all *moveable property*.

The foregoing and all other material objects, the produce of every art and occupation, which require labour or industry to collect, arrange, fashion, and form, or to fit and prepare them for the use, accommodation, or enjoyment of man, compose the wealth and capital or stock of a country. These are all *vendible property*; and they are all of that limited quality that *law and force* are necessarily required to secure them to the possessors or proprietors. And if we scrutinize the whole, and try every article, we shall find that all wealth comes either immediately from the land, or from the hands of productive labour; and that capital (together with all the benefits which it will be shown in the sequel to confer upon mankind) owes its existence entirely to human providence, foresight, and parsimony. All wealth therefore is wholly derived from the united powers of nature and human industry assisted by capital, shortly expressed by the terms *land and labour*. The elements and matter of wealth exist in the earth and in the heavens; human labour is necessary to collect, fashion, and dispose them for the use of man.

CHAPTER III.

ANALYSIS AND CLASSIFICATION OF WEALTH IN REFERENCE TO ITS DIFFERENT USES AND EMPLOYMENTS.

ALTHOUGH all wealth is employed either productively or unproductively; that is, either, first, in supplying and gratifying the wants and desires of mankind, without any other return than the support of their bodies and enjoyment of their lives; or, secondly, in supplying and gratifying the same wants and desires, accompanied with the production, or return of a quantity of new wealth, greater or less, or equal to that which is consumed; yet a small examination will be sufficient to convince us that it cannot be divided into two simple sorts, or be classed entirely and distinctly under the two different heads of productive and unproductive.

It is true, there are a great many items of wealth which can only be employed productively, as a plough, a weaving-loom, &c.; and others which can only be employed unproductively, as a piano-forte, a sideboard, &c.; but there is a third sort, and great amount of wealth, which can be employed either the one way or the other, as corn, cloth, &c. according to the employment of the persons whom it maintains.

All wealth consists of objects either immediately applicable to the satisfaction of the wants and desires of mankind, as bread, wine, cloth, houses, household furniture, musical instruments, paintings, maps, books, &c., or of such as assist in producing them, as a plough, a wine-press, a weaving-loom, a printing-press, axes, planes, saws, and other tools, &c. The first sort may be distinguished when occasion requires, as *wealth immediately consumable;* the second as *wealth not immediately consumable.* The latter sort, or wealth not immediately consumable, can be employed only in one way, and that is productively. Of the former sort, or wealth immediately consumable, *a part* can be employed only in one way, and that is unproductively, as instruments of music,* paintings, maps, books, &c.; but another, and by far the greatest part, may be employed either productively or unproductively, as bread, cloth, &c. according to the employment of the persons who consume it. For as wealth immediately consumable, or food, clothing, and shelter of some sort or other, is necessary to the support of our bodies and to our very existence, and as human labour is absolutely necessary, in a greater or less degree, to the production of every article of wealth, that which is employed in maintaining productive labourers is alone productive of new wealth; while that which is employed in maintaining every other description of persons is not followed by any such result. This part of wealth, therefore, is productive or unproductive according to the way in which it is employed, or to the description of persons whom it maintains.

"There is one sort of labour," says Dr Smith, "which adds to the value of the subject upon which it is bestowed; there is another which has no such effect. The former, as it produces a value, may be called productive; the latter, unproductive labour. Thus the labour of a manufacturer adds generally to the value of the materials which he works upon, that of his own maintenance and of his master's profit. The labour of a menial servant, on the contrary, adds to the value

---

*It may perhaps be thought that musical instruments and even household furniture, when they are employed by teachers or boarding-house-keepers for hire, and the gaining of a livelihood, are employed productively; but it is to be recollected that no new wealth is ever produced in this way, and that that which supports both the teachers and taught must be drawn ultimately from some productive source. Vide Dr Smith on this subject, W. of N. b. ii. c. 1. vol. i. p. 441, Buchanan's edition.

of nothing. Though the manufacturer has his wages advanced to him by his master, he in reality costs him no expense, the value of those wages being generally restored, together with a profit, in the improved value of the subject upon which his labour is bestowed. But the maintenance of a menial servant never is restored. A man grows rich by employing a multitude of manufacturers; he grows poor by maintaining a multitude of menial servants. The labour of the latter, however, has its value, and deserves its reward as well as that of the former. But the labour of the manufacturer fixes and realizes itself in some particular subject or vendible commodity, which lasts for some time at least after that labour is past. It is, as it were, a certain quantity of labour stocked and stored up, to be employed, if necessary, upon some other occasion. That subject, or, what is the same thing, the price of that subject, can afterwards, if necessary, put into motion a quantity of labour equal to that which had originally produced it. The labour of the menial servant, on the contrary, does not fix or realize itself in any particular subject or vendible commodity. His services generally perish in the very instant of their performance, and seldom leave any trace of value behind them, for which an equal quantity of service could afterwards be procured."*

To return to our analysis and classification, and to be as distinct as possible upon this subject, wealth, with regard to its uses and employments, must be classed under *three* different heads; namely, *first*, that which is necessarily productive; *second*, that which is necessarily unproductive; and, *third*, that which may be either the one or the other, according to the way in which it is employed.

I. If we cast our eyes backwards upon the various items or sorts of wealth described and enumerated in the statement or summary contained in the preceding chapter, it

---

* Wealth of Nations, book ii. chap. 3. See the subject of productive and unproductive labour treated more fully in the next chapter.

will be apparent that some of them are calculated for immediate use, consumption, or enjoyment; that is, for the satisfaction of the immediate, natural, and necessary wants or desires of mankind,—as bread, wine, &c., while others are calculated merely to assist in producing such articles, and cannot themselves be converted to any such immediate purpose of consumption,—as a plough, a wine-press, &c. Of this last-mentioned sort, or wealth which cannot be applied to any purpose of immediate enjoyment, but must necessarily be applied to productive purposes, is the land, and the meliorations made upon it,—as enclosures, drains, &c., roads, canals, harbours, docks, water-works, or arcs for water-wheels, dam-heads, and all works and buildings necessary for every different manufacture or mechanic art,—as blast-furnaces in founderies, kilns in potteries and glass-works, and all structures of a similar kind, which cannot be applied to the immediate satisfaction of our natural wants, or converted to any other use or purpose but that for which they were originally and expressly designed. These must be considered altogether or chiefly as productive wealth. Of this sort likewise may be reckoned steam-engines, cranes, water-wheels, windmills, thrashing-machines, ships, &c., and generally all those items of wealth which are subservient to production, and cannot be applied without very great loss and depreciation to any other purpose.

It is true, the proprietor of a piece of land, or of a ship, or of a steam-engine, or of a pottery or a glass-work, or of a share in a canal, road, &c., may sell any of these properties, and apply *the proceeds* to the purpose of immediate consumption or enjoyment, or to any other purpose he pleases; that is, he can exchange any of these properties for money, which he can employ in any way he pleases. He may either set labourers to work in some other department of productive industry; in which case his stock, if applied with common judgment and common fortune, will return to him after a certain lapse of time with some augmentation; namely, with the ordinary profit and wages, or remuneration for his trouble and risk in so employing it; or he may lay out the money wholly in procuring immediate enjoyment; as, for example, in treats and amusements,—in eating and drinking and making merry; in which case it will not return to him again, nor will the articles consumed be replaced by any certain or equal quantity of new wealth, but will be destroyed and annihilated as wealth altogether. But the canal, road, &c., the share of which this person sold, will not be in the smallest degree affected, altered, or injured by such disposal. Not a stone of their fabrics will be moved; but they will continue, as before, to be applied to their destined purposes just as if no such transfer had happened.

There are some portions of wealth, therefore, which must always be employed in the work of production, so long as they continue to retain the character of wealth; and, in regard to those just mentioned, that will be until they either go into decay or disrepair themselves, or until the decay of the country, or of trade in the place where they are situated, and on which their employment or utility depends. Machines, whilst a demand subsists for the articles they are calculated to produce, must be so employed;—a canal, a dock, a harbour, must be so employed, and can only cease to be productive wealth in consequence of the decay of the country, or of trade in the place where they happen to be situated, and which no longer requires or can maintain such expensive items or means of production.

It is also true, that some of those items of wealth here set down as mainly and necessarily productive, may, to a limited extent, or in a constrained sense, be applied to immediate consumption or enjoyment;—as a walk for recreation may be taken in the fields, or upon a road; which last, as well as a canal, may be used for the transport of a pleasure-party; and the steam-engine, which was heretofore exclusively confined to productive purposes, is now extensively applied to navigation,—a very considerable part of which is devoted to pleasure or amusement. Yet still their utility or productive capacity continues to constitute the chief end and purpose of this class of objects;—that of a road or canal to facilitate business and the transport of goods or commodities, and that of a steam-engine to propel machinery employed to increase the productive powers of labour; and, generally speaking, therefore, they must be allowed to derive their character from this predominant quality, and must be set down as stock or capital essentially productive.

There are other items of wealth which are also strictly productive, but which may be converted, though but partially, and not without considerable loss and reduction of value, into purposes of mere enjoyment and consumption. Such are cotton-mills, corn-mills, granaries, work-shops, &c., which might be converted into dwelling-houses, churches, theatres, &c. (which are objects of barren consumption); but to a very limited extent, and evidently not without considerable expense and a very material sacrifice of value. For although a granary or an extensive work-shop, &c., might, at a certain expense and sacrifice of capital, be converted into dwelling-houses, or even into a church or a theatre, yet this could not be done in many instances, or to any considerable extent, because granaries and work-shops must be had, as well as dwelling-houses, churches, and theatres, in proportion to the business and population to be accommodated; while it is evident the original destination of granaries, work-shops, &c., could not be changed to any considerable extent in a country requiring an additional number of dwelling-houses, or even in one which barely kept up a fixed and stationary number. This is evident, because the demand for dwelling-houses cannot increase or continue the same without the increase or continuance of the general wealth and population of the country, and then the demand for granaries, work-shops, &c., must increase or remain undiminished at the same time; and whilst the one class of buildings receives an addition to its number, or continues undiminished, so must the other. It is evident, therefore, that the buildings of either description could not be converted to the contrary purposes mentioned to any extent of consequence; as, likewise, it is plain, that in every advanced country there must always be a very great amount of wealth, stock, or capital, invested in productive buildings, or houses, which cannot be converted from their proper use to purposes of consumption and enjoyment; but must continue to be applied to productive purposes, and to retain the character of productive wealth until their own decay, or until the decay of the trade, population, and general wealth of the country or place where they are situated.

II. Again, there are other articles which are altogether confined to enjoyment, and cannot be applied at all to productive purposes. Such are instruments of music, paintings, maps, books, &c. Those things can only serve for pleasure and amusement, or for instruction; and, however much they may contribute to increase production indirectly, by improving the capacity and skill of the producer, as well as by rewarding and stimulating his exertions, they cannot be accounted productive wealth. They may be the most excellent things in the whole circle of nature or catalogue of wealth, but they cannot be applied directly to the work of production. These articles, indeed, being vendible commodities, may be sold, and the proceeds applied to productive purposes, but the articles themselves never can, but must still be applied to their proper and unalterable uses, and must continue unchangeably to amuse, delight, and instruct mankind, into whatever hands they may fall.

All household furniture is strictly unproductive wealth, and properly belongs to this class, which cannot be converted to any other purpose than that of consumption or enjoyment; —as tables, chairs, beds, sideboards, china, stoneware, crystal, &c. Other household articles, indeed,—as those formed of the metals,—may, some with a greater, some with a less sacrifice of value, be converted and applied to productive purposes;—as, for instance, pots and pans might be forged into other useful articles, and pokers and spits might, with perhaps still less loss, be made into nails. Yet a slight consideration will be sufficient to demonstrate that this could only be done to a very limited extent; because pots and pans, and pokers, &c., must be had to serve their purposes as well as nails, or any other articles of wealth into which those utensils could be converted; the one sort being wanted as well as the other, in proportion to the extent, wealth, and population of a country.

III. The third and last sort of wealth is that which may be applied indifferently either to productive or unproductive purposes, and consists of all articles or goods which are immediately consumable, or such as are necessary to the subsistence of the labourer or of mankind, whose industry may be applied either productively or unproductively. Such are corn, cloth, houses, &c., which may be employed either the one way or the other.

For example:—Any person having the command of a quantity of corn, cloth, and other articles necessary to the subsistence of the labourer, equal, suppose, to the maintenance of a hundred or a thousand men for a year, or any other given amount, may employ it in either of the two different ways following:—

First, he may employ it in any of the three general departments of productive industry,—agriculture, manufactures, or commerce; that is to say, he may employ it in raising or producing corn, cloth, or other vendible commodities, by setting labourers to work in any of those departments; in which case, as the corn, cloth, &c., the subsistence of the labourer, disappears, other wealth, corn, cloth, &c., will arise under their hands, and if their labour has been directed and applied with ordinary skill and judgment, and with ordinary good fortune, the quantity of wealth produced will exceed the original quantity which has been consumed, and replace the capital expended, with the addition of the ordinary profit of stock in such employments;—that is, the ordinary remuneration or reward to the proprietor for the trouble and risk he subjects himself to in that particular application and employment of his labour and stock. Secondly, the person having possession of such stock or capital may use it in keeping hounds and hunting-horses, and grooms, and menial servants, or other unproductive labourers; or he may give it away for nothing to persons who do not labour at all; in which case, as the corn, cloth, &c., the subsistence of the hounds and horses, and of the unproductive labourers, or of the non-labourers, disappears, no new wealth will arise therefrom, nor will the original capital be replaced by such expenditure and consumption, which must be supplied, if repeated, from some other source altogether independent of such application of stock, whereby the whole is spent and annihilated as wealth, without any return or reproduction of property equivalent thereto.

In the first of these two cases, goods of equal or greater value arise from the consumption of goods already in existence; in the second, such consumption is not followed by any return of equivalent goods; and as in both cases wealth or vendible commodities are equally consumed, viz. the subsistence of the labourer, or non-labourer, and are reproduced in the one case and not in the other, it is apparent that this sort of wealth becomes productive or unproductive according to the way in which it is employed; in other words, according as it is expended in maintaining persons who are occupied in the one or in the other of the different ways described.

It depends, therefore, entirely and exclusively on the way in which this sort of wealth is employed whether it be productive or unproductive, and whether an equal, or a greater, or a less quantity of wealth, or no wealth at all, arise from its consumption. And hence it follows, that wealth in general cannot be distinctly classed and confined to the two simple sorts or species of productive and unproductive; so very considerable a portion of it,—namely, almost all that is immediately consumable,—being applicable both ways, and taking the character of productive or unproductive, not from any modifications under which it exists, or from any qualities inherent in or constantly attending it, but simply from the way in which it is employed;—that character depending entirely on the *employment* of the persons or labourers which this species of wealth is expended in maintaining.

And this conclusion leads directly to the consideration of the much-controverted question of productive or unproductive labour,—a subject which I shall endeavour fully to discuss in the two next chapters.

It has been already noticed (pp. 26, 27,) that among those items of wealth which belong generally to the class of productive, there are some which may, to a limited extent, be applied to unproductive purposes;—as a canal and a steam-boat may be employed to convey a pleasure-party, and a walk for pleasure may be taken in the fields (which are the land) or upon a road.—It has been shown, in like manner, (pp. 27, 28,) that there are items of wealth which generally belong to the class of unproductive, which may also, in a limited degree, be turned to productive uses;—as a dwelling-house may be converted into a work-shop, granary, or the like; and we have explained the causes which control and restrain the application of those items to any considerable extent, the one way or the other, contrary to their original and proper destination. But it may not be wholly useless or unnecessary to add, that, in a certain constrained sense, all wealth may be applied, at the pleasure of the possessor or proprietor, either to productive or unproductive purposes; as, for instance, a canal, which is chiefly used in a productive way, may not only, as already mentioned, be applied to the unproductive purpose of transporting a pleasure-party, but it may be applied productively in a way quite distinct from that of its ordinary and proper use, should the decay of a country or of trade render it useless for the purpose of navigation;—as the stones which confine its banks, or those of its locks or aqueducts, might be taken to build a house or a bridge; and, under similar circumstances, a road might be turned to tillage; and this might be called applying the canal and road to productive purposes. On the other hand, sideboards and tables, paintings, maps, books, &c., which are strictly unproductive wealth, might be employed to keep up the fire of a steam-engine, or other furnace used in a productive way, as the numerous volumes of the Alexandrian library actually were employed to heat the baths; and this might be called applying those articles productively. But I believe every reader will readily allow that such a construction or strained application of terms as to call such a use of those articles a productive one, would be altogether extravagant and inadmissible. Nor could any cavil or objection founded on such a forced construction and use of language be considered as an obstacle, or be allowed to stand in the way of a more perfect classification of the different kinds of wealth than we have been able, consistently with truth, to exhibit. And this much, at least, the reader must have seen, that it is not on account of such obstacles that we cannot divide the whole mass of wealth into the two simple kinds of productive and unproductive. It is because so great a proportion of it can be applied as we have shown, either the one way or the other, that this distinction holds not universally, and cannot be so laid down. It is sufficient for us to have endeavoured to found our analysis upon the different properties and distinguishing characteristics which really belong to the different sorts of wealth, without pretending or attempting a more exact or more perfect and simple classification of them than the things themselves will really allow.

But although we cannot lay down an unqualified and universal distinction on this subject, still the analysis we have attempted is not to be considered as useless or unprofitable. Nor will our attention be found to have been uselessly or unprofitably employed upon it. A very great proportion of the general mass of wealth falls distinctly to be classed under the two simple heads of productive and unproductive; and we have learned, at least, in the course of our investigations, what portions or items can and what cannot be so classed. We have, besides, it is to be hoped, gotten to the bottom of our subject, and gained a more perfect knowledge of the different uses and employments of wealth than we could have acquired otherwise, as well as a more perfect view of the distinguishing characters of its different items, and a cue to refer every distinct sort to its proper place in our conception of the whole.

We may observe, then, as the result of our inquiries here, that there are *five* different circumstances attending wealth, or accidents affecting it, relatively to its different uses and employments, which belong to and characterize its various parts and items, with a greater or less degree of distinctness.

First, we have seen (p. 25) that among the various items of wealth there are some which must be applied altogether and invariably to productive purposes, so long as they retain the character of wealth themselves,—as ploughs, winepresses, water-wheels, steam-engines, weaving-looms, and the like.

Secondly, we have seen (p. 28) that there are other items which can only be applied to unproductive purposes,—as instruments of music, paintings, maps, books, and things of the like nature.

Thirdly, there is another sort of wealth or items which approach to the character of the first, but which may, in a certain degree and to a limited extent, be applied as the second,—as the buildings of cotton-mills, cornmills, &c., which might be partially converted into dwelling-houses. (See pp. 27, 28.)

Fourthly, there is a sort approaching to the character of the second, but which may be partially converted to the purposes of the first,—as pots, and pans, and pokers, which might be manufactured into nails, &c. (See p. 29.)

Fifthly and lastly, there is a sort of wealth or items which may be applied indifferently either as the first or second; that is, equally to productive and to unproductive purposes, and to an indefinite extent in either way,—as corn, cloth, &c., (see p. 29,)—there being no impediment to the application or employment of the whole of this sort of wealth in pure unproductive consumption or enjoyment, except that which arises from the private interests of the possessors of capital, which teaches them to reflect, that if those items, or their individual portions of them, should be so consumed, they must be reduced to the condition of labourers, or, if incapable of labour, to that of a total dependence or destitution.

CHAPTER IV.

OF PRODUCTIVE AND UNPRODUCTIVE LABOUR.

PRODUCTIVE labour is that which is directly employed in the production of wealth or vendible property, and of which the effects remain apparent after the labour itself is past, fixed and realized in some material object or commodity. Such are the labours of the husbandman, the manufacturer, and the merchant, and of all whose industry is necessary in the processes of production, as the term has been explained in the foregoing chapters. Not only those whose industry is confined to mere manual labour, but those also who are employed in superintending and directing that labour;—not only the ploughman and gatherer-in of the harvest, but the master-farmer also, who orders their work, and directs and superintends the employment of a stock or capital either of his own or some other person's in the business of agriculture;—not only the shopmen and porters of the merchant, but the merchant himself, with his clerks and assistants, who are equally necessary to the conducting of his business with those who are occupied in the moving or transporting of his goods from one place to another,—as carters, porters, sailors, &c.; and, in one word, all are productive labourers whose industry is useful, necessary, or advantageous, in every office and department of the processes of production.

Unproductive labour is that which is employed, not in the actual production of wealth, but in offices of another description, and of which the effects commonly perish along with it, and are no longer visible after the labour itself is past, or, if permanent and visible, they are not communicated to any object that can be turned to account in the way of sale, or voluntary exchange of equivalent values.

Such is the labour of all the officers and administrators of government and of the law, public functionaries of every description, ministers of state, judges and officers of justice, clergy, army and navy. Such also is the labour of menial servants, stage-players, &c., and generally of all whose exertion or industry is not immediately subservient to the work of production, but is yet notwithstanding necessarily or usefully employed in ministering to our convenience or well-being; or to our enjoyment in any way of our share of the goods which the other sort of labour has produced.

It will be at once apparent to the reader, from these definitions, that unproductive labour is no less necessary to the existence and production of wealth (wherever it is to be found in any considerable quantity) than productive labour. And not only is it necessary to this end, but to others equally important;—namely, to the security of *persons* as well as property, to liberty, and even to the very existence of any extensive or civilized society. For it is by unproductive labour that a civilized people are protected in their persons as well as in their properties, and of course that the productive labourer is secured of the fruits of his industry, and allowed to pursue his occupation and objects unmolested. It is by unproductive labour that wealth is secured to the individual possessors or proprietors thereof; that the forcible transfer or violent invasion of it is prevented; and that its equitable distribution is secured agreeably to the only just mode according to which such distribution can take place, viz. by voluntary exchange, by treaty or compact. In short, without the constant vigilance and protecting agency of this class of labourers, rapine would stalk abroad over the land, production would cease, and population fail; industry would be extinguished, and wealth annihilated, or reduced at least and confined to nearly that small and unbought quantity which the earth spontaneously produces.

On the other hand, it is by productive labour that wealth

is gathered together and accumulated, and that the unproductive labourers as well as the whole community are provided with subsistence; and as all men are consumers of wealth, it is abundantly demonstrable, or rather I should say, it is self-evident, that if none were engaged in the work of production, the whole stock which is at any time in the world would be speedily exhausted, and, as in the other case, nothing would remain after a short interval but that comparatively small and inconsiderable quantity which the earth without culture should continue gratuitously to afford.

Productive and unproductive labourers then we see are both necessary, and equally necessary, to the existence of wealth as well as to the existence of society itself, and, where the government is well constituted, they are all equally employed in *useful* labour,—each in his proper sphere contributing his mite of industry to the necessary and multifarious business of the commonwealth. But it is not therefore to be imagined that this is a useless or unnecessary distinction. On the contrary, it is one of the most important and most necessary in the whole science of political economy, and lies indeed at the foundation of all utility in the objects and application of that science; for, without an intimate acquaintance with this distinction, it is not possible perfectly to comprehend the effects of an undue or unnecessary increase of the unproductive class, or clearly to perceive the injustice and injury of appointing and maintaining a greater number in the department of government, than is required to conduct public affairs in the best manner.

The following brief analysis of unproductive labour will render this more apparent.

Unproductive labour is of two sorts:—*First*, that which is employed in the administration of public affairs; and, *secondly*, that which is required in domestic and other occupations and professions by individuals in their private capacity.

Persons engaged in the first sort of unproductive labour are installed into their offices and appointments by a part of society acting for the whole. Those employed in the second are engaged to their work and offices, or appointments, by every individual for himself, that is, by treaty and agreement, conducted, settled, and assented to by both the parties or persons concerned. A few persons appoint all the public functionaries,—the ministers of state, judges, officers of justice, army and navy, for the whole community; but every individual engages his own servants, and determines for himself when he shall see a play or other amusement, and calls to his aid the advice and assistance of a physician or a lawyer when he sees fit.

There is no danger therefore to be dreaded that the number of people employed in the second sort of unproductive labour should become over-great or excessive, because it possesses a *perfect* principle of self-regulation and correction. For the labourers in this sort being all engaged, and their wages, salary, or fees, settled and determined by voluntary consent *fully given*, no one is obliged to employ or pay more of them than he pleases; and if it happens that any body does engage or employ more than he can well afford at one time, he must necessarily confine himself to the use of fewer at another. The numbers and employment therefore of this sort of unproductive labourers is entirely a matter of private prudence and economy; and a superabundance of hands or applicants, in any class or profession in this department, is only felt as an inconvenience to those classes or applicants themselves, but by no means to the rest of the community, or the public in general. The numbers and employment of this sort of unproductive labourers, therefore, belongs not to legislative regulation or interference, nor demands the public attention or solicitude, but may safely be left, and can only be safely confided, to the determination and direction of private judgment and discretion.

But it is not so with the first sort of unproductive labourers above described. Here the regulating principle is *not* perfect; for the amount of salary or remuneration, as well as the appointment of the labourers in this sort, being determined by a part (and a very small part indeed) of the society acting for the whole, there is the greatest reason imaginable to dread that if the consent and suffrage of the general body, who sustain the charge of those appointments, be not required to control them, or if such consent or suffrage be very imperfectly or *partially given* or required, both too many will be employed, and they will be paid too much for their labour. This indeed is a result as certain and confidently to be expected as any that can be derived from experience of the principles of human conduct. This department therefore requires the utmost attention and vigilance of the public,—first, in framing with due care the original rules, or fundamental laws of government, according to which those appointments and suffrages are to take place, and afterwards in watching and superintending their practical operation.

It is almost unnecessary to remark, that there is no danger to be apprehended of the numbers of the productive class being increased too much, because in proportion to their numbers, with equal skill in the arts of production, they will only have to labour so much the less, or enjoy the greater plenty. The greater their number, therefore, the better must it be for all those requiring their commodities; that is, for themselves and every body else.

It is obvious to remark, and has been noticed by Dr Smith in treating this subject, that the most honourable as well as the meanest offices and employments belong to the department of unproductive labour,—an observation that imports nothing farther than the recognition of a simple fact in the development of science, and brings neither disgrace to the persons engaged in this, nor honour to those employ ed in the other. All of them, as is likewise remarked by the same great moralist, deserve their rewards, or wages, as well as the productive class; provided always, I should add, that they be not unnecessarily multiplied, so as not to have real duties to perform equivalent to those rewards which they receive as recompense. That this will not be the case with regard to one distinct sort of the unproductive labourers there is always a sufficient security, as we have already shown, arising from the private interest of those who employ that sort; and the same motives of private interest can be easily rendered available for the like purpose of security against any undue increase of the other sort of unproductive labourers, or those who are employed in a public capacity, by the simple expedient of extending the right of suffrage or control over their appointments to those who bear the charges of their support and maintenance,—this principle of regulation, or check, founded on the feeling of private interest, being the natural and obvious, as it is the only effectual ground of security and reliance against abuse or injustice in all affairs between man and man which fall to be regulated by political constitutions or codes of law.

All those, then, who are employed in the necessary business of the society we call labourers, whether they be engaged in the productive or unproductive departments of useful labour; and both classes have been shown to be equally useful and equally necessary.* The necessity of the one class

* It will be obvious to the reader that both productive and unproductive labourers belong to "the industrious classes;" and, according to our notions, a minister of state, a judge or lawyer, accountant, &c. may be as *industrious* as well as useful as any productive labourer whatever. I shall add here, that the general interest of all labourers, productive and unproductive, is the same in regard to preventing any great or undue increase of that portion of the unproductive class

arises from the scanty and inadequate provision, or means of subsistence and enjoyment, which the earth unassisted affords, or what may be reckoned the imperfection of external nature; the necessity of the other arises from the imperfection of human nature itself,—from the violence of passion, which provokes to injustice, and the cloudiness of reason, which but feebly and inadequately supplies a remedy.

---

which is employed in the administration of government, because, as that portion is increased, the productive class must be diminished to the same extent, and must consequently work longer or harder than before; and so likewise must the unproductive class, by the principle of competition, in all those departments where that principle is allowed to operate.

Sir Walter Scott, in an introductory discourse to one of his novels, has the following shrewd observations on the subject of productive and unproductive labour:—

"I do say it," says Sir Walter, "in spite of Adam Smith and his followers, that a successful author is a productive labourer, and that his works constitute as effectual a part of the public wealth as that which is created by any other manufacture. If a new commodity, having an actually intrinsic and commercial value, be the result of the operation, why are the author's bales of books to be esteemed a less profitable part of the public stock than the goods of any other manufacturer?"—Fortunes of Nigel, Introductory Epistle, pp. 33, 34.

Now this doctrine of Sir Walter Scott agrees entirely, it is plain, with that which is advanced in this inquiry, namely, that all are productive labourers who are engaged directly in the production of wealth or vendible commodities, and an author, consequently, who produces a book *that will sell*, (to the booksellers or others) is necessarily, according to our notions, a productive labourer. Nor are the doctrines of Smith, when carefully examined into, really different. It is true indeed, that in one place Dr Smith says, that in the class of unproductive labourers "must be ranked men of letters of all kinds;" but he had just before stated as the criterion by which an unproductive labourer is distinguished, that his labour "does not fix and realize itself in any permanent subject or vendible commodity;" and it is to be recollected that in Dr Smith's time, literary labours were but rarely or very in-

CHAPTER V.

OF THE CLASS OF NON-LABOURERS; OR OF THOSE PERSONS WHO DO NOT LABOUR AT ALL, OR NEED TO LABOUR.

SECTION I.

THAT THE ONLY PERSONS ENTITLED TO EXEMPTION FROM LABOUR ARE THE PROPRIETORS OF LAND AND THE PROPRIETORS OF CAPITAL.*

BUT, besides the two classes of *labourers* described in the preceding chapter, and distinguished according to their different sorts of industry, there is a third class of persons to be found in every civilized community who do not labour at all, or need to labour, but are at liberty to pursue (solely if they please,) their own private pleasure and amusement. This class consists of those persons who derive their revenue from their land or capital, and who may be considered as

---

adequately rewarded. But here, in the case supposed by Sir Walter Scott, the labour of "the man of letters" fixes and realizes itself in the form of a book or manuscript, which proves to be vendible, and consequently brings the author, according to Dr Smith's own rule, within the description and denomination of a productive labourer.

* Land, it will be said, is capital; and so indeed it is in every country where wealth and population have increased to that degree that it has become *vendible property;* but then it is capital of so distinct and peculiar a kind, and the revenue or *rent* arising from it is regulated or influenced in regard to its increase and decrease by circumstances so very different and even opposite from those which regulate and influence the increase and decrease of the revenue, or *profit*, arising from other sorts of capital, that it becomes absolutely necessary to distinguish them in order to their being treated of, and always to give the land its appropriate name almost as often as we speak of it.

having been emancipated or exempted from all obligation or necessity to labour by their own or their father's industry and parsimony, or good fortune, which enabled them to amass, or to produce that capital or store of wealth, which continues, if preserved from dissipation, in all future time, to be a source of revenue without requiring the performance of any labour on the part of its possessors, save that which is necessary to preserve it, or to invest and secure it in the best manner.

This class must be carefully distinguished from the labourers, productive and unproductive. It is composed entirely of *land-holders* and *capitalists*; and perhaps the latter appellation might be used singly (as frequently it is used) to designate both. But it will be necessary to distinguish this class still farther, when occasion requires, by the name of *non-labourers*. Not that the individuals of this class are precluded or debarred by their social condition and just privileges from the exertion of their industry in any way that they think fit; nor is it intended to say that they are morally exempted from the general obligation incumbent upon all men to employ their time, their labour, and their talents, in the best manner they are able, with a view to the production of the greatest sum of good, or of human happiness, although it be left entirely to their own choice and discretion to determine what they should do, or in what manner they should contribute towards this end; neither is it meant to be insinuated that this order of men are more remiss in their duties or less strenuous in their labours and endeavours to contribute to the public happiness or prosperity than any other class of men whatsoever. All that is intended by the term non-labourers, as applied to designate this class, is merely to recognise their right and privilege, and to distinguish them from those who must *necessarily* labour; for the only persons entitled to the privilege implied by this term are the proprietors of land and the proprietors of capital. All others *must* labour; or, if they do not, and live, they must either be supported by the free bounty of others, or maintain themselves by robbery, or by fraud or artifice of some sort or other.

It is very far indeed from my intention to deny that the individuals of this class labour frequently as assiduously and as diligently as any other members of the community, though not always, it must be confessed, in the walks of profitable or self-interested industry. They oftener work for nothing than any other class; and that this should be the case might very naturally be expected, because they are better able to do so than the others, and many of them have no other object in the pursuit of which they choose to occupy themselves, or in which they so much delight, as in seeking how they may best promote the good of their neighbours or of their country. Still, however, whether they labour or not, they are entitled to consume wealth to the extent of their income derived from land or capital; or, even if they please, the whole amount and value of their land and capital itself. And by so much as they consume above what they produce by their labour, by so much are they non-labourers. Their capital stands in the place of the labour of their hands, and may be conceived as labouring for them, as it assists the labourer in the work of production, and thereby creates a fund to which no labourer or borrower of capital has any right, but which falls due to the proprietors of the capital as the proper inducement or reward for its preservation and increase.

Probably there is not and never was in the world, any individual who was absolutely and altogether a non-labourer, in the full sense of the word, during his whole life; or who never, upon any occasion, or in any manner of way, by accident or design, performed one single act of useful labour. Every person, it is probable, has done some things which must have furthered the business of mankind in some way or other; for even the most helpless invalid, confined his whole life to a single posture, might yet have done many things which had such an effect. But all men are non-labourers during a part of their lives. They are so during the period of infancy at least, when they are supported by the willing bounty of parents, and generally some time likewise in old age, when children have again the privilege of paying back the sacred duty of gratitude and affection. Besides, during periods of sickness, recreation, and accidental intervals of employment, men are occasionally non-labourers, when the wealth which they consume must either be derived from their land or capital,* or must be acquired from other people, in whatever manner.

In general, however, it may be affirmed, that most men of all ranks and classes are engaged during the greater part of their lives in useful labour of some sort or other, and either do something which contributes to production directly, or assist in the administration of public affairs—of justice and government; which last-mentioned occupation is indeed peculiarly the province of this third class of persons, a great proportion of whom is always found employed in this way; nor is any thing more usual than to observe the individuals of this class emulating all others in assiduous industry,—relinquishing all ease and indulgence, or exclusive pursuit of private pleasure, and giving up their time, and their labour, and their talents to the calls of public duty,—sometimes honourably, for a just and adequate remuneration or reward; and in other cases gratuitously, without fee or recompense, save that which they derive from the consciousness of their own virtuous conduct.†

---

* Their own previous savings, it is to be remembered, come under the denomination of capital as well as the accumulations inherited or derived from others.

† In what is here said I would not be understood as alluding to

And certainly no class of persons can have a higher interest, or more cogent motives to promote, by every means in their power, the public prosperity than this class; and more particularly the landlords, seeing that every increase of wealth and population increases the value of their possessions. The landlords are indeed the natural nobles and magistrates of the country; and all offices of a public nature, as well as the cultivation of the arts and sciences, though free to all in a free country, belong in a more especial manner to the class of capitalists who can command the leisure and other means so conducive, and even, generally speaking, indispensable to the successful or advantageous prosecution of such avocations. Nor are those to be condemned who follow none of these pursuits. They injure no one who, possessing the means, seek only in an innocent manner to attain happiness; and if they arrive at their object without any other particular employments, they will by no means be unprofitable members of the community. They will not have lived in vain. Nay, as it is human happiness which is the great end and aim of all our earthly labours, and as the happiness of the community is made up of the happiness of individuals, it follows as a necessary consequence, that such members or persons as arrive at that end by the shortest road are, as members of the community simply taken, the most profitable of all.

This will perhaps be the more readily admitted when it is understood that the direct benefits accruing from capital, in

---

the "unpaid magistracy of England," or as approving of or recommending that system; on the contrary, I think that the evil consequences of it are but too apparent. The judges and administrators of public justice ought to be paid for their trouble from the highest to the lowest; but there are thousands of other ways in which the industry and self-devotedness of the landlords and capitalists may find scope and opportunity to display itself.

the shape of profit or interest to the proprietors, do not comprise or exhaust the whole of the advantages which flow from it; but that, on the contrary, a great part of those advantages is reaped in an indirect manner by the whole community, and by every individual in it from the highest to the lowest, in consequence of that diminution in the cost of production, and consequently in the price of commodities, which must always arise from every new increase and new investment of capital. For, besides that every addition to capital necessarily creates and establishes a new and additional fund, in the shape of profit or interest for the maintenance of non-labourers, it also enables those who employ it and pay that interest to carry on their business to better advantage, and to bring their commodities either better or cheaper to market;—that is, it enables them to make greater gains themselves, and to supply the market with cheaper goods, than they could have done without its assistance, at the same time that it enables them to pay also the stipulated interest. But, as this is a point of the very highest and vital importance in the standing controversy between capital and labour, or in regard to the effects or services of the one and the other in the work of production, and as the illustration of it, therefore, forms one of the leading objects of the present work, it will be proper in this place to endeavour to go to the bottom of that question; this, therefore, I shall endeavour to do with all brevity in the following section, leaving the fuller discussion of it to other opportunities which will occur hereafter, and where the further illustrations may be introduced with greater advantage. Before concluding the present section, however, I should still farther observe, in connexion with the preceding statements, that every increase of capital, whilst it produces all the effects that have been stated, increases at the same time the rent of land by diminishing the difficulty or expense of cultivation, and bringing into tillage the inferior soils or portions of land more inconveniently situated with regard to the market, or more inaccessible to the great masses of the population, than those which could previously have been cultivated. For it is by the increase of capital, and not, as has been erroneously and absurdly maintained, by the degradation of the labourer, that cultivation and improvement is naturally extended to the inferior soils and more distant parts of the country.*

And thus it will be found, that every increase of capital, whilst it benefits the non-labourer *directly* by maintaining him at his ease without labour, benefits at the same time all the other classes of the community *indirectly*,—the land-proprietors by increasing the rent of their land, and the labourers by reducing the cost and price of commodities, which all persons must necessarily consume and purchase.

SECTION II.

OF THE MANNER IN WHICH CAPITAL IMPROVES THE CONDITION OF THE LABOURING CLASS.

THE utility of capital, and the advantages which arise from it to the country in which it abounds, are obvious, and are

---

* It is easy to see how the increase of capital, and its investment in the shape of a canal, road, or the like, should ultimately produce an addition to the rent of land. For although, *at first*, by lowering the cost and price of corn in the most populous places or great markets, it might take as much from the rent of the contiguous lands as it should add to those at a distance, still, *ultimately*, the former would necessarily regain what they had lost as soon as the price of corn should rise to nearly its former level, which it would speedily do in consequence of the increase of population which would naturally fol-

indeed almost universally acknowledged; but the manner in which the labouring classes of people, and the whole community, including both those who are and those who are not endowed with any portion of capital themselves, are made to participate indirectly in the wealth which capital creates, is not so apparent, and has never yet been distinctly shown, or even so much as directly noticed, in so far as I am acquainted, by any foregoing writer. Yet it is by means of capitals which they do not themselves possess, and by their effects in diminishing the price and increasing the abundance of goods, that the poorest individual or labourer that lives in a wealthy, and populous, and civilized or well-governed country, is commonly supplied with comforts, conveniences, and necessaries, which surpass, in a measure which is altogether incalculable, any thing which his own unassisted efforts could obtain for him, though he were al-

---

low upon the low price; and then the whole rent paid for the latter (that is, for the more distant lands) would be a clear addition to the aggregate fund of rent. And the truth is, that every increase of capital has a tendency to produce the effect stated in the text, however invested, although the manner in which that effect is produced is not always so apparent or obvious as in the case of a road or canal.

In regard to the utility or desirableness of an increase of rent, I shall only remark here, that where it is brought about by the increase of capital, and not by the degradation of the labourer, it is clearly a good; as, without bearing injuriously on any persons, it creates an addition to the fund for the maintenance of non-labourers.

The appropriation or individual possession of the land, it is always to be remembered, is a condition which is evidently and absolutely indispensable to its proper cultivation or improvement as well as to the increase or accumulation of capital upon it and the rent, which always increases and can alone increase with increasing wealth and population, is *the effect*, not *the cause*, of a high price of corn, as has been demonstrated by Dr Smith, and by many persons after him; all which will be more particularly explained hereafter in the proper place.—*See* chap. vii. of the 2d Book.

lowed the whole earth as a field for his exertions. For it is to be understood that he must then labour without the assistance of any capital worthy of the name,—without combination, and without any of the advantages which are derived from the system of *the division of labour*,—that system whereby different individuals follow different employments, and exchange their productions with one another,—a system from which so many advantages arise, but which, as I shall show hereafter, cannot for a moment be supported or established without capital.

That capital must necessarily be advantageous to some persons is a certainty which no argument can be required to prove. To the capitalists themselves it must evidently be so to the amount at least of the profit or interest which they derive from it. This advantage is direct and manifest, but exclusive, being confined entirely to the capitalists themselves. But that the same persons are benefited still farther, though indirectly, along with every individual member of the same community, in consequence of the effect essential to capital of diminishing the cost of production, and by that means increasing the abundance of commodities and lowering their price, is also a truth which will, it is hoped, be made fully apparent in the course of this work.

It has sometimes been thought and maintained that the shares of the capitalists, or the direct advantages enjoyed by them in the shape of profit or interest, form a deduction *pro tanto* from the wages of the labourers; whereas, so far from this being really the case, it will be demonstrated, that the enjoyment of those shares or advantages by the capitalists is a necessary, preliminary, and indispensable condition to the attainment of really high wages on the part of the labourers; and that the shares or wages of the latter, where capital and labour are both employed to assist each other in the work of production, (and where consequently a share in the shape of profit or interest is always paid to the former,) are always *necessarily* greater than they can be where labour alone is employed, although in this case the labourer has of course the whole produce to himself. Nay the aggregate produce, where both capital and labour are jointly employed, is always so much greater than where the latter is employed singly, that it not only affords the profit or interest of the capitalist, and also a far greater share to the labourer in the shape of wages than he could acquire without the assistance of capital; *but, over and above all these,* it leaves a certain surplus to be shared and enjoyed by the whole community without the possibility of exclusion or exception of a single individual; which surplus diffuses itself in the form of diminished price or cheapness of commodities, over the whole expanse and surface of society.

The manner in which all this takes place I shall now endeavour very briefly to demonstrate; and for this purpose it will be necessary to revert to that early and simple state of society in which capital first begins to be acquired or employed in production.

Suppose a nation or tribe of savages to be situated in a country abounding with game, and with lakes or rivers well stored with fish, and to draw their supplies of food from those two sources in the simplest and most unartful manner, taking the fish in the shallows with their hands merely, and killing the land-animals with stones or clubs; and suppose that, in this state of things, one individual of their number more ingenious or more considerate than the rest, should construct a canoe, and invent some rude sort of nets, or other tackle, for catching the fish; and that another individual should contrive gins and the bow and arrow, and prepare a quantity of each for killing or taking the land-animals; and suppose still farther, what would naturally and necessarily follow, that, by means of these instruments and contrivances, and preliminary labours, those two individuals should be enabled, the one to catch a great deal more fish, and the other to take or kill a great deal more game, than any other individual of the tribe who continued to use their hands, or the more imperfect instruments of stones or clubs;—let us suppose what is probable enough, that with their newly-acquired instruments, or *capital*, they should be enabled to acquire in general each respectively *ten times* as much of this sort of wealth, viz., food, in a day as the others.

If, observing the advantage which those two individuals derived from their superior artificial and (be it always remembered) laboriously-acquired means or capital, any others of the tribe should wish to borrow, and they should agree to lend, the one his canoe and tackle, and the other his gins and bows and arrows, on condition of receiving *a part* of all that should be taken by the borrowers by means of the instruments intrusted to them, then whatever might be agreed upon to be paid to the proprietors of those instruments would be *profit of stock* or *interest* to them (the lenders) for the use of their capital, and whatever should remain over and above that payment would be wages of labour, reward, or recompense, to the borrowers and labourers, for the toil and trouble or labour undergone by them.

Now, suppose that a fourth part, or even a half, of all that should be acquired were agreed to be paid to the lenders, still the borrowers would obtain a great and evident advantage by the bargain; for, even if they gave one-half to the lenders, the other half which would remain to themselves would be *five times as much* as they could have acquired by their day's labour, without the use of the borrowed capital. But this very high rate of profit or interest, if it once existed, would not certainly continue long, because the inducement to set about the formation or acquisition of similar instruments or capitals would be too great and too evident to be neglected by others. Many persons, therefore, it is probable, would supply themselves with similar capitals, whereby the number of lenders and the competition among them would increase, whilst the number of borrowers and the competition among them would decrease, and the rate of interest or sum paid for use would naturally and necessarily decline; and the obvious consequence would be, that a very great proportion of the wealth produced by capital would devolve indirectly to the community in general, and would accrue to every individual in the diminished cost or price of their food.

At first, indeed, it may be supposed, that the capitalists might have enhanced the value of their capitals, and might have screwed up the rate of profit or interest somewhat higher than we have supposed, and, instead of *one-half*, might have demanded *three-fourths*, or even a still higher rate, which no doubt they might have done when they had no competitors; but it is plain they never could have raised that rate the whole *nine-tenths* which were to be gained by the use of it, because on such terms the borrowers would have had no interest to accept of it, and would naturally have preferred to labour independently, and unencumbered with useless adjuncts, which could, upon this supposition, bring them no advantage. It is plain, therefore, that the capitalist could never, under any circumstances, have raised his profit or interest so as to draw the whole advantages to himself, and far less could he raise it so as to abstract any thing from the labourers or borrowers.

Let us suppose now still farther, that the borrowers and employers of the above-mentioned capitals, acquiring (as by the hypothesis they easily might) a great deal more game and fish than they could use, should come to offer the surplus to their neighbours in exchange for other things, it will be evident that for any article they wished to acquire, which usually cost a day's labour to those employed in producing it, they must offer at least as much or rather somewhat more game or fish than those with whom they were dealing could procure to themselves by a day's labour, otherwise the latter would have no interest to accept such offer rather than go to the fields and rivers, and take their fish and game in the old manner. And thus again we arrive at the conclusion, that the borrowers or employers of capital can never use or employ it to the disadvantage of those who find it their interest to purchase its produce.

And hence we acquire an easy and distinct view of the advantages arising from capital, and of the manner in which they accrue to the different classes of society, and to the whole community, without exception or exclusion of any individual.

But though it may perhaps be allowed that what has been here stated is a correct representation of the effects of capital in the early state of society, yet still it may be thought that the same effects will not necessarily take place in the advanced state, because the lower classes have not then always the same resource or option of working independently for themselves, but must in general submit to be employed by a higher class of labourers or capitalists. But then the competition of their employers comes in the place of this option; and in point of fact it will be found that the same effects do take place, and that (as I shall have occasion to show hereafter) a constantly-increasing portion of the benefits arising from capital naturally and necessarily descend to the lower classes of labourers as society advances, wherever there is good government, or any tolerable degree of liberty and security.

From what has been advanced then it should appear that every stock or capital employed in production is advantageous to the community in a *threefold* manner.

1. In the first place, every capital is *directly* advantageous to the proprietor, whether he employs it himself, or lends it

to another at the ordinary rate of profit or interest. This advantage needs no illustration or argument to prove it.

2. Secondly, every capital is *directly* advantageous to the person who has it in loan; because, if he did not expect to derive advantage, he would not have borrowed, or having borrowed, he would not retain the loan if he did not find his advantage in doing so.

3. Thirdly, every capital is *indirectly* advantageous to the whole community; because every capital either actually assists in the work of production, or fills a vacuity which would draw other capitals from that work; consequently every capital assists either directly or indirectly in augmenting the quantity and diminishing the cost and price of commodities; and as all men are consumers and purchasers of commodities, they are necessarily participators in the benefits of that abundance and cheapness which capital creates.*

---

* As a farther illustration of the subject discussed in the text, the following extract from a pamphlet, published (by the author of this Inquiry) several years ago, may be added:—

"Capital," it is there said, "extenuates labour to the full amount of the revenues drawn from it; nay, it always does so in a considerably greater degree, and the poor and unendowed man's lot, as well as the inheritor of those revenues, is improved by it, and always made better by every extension and investment of capital, excepting when that investment is in public funds or securities, the interest of which must be paid from taxation.

"Capital extenuates labour in a greater degree than the amount of the revenues drawn directly from it by the proprietors of that capital, because, if the works or properties in which it must always be invested, (if not in public funds,) did not operate such an advantage to the public, those revenues could not be paid. Thus the collections drawn from canals, roads, harbours, docks, ships, &c. and which go to keep up those properties, and to pay the proprietors their shares of revenue, do not exhaust the whole of their benefits. Every one who pays or contributes any part, however small, of those revenues does previously

SECTION III.

CONCLUSION OF THE CHAPTER.

INDEPENDENTLY therefore of any labour they may themselves choose to perform, the capitalists are in reality the greatest of all benefactors to the community; for not only are their properties necessarily beneficial in a greater or less degree to all the other classes as well as to themselves, as has been shown in the previous section; but, as will be

---

derive a positive advantage and benefit to himself, either by the immediate use and occupation of that canal, road, harbour, dock, ship, &c. or from the cheaper purchase of the goods he has occasion for, and which are, by means of those and other investments of capital, brought to market at an easier rate, and in greater abundance, and placed more within the reach and ability of every one to procure. And this advantage is independent of and over and above that which is derived, in the shape of revenue, by the proprietors of those capitals.

"If the merchant could have got any cheaper, more convenient, and easier mode of transport, he would not have employed that canal, road, harbour, dock, ship, &c.; and if the smallest purchaser of goods could have got them cheaper borne by any other conveyance, he would not have preferred those, or contributed any part to support and keep up those capitals, and to pay the revenues of their owners. And thus it is that the poorest man shares naturally in every accumulation of wealth and investment of capital. His command over the luxuries, conveniences, or necessaries of life, is increased. And so it is with all capitals,—they extenuate labour in a greater degree than the amount of the revenues drawn from them, to which no one is *compelled* to contribute, but does it *voluntarily*, and solely for his own advantage; and thus it is that the owners of those capitals live and enjoy their revenues, not only without being burdensome to the rest of the community, but conferring, at the same time, a boon and a benefit upon it."—*General Statement of an Argument on the Subject of Population in Answer to Mr Malthus's Theory. Edinburgh*, 1821.

shown more fully in the sequel, it is by means of the assistance of those properties, that is, of the capitals preserved, saved, and accumulated by them and their predecessors, that any wealth is produced or enjoyed by any individual beyond the most scanty and most miserable subsistence.

The distinct nature and condition of this class, or the real effects produced by the establishment of those rights of which the condition and privileges of this class is a necessary consequence, has never yet been fully explained or elucidated; and hence it is that it has been thought a sufficient answer to objectors and cavillers, to say that the *law of the land* is the foundation of their rights, as if just grounds in reason could not be shown why the institutions which establish these rights *should be* the law of the land.

It is owing probably to the neglect of this point also, that any obscurity has ever appeared to rest on the question of productive and unproductive labour, after the very clear and accurate manner in which Dr Smith has explained that obvious distinction. For it is not to be imagined that in laying down that distinction this very perspicacious author intended to include in those two classes, whom he calls labourers, the whole population or members of the community. Some, he confesses, "do not labour at all." Those of course he could not intend to include. All that Dr Smith meant therefore, in drawing the distinction which he has done between productive and unproductive labour, evidently was simply to divide and distinguish the persons who really and necessarily must and do labour into those two classes, so very plainly marked and distinct in themselves. That this was indeed his only intention is not left to be made out by any uncertain process of reasoning, or conjecture, but follows closely and unequivocally from the propositions he expressly admits and the terms which he uses,—as when he says,—"Both productive and unproductive labourers, and those who do not labour at all,"* &c.,—" Unproductive labourers, and those who do not labour at all,"* &c.,—expressions which conclusively show that he acknowledged this third class of persons in society, and consequently did not intend to include the whole people under his classification of the labourers, productive and unproductive.

There is then, it must be acknowledged, a class in the community who do not labour at all or need to labour; and it has been now shown, and will appear more fully in the sequel, that this privilege or exemption from labour on the part of particular persons, when it is derived from the possession or proprietorship of land or capital, not only does not entail any burden or hardship upon the labouring classes, but is, on the contrary, most closely and inseparably connected with their advantage and interest; the establishment of those rights on which this privilege is founded being a condition necessary to the acquisition and employment of capital, without which neither the labouring classes, nor any classes or class whatsoever, even the lowest that exists, could possess or enjoy that degree of wealth or affluence which naturally and necessarily falls to them wherever there is any capital accumulated under good government.

This being considered, it will not, I hope, surprise the reader when I observe here, that it is the grand object and effect of all real improvement to increase this class and diminish every other,—to increase the number of the non-labourers, and diminish the number of the labourers, productive and unproductive,—at the same time, be it well observed, that either the quantity of labour to be performed by those who remain labourers is diminished, or their enjoyments or wages increased, or both; in a word, that the pro-

* Wealth of Nations, book ii. chap. 3.

per object and effect of all real improvement is to increase enjoyment and to lighten labour. And to this end it is that the whole exertions and endeavours of mankind, in the accumulation or acquisition of wealth, are constantly directed, and uniformly tend, wherever there is any tolerable degree of security and liberty, or good government.

This object is chiefly to be attained by the accumulation and application of wealth to the work of production,—that is, by capital; in other words, by all those various properties whereby the productive powers of labour are assisted and augmented, and a given quantity of wealth produced by fewer hands;—as by roads, canals, harbours, docks, ships, steam-engines, water-wheels, and all other articles or items of productive wealth, as well as by such accumulations or stores of consumable goods as are necessary to the establishment of the division of labour; all which properties are the fruit of *saving*, and as soon as they are accumulated or completed, present at once,—first, the means of production with diminished labour; and, secondly, a certain fund for the maintenance of non-labourers; which fund is, as we have shown, additional to and over and above the other advantages which necessarily accrue from those properties or capitals to all other persons; and it is always to be borne in mind, that the existence of this fund—namely, the interest due to the capitalists—is a condition necessary to the existence of the capitals themselves, and consequently to any other species of advantage derivable from them. And thus it is that the object we have endeavoured to describe is accomplished, and that non-labourers are provided for and their number increased with advantage to the community; being the only way in which the increase of this class can be either just and useful, or desirable.

There is indeed another mode quite different from this of increasing this class; but then its effects in regard to the community at large, and to the labouring classes in particular, are equally different, and are as baneful and pernicious as those of the method just described are beneficial and salutary. What I allude to is, that increase of the non-labouring class which is effected by public debts, or by the payment of interest for capitals which have been spent and annihilated, and which cannot of course continue to assist the labourer, or in any possible manner contribute to production. All revenues drawn in this manner fall as a burden on the community at large, and either diminish the comforts or increase the toil of the labouring classes.

But there is yet another method of increasing this class, which, though precisely similar in its effects with that just mentioned, is still more objectionable, namely, that which is effected by means of taxation, which is altogether gratuitous and uncalled for by any useful object or necessity, as when contributions are levied upon the community, and paid over to persons who either do nothing at all in return, or nothing which is adequate; or, what is still worse, when such contributions are paid away for purposes of mere influence or corruption.

This mode has sometimes been practised to a certain extent even in countries where taxes must be levied by regular laws, and was then legal of course; but no power or authority on earth can make it *just*; and no government which sanctions or permits such practices to be carried to a great extent can ever expect to make a happy or a peaceable or a contented people.

This last-mentioned method of increasing the class of non-labourers is indeed infinitely more rapid in its progress and simpler in the execution, than that which proceeds by means of the tardy and painful accumulations of capital, and its gradual application to productive purposes. But then it produces effects directly the reverse. Instead of lightening labour, it makes it harder to those who are left to perform it; and it only enriches one set of people at the expense of another—at the expense chiefly of the labouring classes, productive and unproductive;* whom it dooms to increased exertion and diminished reward or enjoyment, by compelling them to maintain the idle and the useless; and by consigning the lower classes of labourers to oppressive toil and inadequate remuneration, and by subjecting them to immediate hardship, it sinks both their spirit and their character, lowers the natural wages of labour, and permanently degrades their habits and condition.

CHAPTER VI.

OF THE MATERIAL MEANS OR INSTRUMENTS OF PRODUCTION, AND THAT THESE ARE THE ONLY ORIGINAL SOURCES OF WEALTH.

THE material means or instruments of production are all conveniently reducible to three general kinds, or heads of

---

* The interest of these two classes, that is, of all labourers, I may remark here, is, in the respect alluded to, exactly the same, and whatever raises or depresses wages to the one must produce the same effect in regard to the other. Thus, if the class of unproductive labourers be very much increased, and taken away from productive employments, more work must be done by those who are left; and if more work be done for the same wages it is equivalent to a reduction of wages. But if more work be done, or less wages taken for a given quantity of work by the productive classes of labourers, the same must be done by the unproductive class, including of course those employed under government, in all the subordinate situations at least, where the principle of competition is allowed to operate.

arrangement, and naturally belong to some one or other of the following distinct denominations; viz.

I. Land.

II. Man himself.

III. Capital.

1. It has been shown in a former chapter,* that all the physical elements of wealth come immediately from the earth, and either grow out of it as vegetables, or rest upon its surface as animals, or are found within its bowels, or in its waters, as minerals and marine productions. It is true, that many of these elements come previously from the distant regions of the atmosphere, from the sun, and perhaps, for any thing that mankind know, even from the stars; but certain it is they must all reach our globe of earth and ocean before they can enter into the composition of any article of wealth, or indeed of any thing that can be acquired by mankind. Political economists therefore, in order to avoid all useless encumbrance of words, or unnecessary multiplication of terms and distinctions, have generally agreed, by common usage and consent in this science, to understand by the term *land* whatever material substance our globe or nature offers to the hands of man on which he may bestow his labour, with a view to convert it to his convenience or use; and in this extensive sense, in which it is always to be used, it is one and the first necessary and indispensable instrument of production and original source of wealth, without which not the smallest particle or atom, so called, could ever be acquired or exist.

---

* Chap. ii. sect. 1.

II. The second necessary and indispensable instrument of production is *man himself*, of whose labour it requires some portion, greater or less, to produce every item of wealth, however trifling. In general it requires a considerable quantity of human labour to produce all sorts of wealth; but every article must be gathered at least and taken care of, which cannot be done without labour. Human labour therefore, it may be added, is another original source of wealth.

III. Capital is the third instrument of production and original source of wealth. It is at its origin a product of the other two instruments; but it immediately unites with them in causing its own future increase, and co-operates thenceforward in the production and augmentation of every sort of wealth. It is at first a very rude instrument,—a club, a wooden spear, or even a stone, in the hands of the savage; but it gradually improves and increases as society advances by means of industry and frugality, and comes more and more into employment, until at length, in the progress of improvement and accumulation, it becomes the most efficient and powerful of all the three instruments, and the grand source of exuberant production—of abundance, luxury, and leisure. Of this truth we shall be fully convinced when we consider how limited the powers are of man's naked arm, and how little can be produced by land and labour simply, without the co-operation and assistance of capital.

These are the three material means or instruments of production, and the only immediate and original sources of wealth. Strictly speaking, indeed, the first and second only are simple and original; the third being at first, as was just observed, a product of the other two. The first articles of capital used by the savage, the club, the wooden spear, and the stone, are the simple products of land and labour. Or if it be supposed that the club and wooden spear must have been cut and formed by the assistance of some other instrument, as a sharp-edged stone, then this last must be admitted to have been the produce of the two primary and original instruments; but as soon as capital has accumulated into masses, it becomes a separate and independent instrument, and an original source of wealth to its possessors or proprietors, as well as land or labour. The latter are essential and absolutely necessary to production, and even to the very existence of wealth. The former is essential to its production in any great quantity or abundance, in proportion to the numbers of mankind and extent of territory, or to the quantity available of the two other instruments. Without land and man himself there could be no production at all, or even existence of wealth; and without capital there could not be any considerable or abundant production. Without capital, in short, no man could procure or enjoy more than the bare necessaries of life, and even these of the worst quality, and painfully acquired by his constant daily toil; so that, without this instrument, all men would be wholly occupied in procuring a bare and uncomfortable subsistence; whereas by means of it, whilst all men are supplied liberally with the necessaries of life, and have some of the conveniences and even luxuries superadded, a great many men have all these in the greatest abundance, without almost any labour or trouble on their part being necessary to procure them, and are thus left at liberty to cultivate their nobler faculties, and to promote the improvement and advantage of their neighbours and of the whole human race.

CHAPTER VII.

OF THE MANNER IN WHICH CAPITAL CONTRIBUTES TO PRODUCTION.

SECTION I.

CAPITAL DEFINED—ITS POTENT AGENCY IN PRODUCTION —DISTINCTION OF FIXED AND CIRCULATING CAPITALS —THE ACQUISITION OF EXISTENCE OF BOTH THOSE SORTS OF CAPITALS, OR OF CAPITAL IN GENERAL, A CONDITION NECESSARY TO THE EXISTENCE OR ATTAINMENT OF THE SYSTEM OF THE DIVISION OF LABOUR.

THE manner in which *land* and *labour* contribute to production is obvious enough, and has been already perhaps sufficiently explained in the foregoing chapters. It remains to explain the manner in which *capital* contributes.

Capital consists of all accumulated wealth, which is or may be applied to assist in the work of production, which is nearly equivalent to saying that it consists of all wealth whatsoever.* It contributes to production by assisting and in-

---

* There is no real use in the distinction which has been attempted to be established by some writers, (Torrens, Prod. W. p. 4, et seq.; Malthus' Definitions in Pol. Econ. chap. x, p. 237,) between stock or wealth generally, and capital. To know whether any portion of stock, capital, or accumulated wealth, be productive or unproductive, it is necessary to know in what manner it is employed; and all that is requisite to enable the student to form a judgment upon this point has been already explained in the third chapter.

creasing the productive energies of the other two instruments;—of land by improvements and cultivation of the soil; and of labour by abridging its processes, and increasing the dexterity and efficiency of the human arm.

The land yields more rude produce (of that sort at least which is fit to be converted to the use of mankind) when it is highly cultivated and improved by means of capital, than when it lies waste; and the human arm produces an incomparably greater effect by means of the spade and the plough, or of the cotton-frame and the steam-engine, than it could do naked and unprovided with those potent instruments and items of capital.

Capitals are commonly distinguished into two different kinds, called *fixed* and *circulating* capitals.*

The fixed capitals consist of those articles which are calculated to assist in the work of production, "without changing masters,"† or going out of the possession or ownership of the proprietors or employers thereof. Such are all permanent improvements or meliorations of the land, and all farm-buildings constructed thereupon, as well as all agricultural implements, labouring cattle, &c. Such also are all the manufactories within a country, and all the canals, roads, harbours, docks, ships, &c., as also all the useful machines and tools or instruments of trade, and things of the like sort.

The circulating capitals, again, consist of those articles which are continually changing either their shape or their place, or both, while the process of production is going for-

* The distinction here noticed, though not perhaps of essential importance, will sometimes be found useful for the purpose of preventing circumlocution, as in the instance of the present chapter, in explaining the manner in which the different sorts of capitals contribute to production.

† Wealth of Nations, book ii. chap. 1.

ward to its completion, and which frequently change masters or proprietors in the course of that process. They comprise among other things the raw materials of every manufacture, and the food, clothes, and other articles immediately necessary to the maintenance of the labourer.

The manner in which the fixed capitals contribute to production is generally not difficult to be discerned; and with regard to such portions of them as take the form of particular instruments, as the spade, the plough, &c., the manner in which these contribute is manifest, because the manner in which they increase the power and efficiency of the human arm is open and apparent; but the manner in which a great part of the circulating capitals contribute to the same end appears to be not generally so well understood.

The necessity indeed of that part of the circulating capitals, which consists of the raw materials of the different manufactures, is self-evident; but the necessity in production of the capitals consisting of food, clothes, and the other articles of subsistence, is not perhaps, on a first view, quite so obvious. They are, however, not less useful or less necessary than the others. Nay, they are absolutely indispensable to render the fixed capitals as well as the other part of the circulating capitals of any value or effect. To be aware of this, we have only to reflect that the machinery and work-looms will not work themselves, but require hands or labourers to conduct the operations; and these must be provided with the means of subsistence.

And let it not be imagined that such capitals are inconsiderable or trifling in amount. Let any one calculate the value of the maintenance for one year of the whole of the productive labourers of any extensive, highly-populous, and civilized country, and he will at once be made sensible of the amount and importance of this part of the circulating capitals.

This part of the circulating capitals then is evidently indispensable to give effect and activity to all the other capitals employed in production, because it is indispensable to the maintenance or existence of the labourers in all the variety of employments or species of productive industry.

And this consideration brings us directly to the grand instance wherein the supreme utility and importance of capital in general will most distinctly and decidedly appear, namely, in its indispensableness to the attainment of the system of the arrangement and *division of labour*,—a system which increases the productive powers of labour and the dexterity and efficiency of the human arm to a degree that is almost incredible. And to this system capitals of every description are necessary or subservient ; but, first of all, capitals consisting of food, clothes, and any other articles necessary to the maintenance of the labourer, without which no species of industry could be undertaken or successfully followed out, which does not afford a direct and immediate return of such necessaries.

By the system of the division of labour is meant, that arrangement which takes place in the progress from barbarism to civilization, and which is the very first step in that progress, whereby each individual labourer finds it his interest to confine himself and his labour mainly to one distinct and peculiar occupation, and to exchange his productions against those brought to market by the other labourers, instead of engaging himself in all the variety of pursuits which would be necessary were he to attempt to do every thing for himself, and to produce directly, by his own isolated and unassisted exertions, every article of wealth he had occasion to consume. By this system the great body of the people gradually form themselves into distinct classes of producers, and, as society advances, attach themselves more and more to separate and distinct businesses, exchanging their productions one with another "by treaty, by barter, and by purchase,"* to the great advantage of every particular labourer and of the whole community.†

It is this system which we observe grown to a degree of perfection in all highly-populous and civilized countries, and which occasions that abundance of commodities and general diffusion of wealth which, under a good administration of government, extends itself downwards to the very lowest ranks of the people.

But before a single individual can confine himself and his labour to any single species of business or employment, (except the production or acquisition of the immediate necessaries of life,) and continue to follow it exclusively as a constant and regular occupation, a certain accumulation of provisions must have previously taken place, which may be accessible to him for the purpose of supplying his natural daily wants; and before the division of labour can be fully and universally established in a country, and every different trade or employment be followed by a separate and distinct set of people, stores and savings or accumulations of every different description of wealth or capitals must be provided and established beforehand within such country or in its neighbourhood. There are, in the first place, the houses to dwell in and the houses to work in; next there is the machinery required, and the tools or instruments to work with; there are farther the materials to be wrought up into all the variety of products or commodities; there are still farther

* Wealth of Nations, book i. chap. 2.

† In the sequel it will be shown, that the principle which gives rise to this system of the division of labour is at the same time the great regulator of distribution; and that the more every individual labourer can produce under this system, the more he will find it necessary to give in exchange to other labourers for their productions.—See book ii. chap. 1.

the provisions necessary to subsist the workmen while engaged in the work; and, lastly, there is the money necessary to act as the instrument of distribution and exchange, to facilitate the division and allotment of the different circulating capitals, and to conduct them in their just proportions to the persons and places where they are effectually demanded. All which different sorts of capitals must be accumulated, saved, and accessible within a country, before it can fully enjoy all the advantages to be derived from the division of labour.

"In that rude state of society," says Dr Smith, "in which there is no division of labour, in which exchanges are seldom made, and in which every man provides every thing for himself, it is not necessary that any stock should be accumulated or stored up beforehand in order to carry on the business of the society. Every man endeavours to supply by his own industry his own occasional wants as they occur. When he is hungry, he goes to the forest to hunt; when his coat is worn out, he clothes himself with the skin of the first large animal he kills; and when his hut begins to go to ruin, he repairs it as well as he can with the trees and the turf that are nearest it.

"But when the division of labour has once been thoroughly introduced, the produce of a man's own labour can supply but a very small part of his occasional wants. The far greater part of them are supplied by the produce of other men's labour, which he purchases with the produce, or, what is the same thing, with the price of the produce of his own. But this purchase cannot be made till such times as the produce of his own labour has not only been completed but sold. A stock of goods of different kinds, therefore, must be stored up somewhere sufficient to maintain him, and to supply him with the materials and tools of his work, till such time, at least, as both these events can be brought about. A weaver cannot apply himself entirely to his peculiar business, unless there is beforehand stored up somewhere, either in his possession or in that of some other person, a stock sufficient to maintain him, and to supply him with the materials and tools of his work till he has not only completed but sold his web. This accumulation must evidently be previous to his applying his industry for so long a time to such a peculiar business."*

It thus appears evident enough, that the acquisition or existence of capitals is absolutely necessary to the existence or attainment of the system of the division of labour. Before, however, proceeding farther in the illustration of this point, it will be expedient to describe the manner in which that system assists and increases the powers of production, in order to elicit some adequate conception of the immense and incalculable service that capital performs to society and to mankind in this respect.

SECTION II.

OF THE MODE IN WHICH THE DIVISION OF LABOUR PRODUCES ITS EFFECT OF ASSISTING AND IMPROVING THE POWERS OF PRODUCTION.

This subject has been already so fully and so excellently explained by Dr Smith, that it would be an unpardonable waste of time to attempt any new or original treatment of it in this place, more especially since a far less perfect exposition than that which is to be found in the "Wealth of Nations" might be sufficient to serve the purpose required in our present argument. I shall therefore, in this instance, avail myself of the illustrations which I find formed to my hand;† and in doing this I shall adhere as much as pos-

---

* Wealth of Nations, book ii. Introd.

† In this and other instances which will occur in the course of this work, when I find any part of my argument already illustrated by a

sible, or as may be consistent with brevity and conveniency, to the words of the author so generally followed on this subject.

---

former writer as well or better than I could do it myself, I always take such part and apply it to my purpose, and always in the words of the author. This is the method of the mathematicians, and is one among others of the causes that have powerfully contributed towards the progress and perfection of their science. Those who cultivate the mathematics never dream of altering or varying any demonstration, or part of a demonstration, except with a view to improve it; and if they cannot either shorten the steps, or chain of reasoning, between the original principles and the conclusion, or make the whole process clearer or simpler, they uniformly allow it to stand as it is, and proceed forward in their inquiries. They take what they find already done, and apply it to their purpose exactly as they find it, adding what is new only where they can improve or extend their science.

And why should not political economists do the same?—Why should they uselessly occupy and mispend their time in re-performing a task which has been already completed, more than the others? —It cannot be with the idea of making their work *original*, for this it cannot do. Nay, it hinders them from producing what *is* original, or from proceeding to what is farther wanted in the science. Let political economists then imitate in this respect the example of the mathematicians, and the best effects will follow. They will thus have a better chance to proceed from improvement to improvement, till their science be perfected; and in its present state there is still ample room for labours of this sort. We are still very far from the goal of our labours in this science.

The way of proceeding recommended here is, besides, but a proper act of courtesy from one author to another, or rather it is but a bare act of justice to those who have gone before us; and not to do it is to deal unfairly by them, independently of the waste of labour and time which it involves.

It sometimes indeed happens, that an argument in another work will not easily incorporate with a different writing in the precise words of the original, and in that case it must of course be remodelled to suit the particular purpose. But whenever it can be done, whenever

Dr Smith, and after him every other writer, as far as I have observed, who has treated the subject since his time, have arranged the circumstances, or particular causes to which it is owing that the division of labour increases so very greatly the powers of production, under three different heads, as follows:—*First,* (say they,) it increases the skill and dexterity of every particular workman; *secondly,* it saves the time commonly lost in passing from one species of work to another; and, *thirdly,* it gives rise to the invention of a great number of machines which facilitate and abridge labour, and enable one man to do the work of many.*

On the first of these heads, Dr Smith observes,—"A common smith, who, though accustomed to handle the hammer, has never been used to make nails, if upon some particular occasion he is obliged to attempt it, will scarce, I am assured, be able to make above two or three hundred nails in a day, and those too very bad ones. A smith who has been accustomed to make nails, but whose sole or principal business has not been that of a nailer, can seldom with his utmost diligence make more than eight hundred or a thousand nails in a day. I have seen several boys under twenty years of age who had

---

an argument is found exactly suited to our purpose, no time ought to to be lost in translating or manufacturing a new version.

On the subject now to be illustrated in the text,—the Division of Labour,—Dr Smith is almost universally followed, both abroad and at home, and either fairly quoted, or the substance of his statements extracted and remodelled. In the case of the foreigner not quoting Dr Smith, there is a proper excuse, because, writing in another language, he cannot give the exact words; but there can be no excuse for a writer of his own country, who, instead of using and fairly quoting an argument already made perfect to his hand, chooses rather to dress it up in language slightly different.

* Wealth of Nations, book i. chap. 1.—See also a very able and elaborate "Report," by Alexander Hamilton, Esq. of North America, Secretary to the Treasury of the United States, 1790: Article, Division of Labour.

never exercised any other trade but that of making nails, and who, when they exerted themselves, could make each of them upwards of two thousand three hundred nails in a day. The making of a nail, however, is by no means one of the simplest operations. The same person blows the bellows, stirs or mends the fire as there is occasion, heats the iron, and forges every part of the nail: in forging the head too he is obliged to change his tools. The different operations into which the making of a pin, or of a metal button, is subdivided, are all of them much more simple, and the dexterity of the person, of whose life it has been the sole business to perform them, is usually much greater. The rapidity with which some of the operations of those manufactures are performed exceeds what the human hand could, by those who had never seen them, be supposed capable of acquiring."*

"Secondly," continues Dr Smith in illustration of the second head, "the advantage which is gained by saving the time commonly lost in passing from one sort of work to another is much greater than we should at first view be apt to imagine it. It is impossible to pass very quickly from one kind of work to another, that is carried on in a different place, and with quite different tools. A country weaver who cultivates a small farm must lose a good deal of time in passing from his loom to the field and from the field to his loom. When the two trades can be carried on in the same workhouse the loss of time is no doubt much less. It is even in this case, however, very considerable. A man commonly saunters a little in turning his hand from one sort of employment to another. When he first begins the new work he is seldom very keen and hearty; his mind, as they say, does not go to it, and for some time he rather trifles than applies to good purpose. The habit of sauntering, and of indolent careless application, which is naturally, or rather necessarily, acquired by every country workman who is obliged to change his work and his

* Wealth of Nations, book i. chap. 1.

tools every half-hour, and to apply his hand in twenty different ways almost every day of his life, renders him almost always slothful and lazy, and incapable of any vigorous application even on the most pressing occasions. Independent therefore, of his deficiency in point of dexterity, this cause alone must always reduce considerably the quantity of work which he is capable of performing."*

"Thirdly and lastly," continues the same author, in reference to the third head above stated, "every body must be sensible how much labour is facilitated and abridged by the application of proper machinery."† "'Tis an artificial force," says Mr Hamilton, "brought in aid of the natural force of man, and, to all the purpose of labour, is as an increase of hands; an accession of strength, unencumbered too with the expense of maintaining the labourer.‡ "A man," adds this writer, "occupied on a single object will have it more in his power, and will be more readily led to exert his imagination in devising methods to facilitate and abridge labour, than if he were perplexed by a variety of independent and dissimilar operations. Besides this, the fabrication of machines, in numerous instances becoming itself a distinct trade, the artist who follows it has all the advantages which have been enumerated for improvements in this particular art; and in both ways the invention and application of machinery are extended."§

To this very concise and distinct exposition and enumeration of the circumstances, or particular causes to which it is owing that the division of labour increases so very greatly the powers of production, there might perhaps be added as

---

* Wealth of Nations, book i. chap. 1. † Ibid.

‡ Report mentioned above in note, p. 73, as quoted in a North American publication, entitled "Address of the Philadelphia Society for the Promotion of National Industry."

§ Report referred to in the preceding note.

another and *fourth* cause or circumstance, contributing to the same result, and of sufficient consequence to deserve a particular notice, that it sharpens the wits and ingenuity of those persons who are intrusted with or engaged in the business of direction and management, and gives room for the exercise of judgment in the proper arrangement and combination of the different processes of labour and efforts of the labourers. In an extensive manufactory the arrangement of the buildings and machinery, or plan of the work, is itself a highly important point; and where a great number of people are employed of diverse talents and dispositions, and of various degrees of skill or dexterity, and where also a multiplicity of different processes are going on, the opportunities and methods are innumerable, wherein, by a judicious arrangement of the different operations, and by placing every particular workman, as far as it can be done, in his proper situation, or in that post for which he is best adapted, the manager of a work, and even the subordinate managers, or *foremen*, in an extensive establishment, can very materially assist in producing the greatest effects with the smallest expenditure of human labour. But on this head it is unnecessary to enlarge after the previous detail. From that detail it cannot but have happened, that the minute causes or circumstances, whereunto it is owing that the division of labour increases so very greatly the powers of production, must have already appeared in a clear light. Still, however, I must add, from the author already so largely quoted, his celebrated example of the effects of the division of labour in the trade of the *pin-maker*, since it not only illustrates those effects more fully, and perhaps still more strikingly, than any of the passages we have before adduced, but will serve also to throw light on one more observation or two, without which this portion of our argument would be imperfectly stated.

"A workman," says Dr Smith, "not educated to this business (which the division of labour has rendered a distinct trade,) nor acquainted with the use of the machinery employed in it, (to the invention of which the same division of labour has probably given occasion,) could scarce, perhaps, with his utmost industry, make one pin in a day, and certainly could not make twenty. But in the way in which this business is now carried on, not only the whole work is a peculiar trade, but it is divided into a number of branches, of which the greater part are likewise peculiar trades. One man draws out the wire, another straights it, a third cuts it, a fourth points it, a fifth grinds it at the top for receiving the head; to make the head requires two or three distinct operations; to put it on is a peculiar business, to whiten the pins is another; it is even a trade by itself to put them into the paper; and the important business of making a pin is, in this manner, divided into about eighteen distinct operations, which, in some manufactories, are all performed by distinct hands, though in others the same man will sometimes perform two or three of them. I have seen a small manufactory of this kind where ten men only were employed, and where some of them consequently performed two or three distinct operations. But though they were very poor, and therefore but indifferently accommodated with the necessary machinery, they could, when they exerted themselves, make among them about twelve pounds of pins in a day. There are in a pound upwards of four thousand pins of a middling size. Those ten persons, therefore, could make among them upwards of forty-eight thousand pins in a day. Each person, therefore, making a tenth part of forty-eight thousand pins, might be considered as making four thousand eight hundred pins in a day. But if they had all wrought separately and independently, and without any of them having been educated to this peculiar business, they certainly could not each of them have made twenty, perhaps not one pin in a day; that is, certainly not the two hundred and fortieth, perhaps not the four thousand eight hundredth part of what they are at present capable of performing, in consequence of a proper division and combination of their different operations."*

The separation of different trades and employments from one another in the great business of a whole community, is analogous to this subdivision of labour in a particular manufactory, and produces a similar but vastly more extended influence in assisting and improving the powers of production, and increasing the quantity and abundance of wealth. By following a separate and distinct trade, every individual labourer acquires the capacity of performing a great quantity of work, or, in other words, of producing largely in his peculiar department; and every capital also produces largely by the same means. Every one has therefore a great quantity of the produce of his industry or capital to exchange against the produce of other people's industry or capital; and the whole society are in this way far more abundantly supplied with all commodities, than they could be if each attempted independently to supply the whole of his individual wants by his own isolated and unassisted labour.

Dr Smith continues:—"In every other art and manufacture, the effects of the division of labour are similar to what they are in this very trifling one, though in many of them the labour can neither be so much subdivided, nor reduced to so great a simplicity of operation. The division of labour, however, so far as it can be introduced, occasions, in every art, a proportionable increase of the productive powers of labour. The separation of different trades and employments from one another seems to have taken place in consequence of this advantage. This separation, too, is generally carried furthest in those countries which enjoy the highest degree of industry and improvement, what is the work of one man in a rude state of society being generally that of several in an improved

---

* Wealth of Nations, book i. chap. 1.

one. In every improved society the farmer is generally nothing but a farmer; the manufacturer, nothing but a manufacturer. The labour too which is necessary to produce any one complete manufacture is almost always divided among a great number of hands. How many different trades are employed in each branch of the linen and woollen manufactures, from the growers of the flax and the wool to the bleachers and smoothers of the linen, or to the dyers and dressers of the cloth!"*

Lastly, Dr Smith observes,—"The division of labour is commonly supposed to be carried farthest in some very trifling manufactures; not perhaps that it really is carried farther in them than in others of more importance; but in those trifling manufactures, which are destined to supply the small wants of but a small number of people, the whole number of workmen must necessarily be small; and those employed in every different branch of the work can often be collected into the same workhouse, and placed at once under the view of the spectator. In those great manufactures, on the contrary, which are destined to supply the great wants of the great body of the people, every different branch of the work employs so great a number of workmen, that it is impossible to collect them all into the same workhouse. We can seldom see more at one time than those employed in one single branch. Though in such manufactures, therefore, the work may really be divided into a much greater number of parts than in those of a more trifling nature, the division is not near so obvious, and has accordingly been much less observed."†

Such then are the effects of the division of labour in assisting and improving the powers of the production, and in increasing the quantity or abundance of wealth.

* Wealth of Nations, book i. chap. 1. † Ibid.

SECTION III.

THAT THE ACQUISITION OR EXISTENCE OF CAPITAL IS A CONDITION NECESSARY TO THE ESTABLISHMENT OR EXISTENCE OF THE DIVISION OF LABOUR.

But all this—all that is effected by the division of labour, as explained in the foregoing section, is owing to capital; because without capital the division of labour cannot be established or attained. For the whole of the articles or items of wealth required in every department of industry, and in every employment or division of labour, as necessary to enable one and all of them to be established or carried on, are portions of capital. All the machinery required is capital, and every tool or instrument used in every sort of business, and not only these, but all the materials prepared or required to be worked up into more perfect goods, as well as the stores of food, clothing, and provisions of all sorts, necessary to maintain the whole of the labourers engaged in any kind of work, are capitals. Now it is self-evident, that without supplies of capital of the last-mentioned kind, namely, food and other necessaries, either possessed by himself or furnished him by other people, the labourer could not confine or apply himself to any single trade or employment (except that of seeking for such necessaries) but for the shortest periods; not probably for a whole day at one time, and certainly not for a whole week. Without such necessaries or capitals previously laid in store, every man's immediate efforts must be directed to the procuring of what will satisfy those natural wants which can neither be delayed nor dispensed with. But if even one individual could not confine himself to one employment without a certain capital or quantity of provisions being previously laid in store, much less would it be possible for very large numbers to divide and betake themselves to all the variety of distinct occupations necessarily followed among a civilized people, without such stores and accumulations being provided beforehand as should be sufficient to supply their immediate wants.

Those who cultivate the ground, and look forward to its produce for their remuneration, must be provided beforehand with sufficient stores to supply their necessities till the gathering of the harvest; and the farmer must of course be prepared to afford his labourers food, clothes, and lodging, or, what comes to the same thing, money-wages with which they may purchase these necessaries, as well during the period that he is only putting the seed into the ground as when he is receiving his return, and during the whole interval likewise between the one period and the other. The manufacturer also, who undertakes the establishment of a work, must be prepared, in like manner, to supply his labourers with their necessary maintenance, or with money-wages sufficient to procure it for them, besides providing them with the proper machinery or implements required in the peculiar business. The cotton-spinner, for example, must build his mill-house, and fit it up with the proper machinery; he must erect the water-wheel or steam-engine which is to give motion to that machinery, and he must provide the material of *cotton* which is to be spun; and not only so, but he must provide all his work-people with their necessary subsistence, comprising food, clothes, and lodging, or with such wages as will enable them to purchase those articles; and every person in every business must be prepared to do the like for his labourers. But it is self-evident, that no wages could enable either the manufacturer or his workmen to purchase such articles, (or any articles,) if they did not already exist, or had not been previously produced and accumulated in the hands of neighbouring speculators or proprietors, with a view to supply the general demand.

Wherever, therefore, the system of the division of labour is established, such stores or capitals must necessarily be accumulated, and must have grown up simultaneously with that system, sufficient to supply the necessary wants of the whole of the labourers employed under it.

Those stores and accumulations, or capitals, belong of course to a vast variety of persons; indeed nearly to as many as there are individuals or members in the community, and in the greatest variety also, and difference of proportions. It is by no means necessary that they should belong to the persons who actually apply them to the work of production. They are often consigned in the shape of a loan from the rich capitalist to the undertaker of a work; and the inferior labourers are supplied from those stores or accumulations which the general demand of the country gives birth to, weekly or daily as they require them, through the instrumentality of the money-wages which they receive, and with which they purchase what they have occasion for from the capitalists, who make a trade of providing such stores. And the ways are innumerable by which every different store and every different item of every different sort of capital finds its way from the possession of its temporary proprietor to its proper and destined use by exchange, by treaty and agreement, by barter, by purchase, and by loan.

Nor must we be confounded by the circumstance, that loans of capital from one person to another are commonly made in the shape of money. This is merely the temporary and transitory form which capital is made to undergo in the act of changing masters; and the transfer of the money from the one to the other is simply the transfer of a command over the general wealth or capital of the country to the extent of all that can be purchased by the amount of the loan.

"Almost all loans at interest," says Dr Smith, "are made in money, either of paper, or of gold and silver. But what the borrower really wants, and what the lender readily supplies him with, is not the money, but the money's worth, or the goods which it can purchase. If he wants it as a stock for immediate consumption, it is those goods only which he can place in that stock. If he wants it as a capital for employing industry, it is from those goods only that the industrious can be furnished with the tools, materials, and maintenance, necessary for carrying on their work. By means of the loan, the lender, as it were, assigns to the borrower his right to a certain portion of the annual produce of the land and labour of the country, to be employed as the borrower pleases."*

To return:—It should appear then, from what has been advanced, that stock, or stored wealth, or capital, is absolutely necessary to the existence or establishment of the division of labour; and it consequently follows, that all the effects which we have seen to result from the division of labour in assisting and improving the powers of production, are really and properly the effects of capital.

SECTION IV.

CONCLUSION OF THE CHAPTER.

THAT ALL WEALTH IS NOT PRODUCED BY LABOUR ALONE, BUT BY LABOUR AND CAPITAL TOGETHER.

How absurd then must it appear to contend that labour produces all and is the only source of wealth, as if capital produced nothing, and was not a real and distinct source of wealth also! But those who maintain this most extraordinary doctrine could only do so from mistaking the most im-

* Wealth of Nations, book ii. chap. 4.

portant objects of the science which they cultivate, and from overlooking the proper end which is meant to be served by distinctly ascertaining and discriminating the original sources of wealth; which end is, that we may establish thereupon the distinct original grounds of right to property; for if capital did nothing, and labour every thing, in the work of production, what right could the capitalist show to any part of the produce?

If it should be said, that capital could not do what is done by means of it without the assistance and co-operation of labour, neither, I reply, could labour do what is done by means of it without the assistance and co-operation of capital; and if an attempt were made to estimate what could be done by labour without capital, and compare it with what actually is done in any highly-improved and civilized country by its assistance, it would quickly appear which of these two sources was the most copious, and to which of them the society were indebted for the greater part of their wealth.

Without, however, attempting to make such an estimate, it may be useful, in concluding, here briefly to glance at the effects of capital in the three great departments of productive industry—agriculture, manufactures, and commerce,—in order to bring to view, in a connected manner, how much is owing to this instrument in the production of wealth. In doing this, it will only be necessary very slightly to review those different departments of industry, and to enumerate a few of the most striking and important particulars of the capitals employed in them.

I. In *agriculture* it is obvious to perceive how much production is increased and labour saved by the possession and employment of capital. "In a farm," says Dr Smith, "where all the necessary buildings, fences, drains, communications, &c., are in the most perfect good order, the same number of labourers and labouring cattle will raise a much greater produce, than in one of equal extent and equally good ground, but not furnished with equal conveniences."* But these are all parts and portions of capital; and the additional work they enable the labourers to perform, above what they could do without those conveniences, is wholly to be ascribed to this instrument of production. Let any one then think but for a moment, and calculate in his mind, how much of this sort of capital is existent in Britain at the present time, and he may acquire some adequate notion of its magnitude, and of the saving of labour, or assistance given to the labourers, by this single species of capital in this department.

Under this head also come mines and fisheries; the former of which could not be worked at all, and the latter could not be successfully prosecuted, or prosecuted to any extent, without capitals. Almost the whole produce, therefore, in these two employments might be ascribed to capital; but as a certain number of labourers are also necessary, they must also come in for a share of the produce. But all that part of the produce which is over and above what pays the whole of the labourers who are anywise concerned in the business may fairly be claimed as the produce and reward of capital.

II. How vitally *manufactures* depend upon capital, and in what measure the magnitude of production in this department is owing to the use of proper engines, machinery, &c., needs hardly to be stated. The buildings necessary, and the whole machinery, materials, &c., are all capitals; and the amount in Great Britain invested in these forms, as well as the amount of production, or saving of labour under this head, is altogether incalculable. Of the vast aggregate of commodities produced by means of those investments,

* Wealth of Nations, book ii., chap. 2.

how much could be produced without them, I shall not pretend to say, but we may be confidently assured that it would be absolutely trifling in the comparison.

III. *Commerce* likewise, when it is carried on to any large extent, depends even still more, if possible, upon capital, than any of the other two departments of productive industry. In this department the merchants' stocks are all capitals; and their shops, as also the buildings set apart for containing and preserving their merchandizes, are capitals.

Under this head also we have to reckon canals, roads, harbours, docks, &c., which are chiefly constructed for the convenience of commerce, and which stand in the place of very great exertions of labour, saving those exertions, and assisting the labourers in such manner as to enable them to produce much greater quantities of work or of commodities, than they could do without such powerful helps.

In few words, therefore, it may be stated, that the great mass of wealth within a country, including the whole apparatus of houses, manufactories, structures, machines, tools, materials, and provisions, required or employed in every department of productive industry, to perfect, establish, and maintain the great system of the division of labour, and, in short, every article of wealth which is calculated or applied to assist in the work of production, are all to be considered as parts and portions of this one vast engine or instrument,—capital.

The growth and acquisition of this great instrument is altogether the fruit of *saving*; for capital can only be produced, increased, and improved, by individual accumulations, self-denial, and parsimony. If every person from the beginning had always consumed immediately all that he produced, it is plain that no accumulations of wealth could ever have been made, or capital existed; and, in like manner, in more advanced times, when, in consequence of parsimony, accumulations have taken place, if then, or at any given period, all saving were universally to cease, this important instrument could never be improved or increased subsequently.

This being the case, then, there must necessarily be some proper benefits attached to the saving and preservation, or possession of capital, else such saving never could be made; for no person will deny himself a present enjoyment fairly within his power, unless it be with a view to some superior enjoyment in futurity. And hence we see the reasonableness and justness of the profit or interest ordinarily derived or derivable from capital. Such profit is to be looked upon as no more (and in reality it is no more) than an adequate reward and inducement held out for the increase and improvement as well as for the use of capital; without the prospect of which there could not exist any regular motive or obligation sufficiently powerful to ensure the preservation and indefinite increase of this great instrument of production, and all that wealth of which it is so fruitful a source would be unknown and unenjoyed by mankind.

Every person, therefore, who saves, and adds any thing to capital, may be considered as contributing to the improvement of this great instrument; and every person who does so, or even who merely preserves undiminished a capital previously accumulated, is a public benefactor. Not that he saves, or ought to save with this particular view; his own private advantage is the only proper and legitimate motive from which his conduct ought in this respect to spring. But he cannot do so without benefiting the public as well as himself, and he is not only justly and fairly entitled to all the advantages he derives in the form of profit or interest from those savings or additions which he thus makes to the general mass of capital, but he deserves the gratitude or good-will of every individual to boot. For, as we have already shown,* and as will be illustrated more fully in the sequel, besides the fund of profit or interest which every accumulation and addition to this great instrument of production establishes as a reward and remuneration to the proprietor and preserver of it, every such addition has likewise the effect of increasing still farther the power and facility of production, and of lowering the cost and price of commodities,—an advantage which is shared and enjoyed by the whole community.

And thus it will appear when the subject is fully investigated, that whoever saves and adds any thing to this great instrument, not only benefits himself and his heirs for ever, but his country and all posterity, so long as the wealth and bounty which he bestows remain existent and unconsumed by some prodigal successor.†

---

* Chapter v., section ii.

† Not but that there are other ways of benefiting one's country as well as saving; to be generous or munificent is equally useful in its proper place, provided it do not exceed the proper resources of the person who exhibits those virtues; and even the most prodigal may be sometimes as great or even a greater public benefactor than the most saving, in as much as it may happen that he may be the author or contriver of works and inventions which may be of more consequence a thousand times than his savings could be. In stating or considering one fact or principle in political science, we ought not to forget its proper limits, or lose sight altogether of those other principles by which it is modified.

CHAPTER VIII.

THE NATURAL GROUNDS OF RIGHT TO PROPERTY DEFINED AND ENUMERATED.

It has been shown in a preceding chapter,* that there are three distinct material means or instruments of production, or, in other words, three general denominations or heads of arrangement, under which all the inferior and particular material means or instruments of every description may naturally and conveniently be classed. These are,—first, *land*,—second, *man himself*, or *human labour*,—and, third, *capital*. But the exclusive general means or instruments of production are necessarily the only immediate and original sources of wealth; they are necessarily, therefore, the only immediate and original grounds of right to property.

All wealth is the produce either of land and labour, or of land, labour, and capital; and there is no way of coming by it at first but by one or other or all of these three means. These alone, therefore, can give any *original* right or title to it, and all other claims of right to wealth or property must be secondary and derivative, and must be founded on the *consent* of the persons who originally drew it from those exclusive sources, and on the fact of its *voluntary* transfer from them to the present actual possessors or proprietors; for whoever possesses any portion of wealth, be it great or small, must either have drawn it directly and immediately from some one or other or of all the three original sources just mentioned, or must have procured it by a longer or shorter process from those who must have pre-

---

* Chapter vi.

viously drawn it thence. Now there are but two ways in which wealth can be procured from the original producers or proprietors, viz. by *voluntary consent*, or by *force*. If it be procured by voluntary consent, the right and title to it is always good and undeniable; but if by force, how stands the case?

All the ways of procuring wealth by voluntary consent of the proprietors, whether it be gratuitously delivered up and bestowed, or transferred by treaty and agreement in exchange for a valuable consideration or equivalent, are just and allowable; but all the ways of taking it by force are unjust, and are indeed nothing else but actual robberies, except one, and that is when it is taken by authority of the community to support government, law, and justice. And for this anomaly, and single exception to the general rule, *necessity* is the only apology, the very existence of civilized society depending upon it. But even here the principle of voluntary consent ought to be adhered to as far as it is possible to do so; and in the imposition of *taxes*, as well as in other affairs of government in general, the sense and suffrage of the people ought to be taken as widely and extensively as circumstances will permit, that they may be sanctioned by voluntary consent, or appointment of the *greater number* at least, without which they cannot be altogether just or unexceptionable.

Government, law, and force, are absolutely necessary to the existence of civilized society. The decrees and sanctions of authority, law, and government, and force to support those sanctions, are necessary to the production, security, and just distribution of wealth; and not only to this end, but to the protection, security, and defence of the person as well as property. But government cannot exist without persons to administer it, and these must be paid for their labour and services; and hence the necessity of contributions, and of *regulations* as to their amount, or laws and force to *compel*, where it may be necessary, the fraudulent or refractory to pay their due proportions, that all may be obliged to contribute to the support of so useful and indispensable an institution, in the benefit and protection of which all must share. But the force and compulsion ought always to be endeavoured to be made as little as possible, and should never be allowed to exceed what the exigence requires.

While we then distinctly recognize and admit this particular case of force, in the transfer of property which the imperfection of human nature and the exigence of human affairs demand, and most fully acknowledge, as we are bound in reason to do, the necessity upon which it is founded, we must at the same time claim, in return, the concession, equally absolute, unqualified, and undeniable, that this particular case is a perfect anomalism, that it is a solitary exception to the general rule and principle, invariable and inviolable in all other cases, that it is justified alone by those circumstances of imperious necessity in which its expediency is acknowledged, and that it is always to be confined within the narrowest limits which it is possible to prescribe to it.

To comply with this principle, therefore, it is manifest, that in the imposition of taxes, (whether by the general government, or by inferior local authorities,) the sense and suffrage of all who are to contribute* ought to be admitted

* It is not necessary that we should here enter into the controversy respecting universal suffrage, it being indirectly admitted in the text, that a much more limited system of representation would sufficiently guarantee the rights of property and secure from spoliation the public treasure. Nevertheless I shall state here what appears to me to be the truth, that a great deal of absurd declamation has been vented on this subject, and much affected or unnecessary horror and alarm expressed and excited against what would probably

and consulted as far as it may be practicable to do so; and when this is attended to, all is done that can be done for the attainment of justice. The minority, though dissent-

---

be found upon trial to be entirely harmless at least, if not positively beneficial and preferable to any limited plan of suffrage whatever.

It has been argued, that the system of universal suffrage would subject the community, where it should be allowed, to the government of the mob; and fears have even been entertained, or pretended, for the security of property under such a system. But certainly nothing can be more unfounded or gratuitous than such fears; for although universal suffrage were established, property would still preserve its full and legitimate influence in the election of representatives; and the inferior ranks of people would still continue to look up to those above them, and to be guided in a great measure by their opinion, except, perhaps, in the case of particular persons of superior judgment and intelligence, in whom the exercise of an independent vote would be not only innocuous, but highly salutary and advantageous.

Even the number of those who have property to protect, great and small, in an opulent and well-governed country, is always greater than that of those who have nothing, independent of their greater weight and influence with their neighbours. And with regard to the objection that great bodies of men might be influenced by their employers, and driven to the *poll* like herds of cattle, it is a sufficient answer, that the employers themselves, not being all of one side or one mind, would throw what influence they possessed into the opposite scales, and thus in a great measure neutralize the effects of one another.

"The lower sort of people, and small proprietors," says one who was never suspected of favouring democracy, "are good enough judges of one not very distant from them in rank or habitation; and therefore, in their parochial meetings, will probably choose the best or nearly the best representative: but they are wholly unfit for county-meetings, and for electing into the higher offices of the republic. Their ignorance gives the grandees an opportunity of deceiving them."—*Hume's Essays*, part ii., essay 16.

So far from endangering property, the system of universal suffrage (or some plan of voting or representation approaching to it in a greater or less degree) is the one thing needful to render property perfectly secure; for it is this alone which can prevent all undue ening, must acknowledge, at least, the fairness of the proceeding, and will therefore the more readily yield obedience to the law, and even cheerfully contribute their allotted proportions, (in this case never likely to be exorbitant or oppressive,) under so equitable a system.

By extending in this manner the right of delegation or suffrage as far as may be practicable under any given circumstances, the fullest and most general consent will be obtained which is possible: there will be as little of force and as much of agreement in every act of government as the imperfection of human affairs will permit; and whilst the sovereignty of the law will be established on the surest foundation, and the maintenance of justice fully provided for, the prosperity of the country where such system prevails, and the harmony and tranquillity of the whole society, will be effectually promoted and secured.

From what has been here advanced, then, it should appear that there are just *five* distinct grounds or descriptions of right to property.

The *first* arises from LABOUR, by which it is directly and immediately obtained.

The *second* is from LAND, by which it is directly and immediately obtained.

The *third* is from CAPITAL, by which it is directly and immediately obtained.

These three foregoing are the primary and original grounds

---

croachments upon it in the shape of unjust and unnecessary taxation, and the consequent discontent and oppression of the *labouring classes*, (which is so frequent a cause of disturbance and of danger,) as well as in that of monopolies of every kind, (which influence so largely and so unjustly the distribution of property, and excite the discontent and just detestation of every enlightened mind,) and by annihilating (which it would do in time) every sinister and every partial interest, give that peace, and prosperity, and happiness to a people, which would establish the security of property on the only solid and permanent basis, and dissipate for ever all alarms about its safety.

of right from which the two others following (which are therefore secondary) are derived.

Fourth, The voluntary consent of proprietors *fully given.*

Fifth, The voluntary consent of proprietors *partially given* by majority of their numbers in a joint contribution.

These then are the natural and the only equitable or reasonable grounds of right to vendible property or wealth, or modes of acquiring it consistently with justice; and none can have title to any the smallest portion of such property which is not founded on some one or other of these five grounds or descriptions of right, else they would have a right to the property of other people, that is, a right to what others have a right, which is absurd.

CHAPTER IX.

THE THREE ORIGINAL GROUNDS OF RIGHT TO PROPERTY TRACED TO THEIR FOUNDATION IN THE PRINCIPLES OF HUMAN NATURE.

SECTION I.

OF THE RIGHT TO PROPERTY FOUNDED ON LABOUR.

Before the existence of property in land, when the earth was common to all, like the air we breathe, and when no sort of capital of any consideration had as yet been accumulated, *labour*, as it was the only available means whereby wealth could be acquired, so it was the single original ground of right to property.

He who first gathered the spontaneous and unappropriated productions of nature—the acorns, which, we may suppose, he found scattered beneath the oak tree, or the grapes, which he descried hanging upon the vine—was immediately the proprietor, and would at once have felt it to be an invasion of his rights, if another savage had attempted to take from him, without his consent, any part of the fruit he had thus procured.

He who ran down, and took, or killed any wild animal, would, in like manner, immediately consider it as his property, and would equally have felt it to be an insult offered to his person, and an invasion of his rights, if another human creature attempted to take it from him without his consent. If he made a bow, or a tomahawk, or built a hut, he would still consider these objects as his own exclusive property; and the most ignorant and untutored savage of the wilderness would instantly have felt the sentiment of injustice and of *wrong* arise in his breast upon any attempt being made to dispossess him of them; and would have resisted and resented such attempt to the utmost of his power, and perhaps even at the hazard or expense of his life;—so readily does the idea of property suggest itself to the mind of man, and so naturally does it arise, even in the very lowest state of human existence, from the consciousness of labour or personal exertion bestowed in acquiring it.

Nor does this representation rest on conjecture or speculation merely; on the contrary, it seems to carry its own evidence along with it, and speaks, I think, intelligibly enough to every man's bosom. And facts, still observable in the savage parts of the world, are abundantly found to corroborate the statement, there being scarcely a traveller who has visited those parts, and given any account of their inhabitants, who has not recorded some circumstance of their conduct calculated to illustrate our present subject. It will be unnecessary to adduce many of these, else I might here transcribe a whole volume of them. That, however, this portion of our argument may not be left wholly unstated or imperfect, I must instance one or two; and these I shall select from a book of the most authentic description, the Journal of the American Travellers, Captains Lewis and Clarke, to the Source of the River Missouri, and across the American Continent to the Pacific Ocean.

These officers were commissioned by the government of the United States, with a party of men under their orders, to traverse and explore those almost boundless and unknown regions. In their extensive wanderings they visited many tribes of savages, and from the accounts they give of them many things might be gleaned that are much to our present purpose; those, however, which follow are the most remarkable.

It is related by these travellers, in their very interesting Journal, that when the party arrived on the head streams of the Missouri, Captain Lewis was despatched with three men in quest of the Shoshonee Indians, on the other side of the Rocky Mountains, to endeavour to procure horses from them, and bring some of their people to assist the main body of the Americans in transporting their luggage and merchandise across the ridge of those mountains to the river Columbia. After crossing the ridge, and searching for some days, Captain Lewis came up with a tribe of the Shoshonees, and having engaged them to go with him, the whole party, consisting of himself, his three men, and the Indians, to the number of "fifty warriors," with their wives and children, set out together to rejoin their companions on the "forks" of the Missouri.

The parties who travelled together were, in those sterile regions, but scantily provided with food, and the necessary supplies were hardly to be procured. One morning when (to use the words of the Journal) "they had nothing to eat," Captain Lewis sent forward two of his hunters to endeavour to procure something, which the Indians (who were exceedingly jealous of their fellow-travellers) perceiving, they sent two or three of their number a-head also, to keep an eye over the hunters. In a short time one of the latter killed a deer, upon which the Indian scouts rode instantly back, "full speed across the plain," to inform their friends. These were at first somewhat alarmed at this movement, but the moment they were made to understand what had happened, "the whole troop dashed forward as fast as their horses could carry them" to the scene of action. The narrative after this period goes on as follows:—"When they reached the place where Drewer had thrown out the intestines, they all dismounted in confusion, and ran tumbling over each other, like famished dogs; each tore away whatever part he could, and instantly began to eat it; some had the liver, some the kidneys, in short, no part on which we are accustomed to look with disgust escaped them; one of them, who had seized about nine feet of the entrails, was chewing it at one end, while with his hand he was diligently clearing his way by discharging the contents at the other. It was indeed impossible to see these wretches ravenously feeding on the filth of animals, and the blood streaming from their mouths, without deploring how nearly the condition of savages approaches to that of the brute creation; yet, though suffering with hunger, they did not attempt, as they might have done, to take by force the whole deer, but contented themselves with what had been thrown away by the hunter."*

Perhaps there could not be adduced a stronger proof of the innate force of justice, or a more striking instance of the powerful sense which even savages have of it. It may indeed be alleged that this natural sense of justice and respect for the rights of others, even among savages, are

* Travels of Captains Lewis and Clarke to the Source of the River Missouri, and across the American Continent to the Pacific Ocean; performed by Order of the Government of the United States, in the Years 1804, 1805, and 1806, vol. ii., p. 103. London edition. Octavo, 1815.

materially strengthened and increased by severe experience of the consequences that would follow an attempt to violate them; but so likewise it is in the most civilized countries, where, it must be confessed, men could have but little dependence on the security of their possessions, if the simple and natural sense of justice were not re-enforced by the apprehension and experience of the consequences of attempting to rob or steal.

The narrative continues:—"Captain Lewis now had the deer skinned, and after reserving a quarter of it, gave the rest of the animal to the chief, to be divided among the Indians, who immediately devoured nearly the whole of it without cooking."*

The same travellers inform us a little further on, that the Indians having gone out to hunt, "discovered a mule buck, and twelve of their horsemen pursued it for four miles. We saw the chase, which was very entertaining, and at length they rode it down and killed it. This mule buck was the largest deer of any kind we have seen, being nearly as large as a doe elk. Besides this, they brought in another deer and three goats; but, instead of a general distribution of the meat, and such as we have hitherto seen among all tribes of Indians, we observed that some families had a large share, while others received none. On inquiring of Cameahwait the reason of this custom, he said that meat among them was scarce, that each hunter reserved what he killed for the use of himself and his own family, none of the rest having any claim on what he chose to keep."† Here we have distinct evidence that property was so far established among this tribe of Indians, and separate rights known and acknowledged with regard to the most important article of wealth, food, even in their daily acquisitions of that most necessary article, founded on the *labour* or *trouble of acquiring it.* In other tribes, where it is usual to share in common all the provisions daily ac-

* Travels of Lewis and Clarke, p. 103. † Ibid. pp. 151, 152.

quired, this arrangement is no doubt formed on the plain principles of reciprocity and justice, and proceeds upon an agreement, either expressed or understood, and always acted upon, that whereas any one who happens to be unsuccessful in the search for food is to receive a part of whatever is procured by his companions; so, at another time, when he has been more fortunate, whatever he acquires is, in like manner, to be delivered up also into the common stock, and to go equally to supply the whole tribe, and of course those members of it whose fortune it was on this occasion to be unsuccessful in their turn.

It is labour also which confers the first transient right to property in land, before it becomes finally and permanently appropriated in the natural course of things, by the multiplication of inhabitants and the accumulation of wealth.

When an individual wanderer, savage, or civilized in the midst of unappropriated and uncultivated wastes, chooses a field or spot of earth, and bestows upon it the labour of cultivation, he immediately acquires the idea of property, and would at once feel the injustice if an attempt were made to drive him from his possession, and thus to rob him of the fruits of his industry and past labour. Even after he had gathered his crop, should he retain possession of the field, by occasionally working upon it, and preparing it anew for seed against the proper season, and should another individual come and attempt to drive him away, and to appropriate to himself the advantages of his labour of cultivation, it would not fail to appear an invasion of his rights to the first possessor, whom nothing but force could possibly reconcile to the yielding up of his land to such licentious and unauthorised intruder. But he who had bestowed his pains and labour upon the field would be fully justified in resisting and driving off the invader of his property, who ought to be obliged to clear and to cultivate land for himself, where there remained a boundless extent to be chosen for that purpose, wanting only the improvements which labour had bestowed.

In the same manner, should a wandering *tribe* determine to cultivate the ground, and choose an unappropriated tract of land for their settlement, and should another tribe come to dispossess and despoil them of their crops, or of their land, they would not be slow to resist the attempt, and to resent it as one of the very highest injustice,—so naturally and so reasonably does the idea of *right* arise out of pre-possession and labour bestowed in cultivating the land. Even tracts which are only traversed by the hunter or shepherd, and which are left by them for months together, and sometimes perhaps for half the year, are often considered by them as their right and patrimony. But here they are evidently in error; for nothing but cultivation or permanent occupation can give any exclusive natural right to property in the land; and it is undoubtedly just in theory, as it will always be found to prevail in practice, that the desert must be resigned to the people who will *cultivate.*

SECTION II.

OF THE RIGHT TO LAND.

After a people advance beyond the pastoral and migratory state, and begin to apply themselves to agriculture, the land is immediately appropriated. Those who exist at the time, being the whole people, have right to all the land, and may divide it amongst them if they please; and as their numbers must then be but small, compared to what their country, when fully cultivated, could support, it may be imagined that every individual must acquire a large portion of territory. Nor should this circumstance, unavoidable as it must be at the time, necessarily occasion, under a free and just system of laws and government, any inconvenience afterwards when population would have increased; for under such a system, every person being at full liberty to turn his property to the best account, their own private interest would naturally lead individuals to divide the land into smaller portions as soon as the interest or convenience of the society required it. Even in the case of these original proprietors being dispossessed by conquest, and the land parcelled out anew, and distributed arbitrarily amongst the conquerors in still more unequal and unmeasured quantities, still, if the property were made absolute, and the disposal of it left free and unfettered by entails or restrictions of any kind, it would necessarily happen, as soon as regular government were again established, that the simple and unforced operation of the principle of self-interest would cause the larger portions to be once more subdivided and broken down into smaller ones as population and wealth advanced, and all remembrance and effects of any injustice or inequality in the original appropriation of the land, or in the subsequent reconquest and arbitrary distribution of it, would be speedily effaced, and every trace of them obliterated in two or three generations.

But this would not be the case if strict laws of entail were established whose operation should extend over many generations. Such laws would, by direct and necessary consequence, prevent the land from being divided in such a manner as the convenience or interest of the community might require, and would form an obstruction to the increase of population and wealth. But the increase of population and wealth, taken together, constitute the most important and essential interest of a country. Strict laws of entail, therefore, are directly opposed to that interest. It is, besides, the increase of population and wealth which confers all its value upon the land. Such laws, therefore, obstruct the increase of that value. Such laws are therefore opposed to the interests of all classes of people, and are indeed essentially and radically unjust and injurious, not merely as preventing a man's ostensible property from being applied to the payment of his debts, but much more, as they prevent the land from being applied to its proper uses, keep large tracts of it uncultivated and unimproved, and render the earth comparatively a desert.

That no permanent ill consequences would follow from the original distribution and allotment of the land, however partial, unequal, or arbitrary such distribution and allotment might be, provided it were allowed to be freely disposed of afterwards, will be manifest from this, that in such case, namely, where the land were allowed to be freely disposed of, it would naturally happen, that, in proportion as population and wealth increased, the proprietors of large tracts of territory, received at the original appropriation and distribution of the land, or on the subsequent reconquest and new settlement of a country, great part of which remained useless on their hands, would be induced to exchange a portion of their superfluous possessions for some of the superfluous wealth of another description, belonging to other capitalists, as it arose under the hands of productive industry; which, again, would serve the land-proprietors as a disposable fund or capital, wherewith they might cultivate their remaining unimproved domains; and whilst the parties themselves would be thus mutually accommodated, their common country would be improved, and the whole community benefited to the utmost extent that circumstances would permit. For, as it may reasonably be presumed that the purchaser of the land would generally retain in his hands capital sufficient to improve what he bought, there would arise between him and the former proprietor a twofold cultivation and improvement of the soil, a twofold demand for agricultural labour, and a twofold produce; which demand, and produce, and cultivation, would go on constantly and rapidly increasing, until the wealth and population of the country, and consequently the value of the land, should have advanced to nearly their greatest possible magnitude and most improved state,—a state which never could be attained under the paralyzing effects of a system of restrictions or entails.

All laws of entail, therefore, or any restrictions calculated to prevent the division and sale or disposal of the land, or the free voluntary conveyance of it from one possessor or proprietor to another, are unjust and injurious; first, as obstructing and repressing the increase of its value, by setting a premature limit to the increase of population and wealth; and, secondly, as preventing it from going into the hands of those who are most able and willing to make the best use of it, and thus attempting, unwarrantably and unjustly, to perpetuate the original distribution and allotment of the land, which, however just and necessary and advantageous it might have been at the time of its being made, could never have been intended to be permanent or unalterable, and which, when kept up under circumstances entirely different, and which call loudly for extended cultivation, are turned into a grievance and a nuisance of the most intolerable description.

It has been supposed, however, that if the land might be freely bought and sold, and conveyed from one person to another, without limit or restriction, and might be equally divided amongst children or legatees, according to the inclination or interest of the parties concerned, it would necessarily happen in process of time that it would be reduced and divided into very minute portions, and that the whole world, or any country, or part of it, where such a practice were allowed, would present in the end the monotonous and miserable spectacle of an interminable congeries of uniformly small properties, each but barely sufficient to maintain only one single individual or family. This, however, it is believed, is a very unwarranted and improbable supposition; and those who make it seem totally to forget that there are in general, in the advanced periods of society, as many persons who are both able and willing to purchase new properties, and to increase their possessions, as there are of those who are willing to sell or divide them.

Under the just and liberal system here supposed, it is to be recollected, wealth would naturally increase very rapidly and to a very great degree. But wherever wealth increases to any great degree, it must necessarily be accumulated into masses or capitals of considerable magnitude in the hands of individuals; and where wealth of other descriptions is possessed in large quantities or capitals, distinct from the land, there the land must be possessed in large quantities or capitals also, because there will always be found the means or ability to purchase it in large quantities.

It would necessarily happen also where there was great wealth, that the higher and even the middle classes of people would present the example of a liberal way of living; and hence it would naturally follow that the proprietors of small portions of land would, in most instances, be inclined to sell them, as not being sufficient to enable them to live in the easy and affluent manner, which would then be so very common, that most people of any property would be naturally induced to propose it to themselves as the end of their endeavours.

But when there existed at one and the same time and place both the power to purchase on the one hand, and the disposition to sell on the other, the very small lots or properties of land, it follows to a certainty, that they would be transferred from one to another, and that they would be added together, and accumulated into larger properties in the hands of the greater capitalists as often as they were separated or divided; and if it should happen that portions or estates of land should be sometimes broken down and partitioned, it would soon follow, and would happen equally often, that they would be reunited and added to other portions or estates; for where the means existed of acquiring a species of property, which is the most desirable of all, it would be absurd to suppose that the will should be wanting.

Under a system of the most perfect liberty therefore, in regard to the disposal of the land, there seems no reasonable ground for apprehending that it would be necessarily reduced to very small portions; and I think, therefore, we may very safely conclude, that no restrictions of any kind, not even the law of primogeniture, and far less entails, can be at all justified on such ground.

It is laudable indeed to endeavour to render the state of man in society as steady and secure as possible, or as the laws of nature and of justice will permit, but it is not allowable to advance a single step beyond this point. The fate and the fortunes of one individual or family ought to be as dear to the laws and to the legislator as those of any other individual or family; but when laws of entail, or any other unwarrantable restrictions, are established, which prevent the land from being cultivated, where there is a demand for an increasing population, the objection to them is not merely that the real or supposed interest of one individual or family is postponed and preferred to that of another; it is, that the real or supposed interest of one is preferred to that of millions, and is protected at the cost of penury to some, and of exclusion from existence to multitudes that would otherwise be born.

It has, however, been said, that God gave the earth in common to mankind, and that "the land is the people's farm," which ought to be enjoyed as common property, and as the natural and equal inheritance of all; but it is to be remembered, that in every country where the land is fully appropriated, it will always be found that it has been improved and ameliorated by human labour and capital. The forests have been cleared away, the superfluous waters have been drained off and directed into narrow channels, the soil has been manured, enclosures have been made, houses built, manufactures established; mounds, embankments, excavations, aqueducts and innumerable constructures have been raised and formed upon it, all of them immoveable and inseparable from the ground or site whereon they are placed. Now, I presume, it will hardly be contended that these properties are also the natural and equal inheritance of all. Those persons by whose *capital*, or by whose *labour* and *saving* they have been produced, or the persons to whom they have consigned their rights, must surely be allowed to have a preferable claim. Were this indeed not conceded, none of those properties, nor any others of the kind, would ever be produced at all. In the earliest stages of society, and up to the state of shepherds, the land is naturally and quite conveniently held in common; but in the agricultural and commercial stages it becomes altogether impossible and impracticable to do so. For who in those advanced stages would expend his patrimony in any productive or useful undertaking upon the land, if he could not acquire an exclusive and permanent right to it?—Who, for example, would erect a cotton-mill, or establish any considerable or extensive manufactory, if, after he had done so, he could not call it his own?—It is certainly true that God has given the earth to mankind, together with all the rude materials out of which wealth is to be produced; but he has not commanded those persons who have been frugal and industrious, and have made to themselves possessions out of those materials, nor those who have derived such possessions from frugal and industrious ancestors, to give them away to be enjoyed in common; and neither does reason nor common sense, the gifts of God, prescribe any such conduct or sanction such doctrine.

Those individuals by whose labour and saving, or capital, wealth is first produced and accumulated upon the land, must be allowed the exclusive right to it, else they would never accumulate such wealth; and they must also be allowed the right to sell, bequeath, or bestow it on whom they please. It is only the bare uncultivated earth, where it is unappropriated and unimproved by labour, to which an equal and common right can be pretended; for no man can have a natural right to the wealth produced by others, or to a single atom of accumulated property, but what he has either produced himself, or has had bequeathed to him, unless it be to those things which nature spontaneously presents.

Those, therefore, who contend for an equal and common right to the land, must confine their pretensions to the desert and unappropriated parts of the world, where no labour has been bestowed, nor any capital or improvements connected with it. And to this extent we most readily grant the right,—a right which, I believe, never was denied, and which could hardly indeed be effectually opposed; for who should be present where there were no people to exclude any person from appropriation or possession?—But were those persons who make a parade of claiming this right as their inheritance only to remove themselves to the places where they must go to exercise it, they would speedily find and acknowledge that the benefits which are enjoyed in countries where the land is appropriated, which come in lieu of this right, and which accrue, as has been already shown,* to all men from the effects of capital,—were an inheritance infinitely more valuable and worthy of acceptance than that which it takes away, and for which they would exchange it,—a barren and unavailable right to the uncultivated desert, or a common liberty for all men to wander unchallenged over the unappropriated parts of the world, and to gather therefrom, every individual as he best could, a precarious and therefore a miserable subsistence.

"Paradoxical as it may seem at first sight," says M. Say,

---

* Chap. v. sect. ii.

"it is neverthless perfectly true, that the man who is himself no share-holder of land is equally interested in its appropriation with the share-holder himself. The savage tribes of New Zealand, and of the north-western coast of America, where the land is unappropriated, have the greatest difficulty in procuring a precarious subsistence upon fish and game, and are often reduced to devour worms, caterpillars, and the most nauseous vermin; not unfrequently even to wage war on one another from absolute want, and to devour their prisoners as food; whereas in Europe, where the appropriation is complete, the meanest individual, with bodily health and inclination to work, is sure of shelter, clothing, and subsistence, at the least."*

But, although the land cannot be occupied or enjoyed *wholly* as common property, and as the natural and equal inheritance of all, *in its full extent*, still a part of its annual value, or produce, may be thus enjoyed, by being reserved to the state in the shape of a land-tax or quitrent, which should be applied to the support of government in the place of taxes; such quitrent to be a certain proportion of the rack-rent,—and provided it were not exorbitant in its amount, and that the proportion it should bear to the whole, or rack-rent, were unalterably fixed, nothing could be more just and proper, or more expedient to be established as a fund for the support of government. By being made a proportion of the whole rent of the land, such a quitrent would vary precisely with all the variations of that fund, and would increase as the value of the land increased; and by being applied to the support of the general government, and thereby saving to the people an equal amount of taxes, it would be in reality, and in the strictest sense, enjoyed in common.

---

* Treatise on Political Economy, book ii. chap. 9. Princep's Translation.

Rent, as will be shown hereafter,* is partly the creation of capital, and partly the effect of the general increase of population and wealth upon the land, or in its immediate or near neighbourhood. In as far as it is the creation of capital, it should wholly belong to and be enjoyed by the capitalist; but in as far as it arises from the natural progress of society, and the general increase of population and wealth, independently of any effort or expenditure on the part of the proprietor, it should belong to and be enjoyed by the public, if possible, as common property. Now we see that this *is* possible, to a certain moderate extent at least, in the manner which has just been stated.

What portion of the aggregate fund of rent is to be ascribed to the effects of capital laid out from time immemorial in meliorating the land, and what portion to the general increase of wealth and population upon it, or what may be the respective claims on the fund of rent, on those two distinct grounds, it will always be impossible precisely and satisfactorily to determine under any circumstances, seeing that the effects of those two different causes of rent are always necessarily blended and combined in very undefinable proportions, it being impossible that any rent should exist without both; that is, without the existence of some people and of some capital laid out upon the land. Nor is this circumstance—I mean the circumstance that those two different claims, or grounds of right to claim, upon the general fund of rent cannot be exactly distinguished or separated—of any material consequence, since, whatever they may respectively amount to, the rate or proportion of the quitrent to the whole rent must be fixed with reference to other and still more important considerations, and must be kept within such moderate bounds, that the former shall not

* See book ii. chap. 7.

encroach so far upon the latter as to lessen in any sensible degree the desirableness of the land as private property, or to render the situation of land-proprietors a mere stewardship for the public; because this would be to counterwork and bring to nought the very ends for which the right of property in land was itself instituted; which ends are, not only that the land might be improved and cultivated in the best manner, and that no obstruction should be given to the increase of capital upon it, but also that the best form of society might be established, in the composition of which the class of land-proprietors, as will presently be shown, must always form an essential and indispensable ingredient.

Taking these considerations along with us then, and holding this as a principle not to be trenched upon, that the land must be kept so far free from being in any manner overburdened as that it shall still continue to be looked upon as the most desirable of all investments for capital, and that an estate of land-property shall still continue to be regarded as "the highest prize in the lottery of life,"—it will follow that the land-tax or quitrent here proposed should be calculated on a very moderate scale, and fixed at a moderate amount. Perhaps *one-eighth part*, or about *twelve per cent.* upon the rack-rent, is what the land might fairly bear, (provided it were free from poor-rate and tithes, or any other peculiar imposts,) without lessening in any sensible degree its desirableness as an investment for capital, and without deteriorating the composition or diminishing the happiness of society, but rather, at the same time, improving the one and increasing the other. But whatever the proportion of the reserved rent should be, it is most indispensable that it should be fixed and established as a fundamental law, not to be altered afterwards.

A law such as this would produce a revenue that would in most cases be sufficient to defray the whole of the ordinary expenses of civil government; and would thus obviate the necessity of *any* taxes, except upon occasions of war or other extraordinary emergencies. Nay, it might probably happen, that if the reserved rent were fixed at one-eighth, and that the government were very economically conducted, there would arise a surplus after defraying the ordinary expenses of government in time of peace, which might be accumulated by investment in profitable works and improvements, as in making roads, canals, &c., which might be resold in time of war, and the proceeds applied to the public service; and again, the properties thus alienated might be repurchased on the return of peace by the accumulation of the rent; or any other mode might be chosen for secure investment of the surplus above the ordinary expenses required.

Such a fundamental law would be more particularly proper to be established at the foundation of all new states or colonies;* but it would, perhaps, be not even very difficult to devise a plan for its establishment in this or any other country, without inconvenience or injustice to the land-proprietors. This might be done by giving them an *equivalent*, and thereby repurchasing this small portion of the rent; and for doing which in this country the means might be found in the *abolition* of one old law, and the *alteration* of another, one of them affecting the land injuriously and the other unfairly, and both of which changes would be improvements in themselves and desirable on their own account.

In the *first* place, I would equalize the pressure of the poor-rates, by raising the fund for supporting all who might

* Had such a law been established in the United States of North America for example, or were it even now established there, where so great an increase may be expected to be yet realized in the value of the land, it would, in process of time, if the government should continue to be conducted upon any thing like its present very moderate scale of expenditure, render all other taxes whatever unnecessary.

be in want from a tax upon all property, or rather upon all income or revenue, instead of allowing it to fall wholly upon the land, as at present. This would operate a relief to the landlords, *pro tanto*, wherever a poor-rate is levied, and could be charged upon them as a part of the equivalent for the quitrent proposed to be reinstated upon them, at a fair valuation. And this is the *alteration* which, as I hope to show hereafter,* would be desirable on its own account.

Secondly, abolish the tithes as the present incumbents die off,—remunerating the clergy afterwards by a salary from the national treasury, as is now done in France,—and commute this burden also for the proposed quitrent, at a fair valuation as far as it will go, taking or giving the difference, and repurchasing the whole quitrent in those cases where the proprietors happen to be altogether free both from the *nuisance* of tithes† and the unshared and undivided burden supporting the poor. And for this purpose the funds arising from these two sources would be found amply sufficient;‡

---

* See book ii. chap. 9. on Poor Laws.

† Tithes form one of the chief obstacles to the improvement and full cultivation of the land.

‡ The following is a rough estimate, from such documents as are at present within my reach, of the amount of the two funds supposed to be available as an equivalent for the proposed rent or land-tax, and of the demands upon them on account of it, for the United Kingdom.

Annual value or amount of tithes:		
England and Scotland,..............................	£3,000,000	
Ireland,..	2,000,000	
	£5,000,000	
Annual value or amount of poor-rates, exclusive of what may be considered as paid in part of wages:		
England and Scotland, £4,000,000, of which the land pays probably about three-fourths.	3,000,000	£8,000,000
Carry forward,		£8,000,000

and the advantage to be gained by the public from the whole arrangement would be, that they would thenceforward participate in the expected future increase of the value of the land.

But, perhaps it may be imagined that not a part only, but the whole rent of all the land might be thus retained and enjoyed as common property, and as the natural and equal inheritance of all, by vesting it all in the public, or in the sovereign, or government, on the part of the public, who should farm out the whole land, and apply the whole rent to public purposes, in the same manner as the proposed quitrent. The slightest attention, however, to what would be the consequences of such an arrangement will be sufficient, I think, to bring into view the numerous inconveniences and evils and insurmountable objections to such a system. I shall only briefly notice a few of the most weighty and most prominent.

But, in the first place, I will remark, that such a system, if *short leases* only were granted under it, would be liable (in a degree proportioned to that shortness) to all the ob-

---

Brought forward,		8,000,000
Annual value or amount of rent of land and ground-rent of houses:		
England,	£24,000,000	
Scotland,	6,000,000	
Ireland,	12,000,000	
	42,000,000	
Of which one-eighth amounts to		5,250,000
Leaving a surplus of		£2,750,000

per annum over and above what is required to repurchase the land-tax or quitrent proposed; and which quitrent ought always to be retained *ab origine* by every community, as a fund for the support of the government.

jections that have been stated against the land's being enjoyed as common property; and, on the other hand, if very *long leases* were allowed, this would be in effect the same as the present system of absolute property in it, under which there is generally a small feu-duty or quitrent paid to the *crown*, or to a *subject superior*, who may be conceived to stand for the crown or the public.

To illustrate this circumstance somewhat further:

1. It is plain, that if very short leases only were granted, there would not be a sufficient inducement to the proper cultivation of the land, and still less to any considerable or expensive improvements or works of any magnitude, as manufactories, &c., being made upon it.

2. On the other hand, if very long leases were allowed, leases, let us suppose, of a thousand years duration, it is obvious that this would amount to a very near approximation to the present system of indefinite and unlimited right; but then it would fall short of it in giving satisfaction to the individual possessors or proprietors of the land, at the same time also that it would be less beneficial to the general interests of the community. For although a lease of a thousand years, provided the quitrent were the same, would be in reality nearly as good as a holding for ever, yet it will always be considered as materially different in the imaginations of men, and most people will be found to regard it, and to lay out expense upon it in general, with a very different feeling in the one case and in the other. There are probably but few estates that have remained in possession of the same family, or that have descended through one unbroken line of heirs, for so long a period as a thousand years, yet still every individual is at liberty to hope that such may be the good fortune of *his* family or *his* heirs; and to sooth this feeling may be allowed to be an object of greater importance than that which is involved in the difference of a grant for ever and one for a thousand years, if indeed there

be any real difference, or if, from the indefinite grant, any advantage whatever could be gained to the public.

But, waiving these considerations altogether, what, I would ask, should be done by any government with so great a revenue as the whole rent of all the land,—a revenue that would be so much disproportioned to, and would so greatly exceed what could ever be necessary for its ordinary and legitimate expenses?—Or what government could be safely intrusted with the disposal of so large a surplus as would here arise?

And should it be thought that this surplus might be all invested in profitable undertakings and the improvement of the country, it is easy to see that such a system would be fraught with all the evils and corruptions of an extensive and almost boundless patronage, from the great number of agents or functionaries that would be required for the conducting of so vast a business. The seeds of corruption are here so thickly sown, that it will be unnecessary to attempt to detail or trace the manner of their growth.

But even if all the considerations and difficulties that have now been stated, as opposed to such an arrangement in regard to land-property, could be surmounted, there still remains behind a further objection and consideration, which should be sufficient of itself to settle the question, and should oblige us to reject all idea of such an arrangement. This consideration is, that such an arrangement would be inconsistent with the best form of society or civil polity; in the composition of which, as was before observed, a class of land-proprietors is an indispensable ingredient.

It will, I believe, be generally admitted, that land is the most desirable of all properties.

"Upon equal, or nearly equal profits," says Dr Smith, "most men will choose to employ their capitals rather in the improvement and cultivation of the land, than either in manufactures or in foreign trade. The man who employs his capital in land has it more under his view and command, and his fortune is much less liable to accidents than that of the trader, who is obliged frequently to commit it, not only to the winds and the waves, but to the more uncertain elements of human folly and injustice, by giving great credits in distant countries to men with whose character and situation he can seldom be thoroughly acquainted. The capital of the landlord, on the contrary, which is fixed in the improvement of his land, seems to be as well secured as the nature of human affairs can admit of. The beauty of the country, besides the pleasures of a country life, the tranquillity of mind which it promises, and wherever the injustice of human laws does not disturb it, the independency which it really affords, have charms that more or less attract every body; and as to cultivate the ground was the original destination of man, so in every stage of his existence he seems to retain a predilection for this primitive employment."*

The class of land-proprietors, therefore, it will, I think, be allowed, must, *ceteris paribus*, be the happiest in the community; and an arrangement that would abolish such a class (were such a thing practicable) would destroy this happiness without doing any good at all to the other classes, or any that would compensate for the great deterioration which would be wrought in the texture of society by the want of this class, not to mention the extent of patronage and corruption which it would probably introduce into the administration of public affairs.

But I will not push the argument upon this topic any farther at present, although there remains ample room for enlarging upon it. This, however, will, I think, be needless after all that has been said, and every reader, I trust, will

* Wealth of Nations, book iii. chap. 1.

be able to supply for himself all that may be deficient in our present illustrations.*

I shall conclude the present section with remarking, that as the right of property in land is founded in necessity, and in the manifest impossibility of any progress or advancement in society or civilization being made without it, so the extent of this right must be limited and circumscribed by the extent of the necessity. Had it been possible to have possessed and enjoyed the land as common property, without the relinquishment of a greater advantage, it would naturally have been done, and the system of private property and exclusive possession of it had never been established or permitted. And still the exclusion can never be justly carried farther than the real necessity of the case demands, or, in other words, than the necessity upon which the right itself is founded. It cannot, therefore, extend to the exclusive use or enjoyment of the fruits and produce of the earth any more than it can extend to sanction entails or any other restrictions whatever, on the disposal or transfer of it from one person to another.

All the institutions of human society, and those in regard to property in land of course among the number, are or ought to be calculated, not for the separate or exclusive advantage of any single class of persons or proprietors, but for the general good of the whole society, or, as it is now common to express it, for the greatest good of the greatest number. Under the system of the division of labour, it is necessary that the land should be possessed and cultivated by a part of the people, while the others are employed in different occupations ; but it is equally necessary that all should share in the produce, and the land-proprietors cannot

* See chap. v. sect. 1.

have a right which should extend to exclude the other members of the community from acquiring *by purchase* any part of that produce. For, if they may rightfully prohibit the buying or selling of one part of their produce, as hares or rabbits, why should they not have the same right in regard to any other part or the whole produce, corn, cattle, and every thing?—And granting this, it would follow that they have the right to starve all the other classes of the community, rich and poor, who happen not to be possessed of any land. It must be an implied condition therefore in the institution of land-property, that its produce be allowed to come freely to market, and be sold to all persons under the operation of the fair principles of an open competition.*

SECTION III.

OF THE RIGHT TO CAPITAL IN GENERAL.

As soon as the land is wholly appropriated, and wealth begins to increase and accumulate in the hands of individuals, it is immediately felt and perceived, that those persons by whose labour and frugality it has been produced or acquired, (for it is by frugality and saving alone that wealth or capital can be accumulated,) have a right to do what they please with it; that is, they have a right either to consume and enjoy it themselves, or to give it to others to consume

* The considerations and principles here stated appear satisfactorily enough to dispose of that extraordinary regulation under the game-laws, which interdicts the purchase or sale of game, than which nothing can be more arbitrary and unjust. For no right can exist anywhere to prohibit the use or disposal of this part of the produce of the land that will not extend to corn or cattle, or to any other part of it whatever.

and enjoy, as they shall think proper. In doing this they injure nobody. If they had not saved and produced any wealth they may possess, it would not have existed, and they might have used or consumed it immediately as it was produced, if they had chosen to do so. Other individuals, it may be supposed, in the same community, and under the same circumstances, produced as much, and consumed the whole immediately as it was produced, and were of course now destitute of any capital. But those persons who saved and did not consume the whole of what they produced, but who might have consumed the whole of it, if they had chosen to do so, as freely and innocently as the other persons who consumed the whole of what they produced, must be held to be at equal liberty to use and consume what they have saved at any subsequent period; since it is evident that the one way of disposing of it, or period of consuming it, can be no more blamed or objected to than the other.

Now, admitting the right of those who labour and save and accumulate wealth, either to consume and enjoy it themselves, or to give it to any other persons they please to consume and enjoy during their lifetime, it follows as an unavoidable consequence, that they may bequeath it to whom they please, at or previous to their death. And where the will was not known, or declared before death, it would at once occur as the most natural and reasonable way of disposing of a man's property to let it fall to his children or other near relations, whom he would most naturally and reasonably have supported whilst he lived. And this course being once adopted, the practice would naturally grow into a law, and would be declared as such as soon as any laws came to be regularly established.

And here we arrive at the grand cause of that inequality of conditions amongst men which is universally found to exist in all civilized countries, and even in those which have advanced but a single step beyond the condition of savages;

which inequality arises chiefly *from the accumulation of capital, and its devolution by will or otherwise upon particular persons or families.*

The inequality of conditions amongst men in the advanced state of civilized society is chiefly occasioned by the inequality of their possessions of wealth or property; and inequality of property is again chiefly occasioned by the constant and unavoidable operation of two great causes;—first, *by the difference of application or industry, and of parsimony or saving, between one person and another;* and, secondly, *by the devolution of fortunes upon individuals;* or, in other words, *by the inheritance of the savings of persons deceased in all time past falling to particular individuals or families, and not to others.*

Much has been said of *the difference of personal qualities,* as causing the inequality of property and conditions; and undoubtedly that difference is another fair and natural and legitimate cause of such inequality. But, except in the very infancy of the world, the effects produced by this cause are necessarily extremely limited and inconsiderable; and in all advanced periods the two others just mentioned will be uniformly found to be the chief causes of whatever inequality may happen, or may be observed to exist, at the particular time.

In the earliest stages of society the difference of personal qualities would, without doubt, be the chief cause of whatever inequality might be found to exist among mankind; and the strongest, swiftest, or most active savage would bear away the prize from his less vigorous competitors, and would naturally acquire the greatest quantity of wealth. Or rather indeed in the very earliest stage, and before the establishment of any law, or any confederacy of individuals for mutual protection, the strongest would take to himself by force every thing he coveted, and make every weaker individual the slave and subject of his arbitrary will. But as soon as any sort of social compact was formed, or any combination of a number of individuals to protect the weaker members from the depredations of the stronger, it would immediately happen that the difference of application and industry, or labour, would, even in this early period, be the chief cause of difference in the acquisition of wealth, or in the quantity of food, raiment, and shelter, that every one would be able to procure.

As society advanced immediately after this juncture, the difference of industry and parsimony would continue for some time to be the chief causes of inequality, until numerous and considerable accumulations had been made by individuals, which they could bequeath and hand down to their immediate posterity; from which period it would happen that it would be the inheritance of those accumulations, with all that should be added to them ever afterwards, which would continue thenceforward to be the great and principal cause of the difference or inequality of wealth and conditions.

Nor is it possible to conceive any thing more just, or more reasonable and unchallengeable, than this inequality; or any right more sacred to things external, than that which arises in the manner just described, to the accumulations of capital by whomsoever they have been made, and to whomsoever they have been fairly or voluntarily bequeathed.

Yet it has been said by no less eminent a person than Mr Godwin, that "it is a gross imposition that men are accustomed to put upon themselves, when they talk of the property bequeathed to them by their ancestors. The property is produced by the daily labour of men who are now in existence. All their ancestors bequeathed to them was a mouldy patent, which they show as a title to extort from their neighbours what the labour of those neighbours have produced."*

* Inquiry concerning Political Justice, book viii. chap. 2.

It has been one of the chief objects of this work to demonstrate the fallacy of the argument contained in the above passage; and to those readers who have attended to what was advanced in some of the preceding chapters,* that fallacy will be at once apparent. It is here assumed, that labour is the sole instrument of production, and it is roundly asserted that all the wealth at present extant "is produced by the daily labour of men who are now in existence." What! will Mr Godwin venture to maintain that all the cotton-yarn now daily spun in Great Britain is the proper and exclusive produce of the men, women, and children, who guide the spindles?—Will Mr Godwin maintain that the mills, buildings, and machinery, are of no use, or that no part of the effect is to be ascribed to them?—Or will he call mills, buildings, and machinery, "a mouldy patent?"—Will Mr Godwin, or any other person, venture to maintain that all the buildings and constructures of every kind, and the apparatus of every manufactory, and all the stores of food, clothes, money, and materials, necessary and useful, or actually in use, in all the processes of production at present going on in Great Britain or anywhere else, have been produced by the labour of men at present in existence?—Or will he, or any other person, maintain that any one of those accumulations or constructures† has been produced by labour alone, or, in other words, without the assistance and co-operation of previously existing accumulations or capital?—If he can do this, then indeed, but not before, he may call the property bequeathed to men by their ancestors "a mouldy patent."

Our ancestors left us our country filled with the fruits of their labour, and of the capital left to them by *their* ances-

---

* Chapters v. and vii.

† For a catalogue of what these may be, see chapters ii. and iii. of this book.

tors;—they left well-built cities, villages, and hamlets;—they left enclosed and cultivated fields, much improved from their original barrenness, and properly prepared and adapted to all the purposes of agriculture;—they left canals, roads, bridges, and innumerable other works of art, calculated to facilitate and abridge labour, or, in other words, calculated to assist in the work of production; not to mention the stores of finished manufactures, clothes and food, as well as of unfinished materials proportioned to the numbers and wealth of the community; and, because writings might exist relative to all those things in the hands of the proprietors, and might be required to register their existence, and to designate the persons to whom they at present belong, and are afterwards to descend, are those stupendous works themselves to be called "a mouldy patent?"

But to descend a little to particulars.

Suppose a person to have cleared a piece of ground,—to have enclosed it, drained it, manured it, and brought it to a high state of cultivation, and having done so, that he dies, and leaves it in this improved condition to his son; the new proprietor, we may imagine, ploughs and sows this piece of ground, and reaps, in his first harvest, a quantity of corn ten times, twenty times, or even perhaps a hundred times as great as his father did in the first years of his occupation and improvements upon it; now I ask, is this multiplied harvest to be accounted the produce of the son's labour exclusively, or is this inheritance to be accounted a mere "mouldy patent?"—A piece of parchment may be necessary to contain the record of the land-marks and boundaries of this piece of ground, or of the *will* of the previous possessor of it that it should descend to the present. This parchment is no doubt *left*, and may perchance, through neglect and length of time, grow "mouldy;" but this is not all that is left, nor the main thing; nor is this parchment left at all as a thing valuable on its own account. It is left merely as a record of the existence of that which is valuable, and as a guarantee or evidence in favour of the person who has the right to it, and to whom it is bequeathed.

But let us suppose farther, that the son to whom this improved piece of ground has been left, instead of labouring it himself, employs some other person whom he finds willing to do the work for a certain quantity of the corn, or of any other sort of wealth or produce to be given to him as wages; and be it observed, that whatever is agreed upon to be thus given must necessarily be at least as much as this person could have procured in any other equally eligible way of employing himself, and always far more than he could have earned in a state of nature without capital, or permanent possession or property in land, but with the whole world "all before him where to choose." Now it would happen as before, that the same accumulated harvest would be reaped; and is this, I again ask, to be accounted the exclusive produce of this hired labourer, or is he entitled to the whole produce of this improved piece of ground, because he added a comparatively small portion of labour to that which had been bestowed before, or, more properly speaking, to the *capital* which was accumulated upon it previously to his touching it, and which was the real efficient cause of the far greater part of the produce?—Is this man dealt unjustly by if he gets his stipulated wages?—On the contrary, is he not manifestly benefited by the transaction, and by the institution of property in land, since it is the condition necessary to his receiving or earning more than he could have done if no such institution existed, nor any such capital as this institution allows to be accumulated?—And is it not farther evident, that the wages agreed upon must be considered as properly representing the labourer's produce,—if, indeed, it may not be reasonably objected that they always represent really more than his actual produce, by giving him the command of more than he could have been able to acquire by his own separate exertions unassisted by capital and the institution of property.

Another argument and objection of precisely the same import as that we have just been considering, or rather indeed the same argument, but in somewhat of a different and more limited form, has been strongly urged in a more recently published book, the writer of which contends, that "all the benefits attributed to capital arise from co-existing and skilled labour."*

"To enable either the master manufacturer or the labourer," says this very able though anonymous author, "to devote himself to any particular occupation, it is only necessary that he should possess, not as political economists say, a stock of commodities, or circulating capital, but a conviction that while he is labouring at his particular occupation, the things which he does not produce himself will be produced for him, and that he will be able to procure them and pay for them by the produce of his own labour."†

After all that has been stated on the subject in some of the foregoing chapters,‡ it would be an unpardonable waste of time to enter into any very particular refutation of the above assertion. I shall only, in reference to it, ask this simple question, Of what consequence would the man's conviction be that he would be provided for if the goods themselves did not actually exist and were not forthcoming? —This writer, however, maintains, that "the farmer knows he will be able to get clothes when he requires them, and the tailor knows he will be able to get food; but the former knows nothing of any stored-up stock of clothes, and the

---

* Labour defended against the Claims of Capital; or the Unproductiveness of Capital proved. By a Labourer. London 1825.—Prefatory Notice.

† Labour Defended, &c. p. 11.

‡ See particularly chap. vii.

latter nothing of any stored-up stock of provisions."* Now this appears to me a very bold assertion indeed,—an assertion which, I must say, I should hardly have supposed would have been hazarded by one who has paid so much attention to the subject as this author seems evidently to have done. It appears to me impossible, that men should live in a civilized and opulent country such as Britain is at present, with their eyes open, and not "know such things,"—and not know and observe everywhere around them "stored-up stocks" both of clothes and provisions. And all persons that reflect but a moment must be aware that if the fact were not so;—if there were not, *in fact*, "any stored-up stock of provisions," they could not continue to be supplied, or live from day to day, or from one season or harvest time to another. The clothes may not indeed be "ready made," or the provisions ready cooked, but every individual who goes to buy the former must know that, if there were not a stored-up stock of cloth, he could not get clothes; and every one who goes to buy the latter,—be it, for example, corn, the staple commodity of life,—must know, if he succeeds in getting it, and reflects at all, that it had been stored up since the period of the last harvest at the least, either in the hands of the farmer or in those of some other capitalist.

But, says our author, "if we push our inquiries still farther, all that we can learn is, that there are other men in existence, who are preparing those things we need, while we are preparing those things which they need."† Now I think, "if we push our inquiries," we may learn somewhat more; we may learn that it is capital which enables both them and us to prepare the articles we both need and respectively labour to produce. We may learn that there are stocks and

---

* Labour Defended, &c. p. 11. † Ibid. p. 11.

stores of food,—of corn, cattle, cheese, butter, &c.,—in the hands of farmers, dealers, millers, and others, and of clothes in those of manufacturers, merchants, tailors, and others, who are all capitalists to a greater or less extent. We may, in short, learn, that there are *thousands*,—nay, let me say *millions*,—of stocks and stores, or capitals, some larger, some smaller, and of all possible varieties of minuteness or magnitude, and all employed in assisting the labourer in the work of production.

Thus far the author has been arguing in reference to *circulating capital* particularly, which he treats of first in order. Let us now follow him, and attend a little to what he says in reference to the other sort, or *fixed capital*.

"I come now," says he, "to examine, secondly, the NATURE and EFFECTS of FIXED CAPITAL. Fixed capital consists of the tools and instruments the labourer works with, the machinery he makes and guides, and the buildings he uses either to facilitate his exertions or to protect their produce. Unquestionably by using these instruments man adds wonderfully to his power. Without a hand-saw, a portion of fixed capital, he could not cut a tree into planks; with such an instrument he could, though it would cost him many hours or days; but with a saw-mill he could do it in a few minutes. Every man must admit that, by means of instruments and machines, the labourer can execute tasks he could not possibly perform without them; that he can perform a greater quantity of work in a given time, and that he can perform the work with greater nicety and accuracy than he could possibly do had he no instruments and machines. But the question then occurs, what produces instruments and machines, and in what degree do they aid production independent of the labourer, so that the owners of them are entitled to by far the greater part of the whole produce of the country? Are they or are they not the produce of labour? Do they or do they not constitute an efficient means of production separate from labour? Are they or are they not so much inert, decaying, and dead matter, of no utility whatever, possessing no productive power whatever, but as they are guided, directed, and applied by skilful hands."*

The fallacy of the above argument lies in this, that it represents the right of the capitalist to share along with the labourer in the joint produce of labour and capital as depending on the "degree" in which the "machinery," "buildings," and "tools and instruments" he possesses, and supplies the labourer with, can "aid production independent of the labourer!"—a representation which would exclude him from any share whatever, however much that produce might have been promoted by his contribution of capital. The argument, therefore, most clearly *proves too much.* The claim and right of the capitalist to share in the produce to which his capital contributes rests partly upon compact and agreement with the labourer, to whom he pays his wages in virtue of that agreement, and depends not upon the "degree" in which his capital can "aid production independent of the labourer," but partly upon the *comparative* degree in which labour can produce *with* and *without* capital, and partly upon the cost and difficulty or privation which the particular contribution of capital requires.

It is true, that fixed capital,—"machinery," "buildings," "tools and instruments," &c.,—can do *nothing* without men to guide and apply them; but it is equally true, that the labourer can do but *little* without such capital,—machinery, instruments, &c.;—and it is but this little that is properly to be accounted the effects or produce of labour; all the rest being evidently, and by the very terms of the proposition, the effects or produce of the machines and instruments or capital. The question in regard to the proper effects of labour and of capital in production, in as far as it respects the

* Labour Defended, &c. p. 14.

separate rights of the capitalist as well as the labourer to share in the joint produce of labour and capital,—being not whether the machinery, buildings, &c., can produce themselves without labourers to use and apply them, but *what* or *how much* the labourer can produce without machinery, buildings, &c., to use or apply.

Such capitals as are easily procured, and cost but little of saving or privation to acquire them, the labourer himself commonly possesses and draws of course the profit of; but such as are of greater magnitude, or are supplied to him by others, must be allowed to produce a profit to the proprietors distinct from his wages, in spite of every attempt or effort to deny it; for who is it, I would beg to ask, that should supply such capital gratuitously?

The tailor uses his own needles and the gardener his own spade, and their share of produce is, no doubt, augmented accordingly; but the labouring hand that works for stipulated wages in a cotton-mill, or an iron-foundry, and who acquires of course as great a share as either the tailor or the gardener, bating only, we may suppose, what belongs to the account of their small capitals, must allow the proprietors of those important works,—machinery, buildings, &c., on which they have expended perhaps a patrimony,—to share along with them in the produce to which they so largely contribute, and that in a degree bearing some proportion to the sacrifice and expenditure such proprietors have made in supplying the means of an ampler production.

That labour constitutes an efficient means of production without capital is true; but to what extent does that efficiency reach? This question has been already answered, and it has been seen how little can be produced by labour without capital. There is this distinction certainly between labour and capital as means of production, that, whereas capital can produce nothing without the assistance of labour, labour can produce *something* without the assistance of capital. But what avails this distinction in the present argument, since the question still recurs, *How much* can labour produce without the assistance of capital? How many people upon the earth could it supply with subsistence, or what sort of subsistence could it supply? The answer to these questions at once shows the futility of this distinction in reference to our present argument.

Without capital, almost of any sort, it is admitted that a certain number of human beings could exist in the world: all certainly who could live upon and be contented with "fresh herbs, and water from the spring." Nay, I will allow a few more who might catch, and kill, and live upon animals; and, to be as liberal as possible, we shall make no account of bows and arrows, clubs, or any other rude instruments, as capital, such as every savage might make and possess himself of in a short time, and with very little *saving* or sacrifice of immediate enjoyment. And, after all this extent of concession, I will again ask, What would be the numbers or accommodations of such inhabitants as could, under these circumstances, exist upon the earth? And would they not still necessarily continue in the condition of savages, and be obliged to clothe themselves in the skins of wild beasts, and to shelter themselves beneath the spreading tree, or in the cavern of the rock? They could not, without the acquisition of considerable capitals, advance to even the shepherd state, or make any considerable progress in it at least; for the numerous and extensive herds of cattle possessed by pastoral nations are themselves large capitals, the fruit of much saving and industry, and that too frequently of several generations.

This writer, we observe, says himself, "Without a hand-saw, a portion of fixed capital, he (viz. man) could not cut a tree into planks; with such an instrument he could, though it would cost him many hours or days; but with a saw-mill he could do it in a few minutes." Now only consider this:—He could do it! I must tell this author it is *not he* that does it now,—it is the saw-mill.

If our author says that the saw-mill could not do the work unless it were set on, and guided, and directed by the attendant workman, neither, I reply, could the workman do the work unless he had the saw-mill to set on. If he says, farther, that the saw-mill is not an efficient means of production without the man, neither, say I, is the man efficient to the extent of cutting a tree into planks without a saw; and I refer our author to his own statement. If he still urge that the saw-mill is so much inert, decaying, and dead matter, unless it be set on and guided by the man, what, reply I, is that to our present argument? What is it to the person who has the saw-mill, and demands something for the use of it? Or what is it to the person who has no saw-mill, but has timber that he wishes to be cut into planks, and who must pay something for the use of one? What is it, in short, to the question in hand, as to the right of the capitalist, or in bar of his right, to demand or receive something as an equivalent for the use of his capital?

As to the question, "Are they, (viz. instruments and machines) or are they not the produce of labour?" I distinctly answer, *No, they are not.* They are not the produce of labour alone, but of labour assisted by capital. I will only illustrate this answer farther than it has already been done, by remarking, that, as we saw before, the produce of an improved and cultivated field was not wholly the produce of the labourer who merely ploughed and sowed it last; and as we now see that the cutting of a tree into planks in a few minutes by a saw-mill is not wholly the work of the person who guides the machine, but rather of the machine itself chiefly, so the construction of the machine was not effected without the assistance of other machines, and innumerable previously accumulated capitals.

And so of all other machines or instruments, or fixed capitals.

Before concluding the section, there is one point more to which I must advert, in order to complete the outline of discussion on the whole subject of the present chapter. This point relates to the manner in which capitals are, for the most part, acquired originally; or perhaps the topic here to be introduced may be better stated in the form of a query, thus,—In what manner, and by what conduct is it, that property or wealth is in general produced and saved, and the right to it acquired by individuals at first? The answer to this question, and the mode in which we shall endeavour to illustrate it, will, it is hoped, diffuse a clear light over the whole subject, and show more fully than has previously been done, the powerful considerations of *humanity as well as justice*, which concur to sanction and enforce this right.

In order to illustrate this part of our subject, then, let us suppose a case in the advanced state of society, (and one of most frequent and daily occurrence,) of two individuals of equal, or nearly equal, abilities, but varying in respect to their industry and frugality, and let us attend to the consequences that may be naturally expected to result from their different conduct in a course of years. Their trades or occupations may be supposed what you please, but we must make them start from the same point, that is, we must suppose them to be both destitute, at the commencement of their career, of any capital or property, and have no other way of acquiring it than by their industry or labour.

The one, we shall suppose, is ordinarily diligent; he labours daily in his vocation, and he earns what is sufficient for the support of himself and his family. He is contented with this, and he cannot attain more, or at least he saves nothing, nor attempts not to save or accumulate any capital, all the money or wages, therefore, which this man receives—that is, the whole value or produce of his industry—is disposed of as he receives it, and affords him a subsistence.

The other is indefatigable. He is not satisfied with being ordinarily industrious, or with acquiring merely a daily subsistence for himself and family; he aims at something more than this,—he looks forward to the feebleness and helplessness of age, and determines within himself to endeavour to make some provision for its wants. He revolves in his mind the prospects of youth, and is anxious to emancipate his children from the lowly and laborious station which he has himself occupied in the world; and, deeply impressed with the importance of these objects, he is wholly given up to business and application.

This man does a great deal more work than the other, and receives a great deal more money in exchange for it as its price; and he is enabled thereby, not only to support himself and his family as well as the other, but, after doing this, there remains an overplus which he can accumulate and apply to other exigencies.

The first of these individuals, with common industry and application, earns, we shall suppose, a hundred pounds yearly, and expends the whole of it upon himself and family, and he will consequently have nothing over that he could store up or accumulate. The second, on the contrary, by his superior and indefatigable labour, earns again, by the supposition, considerably more than a hundred pounds yearly, and, by his greater frugality or economy, expends something less; let us suppose that he earns *one hundred and thirty* pounds, and expends but *eighty;* then it follows that he will have *fifty* pounds of his income which he can store up and accumulate yearly.

It will not be denied that this man has a full and equal right to what he stores up no less than to what he expends. He or his children, or whomsoever he should choose to appoint, must continue to have a full right to the accumulated property, or to any goods or vendible commodities that it will purchase or exchange for; and this will hold whether it be during the period of his life, or at any future time after his decease.

Both these individuals had an equal right to the *whole* of their earnings, since they both equally acquired them by the sweat of their bodies; and arbitrarily to deprive either of them of any part of those earnings, or of their full and absolute control over the whole, would be evidently both cruel and unjust. If the one acquired more than the other, it was by giving a greater value in exchange for it, namely, an additional quantity of labour proportioned to the additional quantity of wealth acquired; and if the same individual retained a part of his gains as the means of a future enjoyment, the other, by expending the whole of his, and by taking ease to himself while the other toiled, had enjoyed more antecendently. And possibly, *for himself*, he might be the wisest of the two; for while his more anxious neighbour perhaps wasted and macerated his body, and brought upon himself a premature decay and decrepitude, *he* saved himself, and retained his health and strength to a greater age, as a compensation and equivalent for the means of a prospective independence acquired by the other, not perhaps to be enjoyed by himself, but by his children.

And admitting, for the sake of argument, this latter supposition to be the actual case, how unjust and *inhuman* would it be to deprive those children of any part of the benefits intended to be conferred upon them by the father, and to confer which he toiled so laboriously and denied himself so many enjoyments! How unjust and inhuman would it be to confiscate those savings, or to deprive the individual who made them of his undoubted and hard-earned right to dispose of them!

If we frame our hypothesis so as to allow greater genius

as well as greater industry and frugality to one of the individuals in the case supposed than to the other, we may imagine a still greater difference of gains and of savings, and still the same principle will hold good, and the title of the one who gains most will be equally valid to the whole of his earnings with that of the one who gains the least to the whole of his. Besides his greater industry and application to business, for example, one of these individuals may be the inventor of improvements in the art which he professes, or in the machines he works with, or which it is his business to construct; or he may adopt improved plans, and make better arrangements in the conduct of his business, whereby more work may be done by a given expenditure of labour, and his productions be brought better and cheaper to market; and in numberless other ways, which it would be endless to particularize, the individual possessed of superior genius as well as industry might increase his own gains at the same time that he did (and by the very same means too which produced those gains) a service and a benefit of incomparably greater extent and importance to the public. Indeed a man cannot well increase his own gains, either by simple but honest industry, or by improvements in the arts of production, without benefiting the public at the same time; and the advantages arising to the public from the inventions, industry, and enterprise of individuals may always be taken as not only equivalent, but as greater, and generally very much greater, than the price which they pay for them;* in which price is of course included the whole of the wealth or fortunes acquired by those inventive, industrious, and enterprising individuals.

---

* This position has been partly illustrated already, and will, I trust, be fully established in the course of this work. See chap. v., sect. 2. of this book, and chap. i., sect. 2. of the second book.

Again, we may either suppose the diligence and industry of any two individuals to be equal or unequal, and still the same results will come out, or the same principles of right hold good. We may suppose any two individuals either, *first*, to labour and produce equally, but to consume differently; or, *secondly*, we may suppose them to labour and produce differently, but to consume equally; or, *thirdly*, we may suppose them both to labour, and produce, and to consume differently; still, in any case, if one of two individuals shall resolutely save a portion of his earnings or income, while the other shall consume the whole of his, it will necessarily happen, that, after a lapse of time, he will have accumulated a certain amount of capital, and that his right to such wealth or savings will be equally good with that of the other to what he consumed.

We may vary this example still farther, so as to include those persons who have begun their career with a capital previously accumulated, and inherited from their forefathers, and still the same principles will equally hold, and will make valid the right to the original capital, as well as to whatever may be afterwards added to it. For still this capital which was begun with, let it have been great or small, must have been accumulated at first by industry and saving; and whatever was added to it afterwards could only be added by the same means. The right to the original capital, therefore, and to whatever was afterwards added to it, must evidently stand upon the same footing.

It does not invalidate this argument, or in the slightest degree impugn the right to property, to say that it is not always acquired by the persons actually possessing it in the fair and and honourable manner here supposed. Some property is acquired by fraud, and some by highway-robbery; but it is so very small a proportion of it that is acquired in this manner, that, whe compared with the whole, or with that which is acquired fairly and honourably, it sinks into entire insignificance, in so far at least as it should affect the present question. Such acts as fraud and robbery, being the most direct violations of the right here maintained, the law, if there be law at all, must endeavour to prevent, as one of its first objects; and when it happens to fail in this object, as in some instances it must, it is then only by discovery and conviction that it can exempt the property so acquired from that protection which it extends in general to all property. The administrators of the law cannot make it successful in every particular instance for the establishment of right and prevention of wrong, even as recognized by the law itself; in other words, they cannot in every instance hinder the law from being violated with impunity; and as laws must be general in their operation, they must necessarily protect even the property of the successful but undiscovered robber.

Were all wealth, or the greater part of it, acquired (or re-transferred from the original acquirers,) by fraud and robbery, there would be no such thing as *right* to it at all, and it would neither deserve nor obtain respect from any quarter. Where all was the property of *plunder*, and all were *plundered*, every one might be excused to plunder in his turn. But how long would such a state of things endure? How long would booty continue to be found, while all consumed and ravished it from one another, and none applied themselves to replace and reproduce by honest industry what every one consumed, and must consume, to live? The universal ruin which must immediately follow upon such a state of things needs no illustration or argument to prove it.

Perhaps it may be thought that it would be better if the whole wealth of one whole generation could be divided and distributed equally among all the individuals of the next. But this, even were it practicable, could not be done without annihilating the chief motive to save and accumulate; or, in other words, without preventing the existence of that very wealth which it would be its object to distribute. It is evident, however, that it would be physically impossible to divide and distribute the whole wealth of any one generation among all the individuals of the next, unless one entire generation quitted the world and died out at once; not to mention the manifest injustice that would be involved in compelling parents to allow the children of those who had saved nothing, or who had saved less than their neighbours, to share equally with the children of those who had saved the most.

But although such a universal and sweeping distribution of property would be both unjust and impracticable, and would be highly pernicious in its effects if it were practicable, there is yet (as we have partly seen already, and as will be still further pointed out to the attention of the readers in the sequel,*) a principle in the mechanism of human society, which causes a distribution *in effect*, though of a much more limited nature, than the one which has been just adverted to,—a principle which it is one of the chief objects of this work to develop, and which, by an easy, and natural, and unforced process, diffuses the wealth which is accumulated, in a certain measure, through all the various ranks and gradations of the people, dispensing a portion of it necessarily to every individual member of the community, in such a measure, at least, as should enable the lowest and poorest to live, and to procure enjoyments (under any tolerable administration of government) infinitely exceeding those that could be procured by the most gifted in countries wholly destitute of capital, although he had full liberty to seek them, unobstructed and unrestrained, over the whole land.

---

* See chap. v., sect. 2. of this book, and chap. i., sect. 2. of the second book.

I have thus endeavoured to trace, by a simple and obvious deduction, founded partly on facts and real history, and partly on the principles of human nature, and on that species of "theoretical or conjectural history" which rests its authority on those principles, and on what may reasonably be supposed to have happened in the world in former periods, from our experience of things existing at present,—the natural grounds of right to property or wealth; and although some flaws may perhaps be found in the first allotment and distribution of the land among the aboriginal inhabitants, or among those who by force of arms had afterwards dispossessed those primeval occupiers, yet these have appeared to be but trivial in their effects upon its future destiny, and by no means of a character to disturb the existing proprietors after a lapse of time.* We have seen that the first ground of right to property was founded in labour and first possession; but that as society advances other considerations come in aid of these, and it is found that the inviolability of this right, whether arising from labour, from capital, or from land, is a condition necessary to the existence of civilized society, because necessary to the existence of agriculture, of manufactures, and of commerce; and hence it follows that the question in regard to the inviolability or sacredness of property, under the three original grounds of right to it, explained in this chapter, resolves itself into that of the preference to be given to the civilized over the savage state; or, in other words, into this single consideration, Whether it be best that the world should be peopled up to the full measure of its capability of maintaining inhabitants, when cultivated and improved by the knowledge and industry incident to the most enlightened

---

* Especially when it is considered that the same system of private property must be resorted to and continued, into whatever hands the land might fall. This, I think, will be admitted to have been proved.

condition of mankind, and be filled with life and enjoyment, population and wealth, or that it should be one vast, dreary, and interminable desert, the cheerless abode of a poor and inconsiderable number of wandering savages, afraid of each other, and living like the brutes? Whether it is best and most desirable that the world should contain *ten thousand millions* of human inhabitants, (which it is probably capable of maintaining if cultivated and improved to the utmost,) the whole abundantly supplied with the necessaries and many with the conveniences and luxuries of life, or that it should contain certainly not *a hundred millions*, perhaps not a tenth of that number, and they naked of every thing and enduring every hardship and privation? Whether, in a word, the LIFE which the world *must* support, should be that of *man*, God's image, or that of snakes and serpents; for the number of mankind that could exist without respect to the rights of property, and consequently without capital and without agriculture, is hardly worth taking into the account.

CHAPTER X.

OF THE MORAL CAUSES OF PRODUCTION.

SECTION I.

THE TWO GRAND MORAL CAUSES OF PRODUCTION DELINEATED, AND A HIGHLY-IMPORTANT CONCURRENT EFFECT OF THESE CAUSES POINTED OUT.

IN the foregoing chapters of this book our inquiries have been confined, almost exclusively, to the investigation of the *physical causes* of production, and to the ascertainment and explication of those *material means or instruments* by which wealth is visibly acquired and produced; but the production and accumulation of wealth, (as well as its distribution,) like all other phenomena or effects brought to pass by the agency of human creatures, are primarily and necessarily influenced by *moral causes*; and it remains in this place to give an account of these.

There are two grand moral causes of production, which in an especial manner demand the deep attention of the political inquirer. These are the two following, which will indeed be seen to be the fundamental and primary causes of all improvement in the social condition of mankind, as well as of the production and accumulation of wealth:

First,—*The desire natural to all mankind to possess and enjoy wealth*, or, as it is commonly expressed, *to better their condition.*

Second,—*Political justice, law, and government*, or, in other words, *security and inviolability to persons and property.*

We call these moral causes of production in contradistinction to the physical causes, or to those material means or instruments which have been already distinctly considered in a former chapter.*

It will be apparent at the first glance that there is a wide and important difference in the nature of these two moral causes of production, as well as in the circumstances on which their existence or their presence and absence depend; the first being necessarily *always* present while the second is only contingently so. The first of these causes is plainly innate, inherent, and inseparable from human nature; and is therefore necessarily always present, and ready to exert

---

* Chapter vi.

its influence where opportunity offers, at the bare volition of every individual agent; whereas the second is extrinsic, accidental, and independent generally of the will of individuals, and is not therefore, like the other, always present and available to all mankind at all times.

It will be evident also on the slightest reflection, that, without the presence and co-operation of the second moral cause, the first can be of little or no avail. Without the establishment of government, law, and justice, producing a certain degree of security to persons and property, it is quite obvious that the desire of bettering our condition could never be effectual for its purpose. Where all might rob and plunder with impunity, wealth could never be produced or accumulated to any considerable extent; and where none could be sure of possessing or enjoying what they might produce, the very motive to accumulate would be annihilated. It is this second moral cause of production, therefore, which alone requires any attention or effort on the part of mankind to provide or establish it; because, wherever this cause is found, the other must necessarily be found also; since, as has been just observed, this other is necessarily and universally existent wherever there are men.

But there is one peculiar and highly-important effect depending upon the moral causes of production, and especially on the *quality* of the second moral cause,—that is, upon good and bad government,—which, as it has been the main occasion of our treating those causes distinctively, it will be necessary here in some degree to explain, although the discussion belongs more properly to the province of distribution, and will have to be resumed more at large in the second book upon that subject.*

The effect I here allude to is that which good and bad

---

* See book ii. chap. 9. on the Wages of Labour.

government is calculated to produce upon the wages of labour, and upon the habits and modes of subsistence of the lower classes of labourers; and what I shall endeavour to prove is, that under good government the wages of labour and the habits and modes of subsistence of the lower classes of labourers must constantly and indefinitely improve and increase from their endeavour to better their condition, which becomes then effectual for its purpose.

Before, however, proceeding to enlarge upon this part of our argument, it will be expedient to consider the effects of good and bad government, and of the desire of bettering our condition somewhat farther; which we shall do in the two following sections, by setting down a few observations on each of these heads separately.

SECTION II.

OF THE FIRST MORAL CAUSE OF PRODUCTION.

WITH regard to the first, or what may be termed the *innate* moral cause of production, namely, the desire to possess and enjoy wealth and to better our condition, it arises, as has been already hinted, from the very nature and passions of human kind, which subject them to the necessity and implant in them the desire to procure and consume wealth; it is therefore constant, universal, and invariable.

All men naturally desire to possess and enjoy wealth and to better their condition; in other words, all men naturally desire to possess and enjoy the necessaries, conveniences, and luxuries of life. Food, clothes, and lodging, of some sort or other, are absolutely necessary. These are first desired in abundance, then of better quality; and, as society advances, and wealth, and knowledge, and civilization increase, the desire of improvement increases still more; and, finally, a taste for luxuries and for all sorts of gratifications and enjoyments becomes general, and extends itself downwards to the very lowest ranks of the people.

Accordingly we find that the importance of this principle has been noticed and acknowledged by the most profound and sagacious authors who have treated the subject. Dr Smith observes of it, that it comes with us from the womb, and never leaves us till we go into the grave. "The principle which prompts to expense," he says "is the passion for present enjoyment, which, though sometimes violent and very difficult to be restrained, is in general only momentary and occasional. But the principle which prompts to save is the desire of bettering our condition,—a desire which, though generally calm and dispassionate, comes with us from the womb, and never leaves us till we go into the grave. In the whole interval which separates those two moments, there is scarce perhaps a single instance in which any man is so perfectly and completely satisfied with his situation as to be without any wish of alteration or improvement of any kind. An augmentation of fortune is the means by which the greater part of men propose and wish to better their condition. It is the means the most vulgar and the most obvious; and the most likely way of augmenting their fortune is to save and accumulate some part of what they acquire, either regularly and annually, or upon some extraordinary occasions. Though the principle of expense, therefore, prevails in almost all men upon some occasions, and in some men upon almost all occasions, yet in the greater part of men, taking the whole course of their life at an average, the principle of frugality seems not only to predominate, but to predominate very greatly."*

And throughout the whole of his immortal work on "the Nature and Causes of the Wealth of Nations," this principle is constantly referred to by Dr Smith as the primary cause

* Wealth of Nations, book ii. chap. 3.

of accumulation and production, and indeed of improvement in general of every description in the affairs of mankind.

Mr Malthus also, in his "Essay on the Principle of Population," alludes to this primary cause of production invariably in the same manner, and calls it expressly "the master-spring of public prosperity." He observes, "Even poverty itself, which appears to be the great spur to industry, when it has once passed certain limits, almost ceases to operate. The indigence which is hopeless destroys all vigorous exertion, and confines the efforts to what is sufficient for bare existence. It is the hope of bettering our condition, and the fear of want, rather than want itself, that is the best stimulus to industry; and its most constant and best-directed efforts will almost invariably be found among a class of people above the class of the wretchedly poor."*

Again, he asks, (on the supposition of the idle and negligent being placed on the same footing as to wealth or support with the industrious and diligent,) "Can we expect to see men exert that animated activity in bettering their condition, which now forms the master-spring of public prosperity?"† And in another place he says, "That great *vis medicatrix reipublicæ*, the desire of bettering our condition, and the fear of making it worse, has been constantly in action, and has been constantly" producing the best effects, where it has not been rendered nugatory by bad government.‡

To the same purpose Mr Hume observes,—"Avarice, or the desire of gain, is an universal passion which operates at all times, in all places, and upon all persons."§

This then is what we call the first moral cause of pro-

* Essay on Population, book iii. chap. 14.
† Ibid. book iii. chap. 1.
‡ Ibid. book iv. chap. 14.
§ Essays, part 1. Essay, 14.

duction,—the desire natural to all mankind to possess and enjoy wealth, and to better their condition, and it may also be called the first principle in the science of political economy;—for, although in the more comprehensive sciences of morality and *pure* metaphysics, this principle or desire may be traced still higher, and reduced to a principle still simpler and more general, namely, the desire of enjoying pleasure and of avoiding pain, yet still this is the highest point we find it necessary to ascend to in the science before mentioned, or first principle to which we have occasion to refer in tracing the laws which regulate the production, accumulation, and distribution of wealth.

SECTION III.

OF THE SECOND MORAL CAUSE OF PRODUCTION.

But it unfortunately happens that the principle just explained, the desire of bettering our condition, though exceedingly active wherever it has opportunity to exert its influence, and though ever ready to be excited in the human breast, is yet of itself comparatively powerless and unavailing, and can produce but little effect without the conjunct existence and co-operation of the other moral cause of production,—that is to say, without the institution of government, law, and justice, or the association of men for the defence and protection of their persons and property.

Without the protection of government, and a certain measure of justice and security to persons and property, it is quite obvious that mankind could never effectually or considerably better their condition, or increase their wealth to any large amount; and, as was before observed, whatever desire they might feel to do so, must necessarily remain a dormant and inoperative principle.

Without some sort of government and some degree of justice, or some sort of protection to persons and property, wealth could never indeed have increased above the immediate, daily, and most pressing wants of mankind; and the species could never have emerged from the lowest state of barbarism. Where the "right of the strongest" was the only law which an appeal could be made to, no individual could ever think of accumulating wealth, because no one could be sure of possessing or enjoying what he might produce beyond the existing moment. All idea of any considerable provision for the future would be necessarily abandoned, and the motive to accumulate being taken away, present enjoyment would be the only object which could be desired or sought after. Every one would merely strive to live, and to consume or enjoy, as fast as he could, whatever chance or his good fortune might throw in his way, lest by any delay he should run the hazard of being deprived of the fruit of his labour altogether.

Such, however, is the promptitude and elasticity of the first exciting cause of production, that it requires but small encouragement to draw it into activity; and under very indifferent government and imperfect laws, the endeavour of the people to better their condition will show itself, and will often astonish the observer by the pertinacity of its efforts, and the unconquerable perseverance with which it will work, and maintain the conflict against untoward circumstances; but it is under *good* government alone that this principle can produce its full effects.

Accordingly we find also, that the necessity and importance of this second moral cause of production is repeatedly and pointedly taken notice of, and most amply acknowledged by the same able writers whom we have already quoted as acknowledging the first.

"The improvement and prosperity of Great Britain," says

Dr Smith, "which has so often been ascribed to those laws,* may very easily be accounted for by other causes. That security which the laws in Great Britain give to every man that he shall enjoy the fruits of his own labour is alone sufficient to make any country flourish, notwithstanding these and twenty other absurd regulations of commerce; and this security was perfected by the Revolution much about the same time that the bounty was established. The natural effort of every individual to better his own condition, when suffered to exert itself with freedom and security, is so powerful a principle, that it is alone, and without any assistance, not only capable of carrying on the society to wealth and prosperity, but of surmounting a hundred impertinent obstructions with which the folly of human laws too often encumbers its operations; though the effect of these obstructions is always more or less either to encroach upon its freedom or to diminish its security. In Great Britain industry is perfectly secure; and though it is far from being perfectly free, it is as free or freer than in any other part of Europe."†

"Order and good government," says the same author in another place, "and along with them the liberty and security of individuals, were in this manner established in cities, at a time when the occupiers of land in the country were exposed to every sort of violence. But men in this defenceless state naturally content themselves with their necessary subsistence, because to acquire more might only tempt the injustice of their oppressors. On the contrary, when they are secure of enjoying the fruits of their industry, they naturally exert it to better their condition, and to acquire not only the necessaries, but the conveniences and elegancies of life. That industry, therefore, which aims at something more than necessary subsistence, was established in cities long before it was com-

---

* Meaning the system of laws which was connected with a bounty on the exportation of corn formerly in existence.

† Wealth of Nations, book iv. chap 5.

monly practised by the occupiers of land in the country. If, in the hands of a poor cultivator, oppressed with the servitude of villanage, some little stock should accumulate, he would naturally conceal it with great care from his master, to whom it would otherwise have belonged, and take the first opportunity of running away to a town. The law was at that time so indulgent to the inhabitants of towns, and so desirous of diminishing the authority of the lords over those of the country, that if he could conceal himself there from the pursuit of his lord for a year, he was free for ever. Whatever stock, therefore, accumulated in the hands of the industrious part of the inhabitants of the country naturally took refuge in cities, as the only sanctuaries in which it could be secure to the person that acquired it."*

And further :—

"Commerce and manufactures gradually introduced order and good government, and with them the liberty and security of individuals, among the inhabitants of the country, who had before lived almost in a continual state of war with their neighbours, and of servile dependency upon their superiors. This, though it has been the least observed, is by far the most important of all their effects. Mr Hume is the only writer who, so far as I know, has hitherto taken notice of it."†

Still farther in another place the same author observes,— "In all countries where there is tolerable security, every man of common understanding will endeavour to employ whatever stock he can command in procuring either present enjoyment or future profit. If it is employed in procuring present enjoyment, it is a stock reserved for immediate consumption. If it is employed in procuring future profit, it must procure this profit, either by staying with him, or by going from him. In the one case it is a fixed, in the other it is a circulating capital. A man must be perfectly crazy who, where there is tolerable security, does not employ all the stock

* Wealth of Nations, book iii. chap. 3.

† Ibid. book iii. chap. iv.

which he commands, whether it be his own or borrowed of other people, in some one or other of those three ways.

"In those unfortunate countries, indeed, where men are continually afraid of the violence of their superiors, they frequently bury and conceal a great part of their stock, in order to have it always at hand to carry with them to some place of safety, in case of their being threatened with any of those disasters to which they consider themselves as at all times exposed. This is said to be a common practice in Turkey, in Indostan, and I believe in most other governments of Asia. It seems to have been a common practice among our ancestors during the violence of the feudal government. Treasure-trove was in those times considered as no contemptible part of the revenue of the greatest sovereigns in Europe. It consisted in such treasure as was found concealed in the earth, and to which no particular person could prove any right. This was regarded in those times as so important an object, that it was always considered as belonging to the sovereign, and neither to the finder nor to the proprietor of the land, unless the right to it had been conveyed to the latter by an express clause in his charter. It was put upon the same footing with gold and silver mines, which, without a special clause in the charter, were never supposed to be comprehended in the general grant of the lands, though mines of lead, copper, tin, and coal were, as things of smaller consequence."*

On the same subject Mr Malthus writes as follows:—"The fundamental cause of the low state of population in Turkey," says he, "compared with its extent of territory, is undoubtedly the nature of the government. Its tyranny, its feebleness, its bad laws and worse administration of them, together with the consequent insecurity of property, throw such obstacles in the way of agriculture that the means of subsistence are necessarily decreasing yearly, and with them, of course, the number of people. The *miri*, or general land-tax

* Wealth of Nations, book ii. chap. 1.

paid to the sultan, is in itself moderate; but by abuses inherent in the Turkish government the pachas and their agents have found out the means of rendering it ruinous. Though they cannot absolutely alter the impost which has been established by the sultan, they have introduced a multitude of changes, which without the name produce all the effects of an augmentation. In Syria, according to Volney, having the greatest part of the land at their disposal, they clog their concessions with burdensome conditions, and exact the half and sometimes even two thirds of the crop. When the harvest is over, they cavil about losses, and as they have the power in their hands, they carry off what they think proper. If the season fail, they still exact the same sum, and expose every thing that the poor peasant possesses to sale. To these constant oppressions are added a thousand accidental extortions. Sometimes a whole village is laid under contribution for some real or imaginary offence. Arbitrary presents are exacted on the accession of each governor; grass, barley, and straw are demanded for his horses; and commissions are multiplied, that the soldiers who carry the orders may live upon the starving peasants, whom they treat with the most brutal insolence and injustice.

"The consequence of these depredations is, that the poorer class of inhabitants ruined, and unable any longer to pay the miri, become a burden to the village, or fly into the cities; but the miri is unalterable, and the sum to be levied must be found somewhere. The portion of those who are thus driven from their homes falls on the remaining inhabitants, whose burden, though at first light, now becomes insupportable. If they should be visited by two years of drought and famine the whole village is ruined and abandoned, and the tax which it should have paid is levied on the neighbouring lands.

"The same mode of proceeding takes place with regard to the tax on the Christians, which has been raised by these means from three, five, and eleven piastres, at which it was first fixed, to thirty-five and forty, which absolutely impoverishes those on whom it is levied, and obliges them to leave the country. It has been remarked, that these exactions have made a rapid progress during the last forty years; from which time are dated the decline of agriculture, the depopulation of the country, and the diminution in the quantity of specie carried into Constantinople.

"The food of the peasants is almost everywhere reduced to a little flat cake of barley or doura, onions, lentils, and water. Not to lose any part of their corn, they leave in it all sorts of wild grain, which often produce bad consequences. In the mountains of Lebanon and Nablous, in time of dearth, they gather the acorns from the oaks, which they eat after boiling or roasting them on the ashes.

"By a natural consequence of this misery, the art of cultivation is in the most deplorable state. The husbandman is almost without instruments, and those he has are very bad. His plough is frequently no more than the branch of a tree cut below a fork, and used without wheels. The ground is tilled by asses and cows, rarely by oxen, which would bespeak too much riches. In the districts exposed to the Arabs, as in Palestine, the countryman must sow with his musket in his hand; and scarcely does the corn turn yellow before it is reaped, and concealed in subterraneous caverns. As little as possible is employed for seed-corn, because the peasants sow no more than is barely necessary for their subsistence. Their whole industry is limited to a supply of their immediate wants; and to procure a little bread, a few onions, a blue shirt, and a bit of woollen, much labour is not necessary. The peasant lives therefore in distress; but at least he does not enrich his tyrants, and the avarice of despotism is its own punishment.

"This picture, which is drawn by Volney, in describing the state of the peasants in Syria, seems to be confirmed by all other travellers in these countries; and, according to Eton, it represents very nearly the condition of the peasants in the greatest part of the Turkish dominions. Universally, the offices of every denomination are set up to public sale; and in the intrigues of the seraglio, by which the disposal of all places is regulated, every thing is done by means of bribes. The pachas, in consequence, who are sent into the provinces, exert to the utmost their power of extortion; but are always outdone by the officers immediately below them, who, in their turn, leave room for their subordinate agents.

"The pacha must raise money to pay the tribute, and also to indemnify himself for the purchase of his office, support his dignity, and make a provision in case of accidents; and as all power, both military and civil, centres in his person from his representing the sultan, the means are at his discretion, and the quickest are invariably considered as the best. Uncertain of to-morrow, he treats his province as a mere transient possession, and endeavours to reap, if possible, in one day the fruit of many years, without the smallest regard to his successor, or the injury that he may do to the permanent revenue."*

Again:—

"Some tribes, from the nature of the deserts in which they live, seem to be necessarily condemned to a pastoral life; but even those which inhabit soils proper for agriculture, have but little temptation to practise this art while surrounded by marauding neighbours. The peasants of the frontier provinces of Syria, Persia, and Siberia, exposed, as they are, to the constant incursions of a devastating enemy, do not lead a life that is to be envied by the wandering Tartar or Arab. A certain degree of security is perhaps still more necessary than richness of soil to encourage the change from the pastoral to the agricultural state; and where this cannot be attained, the sedentary labourer is more exposed to the vicissitudes of fortune than he who leads a wandering life, and carries all his property with him. Under the feeble, yet oppressive government of the Turks, it is not uncommon for peasants to desert their villages and betake themselves to a pastoral state, in which they expect to be better able to escape from the plunder of their Turkish masters and Arab neighbours."†

And universally throughout his Essay on Population, as

---

* Essay on Population, book i. chap. 10.

† Ibid. book i. chap. 7.

well as in his "Principles of Political Economy," Mr Malthus acknowledges and enforces this important truth,—that the numbers, condition, and habits of the people depend in the greatest degree on the character of the government under which they live.

This, then, is our second moral cause of production,—political justice, law, and government; or protection and security to person and property,—which, it evidently appears, are absolutely indispensable requisites to the accumulation or existence of wealth in any considerable quantity or abundance; and such is a specimen of the facts or examples which demonstrate the importance of the *quality* of this second moral cause; that is to say, of the goodness or badness, perfection or imperfection of the laws and government. Such examples show that if the government be very bad, as in the instance of Turkey, it becomes itself the great robber of its subjects, and prevents, after a small and comparatively inconsiderable accumulation, all farther advance in wealth or improvement. Protection and security are *then* required against the acts and rapaciousness of the government itself; and no effectual way of securing this object has yet been discovered but that which is afforded by the intervention of an assembly of representatives *chosen by the governed.*

SECTION IV.

OF THE EFFECTS OF GOOD GOVERNMENT.

Such then, as they have now been explained, are the two grand moral causes of production, and of improvement in general of every description,—the greatness or smallness of whose effects depends entirely upon the *quality* of the second moral cause,—government; viz. upon its being *good* or *bad.*

Under *bad government* the desire felt by mankind to better their condition, can only produce partial and comparatively inconsiderable effects; but under *good government* it becomes a steady and universally-operating principle of action, producing a continual and indefinite improvement in the conduct and condition of mankind, and especially of the labouring classes. *Wealth* is made continually and indefinitely to increase, and *wages* and *population* also at the same time; though of course, as a country approaches the limits of its resources, at a continually diminishing rate of increase. The means of education and intelligence are brought within the reach of the lower classes of people, who, in consequence of this circumstance, joined to the security which they enjoy, acquire higher and constantly-improving notions of what is necessary to their creditable and comfortable subsistence; which improved notions necessarily affect the amount of provision they are disposed to make for their establishment in marriage; and, without any express resolution or intention on their part of restraining their numbers in order to raise wages, their numbers actually are restrained, and confined within the limits required to raise wages to that precise point which enables them to make such provision as they have resolved not to do without,* and to live in such improved manner as their newly-acquired ideas and habits have brought them to consider as indispensable to existence.

What Dr Smith calls the *custom of the country* is constantly improving; and what were deemed *luxuries* before are constantly passing into the state, and acquiring the character of *necessaries*.

"By necessaries," says Dr Smith, "I understand not only the commodities which are indispensably necessary for the

* This of course includes the meaning *not to marry without*.

support of life, but whatever the custom of the country renders it indecent for creditable people, even of the lowest order, to be without. A linen shirt, for example, is, strictly speaking, not a necessary of life. The Greeks and Romans lived, I suppose, very comfortably, though they had no linen. But, in the present times, through the greater part of Europe, a creditable daylabourer would be ashamed to appear in public without a linen shirt, the want of which would be supposed to denote that disgraceful degree of poverty which it is presumed nobody can well fall into without extreme bad conduct. Custom, in the same manner, has rendered leather shoes a necessary of life in England. The poorest creditable person of either sex would be ashamed to appear in public without them. In Scotland, custom has rendered them a necessary of life to the lowest order of men; but not to the same order of women, who may, without any discredit, walk about barefooted. In France they are necessaries neither to men nor to women; the lowest rank of both sexes appearing there publicly without any discredit, sometimes in wooden shoes, and sometimes barefooted. Under necessaries, therefore, I comprehend not only those things which nature, but those things which the established rules of decency have rendered necessary to the lowest rank of people. All other things I call luxuries; without meaning by this appellation to throw the smallest degree of reproach upon the temperate use of them. Beer and ale, for example, in Great Britain, and wine, even in the wine-countries, I call luxuries. A man of any rank may, without any reproach, abstain totally from tasting such liquors. Nature does not render them necessary for the support of life; and custom nowhere renders it indecent to live without them."*

Under very good government continued for a length of time, where justice is well administered, where industry is free, and not extravagantly loaded with heavy taxes or debt,

---

* Wealth of Nations, book v. chap. 2.

and where no impolitic or unjust restrictions are imposed on the objects of commerce including land,—this "custom of the country," or, in other words, the habits and modes of subsistence of the people, must necessarily, constantly, and indefinitely improve from the principles of human nature and the endeavours of individuals to better their condition. This consequence I say, *must necessarily* fall out, because, under such circumstances, "the principle of frugality will not only predominate, but predominate very greatly;" and the bad conduct, profusion, and imprudence of some will be compensated, and far more than compensated, by the prudence, frugality, and good conduct of the great and preponderating majority.

And hence this subject, when properly considered, will be found to furnish a complete refutation of Mr Malthus's *Theory of Human Misery*, which ascribes to "the principle of population" that extreme general poverty among the lower classes of people, which, wherever it exists, is really occasioned by "ignorance and bad government."

A certain degree of poverty indeed, or limited command and possession of wealth, is necessarily entailed upon men who are the heirs of labour; but not extreme poverty, or such deficiency of the necessaries of life as should be positively injurious to the health or happiness of any class of people even the lowest; for such deficiency or poverty never could be general or exist extensively under long-continued good government. And it will readily be allowed, that that poverty and misery which can be obviated or removed by institutions which men themselves are capable to establish, never can, with any show of justice or veracity, be charged to an inherent principle of their nature as its necessary and inevitable consequence. Even if mankind were a race without the necessity or power of propagation, and the waste of human life were supplied in a manner quite different, although the chief sources of their happiness would be dried up, their poverty and misery would not thereby be abated or removed so long as they must labour in order to eat and live. It is in vain, therefore, that Mr Malthus would ascribe the poverty and misery of the lower classes of people to "the principle of population," in any other sense than as that principle is the cause of their existence.

But Mr Malthus maintains the most contradictory propositions and doctrines. In one place and another he in effect tells us that low wages, low habits and modes of life, and extreme poverty, are chiefly occasioned by "ignorance and bad government,"—and again in other places he represents "human institutions" as having little or no influence on the condition of the lower classes of people, but every thing as depending on their own conduct. He demonstrates that without good government the lower classes of people cannot possibly acquire that character of prudence and forethought, or those comparatively elevated notions and habits and modes of life, which he acknowledges to be necessary to enable them to improve their condition, or to "limit the supplies of labour," so as to raise wages; and yet he continues, with a most singular and perverse inconsistency, to charge their poverty and misery upon themselves and upon "the principle of population," and peremptorily maintains this his favourite and indispensable dogma, while he gives up the whole of the argument on which it should rest.

Mr Malthus admits that there is "a standard of wretchedness, a point below which the lower classes of people will not continue to marry and propagate their species."* He admits that this "standard" is raised by "liberty, security of property, the diffusion of knowledge and a taste for the

---

* Essay on Population, book iv. chap. 9.

conveniences and comforts of life,"* and that it is depressed by "despotism and ignorance."† He admits, in short, that the amount of real wages depends upon the habits and modes of life at any time existent among the labourers, and that those habits and modes of life depend again upon good and bad government; and yet he continues to charge their poverty and misery upon the people themselves,—not because they have the power of changing or improving their political institutions, but because they should withhold from the market the supplies of labour!

His words are,—

"If we be really serious in what appears to be the object of such general research, the mode of essentially and permanently bettering the condition of the poor, we must explain to them the true nature of their situation, and show them, that the withholding of the supplies of labour is the only possible way of really raising its price; and that they themselves, being the possessors of this commodity, have alone the power to do this."‡

Now in what sense, I ask, does Mr Malthus mean that "they themselves have the power to do this?"—If in a mere physical sense, nothing can well be conceived more futile, or more inapplicable to the support of his doctrine; but if in a moral sense, the assertion is equally at variance with truth and with his own reiterated arguments; according to which it is only under particular circumstances,—namely, under good government,—that the lower classes can have the power to withhold the supplies of labour.

"The first grand requisite," says Mr Malthus, "to the growth of prudential habits is the perfect security of property; and the next perhaps is that respectability and importance which are given to the lower classes by equal laws, and

* Essay on Population, book iv. chap. 9. † Ibid.

‡ Ibid. book iv. chap. 3.

the possession of some influence in the framing of them. The more excellent therefore is the government, the more does it tend to generate that prudence and elevation of sentiment, by which alone in the present state of our being poverty can be avoided."*

But Mr Malthus does not advise the lower classes of people (or any other persons for them) to endeavour to improve their government as the one thing needful to give them liberty, security, education,—without which he knows it would be in vain for them to expect or attempt any considerable improvement in their condition, or any permanent rise of wages; but he advises them not to marry, and coolly requires them to withhold the supplies of labour, while he knows it at the same time to be a moral impossibility for them to do this, except by the acquisition of such improved habits and modes of life as he is well aware can only be generated or retained under good government.

Mr Malthus knows that "ignorance and despotism seem to have no tendency to destroy the passion which prompts to increase; but they effectually destroy the checks to it from reason and foresight. The improvident barbarian, who thinks only of his present wants, or the miserable peasant, who, from his political situation, feels little security of reaping what he has sown, will seldom be deterred from gratifying his passions by the prospect of inconveniences, which cannot be expected to press on him under three or four years. But though this want of foresight, which is fostered by ignorance and despotism, tends thus rather to encourage the procreation of children, it is absolutely fatal to the industry which is to support them. Industry cannot exist without foresight and security."† He knows that "the foundations of that passion on which our preservation depends, (he means here the passion of self-preservation as contradistinguished from that of benevo-

---

* Essay on Population, book iv. chap. 6.

† Ibid. book iii. chap. 14.

lence,) are fixed so deeply in our nature that no reasonings or addresses to the feelings can essentially disturb it;"* and he cannot be ignorant that the same thing may be affirmed of another passion on which, not indeed the preservation of individuals already born into the world, but the preservation or continuation of the human race itself depends. And how then can he call upon the people to withhold the supplies of labour without restriction or qualification of circumstances, when he sees so plainly and avowedly that the obstacles to that restraint which should enable them to accomplish the object he recommends are necessarily incident to and inseparable from the condition in which they are most generally placed? or how can he maintain that the people themselves are able to do this, while he shows by his own arguments that the obstacles just alluded to can alone be removed, and the restraint he recommends practised under certain peculiar circumstances which they cannot always command?—Above all, how can he expect to produce the effect he proposes by any "explanations" which he would make to the lower classes of "the true nature of their situation," when it appears so evidently from his own statements that their conduct must ever mainly depend, not upon abstract "reasonings or addresses to the feelings," but on the circumstances in which they are actually placed with regard to good and bad government?

Yet he says, "We cannot justly accuse the common people of improvidence and want of industry, till they act as they do now, after it has been brought home to their comprehensions that they are themselves the cause of their own poverty; that the means of redress are in their own hands, and in the hands of no other persons whatever; and that the society in which they live, and the government which presides over it, are without any *direct* power in this respect."†

---

* Essay on Population, Appendix. † Ibid. book iv. chap. 3.

It is remarkable that Mr Malthus has put the word *direct* in the above passage in italics, as being conscious that the indirect power of government was equally undeniable as it is important. But of what consequence is it whether the power of government in improving the condition of the people be direct or indirect, provided only that it be real and effectual?

But let us attend for a moment, and inquire a little more particularly what it is that Mr Malthus expects or desires the lower classes of people to do. He advises them not to marry in order to limit the supplies of labour and raise its price in the market. Now it is plain that the effect to be produced upon wages by any man's abstaining from marriage with a view to raise them, cannot take place till after the lapse of eighteen or twenty years. That such abstinence could produce no immediate effect upon wages is manifest; and unless it were general it could never produce any effect at all. But is it possible to believe that any persons in their senses are ever to be actuated by such motives, or that such abstinence is ever to become general from such distant and uncertain prospect of advantage?—Is it not manifest, on the contrary, from what has been already quoted in the present chapter, even from Mr Malthus himself, that such abstinence can alone become general by the elevation of the popular character, by means of education, security, liberty, and good government?

When, therefore, Mr Malthus calls upon the "common people" to withhold the supplies of labour with a view to raise wages, what is it but to require them to marry, not for their own advantage or happiness, but for the advantage of other people?—not from a consideration of their own particular circumstances, or singly with a view to their own individual happiness, but from a disinterested regard to the general good of mankind? What is it but to tell them that they should marry for the good of their neighbours, or of the class of labourers to which they belong; and that they should abstain from marriage, not in order to increase their own wages immediately, (for that effect could not possibly be produced by such abstinence,) but in order to increase the wages of other people some eighteen or twenty years afterwards?—not in order to raise wages to their own children, (for if they follow Mr Malthus's advice they will have none,) but to raise them, at the distance of eighteen or twenty years, to the children of other people!

It is the consideration of his own particular situation and of his own private advantage or happiness, (or, at the utmost, of his very nearest relations,) which ever must and ought in general to direct every person in their resolutions with regard to marriage; and to expect or imagine that the common run of mankind should be influenced in regard to this matter in the smallest degree by any consideration so very remote from their immediate interest as the regulation of the wages of labour at the distance of eighteen or twenty years, evinces so total a dereliction of common sense,—not to say of fact or experience as applied to human conduct,—as can only be accounted for in the present instance, by ascribing it to that almost wilful blindness and obliquity of intellect which is not unfrequently produced by too fond an attachment to a favourite preconceived theory or opinion.

It may certainly have been that men may have married in particular instances, not solely from private or personal considerations, but from additional motives of public utility. Perhaps Napoleon Buonaparte divorced one wife and married another partly with the view to consolidate an empire and establish a dynasty; and still more recently, perhaps, some of our own princes were induced to marry from motives somewhat similar. Even private persons possessed of large properties may sometimes, perhaps, have been determined in regard to this matter by the wish to continue the line of an ancient family. But to imagine that mankind in general should be governed in their resolutions to marry or not to marry by any other motives than the consideration of their own private advantage or interest, or that the lower classes, in particular, should be influenced in this respect by any abstract speculation as to the general rate of wages, or by so remote an advantage as they could propose to themselves as the hope of raising that rate after the lapse of twenty years, must be allowed to be a notion as extravagant and chimerical and absurd as was ever yet maintained by reasonable men.

Even in the worst of times and most unfortunate of countries, where work is difficult to be got, wages falling, and multitudes of people thrown out of employment, it will invariably happen, that the far greater number will continue to receive employment, and that some individuals from the accidents of their situation, and of the particular trades in which they are engaged, will find themselves well rewarded for their labour, and in circumstances to marry with better prospects and provision than ordinary,* or than had been usual among their neighbours or equals. Now how, I should beg to ask of Mr Malthus, ought these people to act in regard to marriage?—Ought they to proceed upon the consideration of their own particular situations, or have regard to the general rate of wages before they took such a step? Ought they to say to themselves, "It is true we have good wages at present, and the reasonable prospect of their continuance, but wages in general are low and declining, and if we marry, we shall probably increase the number of la-

* The least reflection will convince any one that the case here supposed must have been a very common one in all the late fluctuations and revulsions of prices and of trade in this country; and any one who has had actual experience or acquaintance with the situation of the labouring classes must know it to have been so.

bourers and depress wages still farther some eighteen or twenty years hence; it is our duty therefore to abstain from marriage, notwithstanding the accidental circumstance of our own good fortune, and the prospect we have of being happy with the object of our choice and of our dearest regard on earth:—could such sacrifices be expected or desired; or if made, is it certain that they would be really useful?

But, perhaps, it may be answered, that such sacrifices are neither desired nor expected: let but those who are in bad circumstances abstain, and the desired object will be attained. And does not this then bring us back to the only rational view of the question, that men are to have regard to their own particular situation alone in forming their resolutions on this subject?

It is in vain then that Mr Malthus would pretend to improve the condition of the lower classes of people, by simply calling upon them to withhold the supplies of labour, or by lecturing them on "the true nature of their situation," and dissuading them from marriage. It is in vain that he would "be disposed to lay considerable stress on the frequent explanation of the real state of the lower classes, as affected by the principle of population, and their consequent dependence upon themselves for the chief part of their happiness and misery."* Even if Mr Malthus could succeed in bringing it distinctly to the view of the labouring classes, that the heightening of wages depends immediately upon the limitation of their numbers, (and few are, I believe, so ignorant as not to know this,) still their conduct in regard to marriage could never be regulated by any regard whatever to this consideration, but altogether by the consideration of their individual circumstances, combined with "the custom of

* Essay on Population, book iv. chap. 9.

the country," or the habits and modes of life prevailing among them at the particular time. The object of limiting the supplies of labour, in short, is never to be attained by mere didactic explanations of general principles, but by the influence of laws formed upon them and upon the principles of human nature.

If any thing could give surprise in Mr Malthus's writings, after the contradictions and absurdities already brought under review, the following passage undoubtedly should:

"It is a truth," says Mr Malthus, "which I trust has been sufficiently proved in the course of this work, that, under a government constructed upon the best and purest principles, and executed by men of the highest talents and integrity, the most squalid poverty and wretchedness might universally prevail from an inattention to the prudential check to population."*

If people will fly into the regions of *chimera*, and make impossible suppositions, it may be easy to draw conclusions logically from them, and to confound the ignorant and the unwary.

Mr Malthus here speaks as if the prevention of the increase of population required the positive interference and direct attention both of the people and of government, and generally all his isolated and unsupported *assertions* either insinuate or broadly maintain this doctrine; whilst all his *facts* and *reasonings* go to prove, that such attention and interference can be of little or no use, and that it is from the indirect operation of good government and education that we have alone to hope for any considerable or real effect in beneficially limiting such increase. If the prevention or retardation of the increase of population requires any attention at all on the part of government, it is merely of that negative kind which should hinder them from giving to

* Essay on Population, book iv. chap. 6.

it any direct encouragement: it is merely necessary they should be aware that such encouragement is not only unnecessary, but generally pernicious. But surely the want of knowledge and attention to the extent just mentioned could not be reasonably supposed of " men of the highest talents and integrity;" and if we have been at all successful in exhibiting a just view of the subject, it must have been made evident, that " under a government constructed upon the best and purest principles," and executed by such men, " the preventive check," as Mr Malthus calls it, must necessarily have been brought to operate with the greatest force. The above passage, therefore, supposes what is morally impossible, and consists indeed of a contradiction in terms. It proceeds upon the assumption, that " a government constructed upon the best and purest principles" might operate so mischievously as to produce the worst effects that can exist under any government, and that " men of the highest talents and integrity" might be ignorant and inattentive to their duties. Now what is this, in plain language, but to assume, that a good government may be a bad one, and that good and wise men may be unwise and bad?—what is it but a distinct and positive contradiction?

Similar in extravagance to that just noticed is the following assertion:—" If the supply of labour were greater than the demand, and the demand for food greater than the supply, the people might suffer the utmost extremity of want under the most perfect and best-executed government that the human imagination can conceive."*

This must, at all events, be allowed to be a truism, as must likewise the following, which is its parallel; but what do they avail in any fair argument?

---

* Essay on Population, book iv. chap. 9.

"If, in the best season for vegetation that mankind have ever seen, or imagination can conceive, the corn would not grow, the people must be starved."

If suppositions may be indulged in which are inconsistent with the nature of things and the established laws of the universe, and used in serious argument without being scouted, no doctrine can be too absurd to be maintained, and no cause too bad to be defended.

Mr Malthus, it has been seen, has himself advanced arguments and facts which conclusively prove that one of the most necessary and inseparable effects of good government is to prevent the supply of food from falling short, and that of labour from exceeding the demand; and without producing this effect it could not of course be called good government, and, *a fortiori*, could far less deserve the name of the most perfect.

It is very remarkable, that in all Mr Malthus has said in his voluminous writings to excuse governments from any blame in reference to the misery and "squalid poverty" of the lower classes, he has always been most scrupulously careful to avoid denying their *indirect* power to mitigate or remove such poverty. Besides the instance already noticed in which this cautiousness plainly appears, the following may be adduced in proof of the same remarkable wariness of Mr Malthus upon all occasions in regard to this particular:—

"Mr Paine very justly observes," says Mr Malthus, "that whatever the apparent cause of any riots may be, the real one is always want of happiness; but when he goes on to say, it shows that something is wrong in the system of government, that injures the felicity by which society is to be preserved, he falls into the common error of attributing all want of happiness to government. It is evident that this want of happiness might have existed, and from ignorance might have been the principal cause of the riots, and yet be *almost wholly* unconnected with any of the proceedings of government."*

A little afterwards he says, " the principal cause of want and unhappiness is only *indirectly* connected with government, and totally beyond its power *directly* to remove."† And in another place he repeats the assertion (for, I should calculate, at least the twentieth time,) in the following words and *letters* (*i. e.* italics) :—" The principal and most permanent cause of poverty has little or no *direct* relation to forms of government."‡

From these statements, and others to the same effect which might be multiplied without end, it is apparent that Mr Malthus tacitly acknowledges the indirect effects of good government in improving the condition of the people, though all his efforts are glaringly exerted to turn the attention of his readers away from that view of the subject. In reference to such statements, I shall only repeat what I have already observed with regard to them; namely, that it is of no earthly consequence whether the power of governments in improving the condition of the people be direct or indirect, the only important question being whether the effect itself be certain and infallible; and provided that this be the case, we need give ourselves very little concern about its being indirect.

I shall add here an instance or two of assertions of similar import with those just noticed, though somewhat different in the form in which they are put.

" The cause," observes Mr Malthus, " which has the most lasting effect in improving the situation of the lower classes depends chiefly on the conduct and prudence of the individuals themselves ;"§ and again repeats,—" The means

---

* Essay on Population, book iv. chap. 6. † Idem.

‡ Idem, book iii. chap. 14.

§ Idem, book iii. chap. 13.

of redress are in their own hands, and in the hands of no other persons whatever."*

Now, has not Mr Malthus been obliged to confess, almost in spite of himself, and to the utter destruction of his theory of human misery, that "the conduct and prudence of individuals," in regard to the abstaining from marriage, depends wholly on the nature of the laws and government under which they live?—Has not he borne most ample testimony to this great truth, and stated sometimes, in the very strongest language, the facts which incontestably and undeniably prove it?—as, for example, when he says, "ignorance and despotism effectually destroy the checks arising from reason and foresight;" and that security or good government is "the first grand requisite to the growth of prudential habits?"

How then, I ask, is the means of redress in their own hands, except they be placed under good government?—and when they are so placed, can Mr Malthus, or any one who has listened to his statements, venture to deny but that infallibly "the redress shall follow?"

From all that has been stated, then, I think we may fairly conclude, that the character, condition, and habits of the people are influenced and determined by their political circumstances, and are in fact the result of the laws and institutions under which they live. On the one hand, if these laws be wisely contrived, and founded on the principles of justice and benevolence, habits of order, frugality, and industry will prevail, and the condition of the people will be comfortable and happy, and will go on steadily and indefinitely to improve. If, on the other hand, the laws be of an opposite description, the condition of the people will be poor and miserable; "the standard of wretchedness at which

* Essay on Population, book iv. chap. 3.

they will consent to marry and propagate their species" will be degraded very low; and if by any accident or great good fortune an improvement or elevation of the "standard" takes place (for such an event will sometimes happen under very bad government,) it will speedily fall back again to the same low point.

Good government, then, it evidently appears, is an absolutely indispensable requisite to any great increase or accumulation of wealth, as well as to any considerable or lasting improvement in the condition of mankind. It is equally certain, or rather indeed it is almost the same proposition, that without good government a people can never be enabled to attain any very great degree of prosperity, or to acquire that degree of improvement which should ensure their future progress in the same career, until they arrive at the most highly-advanced stage in which a country approaches to the limits of its resources. Those limits it may perhaps be impossible for a people or country ever fully to reach, but under good government they must always be advancing and making approaches nearer and nearer towards those limits, although at last of course by very slow degrees; but after having made a certain progress, and arrived at a certain stage of improvement, it is but barely possible that they should ever again essentially retrograde.

At first indeed improvement *might* proceed very slowly, and in the end it necessarily *must* do so, but from very different causes or obstacles at those different periods: at last the obstacle is the limited extent of earth; in the beginning it is the ignorance and ineptitude or torpor of the human mind. This last-mentioned obstacle, however, can never permanently resist the influence of good government, and the first-mentioned can have no power to stop improvement altogether, or to prevent the continual and indefinite increase of wealth, wages, and population. As soon, however, as the second-mentioned obstacle is removed, in countries which are yet at a great distance from the limits of their resources, their progress must be comparatively rapid, until they arrive at a very advanced stage of improvement. The quickness or slowness of their advance may indeed be very various in different parts of this their middle progress from a variety of accidents, but it cannot fail to be incomparably quicker during this period than it is possible for it to be either at the beginning or end.

The progress of a country under good government might be somewhat like the following:—Suppose a country or people ever so miserably poor and degraded, and unenlightened and ignorant, placed at once, by whatever miracle, under good government, immediately all open and flagrant disorders or violence (which we may suppose to have been previously frequent and considerable) would be repressed, and justice would be administered with an even hand; some portion of new industry would quickly show itself amongst them, and they would slowly begin to better their condition, and to emerge from the state of thraldom and apathy in which they had previously lain; wealth as well as population would gradually increase; inventions and improvements in all the arts of life would be introduced and multiplied; and at length the sluggish mind would be fully awakened by the general diffusion of knowledge and education. Then would commence their full career; and although particular accidents might occur to retard or accelerate the march of improvement, and cause it to advance at a quicker or slower pace at one period and another, still it could not fail to be rapidly progressive upon the whole, until the country should have become highly cultivated in every part, the wealth very great, and the population dense or numerous, in proportion to the extent of territory.

Arrived at this stage population must necessarily augment at a slower rate, although wealth might continue to increase and accumulate very greatly and rapidly for some time longer; but ultimately both the one and the other would inevitably be brought to advance with contracted steps; and although it may be theoretically true that they could never be brought to a stop altogether, yet it is certain that in the end their progress must come to be so exceedingly small as to be reduced to an imperceptible and evanescent quantity.

But throughout the whole of this progress,—as well when wealth and population had attained their highest and almost stationary state, as during the period of their most rapid increase,—the condition of the lower classes, as well as that of every other class of labourers, would be constantly and uniformly progressive, and would continue to go on improving indefinitely, though of course, as has been already observed, by very slow steps at the end, and those constantly growing slower and slower.

This constant progress in improvement, after the attainment of a certain stage, follows necessarily from the principles of human nature, and would arise from "the uniform, constant, and uninterrupted effort of every man to better his condition," which, as Dr Smith observes,* "is frequently powerful enough to maintain the natural progress of things toward improvement, in spite both of the extravagance of government and the greatest errors of administration." How much more confidently, then, might this effect be looked for under a system from which such great errors would be necessarily excluded?

It is, therefore, maintained, that wherever good government is once established and advanced to a certain point of improvement, education will be speedily introduced and widely extended, and the principle of improvement, the desire of bettering their condition, will be extended in like

* Wealth of Nations, book ii. chap. 3.

proportion, and become effectual for its purpose, down to the very lowest ranks of the people, and that the necessary consequence must be, that the natural wages of labour,* "the custom of the country," and "habits and modes of life," will begin and continue universally and indefinitely to improve and increase throughout the whole extent of the labouring population.†

It will be found quite in vain to merely urge against this induction what *has been* in times past, and with the lofty air of superior wisdom and intelligence, to haughtily point the finger to the volume of *history*, and refuse to enter into farther argument. Before the *invention of printing* this might have passed, and the sketch just delineated could perhaps never have been realized; but that inestimable invention has totally changed the position and prospects of mankind. Before that invention knowledge and education could never be expected to reach, or at least to be widely diffused, among the inferior ranks of people; and although much might have been done for them by the establishment of good government, even independent of education, who, it may be asked, could or would establish good government, or maintain it, even if it were established, without the assistance of the people themselves and of *the press?*—The degraded condition of the great body of the people, therefore, was then utterly hopeless and irremediable; but now the face of affairs is totally changed, and all reasoning *from experience antecedent to that event, or without taking it into the account*, is valueless, nugatory, and inconclusive. The general diffusion of knowledge and education is at all times, and especially in the present condition and circum-

---

* The student should be already acquainted with what is meant by *the natural wages of labour* as explained by Dr Smith. The general reader will see it explained in book iii. chap. 4. of this work.

† See this subject farther treated in book ii. chap. 5 and 8.

stances of the world and of mankind, a necessary consequence of the establishment of good government; and the progress already made, even under very defective systems, seems fully to secure that establishment at no distant date. The early attainment, indeed, of both these important objects may now be considered as certain, and it may be confidently anticipated that their reciprocal effects, acting and reacting on each other, will produce the most important and beneficial change in the composition of human society, and in the future destiny of our race.

Another objection on which much stress has been laid, is thought to arise from the imputed *indolence* of mankind. But ignorance and bad government are the parents of indolence. Show men their true interests, and enable them successfully to pursue them, and indolence will disappear; but education and good government can alone be adequate to secure the attainment of these objects,—the former teaching men to know and appreciate their true interests, as well as how to pursue their objects wisely, and the latter enabling them to do so with success. It would be in vain for the miserable boors and vassals of Poland or Russia to endeavour to better their condition by activity and exertion however great, and no such endeavour can therefore be expected of them. They can acquire no property which is considerable, or which could be of any consequence to improve their condition, because themselves and all they possess are the property of others. Those *slaves* are of course *indolent*, except when they are roused from their torpor by *the cane* or *the knout*; but it is not so in England. Here, it is certain, there is little to complain of on the score of indolence. The severe distresses for want of employment that have occurred throughout the country, at different periods since the conclusion of the late war, have been attributed to a variety of different causes; but I have heard of no persons so utterly regardless of truth and justice as to ascribe them to the indolence or laziness of our people. It was not an aversion to labour, or any want of alacrity to accept of employment, on the part of the starving population of Glasgow and Manchester, and the other chief seats of our manufactures, but the difficulty they experienced in finding work to labour at, that occasioned the unexampled and truly-deplorable distresses of those unfortunate periods; on the contrary, the patience and perseverance of those men, and the constancy and firmness with which they bore up under the most trying circumstances in which men can be placed, (when their utmost exertions, even when they were so fortunate as to find employment, though continued for *fourteen* and even *sixteen hours a day*, procured them so small and inadequate a return,) it is but feeble justice to say, was remarkable and exemplary, and was of itself sufficient to furnish a complete answer to this objection. Let us hope, then, that we shall hear no more of the effects of indolence, unless it be coupled with its natural and proper causes,—ignorance and bad government.

There are in fact but two ways of improving mankind and of bettering their condition, and these are by means of education and good government, and all attempts to succeed by any other methods will always be found abortive and unavailing; but as a liberal system of education can never be thoroughly and securely established where good government is not found, and as the former naturally follows where the latter has place, these two causes are in effect reduced to one, and *good government* may be pronounced to be the one indispensable and only efficient cause of improvement in the condition of mankind in general, and particularly in that of the labouring classes of people.

END OF THE FIRST BOOK.

AN INQUIRY, &c.

BOOK II.

ON THE CAUSES WHICH UNDER THE SYSTEM OF THE DIVISION OF LABOUR NATURALLY REGULATE THE DISTRIBUTION OF WEALTH, AND WHICH UNDER GOOD GOVERNMENT NECESSARILY DETERMINE THE EXACT SHARE THAT EVERY DIFFERENT INDIVIDUAL IS ENTITLED TO CONSUME, OR TO POSSESS AND COMMAND, IN STRICT ACCORDANCE WITH THE NATURAL GROUNDS OF RIGHT TO IT, AS THESE HAVE BEEN EXPLAINED IN THE PRECEDING BOOK.

CHAPTER I.

GENERAL EXPOSITION OF THE CAUSES WHICH NATURALLY REGULATE THE DISTRIBUTION OF WEALTH UNDER THE SYSTEM OF THE DIVISION OF LABOUR, AND OF THE PRINCIPLE ON WHICH THESE CAUSES DEPEND.

SECTION I.

DEMONSTRATION OF THE PRINCIPLE WHICH NATURALLY REGULATES THE DISTRIBUTION OF WEALTH UNDER THE SYSTEM OF THE DIVISION OF LABOUR.

AFTER the period when the system of the division of labour has once been completely established, it is by the voluntary exchange of equivalent values,—of commodities for commodities and labour, and of labour for commodities, "by treaty, by barter, and by purchase," that wealth is naturally distributed among the people, and that every individual acquires the particular share of it which he is entitled to consume, or to possess and command. For after the period just mentioned, as no person finds it necessary to engage in any great variety of employments, or ever for a moment thinks of producing for himself all the different articles or commodities of which he stands in need, he can only look to obtain them by exchanging some part either of his labour, of his capital, or of his land, or their produce, or what is the same thing, the price of their produce, for such articles, or for the land, the labour, or the commodities or capital belonging to other people.

Now in making these exchanges, it is not to be supposed that the transactions are altogether loose or arbitrary. On the contrary, they are regulated and controlled, in the great majority of instances, by causes and principles which are constant, uniform, and insuperable in their influence; and which under good government, where there is a high degree of freedom and security, and where every person is at perfect liberty to choose whatever occupation he pleases, and to change it as often as he pleases, are calculated effectually to secure the rights and just interests of every individual, and necessarily to prevent any one from gaining any undue or considerable advantage over another in these exchanges.

But the causes which regulate these exchanges, and which by regulating them regulate consequently the distribution of wealth, and the principle also on which these causes depend, will best appear by reverting to that early stage of society in which the division of labour is first introduced.

"In a tribe of hunters or shepherds," says Dr Smith, "a particular person makes bows and arrows with more readiness and dexterity than any other. He frequently exchanges them for cattle or for venison with his companions; and he finds at last that he can in this manner get more cattle and venison than if he himself went to the field to catch them. From a regard to his own interest, therefore, the making of bows and arrows grows to be his chief business, and he becomes a sort of armourer. Another excels in making the frames and covers of their little huts or moveable houses. He is accustomed to be of use in this way to his neighbours, who reward him in the same manner with cattle and with venison, till at last he finds it his interest to dedicate himself entirely to this employment, and to become a sort of house-carpenter. In the same manner a third becomes a smith or a brazier; a fourth a tanner or dresser of hides or skins, the principal part of the clothing of savages. And thus the certainty of being able to exchange all that surplus part of the produce of his own labour, which is over and above his own consumption, for such parts of the produce of other men's labour as he may have occasion for, encourages every man to apply himself to a particular occupation, and to cultivate and bring to perfection whatever talent or genius he may possess for that particular species of business."*

It is in this manner and from this motive, namely, *from a regard to his own private interest*, that, as society advances, every individual devotes himself chiefly to one particular occupation, or species of business, and produces or assists in producing only one particular sort of wealth or commodities. That particular sort he amasses in much greater quantity than he can himself consume; and with the surplus he purchases, in the earliest stages of society by means of barter, and afterwards through the intervention of money, those other sorts of commodities which other individuals in like manner, and from like motives, produce and amass in much greater quantity than they can consume;

* Wealth of Nations, book i. chap. 2.

and by this arrangement every individual and every family acquire more of every commodity, and live in greater ease and plenty than they could do if every one attempted or were obliged to produce and fabricate, by his own separate and unassisted industry, the whole of the commodities for which he had occasion. Under this system, as Dr Smith observes, "the most dissimilar geniuses are of use to one another, the different produces of their respective talents being brought, as it were, into a common stock, where every man may purchase whatever part of the produce of other men's talents he has occasion for."*

We have already seen† how very greatly this division of labour increases the quantity of work which the labourer can perform. But the more work the labourer can perform, and the more of every commodity that every individual can produce, in every different employment or species of business, the more he will be able and the more he will be *compelled* to give in exchange for the commodities produced by others in every other employment or species of business. This he will be compelled to do, not by any physical force or violence directly constraining him to part with his property against his will, but by the force of circumstances and of *competition* operating upon his will, and bringing him to part with it voluntarily, in order to procure his due share of any other property he may wish to have in exchange for it.

That this consequence must necessarily fall out wherever there is any tolerable security or good government, and where men are at perfect liberty to choose and to change their businesses as they please, will appear evident from the following considerations:—

If the hut-maker and the maker of bows and arrows (to

* Wealth of Nations, book i. chap. 2.

† In chap. vii. sect. 2. of the first book.

shape our reasonings here with reference to the passage above quoted from Dr Smith) got a very large and disproportionate quantity of venison for their productions or services, insomuch that, by a comparatively small exertion of their bodies, they could live as well as the hunters could do by a much greater exertion of theirs, it would naturally happen that some of the latter would turn to the making of huts and of bows and arrows, as the more eligible occupation, until it should require about an equal quantity of labour to live by the one employment and the other. This, I say, would naturally and indeed *necessarily* happen, because people will always choose as well as they can judge the most advantageous species of business, or that which they expect the best to reward their exertions.

If the hut-maker and the maker of bows and arrows went a great part of their time idle, and yet procured as much cattle and venison in exchange for their productions as the smith, the brazier, and the dresser of hides, who all worked longer, or harder, or more assiduously, the former would be reckoned good trades and the latter bad ones. Most people, therefore, in choosing their employments would incline to follow the former rather than the latter, and greater numbers applying themselves to the one and fewer to the other, a more just distribution of labour and of wealth would take place, and the different rewards, or wages, in those different trades would be brought somewhat near to an equality.

It is this plain principle, then, namely, the single and simple principle of *self-interest*, or the readiness with which every man endeavours to *better his condition*, and to seize every favourable opportunity of advancing his own fortune, —the self-same principle, it may be remarked, which we have already seen to be the primary cause of production,— which, by regulating the distribution of labour and capital, and equalizing the advantages and disadvantages in all the employments of both, regulates the amount of pecuniary rewards in both, so as to compensate such advantages and disadvantages, and to regulate consequently the distribution of wealth, according to a certain and fixed rule, in every period of society under the system of the division of labour, from the earliest to the latest.

As society advances, one set of people apply themselves and their labour to the production of one sort of commodities, and another to another. One set apply themselves to agriculture, another to manufactures, and a third to merchandise or commerce; and these more general departments of industry are each divided and subdivided into a thousand minuter branches, forming altogether an infinite number and variety of particular employments, not to speak of professions unconnected with trade, as physicians, lawyers, clergy, &c.; all persons, in short, not hereditarily or otherwise endowed with a sufficient portion of saved, stored, and accumulated wealth to support them without labour, or whose *land* or *capital* produces not a sufficiency of *rent* or *interest* to satisfy their wants, must do something, and must generally be provided with trades or occupations. Now, if too many persons apply themselves to one occupation, and too few to another, or, what comes to the same thing, if too much capital be applied to one and too little to another,—for it is capital that draws the labourers to work,—it will necessarily follow that the rewards, profit, or wages in the one will diminish and in the other increase, and that hands and capital will be withdrawn from the one and added to the other, until the disorder be corrected or mitigated, and until those rewards, profit, or wages be brought somewhat near to an equality in all the divisions and employments of labour and capital. And, in general, it is to be observed, that the amount or rates of wages and profit, or rewards, in the different employments of labour and capital, can never differ very widely from one another, or for any long period of time, in the same country or neighbourhood,—except in so far as such difference arises out of the difference of advantages and disadvantages belonging to the employments themselves, independent of the pecuniary rewards, profit, or wages to be obtained by engaging in them.* For as soon as any such difference in the amount or rates of wages and profit, or pecuniary rewards, in the different employments of labour and capital, as should cause a difference in the whole of the advantages and disadvantages attending them, should begin to appear, the principle here explained would come into operation, and would lead the individuals immediately concerned in the employments wherein such difference took place to withdraw hands and capital from those in which the advantages had become less, and to add them to those in which they had become greater, and by this means to correct the inequality, in the manner which has been stated, by merely attending to their own interest.

SECTION II.

GENERAL STATEMENT OF THE EFFECTS IN REGARD TO DISTRIBUTION, WHICH THE PRINCIPLE EXPLAINED IN THE FOREGOING SECTION IS NATURALLY CALCULATED TO PRODUCE.

THIS principle, therefore, it will be seen,—the principle, namely, that every one should continue to prefer and follow

---

* The subject here alluded to, namely, the explanation of the circumstances which occasion a difference of pecuniary wages in different employments, owing to the advantages and disadvantages of a different nature attending them, is given at length in chap. viii. sect. 2. of this book.

the most profitable employment, both for himself (*i. e.* for his labour,) and for his capital,—is perfectly calculated to secure the most equitable and beneficial distribution of wealth which it is possible to conceive or to attain under the present constitution of human nature; as it will be apparent, from what is stated in the foregoing section, that under good government, where there is a high degree of security and liberty, the influence of this principle naturally and necessarily produces the following most important and most salutary results:—First, It awards to every individual the just advantages of his property and industry; secondly, It decrees to the community the whole benefit of all new inventions and improvements in the arts and processes of production; and, thirdly, It decrees to the community also a part of the benefit of every new increase and new investment of capital. And it will be observed also, that in producing these results, and in regulating the distribution of wealth in the manner before described, the principle here explained is farther calculated to secure this other most important object, viz. to regulate the consumption of wealth by the amount of production, and consequently to protect the community from the danger of any premature expenditure or exhaustion of the general stock of wealth at any time existing; because it is calculated to prevent that stock from being drawn upon by any person beyond the amount which he contributes to it, either in land, labour, or commodities.

Thus, if one individual labours and produces more wealth than another, or possesses more wealth produced and accumulated either by himself or by others, he is entitled to consume or command more, because he contributes more to the general stock at market, and he is enabled accordingly to consume or command more under the operation of this principle. Such individual throws more into the general stock, and he draws more out of it in exchange for his larger contributions. Or at least he is *able* to throw more into the general stock; and *if he does so* (and only if he does so) he acquires the power, under the operation of this principle, and of the causes depending upon it, explained in the foregoing section, of drawing more out of that stock, or of commanding or consuming more if he pleases. And in proportion to every man's superior industry, or to what he is able to throw into the general stock of wealth at any time existing, he acquires the power of drawing more out of it in a like proportion, under the operation of the principle here explained.

But if an individual invents any new machine, or makes any improvement in any of the arts or processes of production, in agriculture, manufactures, or commerce, the whole benefit of it goes immediately to the community, unless where a patent or monopoly intervenes, and confines a part of the benefit to the inventor, or to those who hold the exclusive grant under sanction of the law, to use and employ those improved processes; yet still another part of the benefit accrues to the community, even during the existence of the patent; because, in order to acquire possession of any considerable share of the market, the persons who hold the monopoly must lower considerably the price of their products, and the whole benefit must still revert to the community when the patent expires.

Also, if an individual saves and accumulates wealth, and invests it in any profitable or productive employment, the community always derive a part of the advantage; because, as wealth increases, it is only by producing goods of equal or better quality, and by selling the latter nearly as low, and the former as low, or rather somewhat lower than similar goods were formerly sold, that the produce of any new investment can, in general, find a market, or that the individual making that investment can succeed in obtaining his proper share of business or sales; and because every new increase and new investment of capital increases the competition of the capitalists, and forces them to be content with a lower rate of profit or interest. And although the benefit thence resulting may be but small and insensible in each particular instance of new investment, it is always something, and always accumulating.

But, as these considerations are important, I shall here endeavour to render them somewhat more perspicuous, by a more detailed statement of them under the three distinct heads above mentioned.

I. In the first place, then, it is obvious that the principle explained in the foregoing part of this chapter decrees to every individual the just advantages of his property and industry; in other words, it decrees to the *labourer* a quantity of wealth proportioned to the amount of his contributions of labour or commodities to the general stock at market; and to the *land-proprietor*, or other capitalist, it decrees the command of a quantity proportioned to his actual possessions, or to that which he is able to throw into the same general stock.

1. This principle decrees to the labourer the whole just advantages of his industry; in other words, it decrees to him the command of a quantity of wealth proportioned to the amount of his contributions of labour or commodities to the general stock at market.

Thus, if one individual labours more, or produces more wealth than another, he is entitled to consume or command more, because he contributes more to the general stock at market, and, under the operation of the principle here explained, he is enabled accordingly to consume or command more. By labouring or producing more, he is enabled to exchange that labour or produce for more of every other sort of produce, or for more money, with which he can again, by a second exchange, acquire more either of labour or commodities than any other labourer who labours less (in the same species of business) can acquire; and thus, in proportion to every man's superior industry, in any particular species of business or labour, or to what he actually contributes to the general stock of wealth at market, he acquires the power of drawing more out of it, in a like proportion, under the operation of this principle. Nor does the intervention of money make any difference in this result, at least if that money is properly regulated and kept in order.

2. This principle decrees to the *land-proprietor* or other *capitalist* the whole just advantages of his property; in other words, it decrees to him the command of a quantity of wealth proportioned to his actual possessions, or to that which he is able to throw into the general stock at market.

Thus, if one man possesses more land or more capital of any other sort than another, he contributes or is able to contribute more to the general stock at market; and if he does so (and only if he does so) he can draw more out of that stock. As he is able to throw more into it, he has it in his power by doing so at any time to draw more out of it in exchange. This, indeed, is nearly self-evident, and does not appear to require any lengthened illustration. If a man's property be large, he can, by throwing the whole, or a large part of it into the market,—that is, by offering it in exchange for other sorts of property,—draw a large quantity out of the same market or general stock of wealth offered for sale; and thus again, in proportion to every man's superior property, or to what he is able to throw into the general stock at market, he acquires the power of drawing more out of it.

And thus it is that the principle explained in this chapter decrees to every individual the just advantages of his property and industry, and that the consumption of wealth is regulated and kept within the bounds of production or contribution; for it will be manifest, that if no person is allowed to draw more out of the general stock than he contributes or puts into it, or than his labour or property enables him to replace, the community never can be injured by individuals, nor one individual by another, although any one may injure himself by drawing out his whole share and consuming it improvidently.

II. This principle decrees to the community the whole benefit of all new inventions and improvements in the arts or processes of production.

To prove this, after what has been advanced in the former part of this chapter, a very few words will be sufficient.

An invention or improvement in any of the arts or processes of production must either reduce the cost or improve the quality of the articles produced, else it is no improvement at all. If it improves the quality of the articles at the same cost, it in effect reduces the cost; and in any view that can be taken of the subject, the benefit must evidently fall to the community, seeing that all persons must ever afterwards acquire better goods at the same price.

But if the invention or improvement, whatever it may be, reduces the cost of producing the articles, the whole benefit of it is equally certain to fall to the community, and to be shared and enjoyed by every individual; because if the cost of production be reduced, the price of the articles must be reduced also to the same extent, or in the same proportion. This follows directly from the reasonings advanced in the former part of this chapter; for it must be evident, from what is there stated, that if the price of the articles did not fall in proportion to the fall in the cost of producing them, then the business of producing them would be more profitable than other businesses, and hands and capital would be attracted towards it in the manner before described, until the profit in the business and the price of the articles were reduced and brought down to the common level.

Suppose, for example, such an improvement were made in the manufacture of any given article or articles,—let us instance broad cloth and linen,—as should reduce the cost of producing them *one-half*, their price must necessarily fall *one-half*, and the whole benefit must accrue to the community, and must be shared and enjoyed by every individual, because every one would be able, for ever afterwards, to procure what he wanted of these articles at half the real price they formerly cost him; that is, in other words, by the sacrifice or expenditure of one-half of the labour, sweat, or toil, or of the capital, or both, which they formerly would have required; and suppose that the same or similar improvements were extended to all commodities whatever, or that the cost of producing them were reduced universally to one-*half*, one-*third*, or one-*fourth* of what it had formerly been, it would follow, of course, that the price of them would fall in the same proportion, and a double, triple, or quadruple quantity of every commodity would be procured at the same sacrifice of labour or of previously-accumulated wealth, which one-half, one-third, or one-fourth of the quantity had previously required to obtain it.

In this case the efficiency of the powers of production being increased in a twofold, threefold, and fourfold degree, every producer would, if he exerted himself equally as before, have a double, triple, or quadruple quantity of commodities to dispose of beyond what he had before; and as the whole would have to be exchanged in the same proportions as before for one another and for labour, every one would necessarily acquire a double, triple, or quadruple quantity of produce as his share of wealth.

That the whole quantity of commodities produced must be exchanged in the same proportions as before, other things remaining the same, is evident, and follows directly from what is advanced in the foregoing part of this chapter; nor would the greatest conceivable or possible improvement in the arts of production occasion any embarrassment or difficulty in the distribution of the commodities produced under any tolerable system of security and liberty; for under such a system the principle of distribution here explained necessarily ensures the proper application of all commodities to their destined use, since, however great the quantity produced might be, it never could be any body's interest to throw any of them away, and they must all therefore go to their proper use, through the medium of exchange, either for one another or for labour. Even if improvements were made which should produce effects a hundred or a thousand times greater than is above supposed, they would only confer so much the greater benefits on the human race. It would not follow that a single article would be produced to be thrown away, because it would be no man's interest to do so; nor would it follow that any sort of commodities or manufacture would be produced in any greater quantity than should be necessary to supply the effectual demand; for the principle explained in this chapter prevents that circumstance also from taking place, and causes all commodities to be produced and brought to market in a just proportion to one another. Even if the improvements in the arts and processes of production, therefore, were to be so great as to enable all men to provide for all their wants by half a day's, or half an hour's, or half a minute's labour in the day, they would only enable each to employ so much the more of his time and of his life in study, or in any other sort of duty or enjoyment that he liked best.

III. This principle decrees to the community a part of the benefit of every new increase and new investment of capital.

When an individual saves and accumulates wealth, and invests it in any profitable or productive occupation, it is only, as before mentioned, by producing goods of equal or better quality, and by selling the latter always at least as low, or rather generally somewhat lower than the same species of goods had previously been sold, that he can in general succeed in obtaining his proper share of business or sales, or that the produce of his new investment can find a market. People will not in general renounce their old connexions, or change their custom from one dealer to another, without some advantage or prospect of advantage inducing them to do so; and when new competitors appear, bringing additions to a market already well stocked with goods, it is always something to the advantage of the public, who are enabled in consequence to purchase what they want on more favourable terms from both the old and new dealers. The advantage gained may and certainly must be but small, and even insensible in every single instance of new increase and new investment; but it must always be something, and must necessarily produce a pressure towards a reduction of price, if it does not produce an actual or observable reduction.

There are a great many trades and employments, it is to be remembered, in the advanced state of society, which it requires a certain amount of capital to enable the traders to engage in, and as wealth increases, greater numbers come to have it in their power to enter into such trades, and many are willing to do so, and accept a lower rate of profit or interest; and sometimes also a lower rate of what is properly to be considered as wages, or remuneration for their labour; which is all in favour of the community in general, or of the great body of it, consisting of the lower classes of labourers.

But in treating this subject of the distribution of wealth as it takes place under the system of the division of labour, and under the operation of the principle described, and of the causes depending upon that principle explained in this chapter, it is always to be understood and remembered, that it is only under good government, where there is perfect liberty in the choice of employments, and in the disposal of land, capital, and labour, that all the beneficial effects we have endeavoured to delineate are to be looked for, or that a strictly equitable distribution can be attained; and every infringement of the liberty just mentioned, or any obstruction thrown in the way of the free disposal or employment of land, capital, and labour, or of the free choice of employments in general, is to be regarded as an obstruction thrown in the way of the just distribution of wealth, and consequently as a violation more or less of justice and of the rights, not only of the persons directly restrained, but of all others on whom such restraints or factitious monopolies operate injuriously; and indeed of the community in general, whose prosperity and improvement are always obstructed and prevented from expanding to its full extent by all such restraints; and when such restraints or monopolies are carried to a great excess, the real effect is, that a certain portion of the community, or limited number of individuals, are constituted the legal plunderers and oppressors of the others.

CHAPTER II.

OF THE INSTRUMENT OF DISTRIBUTION,—MONEY.

After the period when any sort of regular and settled government has been once established in a country, when the land has been wholly appropriated, when capital has accumulated to some considerable extent, and when the system of the division of labour has been fully introduced, money becomes the great instrument of distribution.

After this period it is no longer practicable for every individual, or for the individuals generally of any class or order of men in society, to supply the whole of their wants, either from their immediate possessions of land or capital, or from the immediate produce of their labour; and not only the non-labourers, whose possessions, however large, consist but of one, or at most but a few different objects, or species of vendible property,—as well as the unproductive labourers, under whose hands no sort of produce or vendible property at all arises,—must exchange, the former their land or capital, and the latter their labour, for some convenient and generally useful or acceptable commodity, as money, in order to obtain, by a second exchange, any other article they require; but even the productive labourers themselves, as they produce, or more commonly but assist in producing only one, or at most but a few different articles or species of commodities, are equally subject to the same necessity, and must all exchange their labour or its produce, in the first instance for money, before they can obtain by a second exchange any of those other commodities which every man constantly requires besides the one or the few articles which he himself produces.

The baker and the brewer, the weaver and the shoemaker, must apply to other people for every thing they want, except bread and beer, and cloth and shoes, and to one another when they want any of these necessaries, except the single article which they respectively produce. But if they possessed nothing else to offer in exchange but those articles themselves, it would be always very difficult and often impossible for them to treat or bargain with one another, or to procure either these or any others of the various articles which all men constantly require. "The butcher," to use the words of Dr Smith, "has more meat in his shop than he can himself consume, and the brewer and the baker would each of them be willing to purchase a part of it; but they have nothing to offer in exchange, except the different productions of their respective trades, and the butcher is already provided with all the bread and beer which he has immediate occasion for. No exchange can in this case be made between them. He cannot be their merchant, nor they his customers; and they are all of them thus mutually less serviceable to one another. In order to avoid the inconveniency of such situations, every prudent man in every period of society, after the first establishment of the division of labour, must naturally have endeavoured to manage his affairs in such a manner as to have at all times by him, besides the peculiar produce of his own industry, a certain quantity of some one commodity or other, such as he imagined few people would be likely to refuse in exchange for the produce of their industry."*

Now this commodity whatever it may be, or whatever other character may belong to it, is money. Every man thenceforward lives by exchanging the surplus part of his property, or of the produce of his industry, for such parts of the property or of the labour of other men, or of the produce of their labour, as he requires; and thus it is that money becomes the great instrument of the distribution of wealth.

The shoemaker uses perhaps one pair of shoes, while he makes fifty. The remaining forty-nine pairs he is therefore at liberty to appropriate to the supply of his other wants; and he endeavours to dispose of them for money, which he knows that every body will be willing to accept for the produce of their labour, and for any commodity he may desire to purchase. It would be in vain for him, he is well aware, to take his shoes to the tanner and the leather-merchant,

* Wealth of Nations, book i. chap. 4.

and propose with them to purchase the stock he might at any time want of the last-mentioned article. Those individuals use no more shoes than himself, and are moreover perhaps already provided with all they require; whilst the shoemaker, it may be, wishes to purchase the article of leather, to the amount perhaps of half the produce of his labour. The leather-merchant, however, will not take his twenty-five pairs of shoes; but let him dispose of his products for money, and bring that commodity to the merchants, and they will gladly supply him with their commodities in exchange. They are not always ready to take his article of shoes, but must have money for their commodities, and when they want shoes, they will come to him, and bring money also in their turn wherewith to purchase them.

But although money be the instrument by which these exchanges are effected, it is still with the surplus produce of his labour that the industrious man really purchases every commodity, because it is with that surplus he purchases the money with which he purchases every thing else. When he gives that surplus for money, he throws it into the general stock at market, and the amount of it, by limiting the quantity of money he receives, limits the quantity of other goods he can draw out of that general stock; consequently it limits his consumption and expenditure or enjoyment of wealth, that is, his destruction of it, to the amount of that which he contributes to the consumption and enjoyment of other people. Money therefore, in short, every person requires, and uses merely as the means of enabling him to exchange his labour or his possessions, or their produce, for the necessaries, conveniences, and luxuries of life in proportion to his scale of property, or to his contributions of labour or commodities to the general stock, daily and regularly, as he requires them.

Every person therefore, in the advanced state of society, requires to keep in reserve a quantity of money greater or smaller in proportion to the amount of his revenue, or to the extent of his transactions or exchanges,—the labourer in proportion to his wages, the non-labourer in proportion to his rent or interest, and the merchant, manufacturer, &c., in proportion to the extent of their dealings, or their sales and purchases, &c. Of these it is evident that the manufacturer will in general pass more money through his hands, in proportion to his annual income or revenue, than the land-proprietor or capitalist; the merchant still more than the manufacturer; and the banker most of all. Every one, however, must endeavour to keep a certain quantity in proportion to his ordinary outgoings or exchanges; but every one will at the same time endeavour to keep as little as possible, viz. no more than may be sufficient to serve his necessary purposes; because if he keeps more, it will lie useless beside him; whereas by employing it in trade, or lending it at interest, he is enabled to make a profit by it.

If the shoemaker, for instance, finds his cash accumulating very much upon his hands, he will observe that by taking a part of it to purchase more leather and any other materials he requires, and employing the remainder to pay the wages of an additional workman, he will get more for the finished work than the materials and wages together amount to; and with what is over, therefore, he can either increase his consumption of other commodities without diminishing his capital, or increase, if he pleases, his capital, and extend his business still farther; or, if he cannot, or does not choose to extend his business, he can lend it at interest, and what he again receives as interest he can still reinvest (though at an ultimately decreasing rate of interest) *ad infinitum*.

The sums therefore which must be kept in hand by every individual will thus be brought within a certain compass, and reduced to as moderate an amount as may be consistent with the conveniency and various necessities of each; and the sum total or aggregate of all these smaller sums will make up the entire *circulating medium*, or whole money of a nation, employed in executing its whole business or exchanges, and in dealing out or distributing the whole of its wealth to every individual in his just proportion, that is, in proportion to what he contributes to the general stock.

This total sum of money which circulates, and which is employed merely as an instrument of distribution and exchange, will be great or small in proportion to the greatness or smallness of the other descriptions of wealth to be exchanged and distributed by it; to which, however, it will bear a higher ratio in poor than in rich countries; because the rapidity of circulation is greater in the latter than in the former, and the same sum of money will therefore do more work in the same time; that is, it will serve to exchange and distribute a greater quantity of other wealth in rich than in poor countries.

Thus far we have spoken of money merely as an instrument of distribution and exchange; but whatever serves this purpose must also be used as the common measure of value, and must therefore be possessed of the quality of value in itself, that is, it must be a vendible commodity; and as it must serve this additional and necessarily connected purpose, not only in all bargains or agreements immediately to be executed, but in those also of a prospective nature, which stipulate and contract for the delivery or receipt of determinate quantities or values of property at periods more or less distant, it is required that the commodity which is to serve this purpose should be comparatively uniform and steady in its own value, which it can only be by requiring at all times nearly an equal quantity of labour to produce it.

Many different commodities, it is probable, as Dr Smith

has observed, were successively both thought of and employed as money in the rude ages of society, and at the first establishment of the division of labour. He mentions *cattle* as having been used in the earliest times; and takes notice of the different articles of *salt*, a particular sort of *shells*, *dried fish*, *tobacco*, and *sugar*, as having been used as money in different situations and countries. But all these or any such articles must have been found very inconvenient and inadequate instruments of distribution, and were all very early superseded in all countries by the metals copper, silver, and gold, which have been found peculiarly adapted to serve both the purposes for which money is required, by the possession of the following qualities:—first, *portableness*,—they contain a comparatively great value in small bulk, which makes it easy to carry them to market:—secondly, *divisibility*,—they can be divided into very minute parts without any perceptible diminution or alteration in the value of the mass, which can be easily reunited by fusion and at a small cost, and thus they can be easily proportioned without loss to the smallest quantity of any other commodity that any one may wish to acquire:—thirdly, *durability*,—they may be kept for almost any length of time without waste or decay:—fourthly and lastly, *uniformity* or *steadiness of value*,—they are the least liable of any known commodities to any considerable or sudden variations in their value, insomuch that, for all practical and ordinary purposes, and within moderate periods of time,—perhaps we may say periods of twenty or thirty years,—they may be looked upon as invariable.

This superior steadiness of value which is found to characterize the precious metals above all other commodities, and which, combined with the other qualities above-mentioned, has caused them to be so universally used as money, and as the common measure of value, arises from the superior steadiness in the cost of their production above what is found in that of other commodities;* or, in other words, from the quantity of labour and commodities, or capital, which must be expended in acquiring those metals at first, being always nearly the same at one time and another, which sort of expenditure constitutes the real price of all commodities, and is the foundation of all value in exchange, and as labour is the chief ingredient in the cost of production, and the only one which continues necessarily and uniformly the same in itself, it is, as I shall endeavour to prove in the following chapter, the only certain measure of that value.

CHAPTER III.

THAT LABOUR IS THE ONLY CERTAIN MEASURE OF VALUE.

As the existence of all value in exchange is wholly dependent on the necessity of some portion of human labour being

---

* It has been asked, "Why should gold, or corn, or labour, be the standard measure of value more than coals or iron?" (Ricardo, Principles of Pol. Econ. chap. 20, p. 343, second edition.) The answer is simply, because the former articles are in general either more steady in their value, or of more convenient application as the standard, than the latter. Some commodity must of necessity be chosen to serve the double purpose of a measure of value and instrument of exchange; and the question being, which is the best adapted to it, there can be no hesitation about the answer as to whether coals or iron, or gold, should have the preference. As to labour, it is indeed the only certain measure, as we shall presently endeavour to demonstrate, fixed and invariable in the nature of things; but then labour is *not* a commodity, and cannot therefore be laid hold of, or applied as the common measure; and as to corn, it is too bulky and inconvenient as well as exceedingly variable within short periods.

employed in the production of those commodities in which value in exchange forms an attribute,* so labour is the only certain measure of that value.

It is true, that after the period when capital comes to be employed to any considerable extent in production, the exchangeable value of commodities is no longer determined by the quantities of labour bestowed in producing them, because they are then no longer produced by labour alone, but partly by labour and partly by capital; and because it happens thenceforward that the quantities or proportions of labour and capital expended in production are not only different in different species of commodities, but are continually varying in the same species.† Still, however, human la-

* Although capital, as I have endeavoured to demonstrate, is a means or instrument of production as well as labour, it is not equally the fundamental cause of exchangeable value; for if capital could produce every thing without labour, there would be no such thing as exchangeable value at all; that is to say, if capital could be made to work itself, without the assistance of human hands or labourers, and to reproduce and extend itself so as to supersede the necessity of labour altogether in the production of every thing that man can wish or want, there would be no such thing as wealth in the sense in which we treat of it, or vendible property, or exchangeable value; because then every thing would be brought to the condition of air and water, and the other *free bounties of nature*; unless perchance, under such condition, the multiplication of mankind in a limited world should make it necessary in the end to *appropriate* the capital and the things produced by it, or even to *destroy* a part of them in order to prevent the earth from being over-peopled; which to do (namely, to appropriate or destroy) would again require care, and attention, and application,—in a word, *labour*; and would thus, by a new fatality, bring mankind back to their first condition, and reconvert every thing that was so before once more into vendible property.

† This happens from a variety of causes, depending, however, chiefly on the increase or diminution of capital; among others, from new inventions and improvements in the arts and processes of production, whether arising from the increase of machinery, the better arrange-

bour, that is to say, *the natural price or wages of common labour*, continues to be the best and only certain standard which can be referred to in any question of doubt or difficulty as to whether the common measure of value, whatever it may be, has varied or not. This alone (namely, the natural wages of common labour,*) of all definable objects or quantities of wealth, is necessarily confined within certain and narrow limits in regard to variations in its value. Almost all other things might vary for any length of time and to any conceivable extent; this alone cannot; and this

---

ment or combination of works or of materials in those processes, or from improvements in the skill or effective power of the labourer himself.

* The ordinary and average wages of common ploughmen, or farm-servants, *hired by the year*, are those perhaps, of all others, in which there are the smallest variations or difference in different ages, or in periods of time considerably distant; and such, of course, must form the best standard measure of value, or the best test to try that standard, and to prove whether it or any other commodity has varied in its value or not

In the higher sorts of labour the wages admit of very great difference and of very great variations, as do likewise the modes of life among the higher labourers. Clergy, lawyers, physicians, master manufacturers, merchants, farmers, and all the other higher classes of labourers, are all of them (the individuals I mean, in each of those classes) paid very differently and live very differently.

But it is not so with the lower classes of labourers; the smallness of *their* wages leaves less room for variations; and in those of all common labourers, as hedgers, ditchers, &c., there can be but comparatively little change in the most distant periods. The ordinary and average wages of these, therefore, would do equally well with those of the common farm-servants for marking the difference of prices in different periods, or for correcting the accidental variations of the common measure of value, were it not that, being hired only for short periods, and not always constantly employed, it is not so easy to know what their wages really are, or how much they earn daily upon an average throughout the year.

it is therefore which is properly considered as the only certain standard fixed and established in the nature of things.

Gold and silver, for example, might vary, not temporarily and partially merely, but once and for ever, to *a hundred times* or *a hundredth part* their present value, from calculable or conceivable variations in the richness or barrenness of the mines; so might all other commodities, except corn, and the very few other articles which can be used, or actually are used, as the chief food of the common labourers, and which, although not altogether so strictly limited in regard to variations as the aggregate of wages, are yet likewise necessarily confined within certain moderate and not indefinite boundaries. It happens necessarily that the article actually used as the chief food of the common labourers cannot vary indefinitely, because a certain extent of variation, one way or other, necessarily effects its own cure. A certain increase in the value of corn, for example, where it forms the chief food of the common labourers, would deprive those persons of food and consequently of life; and a certain diminution of its value would speedily bring into existence additional numbers; and by laying, as it were, the axe to the root of the demand when the commodity was high, and again raising up demanders when it was low, those accidents just mentioned, which must necessarily occur under the circumstances, would keep the value of the article from diverging very far either the one way or the other.

But it is the sum of the articles daily consumed or earned by the common labourer, or, in other words, the exchangeable value of the aggregate of those articles, which constitutes the least variable measure, and which, as being the only permanently steady ingredient in the price of all commodities, is alone to be depended upon in cases of doubt or difficulty, as to whether the common measure of value, or any given commodity, has varied in its value.

And this is all that is, or ever was, or ever could be

meant by those who have stated labour to be the measure of value; at least it is evidently all that is meant by Dr Smith in stating that doctrine; and, after all the comments which have been made upon the subject, and the almost universal rejection of labour as the standard by later political economists, there still appears to me a singular force and propriety as well as truth in all that he has said in support of his position.

"The real price of every thing," says Dr Smith, "what every thing really costs to the man who wants to acquire it, is the toil and trouble of acquiring it. What every thing is really worth to the man who has acquired it, and who wants to dispose of it or exchange it for something else, is the toil and trouble which it can save to himself, and which it can impose upon other people. What is bought with money or with goods is purchased by labour as much as what we acquire by the toil of our own body. That money, or those goods, indeed, save us this toil. They contain the value of a certain quantity of labour which we exchange for what is supposed at the time to contain the value of an equal quantity. Labour was the first price, the original purchase-money that was paid for all things. It was not by gold or by silver, but by labour that all the wealth of the world was originally purchased; and its value, to those who possess it, and who want to exchange it for some new productions, is precisely equal to the quantity of labour which it can enable them to purchase or command."*

"Equal quantities of labour," says he again, "at all times and places, may be said to be of equal value to the labourer. In his ordinary state of health, strength, and spirits, in the ordinary degree of his skill and dexterity, he must always lay down the same portion of his ease, his liberty, and his happiness. The price which he pays must always be the same, whatever may be the quantity of goods which he receives in

* Wealth of Nations, book i. chap. 5.

return for it. Of these, indeed, it may sometimes purchase a greater and sometimes a smaller quantity; but it is their value which varies, not that of the labour which purchases them. At all times and places, that is dear which it is difficult to come at, or which it costs much labour to acquire; and that cheap which is to be had easily, or with very little labour. Labour alone, therefore, never varying in its own value, is alone the ultimate and real standard by which the value of all commodities can at all times and places be estimated and compared."*

It would be unsuitable in this place, and altogether endless, to enter into a detailed controversy with the numerous host of writers who have denied this doctrine; but it may still be proper briefly to notice some of the chief objections they have urged against it.

On the following passage in the Wealth of Nations,—"But though equal quantities of labour are always of equal value to the labourer, yet to the person who employs him they appear sometimes to be of greater and sometimes of smaller value. He purchases them sometimes with a greater and sometimes with a smaller quantity of goods, and to him the price of labour seems to vary like that of all other things. It appears to him dear in the one case and cheap in the other. In reality, however, it is the goods which are cheap in the one case and dear in the other."†—Mr Buchanan‡ remarks,—"Dr Smith himself states, that labour is sometimes purchased with a greater and sometimes with a smaller quantity of goods; but he immediately adds, that it is the goods which vary in their value, and not the labour. But why may not the labour vary in its value as well as the goods?"§

---

* Wealth of Nations, book i. chap. 5. † Ibid.

‡ The editor of the Wealth of Nations, with notes and an additional volume.

§ Buchanan's edition of Smith's Wealth of Nations, book i. chap. 5. As to the general assertion of Mr Buchanan in reference to the above passage, and to the doctrine maintained in it, that "this is quite

To this I reply, that labour itself cannot vary, because it consists of a fixed and invariable quantity of bodily toil, pain, or suffering, which the labourer must undergo, and which times, nor places, nor the power of men cannot alter. *Wages* may indeed vary, and we can understand the proposition when it is said that wages rise or fall; but when it is said that *labour* rises or falls, is there any meaning in the expression?—Is it really intelligible?—What is it that rises when labour rises?—Wages.—But this is not labour itself; it is the reward or recompense of labour. Labour, as I have already observed in a former part of this work,* is simply a movement or exertion of the human body and faculties; and to talk of its rising or falling in value, unless its reward or wages be alone meant, is plainly to use words without the shadow of a meaning.

Again, when Dr Smith observes,—"Labour, therefore, it appears evidently, is the only universal as well as the only accurate measure of value, or the only standard by which we

---

metaphysical," and "a metaphysical notion," I do not know whether it be necessary to make any observations; for what is it in the science of political economy that is *not* metaphysical or connected with metaphysics? or what is political science in general but a branch of the greater sciences of metaphysics and morality?—The subdivision of political economy indeed treats of wealth, and is thus also connected with matter or physics; but all its profoundest and most important conclusions depend upon metaphysical considerations, or the principles of human nature. In short, this department of political science bears the same relation to the more comprehensive science of metaphysics that the mixed does to the pure mathematics; and the use and application of the principles of the latter science in its subordinate branch is not more necessary and inevitable than the use and application of metaphysical principles in political economy; and with regard, therefore, to any doctrine or position contained in it being metaphysical, or "a metaphysical notion," it does not seem to be any objection or disparagement, provided only that it be a just doctrine or position.

* *Vide* book i. chap. 2.

can compare the values of different commodities at all times and at all places. We cannot estimate, it is allowed, the real value of different commodities from century to century by the quantities of silver which were given for them. We cannot estimate it from year to year by the quantities of corn. By the quantities of labour we can, with the greatest accuracy, estimate it both from century to century and from year to year."* His commentator asks, "How can this be, when Dr Smith himself states, that the same quantity of labour is paid very differently?"†

And why should a thing the same in itself *not* be paid differently or "very differently?" or is it any impeachment of the invariability of the value of labour to say that it is paid differently?—On the contrary, is it not plain to the common sense of all mankind, that if a thing really be invariable in its value, it must always be paid differently wherever the value of other things varies?

When indeed an alteration takes place in the *natural price or wages of labour*, or in the quantity and quality of the necessaries, conveniences, and luxuries which can be *permanently* commanded by the lower classes of labourers, the standard of value may be justly said to vary, because in this case an essential change is made in the condition and character or *quality* of those labourers themselves. When, in consequence of good or bad government, the character, condition, and habits of the people are elevated or depressed, the character and absolute value of themselves, of their labour, and of the wealth it produces, suffer a change. When, for example, in consequence of good government, the general condition and habits of the people and the natural reward of labour are improved and increased, every thing is made really more valuable, because every thing is then em-

* Wealth of Nations, book i. chap. 5.

† Buchanan's edition of Smith's Wealth of Nations, book i. chap. 5.

ployed in maintaining a more valuable set of people; or, in other words, all the labourers must then live better, and command more wealth than before. The labourers are then, in fact, more valuable creatures. The absolute value of themselves and of their labour is improved, and their power of purchasing universally increased.

When again, on the other hand, in consequence of bad government, the general condition and habits of the people are deteriorated, and the natural reward of labour diminished, every thing becomes really and absolutely less valuable, because every thing is then employed in maintaining a less valuable population; in other words, all the labourers live worse and command less wealth than before. The labourers are then, in fact, less valuable creatures;* the absolute value of themselves and of their labour is depreciated, and their power of purchasing universally diminished.

All this, however, does not demonstrate but that the natural wages† of those labourers should still continue to be the only certain or safe standard measure of value, and indeed the only one (excepting, as before observed, the chief articles of food,) that possibly can be appealed to in cases of difficulty, because it must still continue to have a fixed and very limited boundary of variation on either hand which it cannot pass; whereas, with regard to every other definable object, or commodity, or quantity of wealth, having exchangeable value, (always excepting the chief articles of food, which are still, however, by many degrees less certain than this,) there is no certain or assignable limits to the extent of their variations.

---

* Humanly speaking.

† Before coming to the consideration of the question here discussed, the reader should be thoroughly acquainted with what is meant by *the natural wages of labour* as explained by Dr Smith.

Mr Ricardo, however, in disputing this doctrine with Dr Smith, contends, that neither corn nor labour is less liable to variation, or more to be depended upon as standards of value, than gold or silver. After stating the causes of variation to which gold and silver are liable, viz. "from the discovery of new and more abundant mines," "from improvements in the skill and machinery by which the mines may be worked," and "from the decreasing produce of the mines after they have yielded a supply to the world for a succession of ages," Mr Ricardo exclaims,—"But from which of these sources of fluctuation is corn exempted?"* Now, suppose the answer should be, *from none of them:* What then? Dr Smith does not say that corn is not liable to variations in its value. On the contrary, he shows that it is subject, within certain narrow limits, to variations even in its *average value;* and he takes particular notice of its temporary fluctuations "from year to year," and explains very distinctly, that *on this account* it is not so good a measure from year to year, or *for short periods of time,* as gold or silver. But he very justly says and demonstrates, that *for distant periods of time,* or, to use his own words, "from century to century," corn is a better measure of value than gold or silver, or than any thing else whatever except labour; which manifestly it is, for this plain reason,—That whereas, by the possible existence or discovery of greatly more fertile mines than any at present known, gold and silver might be reduced to a hundredth part of its present value; or, what is perhaps more probable, from the failure and exhaustion of all the known mines of those metals, and from the prodigious increase in the demand for them which may naturally be expected in the course of a few ages, in consequence of the increase of population and wealth

* Principles of Political Economy and Taxation, chap. i. sect. 1.

throughout the world, their value might be increased a hundred or a thousandfold; no sort of variation approaching nearly in extent to this could possibly take place (or, if it could take place, could continue for any length of time,) in the value of corn; because its cheapness would necessarily raise up consumers or demanders to sustain the price, and its dearness would diminish the number of demanders, or keep them from increasing, and prevent the price from rising or continuing permanently or extravagantly high.

But Mr Ricardo goes still farther, and maintains, not only that neither corn nor labour are any better measures of value than gold or silver, but that neither gold, nor silver, nor corn, nor labour itself, nor any other commodity, or number of commodities, can be considered as a standard measure of value more than another. "Why," says he, "should gold, or corn, or labour, be the standard measure of value more than coals or iron? more than cloth, soap, candles, and the other necessaries of the labourer? Why, in short, should any commodity, or all commodities together, be the standard, when such a standard is subject to fluctuations in value? Corn as well as gold may, from difficulty or facility of production, vary ten, twenty, or thirty per cent. relatively to other things; why should we always say, that it is those other things which have varied and not the corn? That commodity is alone invariable which at all times requires the same sacrifice of toil and labour to produce it."*

Now, do not the average wages of common labour require at all times the same sacrifice of toil and labour to produce them? and are they not, therefore, even upon Mr Ricardo's own principles, necessarily and uniformly of the same value? The ploughman, and other common labourers, earn their daily, weekly, or yearly wages, at all times, by as nearly as can be supposed or calculated an equal sacrifice of toil and

* Principles of Political Economy and Taxation, chap. xx.

labour; they work, as nearly as can be imagined, an equal number of hours in the day, week, and year, at all times (and it must be allowed they work about equally hard upon an average,) and the commodity or commodities they earn as wages, whatever it or they may be, exactly measure and represent their share in the work of production,—all that is over and above wages being produced either by capital or land.* The natural wages of the common labourer, therefore, or the necessaries commonly used or consumed by him, being uniformly produced by the same quantity of labour, are uniformly of the same value, and must therefore be considered, even according to Mr Ricardo's own showing, as the natural and only certain standard measure of value, fixed and established by the constitution of things.

It is true, it would be inconvenient, and indeed altogether impracticable, to constitute all "the necessaries of the labourer," or all the commodities which his labour enables him to purchase or command, the common measure of value, because it would be impossible to apply the whole of these, in the form of a measure, to all the ordinary transactions of business or exchange; yet it is certain, that whatever single or few commodities, conveniently capable of such application, represent most nearly and constantly a day's or a certain given number of days' wages of common labour, will always be the best practical measure; and furthermore, it may safely be affirmed, that no commodity which does not

* If this were not the case, then would the labourer be constantly cheated, for nobody but himself has a right to what he produces. Nor does the capitalist or landlord ever live upon what he produces, but upon what their own lands or capitals produce; of which produce, rent and profit, or interest, are the proper and only certain measures; and nothing is wanting but security and liberty to render all these measures, and the shares they award to the different classes, perfectly just, and that accruing to the labourer a liberal one.

do this, or of which a given quantity is not constantly and uniformly nearly measured by a day's or some given number of days' wages of common labour, could be proposed or established as the common measure, or, if it could be established, could be endured for any length of time, owing to the mischief it would occasion; for if any commodity were established as the common measure which varied much or frequently from the standard of the natural wages of common labour, it would occasion the utter confusion of all value in exchange, the greatest apparent fluctuation in commodities, the real value of which had not at all changed, and the greatest injustice in all the transactions or transfers of property effected by its means upon contracts or stipulations lasting beyond a few days.

Although, however, the only perfect and certain standard of real value in exchange, the natural wages of common labour, cannot be applied as the common measure of value, or as the measure constantly in use, it is not on this account to be thought that it is altogether useless. It can still be applied either to prove the uniformity or correct the variations of the common measure; and if regular and correct registers were kept, as they ought to be, of the ordinary and average wages of all the common and lower descriptions of labour, this standard might often be beneficially applied to the purpose now mentioned.

But we must attend a little farther to the objections of Mr Ricardo:—

"In the same country," says this writer, "double the quantity of labour may be required to produce a given quantity of food and necessaries at one time that may be necessary at another, and a distant time; yet the labourer's reward may possibly be very little diminished. If the labourer's wages at the former period were a certain quantity of food and necessaries, he probably could not have subsisted if that quantity had been reduced. Food and necessaries in this case will have risen 100 per cent. if estimated by the *quantity* of labour necessary to their production, while they will scarcely have increased in value, if measured by the quantity of labour for which they will *exchange*."*

But is it not plain, that the quantity of necessaries given upon an average for labour is exactly that which it produces? Labour produces *wages*, and all wealth or necessaries which exist above what are received in exchange for labour, are produced, as I said before, by *land* or *capital*, else, as I said before, the labourer is eternally cheated. The error lies in supposing that all wealth is produced by labour, —nothing by land and nothing by capital.

Mr Ricardo says again,—"Adam Smith, who so accurately defined the original source of exchangeable value, and who was bound in consistency to maintain, that all things became more or less valuable in proportion as more or less labour was bestowed on their production, has himself erected another standard measure of value, and speaks of things being more or less valuable in proportion as they will exchange for more or less of this standard measure. Sometimes he speaks of corn, at other times of labour, as a standard measure; not the quantity of labour bestowed on the production of any object, but the quantity which it can command in the market; as if these were two equivalent expressions, and as if, because a man's labour had become doubly efficient, and he could therefore produce twice the quantity of a commodity, he would necessarily receive twice the former quantity in exchange for it."†

I shall, in the first place, suppose that "a man's labour" becoming "doubly efficient" has been occasioned by the increase of capital or improvement of machinery, and then I will say, that in this case it is not the man's labour, but

* Principles of Political Economy, chap. i. The *italics* in this passage, of course, are Mr Ricardo's own.

† Ibid.

the capital he is supplied with, which is the *efficient* cause of the double quantity being produced; or, in other words, that it is capital, not the man's labour, which produces *the half* of this double quantity. The man's labour produces, as before, a given quantity, the equivalent of which he receives as wages, and the other equal quantity is produced by capital, and, upon Mr Ricardo's theory of real wages continuing the same, would go wholly to the capitalist.

But to be a little more particular:—If a man's labour becomes doubly efficient, it must proceed from one of three causes, either, 1st, From improvements in his own ingenuity, dexterity, or skill in applying his labour; or, 2dly, From the increase or improvement of capital, machinery, &c.; or, 3dly, From the increased fertility of the land he cultivates. If the increased efficiency of labour proceeds from the last-mentioned cause, it is the land that produces the additional quantity; if it proceeds from the second-mentioned, it is capital which produces it; and it is only when proceeding from the first-mentioned cause that the additional quantity is really and properly to be considered as produced by labour. In this last case the additional produce will always go to the labourer, but never wholly or necessarily in the others. A skilful, ingenious, and dexterous workman, even a common labourer, will naturally receive higher wages than an awkward and unskilful one. But it is in the higher departments of labour wherein ingenuity and skill, from having larger room to develop themselves, (in the construction, arrangement, and conducting of works and manufactories,) produce their most important effects, and draw to the labourers a proportionably large share of the produce of those works as their wages, much (or more frequently the whole) of which is vulgarly supposed to arise from capital, and is called profit of stock, but which is truly the produce and reward of labour.

Mr Ricardo himself, as before cited, observes, that gold

and silver may fluctuate "from improvements in the skill and machinery with which the mines are worked." Now, is it not evident, that, in so far as that effect is produced by machinery, it is not produced by labour, and that it is only in so far as it is produced by bodily toil, ingenuity, dexterity, skill, &c. that it is produced by labour? Superior profit will reward the proprietor of the machinery,—that profit is his produce; and superior wages will reward the skill of the labourer,—those wages again are his produce.

It will be in vain to pretend or assert that the machinery is solely the produce of labour, and that still, therefore, the whole produce is the produce of labour; for it is plainly contrary to the fact to say so. What machinery, I would beg to ask, at present in existence in Great Britain is solely the produce of labour? What machine is there in the production of which capital has not assisted? I defy any man to show a single machine which has not been the joint produce of land, capital, and labour, and I defy him equally to determine in what proportion these different instruments of production have contributed to the final result, except from the share which the different classes of contributors shall acquire in the shape of rent, interest, and wages.

Again, when Mr Ricardo says, "If a piece of cloth be now of the value of two pieces of linen, and if in ten years hence the ordinary value of a piece of cloth should be four pieces of linen, we may safely conclude, that either more labour is required to make the cloth, or less to make the linen, or that both causes have operated,"*—it must be observed, that the conclusion would be altogether fallacious and imperfect, unless we add to it, that *capital* produces more of the linen than formerly, while labour produces less. We should conclude, indeed, that there was now about a

* Principles of Political Economy, chap. i.

half less labour employed in producing a piece of linen than formerly; but this conclusion would still be defective if we did not add to it, that this must probably arise from a half more than formerly being produced by capital; that is to say, about a half more work than formerly must be considered as being now done by capital in the manufacture of linen.

Lord Lauderdale appears to me to be the first who entertained nearly accurate ideas on this point; and if he be wrong in all his other corrections of Dr Smith, as I decidedly think he is, still it must be acknowledged that he is right in this one.

"The author of the Wealth of Nations," says Lord Lauderdale, "appears to consider the profit of stock as paid out of, and therefore derived from, the value added by the workman to the raw material. He states, that—'As soon as stock has accumulated in the hands of particular persons, some of them will naturally employ it in setting to work industrious people, whom they will supply with materials and subsistence, in order to make a profit by the sale of their work, or by what their labour adds to the value of the materials. In exchanging the complete manufacture, either for money, for labour, or for other goods, over and above what may be sufficient to pay the price of the materials and the wages of the workmen, something must be given for the profits of the undertaker of the work who hazards his stock in this adventure. The value which the workmen add to the materials, therefore, resolves itself, in this case, into two parts, of which the one pays their wages, the other the profits of their employer upon the whole stock of materials and wages which he advanced.'* And again, 'The labour of a manufacturer adds generally to the value of the materials which he works upon, that of his own maintenance and of his master's profit.'†

"If this, however," continues Lord Lauderdale, "was a

* Wealth of Nations, vol. i. p. 57, 4to edition. † Ibid. p. 400.

just and accurate idea of the profit of capital, it would follow, that the profit of stock must be a derivative, and not an original source of revenue; and capital could not therefore be considered as a source of wealth, its profit being only a transfer from the pocket of the labourer into that of the proprietor of stock."*

It must be acknowledged, however, that the incorrectness thus noticed by Lord Lauderdale in the Wealth of Nations is more in the expression than any thing else, as Dr Smith is not led into any farther error in consequence of these passages and a few others of similar import; for he founds none of his future reasonings, or of his doctrines in regard to taxation, on the supposition of labour producing all and capital nothing. It is singular, however, that Mr Ricardo, who has so faithfully followed Lord Lauderdale in almost all the erroneous doctrines wherein he differs from Dr Smith,† should not have seconded him when he happened to be right, nor was not led by his Lordship's numerous and just hints,‡ in reference to the independent productiveness of capital, to suspect the soundness of his theory that labour produces all.

To return, and conclude the chapter:

---

* Inquiry into the Nature and Origin of Public Wealth, chap. iii. pp. 149—152, second edition.

† Particularly in the three following:—1st, Denying the distinction between productive and unproductive labour; 2d, Denying that labour is the measure of value; and, 3d, In the distinction he attempts to lay down between wealth and riches.

‡ Among others the following:—" It is apprehended that in every instance where capital is so employed as to produce a profit, it uniformly arises either *from its supplanting a portion of labour which would otherwise be performed by the hand of man, or from its performing a portion of labour which is beyond the reach of the personal exertions of man to accomplish.*"—LAUDERDALE's *Inquiry, &c.* p. 155, second edition.

Under the system of the division of labour, and as soon as that system, together with increasing wealth, has been carried to any considerable extent, it becomes absolutely necessary, as we have already seen, to adopt and establish some one, or some very few vendible commodities, as the common measure or measures of value, which may serve the purpose of regulating contracts, or of expressing the values agreed to be transferred, both at distant periods and in immediate exchanges, as well as to regulate the value of every species of written obligation (as bills, tokens, &c.,) which circulate as money. Gold and silver have been universally adopted for this purpose, and as long as these metals retain nearly their present cost and value, there are no other known articles that could with advantage be substituted for them, or that could supply their place, and serve all the purposes of money nearly so well. Still, however, these articles are but arbitrarily chosen to serve these purposes, and are still subject to the possibility of great variations in their value, and consequently may still require to be corrected, or even to be discarded altogether from performing this office if they should happen to vary in a great degree. And what other articles could then with certainty be appealed to if this possible case were actually to happen?—The natural wages of common labour, or determinate quantities of corn, are the only defined or definable articles which could then be appealed to with certainty to perform the office of correctors, or to determine the value of previous contracts; and to bring this controversy to a short conclusion, we have only to consider what would be the comparative degree of security or certainty to the proprietor of a rent or annuity for a hundred years to come, if it were reserved or stipulated to be paid in gold or silver, in corn, or in days' wages of common labour. Let such rent or annuity be of any given amount:—Suppose it were *one pound of gold*, *fifteen pounds of silver*, *twenty quarters of wheat*, or *five hun-*

dred days' wages of common labour, and that these different commodities or quantities of wealth were equivalent in value and exchangeable for one another at the present time, and a very little consideration will be sufficient to convince us that whilst the gold and silver might vary to almost any conceivable extent, the corn and wages could vary but very little. The gold and silver might, at the end of the hundred years, be exchangeable for very different quantities of labour and commodities from those it exchanges for at present; whereas the corn, as we have already seen, could vary comparatively little in its command of either; and the five hundred days' wages of common labour, in whatever commodities they might then be realized, whilst they would be identical in their command of labour, would vary still less than the corn, if they varied at all in their command over commodities in general.

Suppose that, from additional facility or difficulty of production, gold and silver should, at the end of the hundred years, have fallen or risen in value one-half, and should then of course be equivalent, in the one case, to but 10 quarters of wheat and 250 days' wages, and in the other to 40 quarters and 1000 days' wages, is it not plain that our annuitant would in the one case be stripped of one-half of his income, namely, of 10 quarters of wheat, or 250 days' wages, and that in the other his debtor and bondsman would be robbed to double that extent, as he would be required to part with 40 quarters or 1000 days' wages?—Let us suppose farther, the still possible case, that the gold and silver should have risen or fallen in a quadruple rate, and it will appear that the annuitant might starve in the one case, and his debtor be perhaps ruined or robbed at least to a still greater extent in the other,—events which could not possibly happen if the annuity were payable in corn or in days' wages of common labour.

APPENDIX TO CHAPTER III.

ON THE NATURE OF VALUE.

SECTION I.

INTRODUCTION.

THERE is no question in political economy which has excited greater attention of late, or which has given rise to more conflicting opinions among the present cultivators of that science, than that which relates to the nature of value. In the Ricardo school this question has produced an absolute schism, although most of their writers on both sides agree with their master in pronouncing it "a difficult question." They have all indeed, as it appears to me, very much exaggerated the importance of this question; and yet it may safely be affirmed, that their success in endeavouring to make the subject clearer than it was left by Dr Smith, or to go to the bottom of it, has not by any means corresponded with the magnitude of their labours.

That the subject is not free from intricacy or difficulty when pushed to its utmost metaphysical limits (as is the case indeed with innumerable questions besides this) may be allowed; but it appears to me that all the great practical truths properly and strictly connected with the science of political economy and taxation may be perfectly well settled without going this extreme length, or indeed without any very deep or abstruse treatment of it. As, however, the whole theory and peculiar doctrines of the writers just alluded to seem to be built chiefly, if not wholly, on their peculiar views of this question, we are forced as it were to follow them into the ulterior discussion of it; although it will be found, I think, more curious than useful, and ought to be looked upon rather as a useless appendage than as any proper or necessary part pertaining to the science; for, although political economy be, as we have before observed, a subordinate branch of the more comprehensive science of metaphysics, it is yet separated by an easy and distinct boundary from its genealogical stem, and has properly nothing to do with *the depths* of metaphysics; a proof of which will perhaps appear in the further and supererogatory discussion on which we are about to enter of the present question; in which it will be seen that the moment we advance a single step beyond the point to which Dr Smith has conducted it, we are removed altogether from the precincts of this science, and that those writers who attempt to connect this question with political economy beyond the point just mentioned, either involve themselves in a labyrinth whence they can never escape, or envelope themselves in a cloud of impenetrable darkness.

SECTION II.

OF THE PUZZLE FOUNDED ON THE NATURE OF EXCHANGEABLE VALUE, AND ON THE NOTION OF ITS BEING A MERE RELATION OF COMMODITIES BETWEEN THEMSELVES.

Lord Lauderdale, in whose Inquiry into the Nature and Origin of Public Wealth is to be found the germ of this discussion, and indeed of almost all the peculiar doctrines of the Ricardo school, has, in the beginning of that work, treated very fully of the *market-price* of commodities, or their exchangeable value at a particular time and place, and of the variations to which the market-price is liable; and has explained very distinctly the causes of those variations on the principles of *supply* and *demand*; but he takes no notice of the ulterior dependence of supply and demand, and consequently of market-price, upon cost of production. Now it is this last circumstance evidently which is the main point to be attended to, as being that alone which confers any character of science or of utility on the subject, and without keeping it in view, any reasoning about market-price must necessarily be a totally useless and unmeaning discussion about merely *accidental relations* of quantity or number; it being this circumstance alone, namely, the *ultimate* dependence of market-price on cost of production, which brings the variations of price or exchangeable value into connexion with human conduct or actions, without which the science of political economy could not exist, nor even be conceived.

But, by keeping this circumstance out of view, it has been attempted to reduce the idea of value to a mere *relation of commodities between themselves*, without any connexion with mankind, with labour, or with cost of production; and, in conformity with this idea of it, it has been asserted, that value or exchangeable value cannot even be expressed but by *a comparison of two commodities*; whereas it is manifest that it can be expressed by *a comparison of commodities with labour* as well; and if the term must be designated a *relation*, it must be acknowledged that it is a *double one* at least, and that the connexion of the exchangeable value of commodities with labour and cost of production is indeed the only circumstance which confers any importance on the connexion of the exchangeable value of commodities between themselves.

"Experience shows us," says Lord Lauderdale, "that every thing is uniformly considered as valuable, which, to the possession of qualities that make it the object of the desire of man, adds the circumstance of existing in scarcity. To confer value, therefore, two things appear requisite: 1. That the commodity, as being useful or delightful to man, should be an object of his desire; 2. That it should exist in a degree of scarcity.

"With respect to the variations in value, of which every thing valuable is susceptible, if we could for a moment suppose that any substance possessed intrinsic and fixed value, so as to render an assumed quantity of it constantly, under all circumstances, of equal value, then the degree of value of all things, ascertained by such a fixed standard, would vary according to the proportion betwixt the quantity of them and the demand for them, and every commodity would, of course, be subject to a variation in its value from four different circumstances:—

"1. It would be subject to an increase of its value, from a diminution of its quantity.

"2. To a diminution of its value, from an augmentation of its quantity.

"3. It might suffer an augmentation in its value, from the circumstance of an increased demand.

"4. Its value might be diminished, by a failure of demand.

"As it will, however, clearly appear, that no commodity can possess fixed and intrinsic value, so as to qualify it for a measure of the value of other commodities, mankind are reduced to select, as a practical measure of value, that which appears the least liable to any of these four sources of variation, which are the sole causes of alteration of value.

"When in common language, therefore, we express the *value* of any commodity, it may vary at one period from what it is at another, in consequence of eight different contingencies:—

"1. From the four circumstances above stated, in relation to the commodity of which we mean to express the value; and,

"2. From the same four circumstances, in relation to the commodity we have adopted as a measure of value.

"As the value, therefore, of all commodities depends upon the possession of a quality that makes them the object of man's desire, and the circumstance of their existing in a certain degree of scarcity, it follows that the variation of all value must depend upon the alteration of the proportion betwixt the demand for and the quantity of the commodity, occasioned by the occurrence of one of the four circumstances above stated; and that a variation in the expression of value may be occasioned by the occurrence of any of the eight circumstances we have alluded to."*

And his Lordship concludes his first chapter, in which the above passage occurs, in the following terms:—

"Great, therefore," says he, "as the authorities are who have regarded labour as a measure of value, and who by so doing have contradicted that view of the nature of value which has been here given, it does not appear that labour forms any exception to the general rule, that nothing possesses real, fixed, or intrinsic value, or that there is any solid reason for doubting the two general principles we have endeavoured to establish:—

"1. That things are alone valuable in consequence of their uniting qualities which make them the objects of man's desire, with the circumstance of existing in a certain degree of scarcity.

"2. That the degree of value which every commodity possesses depends upon the proportion betwixt the quantity of it and the demand for it."†

Having thus tacitly endeavoured to disconnect altogether the exchangeable value of commodities from cost of production,—for he takes not the slightest notice of such a connexion either here or in any other part of his book,—the noble author proceeds to advance a number of ingenious puzzles and paradoxes founded upon the nature of exchangeable value considered in this light, that is, considered abstractedly from any connexion with mankind, with labour, or with cost of production.

---

* Inquiry, chap. i. † Ibid.

"It is impossible," says his Lordship, "to subscribe to the idea, that the sum total of individual riches forms an accurate statement of public wealth.* Though the opinion has been universally prevalent, it must be deemed false and unfounded by every man who considers the subject, after having formed and familiarized himself to an accurate and distinct opinion of the nature of value.

"It must then appear, that a commodity being useful or delightful to man cannot alone give it value; that to obtain value, or to be qualified to constitute a portion of private riches, it must combine with that quality the circumstance of existing in a certain degree of scarcity. Yet the common sense of mankind would revolt at a proposal for augmenting wealth by creating a scarcity of any commodity generally useful and necessary to man. For example, let us suppose a country possessing abundance of the necessaries and conveniences of life, and universally accommodated with the purest streams of water, what opinion would be entertained of the understanding of a man who, as the means of increasing the wealth of such a country, should propose to create a scarcity of water, the abundance of which was deservedly con-

---

* Lord Lauderdale endeavours to draw a distinction between what he calls "public wealth" and "individual riches." "Wealth," says he, "may be accurately defined to consist of all that man desires, as useful or delightful to him." (Chap. ii. p. 57.) But what has political economy to do with the value of all that man desires, as useful or delightful to him?—What has it to do with the value of the air, the light and heat of the sun, or with that of dancing, music, oratory, or, in short, of any thing but labour itself, and those material objects, in the production of which some portion of labour must be employed?—"Individual riches," says his Lordship, "may be defined *to consist of all that man desires as useful and delightful to him, which exists in a degree of scarcity.*" (Chap. ii. p. 58.) A rather imperfect definition of wealth, the proper object of political economy, but framed in perfect consistency with the theory, (if theory it can be called,) which would separate the idea of exchangeable value from any connexion with labour or cost of production.

sidered as one of the greatest blessings incident to the community? It is certain, however, that such a projector would, by this means, succeed in increasing the mass of individual riches; for to the water, which would still retain the quality of being useful and desirable, he would add the circumstance of existing in scarcity, which of course must confer upon it value; and, when it once obtained value, the same circumstances that fix the value of its produce for a certain number of years, as the price of the possession of land which produces food, would equally fix the value of the produce of springs for a certain number of years, as the price of the possession of that which produced drink; and thus the individual riches of the country would be increased, in a sum equal to the value of the fee-simple of all the wells."*

Now, who does not see that in this case "the fee-simple of all the wells" would form a subduction from the mass of individual riches, or from the mass of commodities possessed of exchangeable value?—For not only is it obvious that whatever might be the new value acquired by those who held the property of the wells, a like amount must be drawn and subducted from the "individual riches" of the other members of the community who should now be obliged to purchase the water; but the proprietors of the wells being converted into non-labourers to the amount of the "fee-simple," their labour would be withdrawn also from what it must otherwise have been employed upon, namely, the production of a quantity of commodities equivalent to the "fee-simple" whereby they might live, or wherewith they might command or purchase that share of wealth which they would now receive without labour for the water. But perhaps it may be said that the people who had no wells would probably labour a little more than formerly, and thereby acquire all the commodities they had previously enjoyed be-

* Inquiry, chap. ii.

sides the additional quantity required to give in exchange for the water. To this I reply, that there is a certain measure beyond which the people *cannot labour*, and only increase your scarcities;—let every other commodity as well as water be made scarce and more difficult to be procured, (that is, made to require more labour to procure it,) and see what conclusion you arrive at,—see if "the mass of individual riches," or of commodities having exchangeable value, will continue undiminished.

Let us then suppose, that not only water, but all raw produce, were made so scarce and so difficult to be procured, that the whole constant labour of every individual were required to furnish him with a scanty supply of the coarsest food and clothing, and then say if the same mass of individual riches would remain. By the supposition the acquisition of the finer sorts of grain, of flesh, or of any other articles save the coarsest necessaries, is a thing impossible, merely from the increased quantity of labour which the acquisition of such articles would require. The scarcity is made so great, and the earth rendered so barren, that the whole labour of all mankind can only procure for them the inferior and coarser sorts of clothing and food. The acquisition of capital would in this case of course be impossible; but the scarcity of every thing, and the labour necessary to acquire it, would be prodigiously increased. Will it be said that the exchangeable value of those coarser and scantier commodities would still remain the same, as being produced by an equal quantity of labour?—Vain subterfuge!—the value of human labour under these altered circumstances is totally changed; nay the value of human life, of man himself (confining our estimate of him to this his mortal state) is essentially changed and deteriorated; and thus it is that these speculations,—this vaunted theory concerning value, which has been described as the key to the science of political economy,—leads us straight forward into fairy land, and requires of us the contemplation of changes, which were they really to take place, would not only subvert that science, and derange this fine theory, but would dissolve the present natural fabric of civilized society, and annihilate far more than the half of the human race.

Of the same stamp is Lord Lauderdale's next specimen of this *puzzle* exemplified in the varieties of the value of corn. Diminish the supply (of corn), says his Lordship, and you increase "individual riches." You increase, it is true, the exchangeable value of given quantities of corn; but you diminish in a like proportion the value of every thing that is given for it, or disposed of in order to purchase that indispensable article. Diminish the supply sufficiently, and you make the corn in a country equal in value to all the other things in it put together; because every man will rather give all he has for a mess of porridge than allow himself to starve. Diminish the supply of corn still farther, and you annihilate value altogether, and the race of mankind, if you please, into the bargain, "at one fell swoop."

It is not universally or unlimitedly true, therefore, that as you create scarcity you increase value; or when you diminish the supplies of commodities, that either the mass itself or the value of that mass remains unchanged.

SECTION III.

OF ABSOLUTE VALUE.

VALUE is a term which seems to be used by mankind, chiefly, if not exclusively, in relation to themselves and their species; and every thing they esteem *valuable* which is or which may be conceived to be necessary or useful to their existence or happiness, or which is capable of conducing in any manner of way to those ends.

Perhaps, indeed, things may be considered as valuable also in relation to the lower animal creation; and although, in regard to those particular animals which are made subservient to the use of mankind, this relation may be resolved into the former;—as, for example, when men say that *oats* and *hay* are valuable as food for horses, it may be supposed they have some ulterior reference to the value of horses to themselves;—yet it may be still very plausibly contended, that, even if the race of mankind were extinct, still this world and its adjuncts might be considered as valuable in reference to the existence and happiness of those other animals which continued to exist and to inhabit it; and in this light, it may be presumed, such condition of the world would be viewed by a superior being, or even by a very benevolent man. The grass of the fields, the light, and heat, and air, &c., even the mass of the globe itself, with all its other adjuncts and productions, might be considered as valuable in relation to the whole of the animals still contained within its sphere and precincts; and if any of the inferior species of those animals were made subservient to the purposes of the higher, the former might be considered as valuable also in relation to the latter.

Be this question, however, settled as it may, I think it must be admitted, that, in reference to mankind, the world as at present constituted, and all things appertaining to it, must be accounted valuable in proportion to the numbers and the happiness (or the balance of happiness over misery) of the individuals of this species; and that our globe, for example, at this moment, containing, as it does perhaps, about *seven hundred millions* of human inhabitants, is not so valuable as it would be if it contained *seven thousand millions*, which perhaps it might be made to contain, and more valuable than if it contained only *one million*, which at a time past it probably did contain,—always supposing that the happiness were proportioned to the numbers of people;

and whether this were the case or not, would of course depend in a degree on the quantity of wealth being proportioned to the numbers, and upon its being distributed according to justice, or to the natural grounds of right to it, as explained in this inquiry.

If the idea of value then here stated be correct, it would appear that it is a quality belonging to animals themselves in the first place, as being capable of enjoying happiness; and, secondly, to inanimate objects as ministering to that happiness, or as being necessary or subservient to the existence and comfort of animals; and to this idea or *kind* of value every other kind treated of in political science must have reference, else we deviate into endless, unmeaning, and unprofitable discussion.

Nor does this reduce the idea of value, as the Ricardists would do, to a mere relation of number and quantity, or proportions, although such an idea or kind of value is perfectly conceivable and intelligible, and is indeed in constant use in the exact sciences. Thus, 4 is said to be a number double the value of 2, and 4 cubic feet, or 4 pounds weight double the value of 2 cubic feet, or 2 pounds weight; and in this sense it is evidently a mere relation of terms to one another; but in the sense above explained something more is meant, and the ideas of absolute existence and of happiness are included, in addition to that of mere proportion, number or quantity.

Absolute value then may perhaps appear to consist in happiness itself,* or pleasurable sensation; and every thing which has relation, as contributing in any kind of way to

---

* It may perhaps be thought that the idea of absolute value might be traced still higher, to the Deity himself, the fountain of all good and happiness. What has been stated, however, is sufficient for our present purpose, and it is not necessary to inquire further in this place,—I am not composing a system of metaphysics.

happiness, must be allowed to be valuable in one sense or another.

Thus, then, there is, in the first place, the capacity of happiness, which is valuable, and is an attribute of all animals probably in a greater or less degree, and more particularly of man; and, secondly, there is the capacity of ministering or contributing to happiness, which is an attribute of every thing which is useful or necessary, or which contributes in any manner of way to animal existence or well-being, including perhaps the whole circle of nature or of existencies.

But of those objects, which are necessary or conducive to man's existence and happiness, there are some which he enjoys in unlimited abundance without any trouble or exertion on his part to procure them; whilst there are others which he must exert his industry and toil his body to acquire. Both these are valuable in the relations already explained; but the latter are further valuable in another sense, namely, in relation to the labour or privations necessary to produce or acquire them. They thus acquire a double relation to mankind, as well as a relation of number and quantity between themselves; the intensity of which is regulated and measured in general, that is to say, upon the average of trials or comparisons where things are left at liberty to find their proper level by cost of production; cost of production consisting of either labour simply, or expenditure of capital simply, (which latter is a privation of one sort of goods in order to acquire another,) or both.

CHAPTER IV.

OF THE CAUSES WHICH REGULATE THE PRICE OF COMMODITIES; WHAT CONSTITUTES COST OF PRODUCTION, AND WHAT THE CONSTITUENT PARTS OF PRICE REALLY ARE.

SECTION I.

OF NATURAL AND MARKET PRICE.—PRICE DEFINED.

THE price of an article is whatever is given or received for it in exchange by treaty and agreement in the open market; that is, wherever commodities are bought and sold, and where no constraint or violence is imposed on the free will and judgment of the buyers or sellers. This is the actual or *market-price*, which is governed *immediately* by the *supply* and *demand*, or relative proportion of the different sorts of commodities on sale at any particular time ready to be exchanged for one another, the supply of one article constituting the demand for another; for as buying and selling consists simply in the exchange of different sorts of wealth or vendible commodities for one another, through the instrumentality and intervention of money, and as those alone which are in the market can be actually exchanged, they must necessarily limit and determine the price of one another at the particular juncture.

But the supply and demand, or relative proportion of the different commodities on sale, and consequently the market-price, are *ultimately* regulated and controlled by the *natural price* or *cost of production*, from which the market-price cannot in general deviate in a great degree, or for any long period of time.

There are indeed a few vendible commodities, as ancient

coins, statues, and paintings, and a few other things, which cannot be increased by human industry, the price of which is totally disconnected with cost of production, and is essentially and exclusively a market-price, depending upon supply and demand alone, and being determined always by the wealth and particular taste of the persons who are desirous to purchase them. These peculiar articles, however, form but a very slender and inconsiderable portion of wealth when compared with the whole, or with the great mass of commodities whose market-prices are, under all ordinary circumstances, ultimately regulated by their natural prices or costs of production, including in those costs, rent, profit or interest, and wages; of one or more of which three parts or charges, the price of every commodity, as Dr Smith has demonstrated, is necessarily made up.

There is in every community or neighbourhood an ordinary or average rate of wages in every different employment of labour, depending partly upon the particular nature of each employment, and partly upon the general condition and habits of the people engaged in each :—

There is also an ordinary and average rate of profit of stock, or interest, in every community depending upon the abundance or scarcity of capital :—

And there is an ordinary or average rate of rent which must be paid for land, depending partly upon the populousness of the neighbourhood or place where it is situated, and partly upon the fertility or barrenness of the land itself.

"These ordinary and average rates," says Dr Smith, "may be called the natural rates of wages, profit, and rent, at the time and place in which they commonly prevail.

"When the price of any commodity is neither more nor less than what is sufficient to pay the rent of the land, the wages of the labour, and the profits of the stock employed in raising, preparing, and bringing it to market, according to their natural rates, the commodity is then sold for what may be called its natural price.

"The commodity is then sold precisely for what it is worth, or for what it really costs the person who brings it to market; for though in common language what is called the prime cost of any commodity does not comprehend the profit of the person who is to sell it again, yet if he sells it at a price which does not allow him the ordinary rate of profit in his neighbourhood, he is evidently a loser by the trade; since, by employing his stock in some other way, he might have made that profit. His profit, besides, is his revenue, the proper fund of his subsistence. As, while he is preparing and bringing the goods to market, he advances to his workmen their wages, or their subsistence; so he advances to himself, in the same manner, his own subsistence, which is generally suitable to the profit which he may reasonably expect from the sale of his goods. Unless they yield him this profit, therefore, they do not repay him what they may very properly be said to have really cost him.

"Though the price therefore, which leaves him this profit, is not always the lowest at which a dealer may sometimes sell his goods, it is the lowest at which he is likely to sell them for any considerable time; at least where there is perfect liberty, or where he may change his trade as often as he pleases.

"The actual price at which any commodity is commonly sold is called its market-price. It may either be above or below, or exactly the same with its natural price.

"The market-price of every particular commodity is regulated by the proportion between the quantity which is actually brought to market, and the demand of those who are willing to pay the natural price of the commodity, or the whole value of the rent, labour, and profit, which must be paid in order to bring it thither. Such people may be called the effectual demanders, and their demand the effectual demand; since it may be sufficient to effectuate the bringing of the commodity to market. It is different from the absolute demand. A very poor man may be said in some sense to have a demand for a coach and six; he might like to have it; but his demand is not an effectual demand, as the commodity can never be brought to market in order to satisfy it.

"When the quantity of any commodity which is brought to market falls short of the effectual demand, all those who are willing to pay the whole value of the rent, wages, and profit, which must be paid in order to bring it thither, cannot be supplied with the quantity which they want. Rather than want it altogether, some of them will be willing to give more. A competition will immediately begin among them, and the market-price will rise more or less above the natural price, according as either the greatness of the deficiency, or the wealth and wanton luxury of the competitors, happen to animate more or less the eagerness of the competition. Among competitors of equal wealth and luxury the same deficiency will generally occasion a more or less eager competition, according as the acquisition of the commodity happens to be of more or less importance to them. Hence the exorbitant price of the necessaries of life during the blockade of a town or in a famine.

"When the quantity brought to market exceeds the effectual demand, it cannot be all sold to those who are willing to pay the whole value of the rent, wages, and profit, which must be paid in order to bring it thither. Some part must be sold to those who are willing to pay less, and the low price which they give for it must reduce the price of the whole. The market-price will sink more or less below the natural price, according as the greatness of the excess increases more or less the competition of the sellers, or according as it happens to be more or less important to them to get immediately rid of the commodity. The same excess in the importation of perishable will occasion a much greater competition than in that of durable commodities; in the importation of oranges, for example, than in that of old iron.

"When the quantity brought to market is just sufficient to supply the effectual demand and no more, the market-price naturally comes to be either exactly, or as nearly as can be judged of, the same with the natural price. The whole quantity upon hand can be disposed of for this price, and cannot be disposed of for more. The competition of the different dealers obliges them all to accept of this price, but does not oblige them to accept of less.

"The quantity of every commodity brought to market naturally suits itself to the effectual demand. It is the interest of all those who employ their land, labour, or stock, in bringing any commodity to market, that the quantity never should exceed the effectual demand; and it is the interest of all other people that it never should fall short of that demand.

"If at any time it exceeds the effectual demand, some of the component parts of its price must be paid below their natural rate. If it is rent, the interests of the landlords will immediately prompt them to withdraw a part of their land; and if it is wages or profit, the interest of the labourers in the one case, and of their employers in the other, will prompt them to withdraw a part of their labour or stock from this employment. The quantity brought to market will soon be no more than sufficient to supply the effectual demand. All the different parts of its price will rise to their natural rate, and the whole price to its natural price.

"If, on the contrary, the quantity brought to market should at any time fall short of the effectual demand, some of the component parts of its price must rise above their natural rate. If it is rent, the interest of all other landlords will naturally prompt them to prepare more land for the raising of this commodity; if it is wages or profit, the interest of all other labourers and dealers will soon prompt them to employ more labour and stock in preparing and bringing it to market. The quantity brought thither will soon be sufficient to supply the effectual demand. All the different parts of its price will soon sink to their natural rate, and the whole price to its natural price.

"The natural price, therefore, is, as it were, the centra price to which the prices of all commodities are continually gravitating. Different accidents may sometimes keep them suspended a good deal above it, and sometimes force them down even somewhat below it; but whatever may be the obstacles which hinder them from settling in this centre of repose and continuance, they are constantly tending towards it.

"The whole quantity of industry annually employed in order to bring any commodity to market, naturally suits itself in this manner to the effectual demand. It naturally aims at bringing always that precise quantity thither which may be sufficient to supply and no more than supply that demand."*

It is in this manner that the market-price of commodities is regulated and controlled by the natural price or cost of production; and that every distinct article is produced and brought to market in the proper quantity; that is, in such quantity as supplies and no more than supplies the effectual demand for it, or, which is the same thing, that all the different articles required in the most extensive communities are produced and brought to market in a just proportion to one another.

SECTION II.

THAT THE LABOUR EXPENDED IN PRODUCTION REGULATES THE NATURAL PRICE OF COMMODITIES IN THE EARLY PERIOD OF SOCIETY, BEFORE THE LABOURER AND CAPITALIST BECOME DISTINCT PERSONS; AND THAT THE CAPITAL EXPENDED REGULATES IT AFTER THAT PERIOD.

THE subject of the present section has been very clearly illustrated by Colonel Torrens, who was, I believe, the first to lay down the doctrine contained in the latter clause of our

* Wealth of Nations, book i. chap. 7.

title, although it appears so obvious, now it is pointed out, that we may wonder how it should have so long escaped observation, as well as that it should not be at once universally acknowledged. The place, however, where it is originally introduced—in an Essay on the *Production* of Wealth—was not, it must be confessed, the most favourable for its proper consideration; but it must undoubtedly make its way notwithstanding this circumstance, and its truth must be perceived, I think, the more it is considered.

"Before the labourer and capitalist become distinct persons," says Colonel Torrens, "the produce of a day's labour in one occupation will, *cæteris paribus*, be always equivalent to the produce of a day's labour in another occupation, whether the whole labour is employed immediately and directly in obtaining articles for consumption, or whether a portion of it is previously employed in acquiring the capital necessary to the production of such articles. If, previous to the separation of society into labourers and capitalists, vegetable productions were gathered without the aid of capital, while, in appropriating animal productions, it required that for every day's labour employed in the field another day's labour should be employed in preparing implements for the chase, or, in other words, the hunter's capital,—then it is evident that the produce of one day's direct labour in the chase would be equivalent to the produce of two days' labour employed in gathering fruits. In adjusting the terms of the exchange, the labour which prepared the capital would be taken into account, no less than the labour which actually applied it. If, on their returning in the evening from their respective occupations, the collector of vegetable productions should offer the fruits which he had gathered in the course of the day in exchange for the animals which the hunter had killed during the same period, the latter would naturally reply,—'The arrows expended during the chase cost me a day's labour; the animals which I have killed are in reality the produce of two days labour; and therefore, you must give me the quantity of fruits collected by two days' labour in exchange for them. To this demand the collector of fruits would be under the necessity of acceding, in order to prevent the hunter from abandoning the divisions of employment, and collecting vegetable productions for himself."*

But as soon as the labourer and capitalist become distinct persons, the circumstance which determines the exchangeable value or price of commodities is at once changed from the quantity of labour to the quantity of capital expended in their production; for it happens thenceforward that goods upon which equal quantities of capital have been expended must be equivalent in price, or, in other words, must exchange for one another; no matter what quantities of labour may have been employed on the one or the other, and no matter how different soever those quantities may have been, or what reward of labour or wages may have been paid to the labourers; because the capital expended includes always the payment of the labour, or wages, as well as the other two charges of rent, and profit or interest.

"Let there be two identical capitals," says Colonel Torrens again, "each consisting of a hundred quarters of corn, and a thousand pounds of wool; and let the proprietor of one of these capitals employ it in manufacturing broad cloth, while the proprietor of the other capital employs it in preparing carpeting; now, it must be evident, that the cloth and carpeting on which equal capitals were expended would be of equal value. If either of these manufacturers offered a *part* of his productions in exchange for the whole of the productions of the other, the other would immediately reply,—'For the articles which I have had fabricated from a hundred quarters of corn and a thousand pounds of wool, you must give me the whole of the articles which you have had prepared from a like capital. My capital is of equal power with yours; and if you will not barter upon equal terms, I can at any time employ as many labourers as will produce to me that which you re-

* Essay on the Production of Wealth, chap. i.

fuse. To this no reasonable objection could be urged. Hence we see, that *when the capitalists become a class distinct from the labourers, the results obtained by the employment of identical capitals, or identical quantities of accumulated labour, will be equal in exchangeable value.*"*

The exchangeable value or price of commodities is, in the advanced stages of society, almost always reckoned in the common measure of value, money, whatever it may be; and it appears to me, that, had that rule been followed in the above instance, and the capitals been estimated in pounds or ounces of gold instead of pounds of wool and quarters of corn, the reasoning would have been more simple and easily followed, and equally conclusive.

As, for example:—Let there be two equal capitals, each consisting of a hundred pounds of gold, or £4672, 10s. sterling; and let the proprietor of the one expend it in fabricating cottons, with materials equal in value to £2400, and £2272, 10s. paid as wages; and let the proprietor of the other expend it in making gold-plate, with materials equal in value to £4400, and £272, 10s. paid as wages; still the exchangeable value of the gold-plate and of the cottons must be equal, notwithstanding the difference of the quantities of labour employed in the different processes of their production; and they must exchange the one for the other, because equal quantities of capital have been expended upon them.

It will be of no use to urge, in contradiction to this plain account, that different quantities of labour may have been employed in producing the different materials; and that if we will go back to the commencement of the process of production, we shall find that the labour expended on both has been the same. That the quantities of labour employed in producing each *may* have been the same is *a possibility*,

---

* Essay on the Production of Wealth, chap. i.

and cannot therefore be positively disproved, although the supposition be in the highest degree improbable; but to maintain that they *must* have been the same is a mere gratuitous and wholly unproved assumption, proceeding upon the false and absurd opinion already, I trust, sufficiently refuted in this work, that every thing is produced by labour alone, nothing by capital.* Now, it is peremptorily denied that the materials of either of the articles above-mentioned, —cotton or gold,—or indeed any materials or capitals that ever existed, amounting in value to a hundred pounds (weight) of gold, were produced by labour alone,—much capital, not to mention the land (or rent in this place as forming any part of price or value) being always employed in the production both of the material of cotton-yarn and of gold-ingots; and to propose to go back and inquire into the production of the capitals successively employed until we arrive at that produced at first by simple labour, would in reality be to go back to the beginning of time, or, at the least, to that period when the labourer and capitalist began to be distinct

* This notion, so very generally entertained, that every thing is wholly produced by labour, has arisen no doubt from the circumstance which we have endeavoured to establish in the first chapter of the first book of this Inquiry; namely, that *some portion* of labour is always required or employed in the production of every thing, *i. e.* of every article that can be called wealth. But because this is the case, because labour does *a part*, it by no means follows that it does *the whole*. Yet this notion runs through the far greater part of all the writings of political economists, and is strangely jumbled up with their notions of the productiveness of capital. Mr Ricardo's first chapter in his Principles of Political Economy, consisting of *five sections*, if it has any definite object, seems wholly taken up with an attempt to prove that labour produces all, and is the only ingredient in the value or price of all articles; and in his pamphlet "On Protection to Agriculture," (the last of his writings, I believe, published during his lifetime,) he says, "the labour of the country constitutes its only real source of wealth."—Page 7, fourth edition.

persons; for I have already proved,* that capital is a distinct means or instrument of production as well as labour; and that after the first acquisition or employment of the smallest atom of wealth as capital, this new instrument co-operates thenceforward in causing its own increase; that is, it co-operates in the production and increase of every sort of wealth, and indeed becomes ultimately the most powerful and efficient instrument of all "the grand source of exuberant production."

But although it be undoubtedly certain that it is *the capital expended in production* which, in the advanced stages of society, regulates the price of commodities, this does not hinder but that *that* price should be made up of the three distinct parts,—rent, wages, and profit or interest; because all these are included under the expenditure of capital;† and it still continues to be as necessary as ever to trace the causes that regulate the amount or rates of these three distinct charges of production, as being the three grand sources of all permanent revenue, and as involving the consideration of the distinct rights and interests of the three great classes of which the community (*i. e.* every community) is constituted.

In that early and rude period of society which precedes both the accumulation of capital and the appropriation of land, the price of every commodity which then existed would consist or be made up wholly of but one part—wages; because, antecedent to that period, every article possessing the character of wealth was produced by labour alone. But subsequently to that period, that is, as soon as any considerable quantity of wealth was saved and applied to assist

---

* Book i. chap. 6.

† The amount of which expenditure, as of all other value, is still of course *measured* by labour, as explained in chapter 3d of this book.

in the work of production, and, after such increase in the numbers of people had taken place as required all the land in a particular neighbourhood or country to be cultivated and made private property, both rent and profit, or interest, would thenceforward form distinct constituent parts in the price of the great mass of commodities; although it would be altogether impossible, by any analysis, or any practicable means, to determine exactly in what proportions they were combined in any.

Wages, however, it is to be observed, where they do not constitute the whole price, must always make a part of it in every commodity, because some portion of labour must always have been employed in every process of production; whereas rent, and profit, or interest, may or may not make a part of the price of any commodity, and will be found to do so or not just as rent has been paid or not on the production of the raw material,* and as capital has been employed or not either in the production or procuration of such material, or in working it up into a higher value.

It has been thought by some, that because rent is the consequence, not the cause, of high price of raw produce, that it ought not to be considered as forming a component part of that price. But this does not appear to be a good objection; for as rent must necessarily be paid, and actually is paid, on raw produce, after the land is appropriated and population has but moderately increased in any particular place or neighbourhood, before the whole quantity in demand can be produced and brought to market, or before the whole extent of ground can be cultivated which is required to produce that whole quantity, it still forms a neces-

---

* If rent is paid on *any part* of any particular species of raw material required in production, it must be covered by the price of the article produced, and consequently form a part of that price.

sary part of the price of that whole, and must consequently be regarded as forming a proportional part of the price of any given quantity. For if this is not allowed, of what, I ask, is the whole price of the whole produce made up?—Wages and profit do not constitute the whole, and a third portion, therefore, will still be required to balance the account.

To this portion the rent, it will not be denied, is precisely equivalent; and, in point of fact, therefore, this portion really does consist of rent; and rent, therefore, actually does form a constituent part of the price of commodities, whether we choose to acknowledge it or not.

CHAPTER V.

THE DISTINCT NATURE OF THE THREE DIFFERENT DENOMINATIONS OF INCOME OR REVENUE, NAMELY, RENT, WAGES, AND PROFIT OR INTEREST, EXPLAINED AND DISCRIMINATED.

THE three original sources of wealth,—land, labour, and capital,—naturally give rise to three correspondent denominations of income or revenue; namely, rent, wages, and profit or interest; the distinct nature of which it is of the last importance to define and discriminate accurately, since it necessarily happens that the confounding of these different denominations or descriptions of revenue with one another confounds and perplexes all our reasonings concerning them, and especially our reasonings concerning taxation, as it affects those different descriptions of revenue, and consequently as it affects the rights and interests of the three great classes of persons whereof every civilized society is necessarily constituted.

It has unfortunately happened, that even Dr Smith, who has been the most correct delineator of rent, wages, and profit, and the whole of whose doctrines and ideas concerning these different revenues seem in general so just, has, nevertheless, not always perfectly discriminated between them. In particular, he has not upon all occasions perfectly discriminated wages from profit of stock (of which oversight in some parts of his work he was himself perfectly aware, as will be shown presently ;) and, although this does not appear to have led *him* into any ulterior error, or to have in any degree vitiated *his* reasonings in regard to the true ultimate incidence and effect of taxes, it has proved an almost universal stumbling-block to subsequent writers, and particularly to the *Ricardo School of Political Economists*, almost the whole of whose obscure and paradoxical doctrines are distinctly to be traced to this source of error.

It seems to be sufficiently obvious, that nothing can be justly accounted *profit of stock* but what can be got for the use of it without the labour of personally applying it, or superintending its application in business or production; because all that is got by means of that labour is *wages*, and is as properly entitled to this denomination as that which is got by any other species of labour whatever. But this clear line of distinction not being sufficiently attended to by Dr Smith, or at least not being expressly laid down by him, a wide door was thrown open for the admittance of error, and for the superinduction of all that obscurity, perplexity, and contradiction that distinguishes the writings of the school just mentioned; and it is owing to this particular error especially, namely, to the confounding of wages and profit of stock with one another, that the writers just alluded to have been led to promulgate the empty and unsound dogmas, that "wages and profits vary inversely as one another," and that "no taxes can be paid out of wages;" and, in short, to imagine they had discovered so many important errors in the "Wealth of Nations."

It is very remarkable that neither Mr Ricardo nor any of his followers have ever attempted to define what they technically term *profits*, although they have exhibited formal definitions of both wages and rent, and although the chief novelties in their system hinge entirely upon the loose notions they entertain in regard to the particular description of revenue denoted by that term, which they have omitted to define. Had they indeed made the attempt to define profit of stock, the whole illusion wherein they have been wrapt must have been dispelled at once; for it is not easy to see on what grounds they could have held out any thing as that profit above what could be got for the use of stock without labour. But the Ricardo economists probably found it too hard a task for them to define profit of stock, and to maintain their system at the same time unhurt and inviolate by such definition.

Now, in regard to any theory relating to rent, profit, and wages, I would observe, that if we are content with telling what we mean by one or two of these terms, and leave the third undefined, it may be very easy to make such theory perfectly consistent in itself, however false and unfounded it may be in the true nature of things, and however useless and pernicious it may be in its effects and bearing upon practice; because out of the remaining undefined and undeterminate fund or quantity, it will always be easy to solve every difficulty, and balance every account (be it of taxes or what it may,) without allowing it to produce any alteration or effect upon the other quantities, or upon the arbitrary sense we have chosen to give, right or wrong, to the terms we have defined; and if it so happens that we have given incorrect definitions of any one, or both, of those two other descriptions of revenue, it will not be so easy to detect any error in our reasonings concerning them, as if the third term had been precisely defined also.

Had Mr Ricardo, for example, attempted to define profit of stock, he must, in conformity with his system, and in order to prevent the whole fabric of his reasonings concerning taxation from falling to the ground, have stated it to be *all that a man employing a stock of his own in trade gains after the payment of the wages of his workmen, and the other charges necessary to replace that stock.* But this man *labours himself* as well as his workmen, and something must fall to be allowed for his own wages. Now, in making this allowance, I ask, where would Mr Ricardo stop short, if he would set down any thing at all as wages for such labour, but *at that precise point where he comes to interest*, or that profit of stock which can be got without labour?

Or would Mr Ricardo have defined profits to be *all that a man gains in any business after the payment, not only of the wages of his workmen, and the other charges necessary to replace his stock, but after deducting also the ordinary rate of interest?*—Then here again we have the same, nay, if possible, even a greater inaccuracy, nothing being allowed for this man's own wages; and instead of representing any thing that can be properly considered as profit, in the technical acceptation of that term, this definition totally excludes the idea, and in truth represents precisely the individual's wages; for all, it is obvious, that any individual gains, or can gain, after the replacement of his capital, and the ordinary rate of interest upon it, is wages, or remuneration for his labour, and nothing else; and the ordinary rate of interest consequently alone remains as that which can truly deserve or receive the name of profit of stock.*

* Since this chapter was written a disciple of Mr Ricardo has ventured to put forth a definition of profit as follows:—

But had this only reasonable or tenable interpretation of profit of stock been attended to or acknowledged, namely,

---

" By *profit*, in the science of political economy," says Mr J. R. Macculloch, (in his edition of Smith's Wealth of Nations, recently published, vol. iv. p. 184.), " is meant the produce, or the value of the produce, obtained by the employment of a capital, for a given time, in any industrious undertaking, that remains to the owner of the capital, after replacing the capital itself, or such portion of it as may have been wasted in the undertaking, and every other expense necessarily incurred in carrying it on."

Now, here it is plainly seen, that this form of words or definition (so called) agrees substantially with the first of the two *supposititious ones* given above in our text, and confirms what is there stated, inasmuch as *it does not distinguish profit from wages.* No attempt is made to ascertain the wages of " the owner of the capital," who yet, by the writer's hypothesis, superintends himself the " industrious undertaking;" and this notwithstanding of the fact, that, without determining this point, profit *never can* be accurately defined or distinguished from wages. And hence it is, I suppose, that wages *are not even mentioned in the above definition*, and far less are they attempted to be set apart as a distinct charge in the cost of production, separable from profit. On the contrary, they are, without being named, huddled into the concluding clause,—" *and every other expense necessarily incurred in carrying it on!*"

To have set down wages as a separate charge or portion of the " expense," would have obliged the Ricardist to enter into the question,—*How much* should be allowed as the wages of " the owner of the capital" superintending the " industrious undertaking?"—a task that was much too hard for him, and a question he could not have solved without bringing his master's old house about his ears; and what is worse perhaps still, without converting his own ponderous edition of Smith's " Wealth of Nations," as well as the three editions of " the great Ricardo," his Principles of Political Economy, into a heap of rubbish.

But there is another new invention of the Ricardo economists, the most notable of all, and the most recent, which I must here also notice as connected with the foregoing, although, instead of coming *after*, it should have *preceded* the other as its natural parent. It is that interpretation which identifies it with interest, or what can be got for it without labour, the futility of the Ricardo

---

now found out—and Mr J. R. Macculloch has the exclusive honour of the discovery—that *the effects of capital* MAY BE CALLED *the effects of labour;* and that this term (namely labour) "may properly be defined" (see the publication before cited, vol. iv. p. 75.) *any sort of action or operation, whether performed by man, the lower animals, machinery, or natural agents, that tends to bring about a desirable result!!!*"

Now mark the consequences:—If there be no necessity to distinguish the effects of labour from those of capital, but that both may be understood by the same name, or by either name indifferently, then certainly there can be no necessity to distinguish wages from profit, so that they also may be understood by the same name, or by either indifferently! But *why then use two names or terms where one might serve as well?* Why not rescind from our vocabulary either the words *capital* and *profit,* or the words *labour* and *wages,* and be content with the two first or the two last? Or, if we do not choose to rescind the words, let us put the doctrine to the proof, and use them indifferently; then we will talk of *the wages of capital* and *the profit of labour,* and *vice versa* indifferently; and what then will become of "the science of political economy?" A pretty "science" truly would this professor and "speculator" make of it if he had his way. Well indeed might Mr Saddler call such political economists, "jobbers and speculators."

Before concluding here, I must state explicitly, that a more extraordinary piece of elaborate *nonsense* (for there is no other epithet by which it can be properly characterized,) than this "note" (*vide* idem, p. 74,) never certainly fell from the pen of any "political economist;" and after the manner in which the absurdity of the nostrum it maintains had been previously exposed by the author of the "Dissertation on the Nature, Causes, and Measures of Value," (chap. xi. pp. 219, 220; see also, "A Letter to a Political Economist, occasioned by an Article in the Westminster Review, on the subject of Value," by the same author, p. 89,) it is hardly less extraordinary that it should still be persisted in. It is pity it should not have been one among the number of those "positions" which, as we are informed by his friends, (*vide* Scotsman, October 4, 1828,) Mr Macculloch "has had the cou-

theory, which represents the rates of profit and wages as varying inversely as one another, and of the *wire-drawn* doctrine, that the rate of profit is regulated by the barrenness or fertility of the last portions of land brought under cultivation, would have quickly appeared; and the old, and sound, and intelligible doctrines of Mr Hume and Dr Smith, as to the causes of variation in the rates of rent, profit, and wages, and as to the real ultimate incidence and effect of taxes, would have reassumed all their original evidence and authority. It would quickly have appeared that it was not, as they supposed, wages and profits that varied inversely as one another, but the different wages themselves of the different classes of labourers, namely, of the masters or employers of inferior labourers on the one hand, and of those inferior labourers or persons employed on the other, that really varied according to that law. It would have appeared, that when Mr Ricardo says, that the more that is paid to the labourer as wages, the less must go to the capitalist as profit of stock, he could only mean, when the subject was rightly understood, that the more the inferior labourer gets as *his* wages, the less will remain to the superior labourer as his; but the manner in which the aggregate fund of wages is divided between the different classes of labourers, superior and inferior, makes no difference to the capitalist. It is true, that if the superior labourer happens to require or employ a borrowed capital, the more he gets as wages the richer he will be, and the abler of course to pay a high interest. But this circumstance will not determine

---

rage openly to correct." But this perhaps would have been letting out too much at once: it would have been to hazard too much the character of the *professor*, if not as to his being of all persons the most "erudite in the history of economy," yet still for the use he was capable of making of that *erudition*, and for soundness or "success" in propounding "all its great leading principles."

him to do so; and it is not upon this principle that the amount of interest will be regulated, but by the quantity of capital saved and accumulated, or existing at the time, seeking profitable employment or investment, or ready to be lent in any particular country or neighbourhood, compared with the field for its employment and the demand of borrowers. The single question which the borrower will have to consider will be, *what he can get the capital for?* and however much he may make by his business, if he can get a loan at *four* per cent. he will not give *five*. But where capital is abundant as compared with the field for its employment, the number of competitors for that employment, that is, both the persons who wish to lend money or capital, and those who wish to employ themselves in business with capitals of their own, will be such as to produce a low rate of profit, however much may be obtained as wages.

But this explanation of profit and wages contradicts the vulgar notion of them which would extend the meaning of the first term, so as to include all that is acquired in any business, after paying the wages of the inferior persons employed, without reckoning any thing as the wages of the chief labourer himself, and would confine the latter to signify the remuneration or reward of certain of the lowest species of "operatives," or *common day-labourers*, as they are sometimes called; and this appears to be the true secret of the almost universal prevalence and easy dissemination of every erroneous doctrine founded upon the mistake of not properly discriminating wages from profit of stock. Almost every person, indeed, when the question is laid distinctly before him in a separate disconnected form, will acknowledge, that the earnings of the higher species of labourers are really wages as much as those of the lower species; but the far greater part of late writers seem totally to forget this circumstance the moment they turn away from the simple view of the question, and advance a single step in the progress beyond it,—founding all their subsequent reasonings on the vulgar notion of profit and wages, and on that of wages denoting a fixed and invariable quantity; and in this we distinctly recognize the natural and obvious consequence of attempting to reason closely and connectedly upon vague and undefined terms, so frequently observed and complained of in other cases. Had these writers reflected but for a moment, and attempted to define what they meant by common labour, they would instantly have perceived the absurdity of confining the term wages to the earnings of any single class of labourers, and the futility of any reasoning founded on such an understanding of it. Had this attempt been made, what would common labour have been defined to be? or what point of the scale, from the lowest sort of labour to the highest, could have been fixed upon as that where the earnings of labour ceased to be wages and suddenly became profit of stock?

Mr Ricardo defines the natural price (or wages) of labour to be "that price which is necessary to enable the labourers, one with another, to subsist, and to perpetuate their race, without either increase or diminution."*

But this definition could only be intended to apply to the very lowest description of labourers, whom it moreover supposes reduced to the very lowest possible or endurable condition, namely, to a subsistence consisting of the smallest quantity and worst quality of food, clothes, and lodging, by which life can be supported,—a condition to which I believe no considerable number of people or distinct class of labourers ever were reduced in any civilized society, and yet the whole of Mr Ricardo's system is built and rested upon this supposition!

To make his definition applicable to any class above the

* Principles of Political Economy, chap. v., p. 85, second edition.

very lowest, or even to the very lowest itself, if not reduced to the condition above stated, Mr Ricardo should have added the words, *with their existing habits and modes of life.* For what should hinder that class of labourers which is immediately above the lowest,—or even the very lowest of all, unless they were pushed to the very last and extremest verge of existence,—to subsist and increase their numbers if they choose to be content with an inferior quantity and quality of necessaries? But still more, what should hinder every other class of labourers in the ascending scale to subsist and increase their numbers if they choose to be content with a humbler way of living?—What, in a word, should hinder *the higher classes of labourers* to subsist and increase their numbers to the utmost extent that their physical nature admits of, but their disinclination to change their habits and modes of life, and descend to a lower station?

But further; this definition of Mr Ricardo's, of the natural price of labour, is essentially and radically erroneous, and utterly incorrect in every view that can be taken of it, being founded on a false idea of human nature and human society, and an ignorance of the natural progress of the latter under any tolerable system of liberty and security or good government. For not only is it *natural* that mankind should increase their numbers, and quite possible for them to do so *indefinitely*, and to increase *their wealth and the price of their labour* at the same time, but, as has been already shown, and as will be still further illustrated in the sequel, such a progress is the *natural and necessary course of things*, under the condition just mentioned.

It is not only possible, but it is the natural and necessary course of things under good government, for mankind to save, increase, and accumulate *wealth* indefinitely; and it is not only perfectly possible, but it is the natural and necessary course of things also, under the same condition, that one part of the wealth, constantly increasing and accumulating, should go to increase *the numbers of the people,* and another part to improve the condition and increase the *real wages* of the labourers in every employment, and especially of the lower classes of labourers, when education has been fully extended to them, so as to improve their habits and modes of life, by enlarging their minds and raising their ideas in regard to what they should consider necessary to their comfortable subsistence. The natural price therefore. or wages of labour, must be always necessarily, under a good system of government, *not a fixed, but a constantly-increasing quantity;* and every definition which involves a contrary supposition, or which implies that population should be stationary, and the wages of labour a fixed and invariable quantity, must be eternally false and erroneous, and the reasonings founded upon it fallacious and invalid.

It is true indeed, that when the world comes to be very highly peopled and cultivated, the additions which will then be capable of being made to the greater part of raw products which can be used as food, will be small comparatively with the additions or improvements that may still continue to be made in the shape of clothes, houses, and other accommodations or conveniences; and this may very probably cause any progress that takes place subsequently to appear more in the shape of an increase of wages than in the numbers of the people; but such circumstance can never stop that progress altogether, or prevent either the wages of labour or the numbers of mankind, or both, from increasing and augmenting in some degree, however small.

It may be true also perhaps, that, in very highly peopled and cultivated countries, any new additions that can be made to the average annual supplies of food, must generally be procured with greater difficulty, or at greater cost, than previously;* but it is a very false and precipitate conclusion

---

* I have said above, *it may be perhaps,* because in one sense the

which has been attempted to be founded on this circumstance, that the lower classes of labourers must therefore be content with a smaller quantity and worse quality of food, or with lower wages than previously, in order to admit of such additional supplies being obtained. For it does not by any means follow that the additional difficulty must be overcome, or the additional cost defrayed, by the application of *more labour*; such additional difficulty and cost may be, and in point of fact generally is, overcome and defrayed by the increase and application of *more capital*; and whether the effect be produced in the one way or the other will depend entirely on the circumstances which determine the habits and modes of life or subsistence of the labourers, namely, on the character of the government under which they live. If the government be bad, the effect *may* be produced by the degradation of the character and condition of the labourers; but under good government, where the lower classes of labourers will not only, as has been shown, sus-

---

cost or difficulty experienced in acquiring raw products generally cannot differ very greatly, if at all, at one period from another; the greater fertility of the soils first cultivated being counterbalanced by the more imperfect modes of agriculture, deficiency of capital, and other adverse circumstances in the early periods of society, and the sterility of those last cultivated being compensated by the incidence and agency of circumstances or causes of an opposite kind in the advanced periods; those causes or circumstances being innumerable which facilitate and augment the production of corn or other articles of subsistence as population and wealth increase;—as the greater abundance and easier acquisition of manures, the nearer approach of, and more convenient access to markets, or the continual and indefinite *shortening of the road*, or distance, that produce has to be carried to market, which takes place from the growth of population; not to mention the unceasing occurrence of improvements in the skill of the cultivators, or of inventions and discoveries in the arts and processes of agriculture.

tain, but continually improve their condition and character, and habits and modes of life, it can only be by the increase and application of capital that such additional supplies of raw produce must be obtained.

It is not by any means a necessary consequence, as has been supposed, that when the circumstances which determine the character and condition of the labourers are such as to induce them to sustain or improve their habits and modes of life, and consequently to sustain wages, no additional supplies of raw produce requiring greater cost can be obtained. For it is always to be recollected, that the great instrument of production, *capital*, is constantly increasing, and constantly producing greater and greater effects in proportion to the labour that assists and guides it, and it is by this means chiefly, (and not, as has been absurdly and inconsiderately maintained, solely and exclusively by the degradation of the labourer, or by the diminution of his wages,) that any new difficulty, or additional cost in the acquisition of raw produce, is naturally or usually overcome, or that cultivation is extended to the inferior soils, and to the more distant and inconveniently-situated lands.

So far indeed is it from being either impossible or uncommon to see cultivation extended in this manner to inferior soils, that it is precisely what naturally and necessarily happens under good government,—where, if there be any truth in what has been so largely stated in a former chapter,* the additional supplies of raw produce must be acquired not only without any reduction, but coincidently with a constant and indefinite rise of the wages of labour.

It is much more natural and more usual therefore,—as certainly it is much more desirable,—that cultivation should be extended in this manner by the increase and application

---

* Chap. 10. of book i.

of capital, and that the capitalist should be content with a lower rate of profit or interest, than that the labourer should be abridged of his wages; and it is a fortunate circumstance, that in the possible future indefinite increase of raw produce, as well as of manufactured commodities, (both of which must always divide themselves in some way or other,) the lower classes of labourers can never fail to obtain a share as long as they continue to sustain and improve their conduct and character, and habits and modes of life,—all which we have shown they necessarily must do under good government.

Yet this is a result which Mr Ricardo and his followers deprecate beyond all others. There is nothing more terrible to their imaginations than the idea of cultivation being extended to "the poorer soils," lest it should happen in consequence that "wages should rise and profits fall,"—so great a misfortune do they consider it that any part of the benefits arising from capital should descend to the labourer!—There is no danger against which we are more emphatically warned than against this, and none of their nostrums which is more incessantly rung in our ears. "There is no other way," says their chief, "of keeping profits up, but by keeping wages down,"*—a sentiment than which none can, in my opinion, be more ungenerous, not to say hard-hearted;—and, in strict conformity with this sentiment, they represent *high profits* and *low wages* (instead of the very contrary) as the true "standard" or criterion "of national prosperity;" which notion, however, arises from their totally misapprehending the true nature of wages and profits, and from their confounding those two distinct descriptions of revenue with one another.

It has been a question which above all others has most

* Ricardo "On Protection to Agriculture," p. 44, fourth edition.

anxiously occupied the thoughts (and the endeavours to solve it) of good and liberal-minded men in these latter times, how the inferior classes of people might be relieved from the pressure of extreme poverty, and made partakers in some degree of the abundant wealth of the more fortunate members of the community, without any attendant evil, or without plunging them afterwards into deeper difficulties and destitution than those from which it was attempted to deliver them. And if we consider how much the different families of mankind are mixed in two or three generations, this anxiety will appear not more benevolent than just and rational; as it will be seen, that much of the capital at any time existing must probably have been saved by the progenitors of persons who are now poor. Even Mr Malthus professes to go thus far; indeed he goes much farther; for he maintains Mr Godwin's argument, which extends much farther, to be irresistible, if it were not for the consideration just mentioned, of certain alleged greater difficulties and destitution that would fall upon the poor in consequence of those attempts to relieve them. "Taking an individual instance," says the former of these writers, "without reference to consequences, it appears to me that Mr Godwin's argument is irresistible. Can it be pretended for a moment that a part of the mutton which I expect to eat to-day would not be much more beneficially employed on some hard-working labourer, who has not perhaps tasted animal food for the last week, or on some poor family, who cannot command sufficient food of any kind fully to satisfy the cravings of hunger? If these instances were not of a nature to multiply in proportion as such wants were indiscriminately gratified, the gratification of them, as it would be practicable, would be highly beneficial."*

But if it be impossible, consistently with the existence

* Essay on Population, Appendix, vol. iii. p. 344.

of any wealth above the narrow measure of the savage state, "that those who have drawn a blank in the lottery of life," should share *directly* in the prize which the accumulations made in past times present, what are we to think of that philosophy which would grudge to those less fortunate persons that *indirect* participation (or inheritance) in those accumulations, or in the benefits of capital, which the Author of nature has decreed should flow to all mankind, from the constitution of things and from those laws which he has determined should regulate the distribution of wealth?

But to return.

It is another favourite theory of the class of writers already mentioned, (and this will be the proper place to notice it, as being connected with the foregoing discussions,) that every society or people has an incomparably greater tendency to increase in numbers than in wealth or capital; and although this theory is opposed to the strongest evidence of facts, to the most uniform experience, and is utterly inconsistent with their own most ample admissions in regard to the force and effects of the principle of *saving* or *frugality*, these writers do yet maintain it with the most implicit and unhesitating confidence, while, at the same time, they do not advance a single argument in support of it that I have been able to discover, but leave us simply to rely on their oracular word!—I trust I may be free to presume therefore, that it may be sufficient for me flatly and peremptorily to deny this theory, and to appeal to all history,—to the history at least of every country in which any tolerably good government has been established,—for the instant and triumphant refutation of it.

In every country where any tolerably good government has been established,—indeed I might almost say in every country without exception, wherever the people have increased their numbers in any considerable degree,—it will uniformly be found that they have increased their wealth during the same period in a still greater proportion. I shall only refer in proof of this to the United States of North America and Great Britain, the two countries with which we are best acquainted, and in both of which it will be found, that although population has increased very much within the last thirty years, and in the former country, with nearly, it has been supposed, its greatest possible rapidity, still capital has increased in a more than equal proportion, as will be evident if we but look to the additions they have made to their wealth in the open and visible shape of houses, manufactories, and whole towns elegantly and substantially built or renewed; canals and roads of vast extent and cost, meliorations and permanent agricultural improvements, the increase of ships and commerce, and an infinite number of other accumulations throughout the country, which are all greater now in both countries, in proportion to the numbers of the people, than they were at any former period.

It will no doubt be alleged by the disciples of Mr Ricardo, that the rapid increase of wealth in North America is to be accounted for from the circumstance, that the people there have it still in their power to draw their supplies of raw produce from "soils of the first quality;"—and yet I believe it would be found, if proper inquiry were made, that the agricultural produce of Great Britain, taking it in the aggregate both from rich and poor soils, is acquired at a much less cost of labour and capital, than that of the United States, quantity for quantity. But be this as it may, still we have the instance of Great Britain increasing her capital in a still greater proportion than her population, notwithstanding all the waste of by far the greatest and most expensive war she was ever engaged in, *whilst at the same time, for the additions of raw produce necessarily required to feed and clothe her increased numbers, she was* (to the utter discomfiture of the Ricardo doctrine) *obliged to have "recourse to the poorer soils."*

Nor should what has been just stated be at all surprising to those who are aware of the force and general prevalence of the principle of saving or frugality. "It can seldom happen, indeed," says Dr Smith, "that the circumstances of a great nation can be much affected either by the prodigality or misconduct of individuals; the profusion or imprudence of some being always more than compensated by the frugality and good conduct of others.

"With regard to profusion, the principle which prompts to expense is the passion for present enjoyment, which, though sometimes violent and very difficult to be restrained, is in general only momentary and occasional. But the principle which prompts to save is the desire of bettering our condition; a desire which, though generally calm and dispassionate, comes with us from the womb, and never leaves us till we go into the grave. In the whole interval which separates those two moments, there is scarce perhaps a single instance in which any man is so perfectly and completely satisfied with his situation as to be without any wish of alteration or improvement of any kind. An augmentation of fortune is the means by which the greater part of men propose and wish to better their condition. It is the means the most vulgar and the most obvious; and the most likely way of augmenting their fortnne is to save and accumulate some part of what they acquire, either regularly and annually, or upon some extraordinary occasions. Though the principle of expense, therefore, prevails in almost all men upon some occasions, and in some men upon almost all occasions, yet in the greater part of men, taking the whole course of their life at an average, the principle of frugality seems not only to predominate, but to predominate very greatly.

"With regard to misconduct, the number of prudent and successful undertakings is everywhere much greater than that of injudicious and unsuccessful ones. After all our complaints of the frequency of bankruptcies, the unhappy men who fall into this misfortune make but a very small part of the whole number engaged in trade, and all other sorts of business; not much more perhaps than one in a thousand. Bankruptcy is perhaps the greatest and most humiliating calamity which can befall an innocent man. The greater part of men, therefore, are sufficiently careful to avoid it. Some, indeed, do not avoid it, as some do not avoid the gallows.

"Great nations are never impoverished by private, though they sometimes are by public prodigality and misconduct."*

And again:—"When we compare the state of a nation at two different periods, and find that the annual produce of its land and labour is evidently greater at the latter than at the former, that its lands are better cultivated, its manufactures more numerous and more flourishing, and its trade more extensive, we may be assured that its capital must have increased during the interval between those two periods, and that more must have been added to it by the good conduct of some, than had been taken from it either by the private misconduct of others, or by the public extravagance of government."†

Nor is there any doctrine in the whole compass of political science to which the followers of Mr Ricardo bear an ampler testimony, or to which they give a fuller and more unequivocal assent than this. They seem even to vie with one another as well as with Dr Smith, and to strain their invention for stronger language in which to state it, and to express their deep sense of its truth.

"There is no instance," says one of the most noted of Mr Ricardo's disciples, "of any people having ever missed an opportunity to save and amass. In all tolerably well-governed countries the principle of accumulation has uniformly had a marked ascendency over the principle of expense. Individuals are fully sensible of the value of the articles they ex-

---

* Wealth of Nations, book ii. chap. 3. † Ibid.

pend; for, in the vast majority of instances, they are the immediate result of their industry, perseverance, and economy; and they will not consume them, unless to obtain an equivalent advantage."*

It may be stated therefore, I think, as an undoubted axiom, that the disposition to accumulate wealth is at least as strong as the propensity to multiply population; and that the former principle of our nature is perfectly sufficient to keep the latter in subjection and in check, under any tolerable system of laws or good government.

CHAPTER VI.

OF THE PROFIT OR INTEREST OF STOCK OR CAPITAL.

SECTION I.

PROFIT OF STOCK DEFINED.

THE profit of stock or capital is that share of wealth,—the produce of land, labour, and capital,—which belongs to the capitalist after the deduction of rent and wages,—including of course in that deduction *his own wages*, where he bestows *his own labour in the employment of his capital.* In other words, profit of stock is that exact share of wealth which the capitalist can procure by means of his capital without labouring himself, or without, at least, labouring or

---

* Principles of Political Economy, by J. R. Macculloch, Esq. part iv. p. 415.

troubling himself further than may be necessary to lend and secure it in the best manner. Profit of stock is therefore the same thing with *interest of money.*

The distinctive characteristics of rent and wages are not difficult to be ascertained, and the revenues which ought properly to fall under those denominations have been in general pretty correctly understood; but the notions that have prevailed hitherto in regard to what ought to be considered as the profit of stock seem singularly vague, unsettled, and erroneous, as confounding those profits with the wages of labour, in all the employments where capital is required as well as with what is properly compensation for risk,—an undefinable and uncertain quantity.

There is in fact no such thing as profit of stock or capital, properly so called, distinct from that which is paid for the use of stock or capital, and all gain in any business, profession, or employment, which is over and above the ordinary rate of interest on the capital employed, is either wages,—that is, remuneration or reward for labour or industry, or ingenuity, or skill, in the use and application of that capital,—or otherwise it is the result of *fortune or accident*,—that is, of "secret and unknown causes,"* which sometimes occasion greater or less gain in trade, or no gain at all, and sometimes a loss,—and falls properly to be considered as *compensation for risk*, which ought not to be confounded with the profit ordinarily derivable from capital any more than with the ordinary wages of labour;—such accidental gain being regulated by no certain principles, and being therefore without the pale of science, or at least of political science, which is conversant alone with "known and determinate causes,"† rejecting all others with disdain.

---

* Mr Hume's definition of *chance*, i. e. fortune or accident. *Vide* Essays, part i. essay 14.

† *Vide* Ibid.

The word *profit* indeed, in its common and popular acceptation, is understood to mean the same thing with *gain*, and in this sense it includes every thing in the shape of wealth that any person can acquire from any subject whatever, be it land or capital, or from any business, profession, or employment whatever; in which sense it is a very useful and perhaps necessary word;* but as a term designating the revenue arising from a peculiar species of property or capital, and as defining and limiting the right to that revenue, it must be confined precisely to the sense of Interest. Not that interest measures the exact quantity of wealth produced by capital; for, as I have already endeavoured to prove at large,† a great part of that wealth diffuses itself, and communicates its benefits indirectly to the whole community. But interest measures the whole gain arising from it directly to the individual proprietor,—all that he can claim specifically in his character of capitalist, or all that he can directly gain by it without labouring himself; and what he gains by the superaddition of his labour is WAGES.

But Dr Smith, it will be said, did not himself restrict the meaning of the expression *profit of stock* thus far, or confine it to the signification exclusively of interest of money. Still, however, all his reasonings concerning profit and wages, and especially his exposition of the true ultimate incidence and effect of taxes, require that it should be restricted to this meaning; and, as I have already mentioned, Dr Smith himself was perfectly aware that he had not fully explained this point, or always perfectly discriminated between wages and profit. This will now most distinctly and plainly ap-

* Perhaps it might be expedient to discontinue the use of the word *profit* in its technical sense altogether, and, substituting for it the term rent, to say rent of stock or capital, instead of profit of stock, &c., as we say rent, not profit of land. I have not, however, ventured to make so great an innovation.

† Chap. v. section 2. of book I. *et passim.*

pear from the extracts I must here produce from the Inquiry into the Nature and Causes of the Wealth of Nations; and in reviewing the subject it will be, I trust, made fully apparent, that no just or intelligible distinction can be laid down between the one and the other, unless it be at that line where interest commences; that line which separates what is gained without labour from what is gained in consequence of labour being added.

In the following passages it is frankly admitted that wages and profit are too often confounded with one another:—

"The difference," says Dr Smith, "between the earnings of a common labourer and those of a well-employed lawyer or physician is evidently much greater than that between the ordinary profits in any two different branches of trade. The apparent difference, besides, in the profits of different trades, is generally a deception arising from our not always distinguishing what ought to be considered as wages from what ought to be considered as profit.

"Apothecaries' profit is become a by-word, denoting something uncommonly extravagant. This great apparent profit, however, is frequently no more than the reasonable wages of labour. The skill of an apothecary is a much nicer and more delicate matter than that of any artificer whatever, and the trust which is reposed in him is of much greater importance. He is the physician of the poor in all cases, and of the rich when the distress or danger is not very great. His reward, therefore, ought to be suitable to his skill and his trust, and it arises generally from the price at which he sells his drugs. But the whole drugs which the best employed apothecary, in a large market-town, will sell in a year, may not perhaps cost him above thirty or forty pounds. Though he should sell them, therefore, for three or four hundred, or at a thousand per cent. profit, this may frequently be no more than the reasonable wages of his labour, charged, in the only way in which he can charge them, upon the price of his drugs. The greater part of the apparent profit is really wages disguised in the garb of profit.

"In a small seaport town, a little grocer will make forty or fifty per cent. upon a stock of a single hundred pounds, while a considerable wholesale merchant in the same place will scarce make eight or ten per cent. upon a stock of ten thousand. The trade of the grocer may be necessary for the conveniency of the inhabitants, and the narrowness of the market may not admit the employment of a larger capital in the business. The man, however, must not only live by his trade, but live by it suitably to the qualifications which it requires. Besides possessing a little capital, he must be able to read, write, and account, and must be a tolerable judge too of perhaps fifty or sixty different sorts of goods, their prices, qualities, and the markets where they are to be had cheapest. He must have all the knowledge, in short, that is necessary for a great merchant, which nothing hinders him from becoming but the want of a sufficient capital. Thirty or forty pounds a year cannot be considered as too great a recompense for the labour of a person so accomplished. Deduct this from the seemingly great profits of his capital, and little more will remain, perhaps, than the ordinary profits of stock. The greater part of the apparent profit is, in this case too, really wages."*

Of the five circumstances which Dr Smith describes so justly and with so much precision, as affecting wages, and as making up for a small pecuniary gain in some employments, and counterbalancing a great one in others, viz. "first, the agreeableness or disagreeableness of the employments themselves; secondly, the easiness or cheapness, or the difficulty and expense of learning them; thirdly, the constancy or inconstancy of employment in them; fourthly, the small or great trust which must be reposed in those who ex-

* Wealth of Nations, book i. chap. 10.

ercise them; and, fifthly, the probability or improbability of success in them,"*—*three* he acknowledges have no influence on the profits of stock, namely, the *second*, *third*, and *fourth*; but he sets it down that the two others (namely, the *first* and *fifth*) have.—He says:—

(First,) "Disagreeableness and disgrace affect the profits of stock in the same manner as the wages of labour. The keeper of an inn or tavern, who is never master of his own house, and who is exposed to the brutality of every drunkard, exercises neither a very agreeable nor a very creditable business. But there is scarce any common trade in which a small stock yields so great a profit."†

(Secondly,) "The profits of stock seem to be very little affected by the easiness or difficulty of learning the trade in which it is employed. All the different ways in which stock is commonly employed in great towns seem in reality to be almost equally easy to learn. One branch either of foreign or domestic trade cannot well be a more intricate business than another."‡

(Thirdly,) "The constancy or inconstancy of employment cannot affect the ordinary profits of stock in any particular trade. Whether the stock is or is not constantly employed depends not upon the trade but the trader."§

(Fourthly,) "When a person employs only his own stock in trade, there is no trust; and the credit which he may get from other people depends, not upon the nature of his trade, but upon their opinion of his fortune, probity, and prudence. The different rates of profit, therefore, in the different branches of trade, cannot arise from the different degrees of trust reposed in the trader."||

(Fifthly,) "In all the different employments of stock, the ordinary rate of profit varies more or less with the certainty or uncertainty of the returns. These are in general less uncer-

* Wealth of Nations, book i. chap. 10. † Ibid.
‡ Ibid. § Ibid. || Ibid.

tain in the inland than in the foreign trade, and in some branches of foreign trade than in others; in the trade to North America, for example, than in that to Jamaica. The ordinary rate of profit always rises more or less with the risk. It does not, however, seem to rise in proportion to it, or so as to compensate it completely. Bankruptcies are most frequent in the most hazardous trades. The most hazardous of all trades, that of a smuggler, though when the adventure succeeds it is likewise the most profitable, is the infallible road to bankruptcy. The presumptuous hope of success seems to act here as upon all other occasions, and to entice so many adventurers into those hazardous trades, that their competition reduces their profit below what is sufficient to compensate the risk. To compensate it completely, the common returns ought, over and above the ordinary profits of stock, not only to make up for all occasional losses, but to afford a surplus profit to the adventurers of the same nature with the profit of insurers. But if the common returns were sufficient for all this, bankruptcies would not be more frequent in these than in other trades.

"Of the five circumstances, therefore," concludes Dr Smith, "which vary the wages of labour, two only affect the profits of stock; the agreeableness and disagreeableness of the business, and the risk or security with which it is attended."*

Now, in the first place, with regard to the last-mentioned of these two circumstances, which are here represented as affecting the profits of stock in particular businesses, namely, the risk or security with which they are attended, it is undoubtedly true, that the gain, whether profit or wages, "rises more or less with the risk;" and whatever gain does arise, from this or any other cause, augments of course the whole gain; but why such accidental and uncertain gains should be set down to the account of *profit of stock* rather than to that of *wages of labour*, does not by any means so

---

* Wealth of Nations, book i. chap. 10.

clearly appear. In the making of gunpowder, for example, one of the most hazardous of businesses, there are two different sorts of risk which must be more or less compensated by the average returns, both of which it seems much more reasonable to consider as wages of labour than as profit of stock. There is the risk of pecuniary loss from explosions, and there is the risk of personal injury to which people engaged in this business are exposed. As to the recompense for the risk of personal injury, there can scarcely be room for any question as to the denomination of revenue to which it should be referred, the greater part always, and sometimes the whole of it, being in fact paid in the actual shape of wages to the workmen, who require something additional on account of this risk; and with regard to explosions, although they cannot perhaps be entirely prevented by any vigilance or by any precautions that can be taken, yet the frequency of their occurrence may probably be diminished by superior care and vigilance; and whatever is thus saved by the prevention of such accidents in this manner, seems the proper reward or wages of that sort of labour. In the case of the smuggler also, the success of whose enterprises depends so much upon his personal exertions and conduct, it seems much more reasonable to consider his extraordinary gains, " when the adventure succeeds," as the wages of his labour than as the profits of his stock.*

* Perhaps indeed the real truth may be, that such accidental and uncertain gains belong, properly speaking, neither to the one denomination of revenue nor the other, but constitute a sort distinct in itself and different from both; a sort of gain, however, which, as it depends on no fixed or known principles, but, like a lottery-prize, sometimes falls contingently to one and sometimes to another without any settled rule; so it can deserve or occupy no place in the science of the distribution of wealth. Or at least all that can be requisite in that science in regard to it, is simply to disentangle and disencumber

Again, with regard to the agreeableness or disagreeableness of the business as affecting the profits of stock, when, Dr Smith says,—"The keeper of an inn or tavern, who is never master of his own house, and who is exposed to the brutality of every drunkard, exercises neither a very agreeable nor a very creditable business," and when he adds,—"But there is scarce any common trade in which a small stock yields so great a profit," and thence infers that "disagreeableness and disgrace affect the profits of stock in the same manner as the wages of labour,"—does he not evidently confound the one description of revenue or gain with the other? For what is the superior gain which the innkeeper realizes upon his business but wages, or superior remuneration for his more discreditable or disagreeable labour? What is it but an instance of that very "deception arising from our not always distinguishing what ought to be considered as wages from what ought to be considered as profit,"

---

the subject, by dissevering those accidental and uncertain gains from the proper objects of our attention,—namely, rent, wages, and the profit of stock, legitimately so called. The ordinary and average gain in all businesses, professions, or employments, is in general little more than sufficient to maintain the persons engaged in them, according to the manner in which people of the particular condition are accustomed to live; although there are no doubt much greater variety in the modes of living among the higher classes of labourers than among the lower. The far greater part, however, of both the higher and lower, gain nothing more than a livelihood by their businesses; and it is commonly either by living more frugally than their neighbours, or by some accidental gain, that persons of this condition make any considerable accumulations. It no doubt happens sometimes that individuals are indebted for their wealth solely to their superior genius and industry,—as, for example, in the case of Arkwright, the inventor ot the cotton-spinning machinery; but large fortunes suddenly acquired are much more frequently the effects of accident and good fortune; and hence, no doubt, the name, *a fortune*, which is given to every large or remarkable acquisition of wealth.

of which Dr Smith takes especial notice soon afterwards in the same chapter, in continuing his treatment of the subject?*

The ground, therefore, it appears, is not by any means tenable which would distinguish the profit of stock from interest of money, or which would describe any thing as that profit but what is received for it by the capitalist in that character specifically, and without labour; that is, without the labour of personally applying it or superintending its application in business or production. Nor can any line be drawn between profit of stock and wages which shall be more defensible or preferable to another, but that which divides them at the point where interest commences.

And if this be granted, it must at once appear evident, that neither the agreeableness nor disagreeableness, nor the risk or security with which any business is attended, can have any influence on the profits of stock. For what is it to him who lends his capital how disagreeable or hazardous soever the business in which it is employed may be, provided he has sufficient security for its repayment? Let him who engages in such business look to that, and take care to have himself properly rewarded and indemnified both for the risk and hardship whatever it may be. He should certainly receive a higher premium to compensate the greater risk, and higher wages or remuneration for his more irksome or disagreeable labour in the more hazardous and disagreeable businesses; but why the ungalled capitalist should receive higher interest is by no means apparent. Nor is the nature of the case in the slightest degree different with regard to the person who superintends the employment of a capital of his own in such disagreeable and hazardous employment. He should have his risk and labour suitably compensated in

* See the passage quoted at large before, page 265, *et seq.*

the proper shape of wages and insurance against loss; but when this is accomplished, he cannot expect to receive more in his capacity of capitalist than he would do in the least disagreeable and least hazardous business.

Dr Smith has himself observed, that, "in point of agreeableness or disagreeableness, there is little or no difference in the far greater part of the different employments of stock, but a great deal in those of labour; and the ordinary profit of stock, though it rises with the risk, does not always seem to rise in proportion to it. It should follow from all this, that, in the same society or neighbourhood, the average and ordinary rates of profit in the different employments of stock should be more nearly upon a level than the pecuniary wages of the different sorts of labour. They are so accordingly."*

But the same author elsewhere says, "The profits of stock, it may perhaps be thought, are only a different name for the wages of a particular sort of labour, the labour of inspection and direction. They are, however, altogether different, are regulated by quite different principles, and bear no proportion to the quantity, the hardship, or the ingenuity of this supposed labour of inspection and direction. They are regulated altogether by the value of the stock employed, and are greater or smaller in proportion to the extent of this stock."†

Now this is true to a tittle of interest, but of interest only; of course it is true of profit of stock as identified with interest.

---

* Wealth of Nations, book i. chap. 10.

† Ibid. book i. chap. 6.

SECTION II.

OF THE CIRCUMSTANCES WHICH REGULATE AND DETERMINE THE ORDINARY AND AVERAGE, OR NATURAL, RATE OF PROFIT AT ANY PARTICULAR TIME AND PLACE.

THROUGHOUT the whole of our foregoing disquisitions in this work, it may have been observed, that invariably, whenever I have had occasion to speak of the profit of stock, I have always added the words, *or interest.*

This precaution I thought it proper to adopt, that I might not lead the reader into any mistake as to the exact nature of that particular species of revenue which is properly designated by the former term, before I came to the place where I was more fully to explain the reasons why I held it to be identical with that which is designated by the latter. Now, however, having done this, and shown, as I trust I have done, to the satisfaction of every one, that profit of stock is identical with interest of money, it will be unnecessary as well as inconvenient to continue the practice we have adopted and followed hitherto, in regard to this matter, any longer; and I shall therefore, in the present section, and henceforward, content myself with using the terms profit and interest singly, and either of them indifferently, declaring once for all, as I now do, that I use them upon all occasions (wherever I speak of the profit of stock technically,) uniformly and invariably in the same sense.

Having established this point, then, (I mean the identity of profit of stock with interest,) and having before shown*

* Chap. i. sect. 1. of this book.

that the rate of profit* must always be nearly equal in all the different employments of capital at the same time, and in the same place or neighbourhood, we come now to inquire into the circumstances which regulate that rate generally, or which cause it to be higher or lower at one period of time, or at one particular place or neighbourhood, than another.

Mr Hume, and after him Dr Smith, have long ago solved this question, and have shown, in the most unambiguous and satisfactory manner, that the rate of profit depends altogether on the abundance or scarcity of capital, at

---

* It is strictly correct to speak of the *rate* of profit, because it is always reckoned or estimated by the proportion, or *ratio*, which it bears to the stock or capital from which it arises; but it is questionable whether it be equally allowable to speak of the *rate* of wages or rent. Rent indeed may be reckoned by the proportion which it bears to the value of the subject it arises from expressed in money, and considered in this way may be correctly spoken of as a rate; but wages never can be considered as proportionally related to any given sum or value expressed in money,—not even in regard to the whole produce of land, labour, and capital; because they must always be viewed in reference to the natural or necessary wants of an individual or family. They must always be reckoned by the quantity and quality of necessaries, conveniences, and luxuries which they consist of, or which they can purchase or procure, and must be accounted high or low, not from the proportion which they bear to any given quantity (be it the whole or a part) of wealth existing, but as compared with the natural and necessary desires and wants of individuals and families of the human race.

Although, however, it may not be so perfectly correct to apply this word *rate* to either rent or wages as to profit, I shall not go the length to depart from a practice and phraseology which have been so generally used and followed by former writers, and which is sanctioned by the practice and example of Dr Smith, but shall content myself with offering the present explanation, which may, I hope, be sufficient to guard us from falling into any misconception or error in consequence of our giving in to this practice.

any particular time or place, in reference to the demand for it, or to the extent of the field in which it can be employed; and that consequently, after capital has accumulated to a certain extent, profit must decline as it accumulates still farther.

In opposition, however, to this plain and simple account of the matter, another doctrine has been set up by the Ricardo economists, and represented as one of their greatest and most profound discoveries, namely, that the rate of profit in general depends upon that realized in agricultural investments; and this again upon the quality or productiveness of the poorest land under cultivation at the particular time; or, in other words, it is pretended that the general rate of profit depends upon that realized on the capitals last added to the business of agriculture, and employed in producing the latest new additions to the general stock of raw products that have been required to provide for an increased population; and although this doctrine has been considered by many to be only a different way of considering the subject,—because, observe they, to say that profit would not decline if there were an unlimited extent of fertile land in the same country or neighbourhood, is exactly to say, in other words, that it would not decline if the field for its employment were unlimited;—yet I shall endeavour to show, that this new way of considering the subject is not only different from the old, but that it is false and incorrect also in itself.

I shall first endeavour to put the reader in possession of what appears to me to be the truth in this matter, and afterwards consider the objections made to it by the Ricardo economists, together with their new doctrine at the same time.

"The increase of stock," says Dr Smith, "which raises wages, tends to lower profit. When the stocks of many rich merchants are turned into the same trade, their mutual competition naturally tends to lower its profit; and when there is a like increase of stock in all the different trades carried on in the same society, the same competition must produce the same effect in them all."*

"It generally requires a greater stock," says he further, "to carry on any sort of trade in a great town than in a country village. The great stocks employed in every branch of trade, and the number of rich competitors, generally reduce the rate of profit in the former below what it is in the latter. But the wages of labour are generally higher in a great town than in a country village. In a thriving town the people who have great stocks to employ, frequently cannot get the number of workmen they want, and therefore bid against one another, in order to get as many as they can, which raises the wages of labour and lowers the profits of stock. In the remote parts of the country there is frequently not stock sufficient to employ all the people, who therefore bid against one another in order to get employment, which lowers the wages of labour and raises the profits of stock."†

In refuting the notion which was at one time prevalent, that the rate of interest depended on the plenty or scarcity of money, Mr Hume had previously written as follows:—

"High interest," he had said, "arises from *three* circumstances: a great demand for borrowing; little riches to supply that demand; and great profits arising from commerce: and the circumstances are a clear proof of the small advance of commerce and industry, not of the scarcity of gold and silver. Low interest, on the other hand, proceeds from the three opposite circumstances: a small demand for borrowing; great riches to supply that demand; and small profits arising from commerce: and these circumstances are all connected together, and proceed from the increase of industry and commerce, not of gold and silver."‡

---

* Wealth of Nations, book i. chap. 9. † Ibid.

‡ Essays, part ii. essay 4.

And again in the same essay,—"Low interest and low profits of merchandise," Mr Hume had further observed, "are two events which naturally forward each other, and are both originally derived from that extensive commerce which produces opulent merchants, and renders the monied interest considerable. Where merchants possess great stocks, whether represented by few or many pieces of metal, it must frequently happen, that, when they either become tired of business, or leave heirs unwilling or unfit to engage in commerce, a great proportion of these riches naturally seeks an annual and secure revenue. The plenty diminishes the price, and makes the lenders accept of a low interest. This consideration obliges many to keep their stock employed in trade, and rather be content with low profits than dispose of their money at an undervalue. On the other hand, when commerce has become extensive, and employs large stocks, there must arise rivalships among the merchants, which diminish the profits of trade, at the same time that they increase the trade itself. The low profits of merchandise induce the merchants to accept more willingly of a low interest, when they leave off business, and begin to indulge themselves in ease and indolence. It is needless, therefore, to inquire which of these circumstances, to wit, *low interest* or *low profits,* is the cause and which the effect? They both arise from an extensive commerce, and mutually forward each other. No man will accept of low profits where he can have high interest; and no man will accept of low interest where he can have high profits. An extensive commerce, by producing large stocks, diminishes both interest and profits; and is always assisted in its diminution of the one by the proportional sinking of the other. I may add, that, as low profits arise from the increase of commerce and industry, they serve in their turn to its farther increase, by rendering the commodities cheaper, encouraging the consumption, and heightening the industry. And thus, if we consider the whole connexion of causes and effects, interest is the barometer of the state, and its lowness is a sign almost infallible of the flourishing condition of a people. It proves the increase of industry, and its prompt circulation through the whole state, little inferior to a demonstration. And though, perhaps, it may not be impossible but a sudden and a great check to commerce may have a momentary effect of the same kind, by throwing so many stocks out of trade, it must be attended with such misery and want of employment to the poor, that, besides its short duration, it will not be possible to mistake the one case for the other."*

Nothing, it should seem, could well be more obvious or more pregnant with the evidence of its own truth, than this plain account of the causes which force down the rate of profit as capital increases; nor can any theory be based on a more ample foundation of fact and experience, or harmonize more completely or more uniformly with all the phenomena observable in the variations of interest. And now that we have ascertained (as I trust we have done beyond the possibility of doubt or controversy) what the profit of stock really is, and freed that part of the question from all the confusion and uncertainty in which it lay previously involved, this old, and sound, and obvious theory must stand out to view with even more than its original distinctness, and appear clothed with even more than its original evidence.

The Ricardo economists, however, would fain aspire to say, "We have changed all that;" and they affect to think, and assume, that they give a different and a more distinct reason for the fall of profit, which ultimately takes place in the progress of society, when they say it is occasioned by the necessity of having recourse to the "poorer soils" in order to procure the additional supplies of food or raw products required to provide for an increased population. Let us hearken to their arguments:—

"Dr Smith," says a writer of this school "was of opinion,

* Essays, part 2, essay 4.

that the rate of profit varied inversely as the amount of capital, or, in other words, that it was always greatest when capital was least abundant. He supposed, that, according as capital increased, the principle of competition would stimulate capitalists to encroach on the employments of each other; and that, in furtherance of their object, they would be tempted to offer their goods at a lower price, and to give higher wages to their workmen. (*Wealth of Nations,* II. p. 38.) This theory was long universally assented to. It has been espoused by MM. Say, Sismondi, and Storch, by the Marquis Garnier, and, with some modifications, by Mr Malthus. But, notwithstanding the deference due to these authorities, we think it will not be difficult to show, that the principle of competition could never be productive of a general fall of profits. Competition will prevent any single individual from obtaining a higher rate of profit than his neighbours; but, most certainly, competition does not diminish the average *productiveness of industry,* or the average return of capital and labour, which must always determine the rate of profit. The fall of profits, which invariably takes place as society advances, and population becomes denser, is not owing to competition, but to a very different cause—*to* A DIMINUTION OF THE POWER TO EMPLOY CAPITAL WITH ADVANTAGE, *resulting either from a decrease in the fertility of the soils which must be taken into cultivation in the progress of society,—from a more rapid increase of capital than of population,—or from an increase of taxation.*"*

Now, this doctrine so ostentatiously put forward as a new and great discovery, as far as there is any truth in it, is no other than Dr Smith's; and the important concluding sentence, emblazoned in italics and capitals (which are, of course, the reviewer's), is but a different way of considering or stating the question; it is the very same doctrine only put in a different form. For if there be "a diminution of the power to employ capital with advantage," in conse-

* Edinburgh Review, No 79, pp. 9, 10. March, 1824.

quence of there being no more fertile soils to cultivate,* in any country, or place, or neighbourhood, is not this because capital has grown *so large* as to have overrun those soils in that particular country, or place, or neighbourhood? Is it not because of *the growth* and present amount of capital? Is it not plain, that, under the circumstances described, and according to the Ricardo economists their own showing, capital has outgrown the field for its employment *at the old rate of profit*; or, in other words, has outgrown the amount which can be employed with the same *proportional advantage* as before upon the fertile soils? And I will affirm, that capital must increase *first*, BEFORE the less fertile soils can be cultivated, and consequently before profit is reduced. Capital, in short, must outgrow *the demand for it at the old rate of profit*, BEFORE it can be applied to the less advantageous employment, and consequently before the rate of profit can be reduced. It is the growth of capital, therefore, which forces down the rate of profit. Profit is not low because the poorer lands are cultivated, but the poorer lands are cultivated because profit is low. The mistake is the very common one, that the effect is taken for the cause.

It is said in the passage above cited (and the observation is no less than three times repeated in it), that "the principle of competition could never be productive of a general fall of profits;" as if, when commerce comes to be very much extended, and all trades and employments glutted with capital, the law of competition, or, in other words, the private interests of individuals inclined to accumulate, would not induce them to lower the rate of profit in order to ex-

* This is what must be meant by "a *decrease* in the fertility of the soils," &c.; for under good husbandry, or where improvement and the extension of cultivation are going on, *the same soils* do not usually decrease, but, on the contrary, rather improve in fertility.

tend their trade and find employment for their new accumulations, rather than consume them or allow them to remain unemployed altogether.

But it is not affirmed that the principle of competition is the "productive" cause. It is the increase or amount of capital, when it comes to be great as compared with the field for its employment, which is maintained to be so. The principle of competition, however, may be allowed perhaps to be the *instrumental* cause in the process of reduction; for it is that principle which must be the means of forcing down the rate upon either hypothesis,—Whether the "productive" cause arises from the comparative abundance of capital, or from the necessity of having recourse to the cultivation of the inferior soils; and certain it is, it is the comparative abundance of capital which can alone enable us to have that recourse.

After the increase of capital in a wealthy and populous neighbourhood, beyond what can be employed with the same proportional advantage as before, either in agriculture or in any other of the old channels of trade, the principle of competition (or of self-interest, as explained in the first chapter of this book) comes into operation, and forces down the rate of profit, in consequence of the holders of the newly-acquired additions of capital being willing to accept a lower rate of profit rather than allow them to be unemployed altogether. They can only force their capitals into employment either by lending at a lower rate of interest, or by trading themselves on lower profits than before, and thereby extending the trade and the market so as to make room for the additional stocks, until, by repeated operations of this sort, and the continued increase of capital, interest comes to be reduced so low, that nobody will think it worth while to accept of, or to save for a lower rate.

Should it be said, that there would be no fall in the rate of profit if there were plenty of fertile land on which this constant accumulation and increase of capital might flow out and be employed, I answer, that there could and would, because such lands (or any lands) *must extend to a distance*, and because people will often prefer employing their capital at a lower rate under their own superintendence, or in their own immediate neighbourhood, to lending or employing it at a distance. It is to be recollected, that *there cannot be* plenty of fertile land *without extent*, or plenty existing in the same spot,—a million of acres, for example, within a mile square! An addition of new and fertile land cannot be conjured up in the midst of a crowded city, or in a populous vicinity where the whole is already occupied. But should a farmer in the neighbourhood of such a city, or a trader within it, save and accumulate an additional capital, and choose rather to employ it at home where he dwells, and in a business which he knows, though at a considerably lower rate of profit than he had obtained on his old stock, —should he choose this, I say, rather than look abroad for a more profitable investment, or than go perhaps a hundred or even twenty miles in quest of fertile lands,—Whether, I ask, would it be more correct or more reasonable to say, that it was the increase of capital which forced him to lower his profit, or that it was the non-existence of fertile land (by the cultivation of which he might realize a greater) which forced him to do so? Abundance of untouched fertile land does actually exist in the world; and it would be rather a curious reason to assign for the fall of profit, were we to say it was occasioned by the circumstance, that a thousand millions of acres could not be contained within an area that was but barely large enough to contain one million.

The Ricardo economists, too, advance this profound doctrine, that *more profit can be made by cultivating rich than poor land*, as a new and great discovery; whereas the merit of this discovery, whatever it may amount to, belongs plainly to the author of the following passage :—

"In our North American and West Indian colonies," says Dr Smith, "not only the wages of labour, but the interest of money, and consequently the profits of stock, are higher than in England. In the different colonies both the legal and the market rate of interest runs from six to eight per cent. High wages of labour and high profits of stock, however, are things perhaps which scarce ever go together, except in the peculiar circumstances of new colonies. A new colony must always for some time be more understocked in proportion to the extent of its territory, and more underpeopled in proportion to the extent of its stock, than the greater part of other countries. They have more land than they have stock to cultivate. What they have, therefore, is applied to the cultivation only of what is most fertile and most favourably situated, the land near the seashore, and along the banks of navigable rivers. Such land too is frequently purchased at a price below the value even of its natural produce. Stock employed in the purchase and improvement of such lands must yield a very large profit, and consequently afford to pay a very large interest. Its rapid accumulation in so profitable an employment enables the planter to increase the number of his hands faster than he can find them in a new settlement. Those whom he can find, therefore, are very liberally rewarded. As the colony increases, the profits of stock gradually diminish. When the most fertile and best situated lands have been all occupied, less profit can be made by the cultivation of what is inferior both in soil and situation, and less interest can be afforded for the stock which is so employed. In the greater part of our colonies, accordingly, both the legal and the market rate of interest has been considerably reduced during the course of the present century. As riches, improvement, and population have increased, interest has declined. The wages of labour do not sink with the profits of stock. The demand for labour increases with the increase of stock, whatever be its profits; and after these are diminished, stock may not only continue to increase, but to increase much faster than before. It is with industrious nations, who are advancing in the acquisition of riches, as with industrious individuals. A great stock, though with small profits, generally increases faster than a small stock with great profits."*

There can be little doubt, I think, that it was this passage which suggested to Mr Ricardo his recondite theory as to the cause of the fall of profit. That it was plainly calculated to do so no person can deny; and yet we have lived to see the obvious doctrine which was thus stated half a century ago (and stated as fully as its importance seems to demand) represented as one of the greatest discoveries of the present day.

In observing, as we see he has done, in the above passage, that "when the most fertile and best situated lands have been all occupied, less profit can be made by the cultivation of what is inferior both in soil and situation, and less interest can be afforded for the stock which is so employed," Dr Smith was stating a certain and obvious fact; but it was equally obvious (and no doubt appeared so to his sagacious mind), that, in the case of the colonies to which he alluded, as in every other similar case, the increase of capital must have *preceded* the cultivation of the poorer lands and the fall of profit, and must have been the cause of the capitalists consenting, or being constrained to accept such a lower rate of profit as could be afforded from the poorer lands. Such fact, therefore, was perfectly consistent with, and was indeed a part of the theory he maintained and had adopted from Mr Hume; and it did not probably appear to him, therefore, that it would be any improvement to say, that the cultivation of the poorer soils was the cause of the fall of profit or of the superabundance of capital. It appeared to him no doubt a much more natural and more just ac-

* Wealth of Nations, book i. chap. 9.

count of the matter to ascribe the cultivation of the poorer soils and the fall of profit to the growth and superabundance of capital.

The Ricardo economists have the hardihood to affirm (as it is seen in the passage before cited), that "Dr Smith was of opinion that profit varies as the amount of capital;" than which there cannot be a more gross and unpardonable misrepresentation. What Dr Smith really taught was this, that where population and wealth have already increased to a certain extent, within a limited territory, the rate of profit must fall as it increases still farther. Let his words be attended to:—"As the quantity of stock," he says, "to be lent at interest increases, the interest, or the price which must be paid for the use of that stock, necessarily diminishes, not only from those general causes which make the market-price of things commonly diminish as their quantity increases, but from other causes which are peculiar to this particular case. As capitals increase *in any country*, the profits which can be made by employing them necessarily diminish. It becomes gradually more and more difficult to find *within the country* a profitable method of employing any new capital. There arises in consequence a competition between different capitals, the owner of one endeavouring to get possession of that employment which is occupied by another. But upon most occasions he can hope to justle that other out of this employment by no other means but by dealing upon more reasonable terms. He must not only sell what he deals in somewhat cheaper, but, in order to get it to sell, he must sometimes too buy it dearer. The demand for productive labour, by the increase of the funds which are destined for maintaining it, grows every day greater and greater. Labourers easily find employment, but the owners of capitals find it difficult to get labourers to employ. Their competition raises the wages of labour, and sinks the profits of stock. But when the profits which can be made by the use of a capital are in this manner diminished, as it were, at both ends, the price which can be paid for the use of it, that is, the rate of interest, must necessarily be diminished with them."*

Now, in this passage there is express reference made to a limited extent of territory,—*in any country*, it is said; and again it is repeated, *within a country*; and there is also a manifest though general reference to a country which has already advanced considerably in population and wealth. There is nothing here at all like the unqualified assertion, that profit varies inversely as the amount of capital; for this would imply that in any country, no matter how differently it might be situated from another,—although, for example, the one might be of small extent, thickly-peopled, and arrived at the commercial state, while the other was of comparatively much larger extent, thinly-peopled, and had not passed the purely agricultural,—the rate of interest must be the same in both, provided the total amount of capital in each were the same. It would imply, in short, that the rate of profit in every country must be exactly proportioned to the amount of capital within it, without regard to any other circumstance; whereas Dr Smith's doctrine plainly is, that the rate of profit will be proportioned, not to the absolute, but to the relative amount of capital it possesses, —to the amount of capital, namely, as compared with the extent of the field for its employment; and it is perfectly consistent with this doctrine, that profit should be as high in a country possessing a thousand millions of capital as in one that possessed but a single million, provided its trade and territory, or the field for the employment of its capital, were proportionally extended.

On the following observation of Dr Smith, however,— "As the capital of a private man, though acquired by a

* Wealth of Nations, book ii. chap. 4.

particular trade, may increase beyond what he can employ in it, and yet that trade continue to increase too, so may likewise the capital of a great nation,"*—it has been remarked, by way of answer, that "a great nation can always find employment for the capital it accumulates."† Now the contrary to that which is here affirmed is neither directly maintained nor incidentally implied in the foregoing passage, or any where else, in the writings of Dr Smith; and this scholion, therefore, seems unnecessary and uncalled for. It is true, that a great nation can always find employment for the capital it *actually* accumulates, but then it must be, after a certain amount of accumulation, always at a lower rate of profit; and when the rate is reduced very low, the people having no longer any adequate motive, will cease at last to accumulate altogether; or they will at least accumulate no farther than may be necessary to keep up the existing capital, or to supply the waste, and fill up the voids and breaches occasionally made in that great instrument of production by incidental losses or prodigal consumption. It is true, therefore, that a great nation can always find employment for the capital it accumulates, because it accumulates no more than it can employ.

To proceed:—"In a country," says Dr Smith, "which had acquired that full complement of riches which the nature of its soil and climate, and its situation with regard to other countries, allowed it to acquire, which could therefore advance no farther, and which was not going backwards,"‡ the profit of stock would be very low. "In a country fully stocked," the same author adds, "in proportion to all the business it had to transact, as great a quantity of stock would be employed in every particular branch as the

* Wealth of Nations, book i. chap. 9.
† Idem, Buchanan's edition, vol. i. p. 150, notes.
‡ Wealth of Nations, book i. chap. 9.

nature and extent of the trade would admit. The competition, therefore, would everywhere be as great, and consequently the ordinary profit as low as possible.

"But perhaps no country has ever yet arrived at this degree of opulence. China seems to have been long stationary, and had probably long ago acquired that full complement of riches which is consistent with the nature of its laws and institutions. But this complement may be much inferior to what, with other laws and institutions, the nature of its soil, climate, and situation might admit of. A country which neglects or despises foreign commerce, and which admits the vessels of foreign nations into one or two of its ports only, cannot transact the same quantity of business which it might do with different laws and institutions. In a country, too, where, though the rich or the owners of large capitals enjoy a good deal of security, the poor or the owners of small capitals enjoy scarce any, but are liable, under the pretence of justice, to be pillaged and plundered at any time by the inferior mandarins, the quantity of stock employed in all the different branches of business transacted within it can never be equal to what the nature and extent of that business might admit. In every different branch, the oppression of the poor must establish the monopoly of the rich, who, by engrossing the whole trade to themselves, will be able to make very large profits. Twelve per cent. accordingly is said to be the common interest of money in China, and the ordinary profits of stock must be sufficient to afford this large interest."*

But Mr Buchanan again takes exception to this reasoning, and among other criticisms upon it he hazards the following:—"A country never acquires the full complement of riches here spoken of, and its acquisition of capital is totally independent either of its soil, climate, or of local situation."†

---

* Wealth of Nations, book i. chap. 9.

† Ibid. in notes, Buchanan's edition.

To the doctrine contained in the latter part of this sentence, it may perhaps be thought a sufficient answer to repeat the following words of Mr Hume:—"Every wise, just, and mild government, by rendering the condition of its subjects easy and secure, will always abound most in people as well as in commodities and riches. A country, indeed, whose climate and soil are fitted for vines will naturally be more populous than one which produces corn only, and that more populous than one which is only fitted for pasturage. In general, warm climates, as the necessities of the inhabitants are there fewer and vegetation more powerful, are likely to be most populous; but if every thing else be equal, it seems natural to expect that, wherever there are most happiness and virtue, and the wisest institutions, there will also be most people."* I may add, there will also be most riches.

With regard to the other assertion contained in the above-cited criticism, Mr Buchanan says, that a country never acquires that full complement of riches spoken of by Dr Smith, namely, that full complement of riches "*which is consistent with the nature of its laws and institutions*," and with "*the nature of its soil, climate, and situation, with respect to other countries.*" How then, I ask, does it come to pass that a nation becomes stationary? How is it that it comes to go backwards? Why has China continued stationary, as far as can be ascertained, for more than two thousand years? or why does not Egypt, Palestine, and the ancient Asia, why does not Greece and Persia, or the still more ancient empires of Babylon and Assyria, contain the population and the wealth which they possessed when at the height of their prosperity and glory in other days? That the names of these renowned empires should alone survive, that they themselves should exist no more, except as a *sound* merely in the ears of a distant posterity in an-

* Essays, part 2, essay 11.

other part of the world, is too certain and too cogent an answer to this criticism.

I shall but just ask one other question,—Will Mr Buchanan contend that a country can attain to as great wealth under bad laws and institutions, and with a bad soil, climate, and situation, as under the contrary in all these respects? If he would, I shall beg leave to refer him to the last chapter of the first book of this Inquiry, and desire him to answer, not my arguments, but the arguments he will there find collected from Mr Hume, Dr Smith, and Mr Malthus.

It is true indeed, as was before explained,* that a country *under good government* can never, strictly speaking, become absolutely stationary, but must continue necessarily, from the principles of human nature, to improve and increase indefinitely both in wealth and population; but then we must remember the mode and nature of that increase which must come at last, as was shown, to be so very slow, as to be almost, if not altogether, insensible. And this should, I think, be sufficient to vindicate Dr Smith in the language he has used; for I believe it will not be disputed, that such an indefinitely small increase as is here admitted to be possible, even in the last and highest stage of national improvement, should not hinder but that we may speak in a loose and general way, and in order to illustrate a particular subject, which was Dr Smith's intention, of a country advanced to that point, as having acquired its full complement of riches, in comparison with others which are still at a great distance from it, and which consequently still retain the capability of improving and increasing very largely and rapidly both in wealth and population.

To return:—There is just one observation more I would wish to make, before concluding, upon this new theory of

---

* See book i. chap. 10, sect. 4, and book ii. chap. 5.

the causes which force down the rate of profit. No theory, I will venture to affirm, was ever conceived or constructed in a spirit of such utter contempt and defiance of experience and fact. A slight retrospective glance at the *history* of interest for the last hundred years will render this apparent. During that period we have been uniformly increasing our population and extending our agriculture, but we have not observed any thing like a concomitant sinking of interest. On the contrary, we have seen, that uniformly, during the continuance of peace, and when capital was accumulating, interest gradually sunk, and as uniformly during war it again rose, in consequence of the expenditure and diminution of capital. In 1812, for example, interest was as high as five per cent.; whereas in 1732, when our population was less by several millions, and when our agriculture was consequently much less extended over the poorer soils, interest was as low as three per cent.

In denying, therefore, the effects of the accumulation of capital, and referring exclusively to its productiveness as applied to and extended over the land, the Ricardo economists have endeavoured to establish a distinction without a difference, and to substitute a theory which is not only obscure and far-fetched, but really inapplicable to things as they are, for one which is simple and obvious, and which agrees in every particular with the phenomena to be accounted for.

CHAPTER VII.

OF THE RENT OF LAND.

SECTION I.

RENT DEFINED.

The rent of land is that portion (or the price or value of that portion) of the produce raised from it, which is over and above what is required to pay the *wages* and *interest* of as much *labour* and *capital* as is necessary to cultivate it, to replace the capital employed, and to draw the returns in its actual condition and circumstances.*

Rent, as the term is commonly used, means the price, whatever that may be, which is agreed upon between landlord and tenant, to be paid annually by the latter to the former for the use of his land in its actual condition and circumstances; but as the principle of competition causes this price (which is the actual rent) either perfectly to coincide with or very nearly to approximate the precise portion of produce indicated by the definition just given, it is that portion, or the price or value of that portion, which is to be considered as the natural rent of land, or which is to be esteemed rent by the landlord who farms his own land.

"Rent," therefore, as Dr Smith has observed, "considered as the price paid for the use of land, is naturally the highest which the tenant can afford to pay in the actual circumstances of the land. In adjusting the terms of the lease, the landlord

---

* Including, of course, situation or local position under these terms.

endeavours to leave him no greater share of the produce than what is sufficient to keep up the stock from which he furnishes the seed, pays the labour, and purchases and maintains the cattle, and other instruments of husbandry, together with the ordinary profits of farming-stock in the neighbourhood. This is evidently the smallest share with which the tenant can content himself, without being a loser, and the landlord seldom means to leave him any more. Whatever part of the produce, or, what is the same thing, whatever part of its price, is over and above this share, he naturally endeavours to reserve to himself as the rent of his land, which is evidently the highest the tenant can afford to pay in the actual circumstances of the land. Sometimes, indeed, the liberality, more frequently the ignorance of the landlord, makes him accept of somewhat less than this portion; and sometimes too, though more rarely, the ignorance of the tenant makes him undertake to pay somewhat more, or to content himself with somewhat less, than the ordinary profits of farming-stock in the neighbourhood. This portion, however, may still be considered as the natural rent of land, or the rent for which it is naturally meant that land should for the most part be let."*

Mr Ricardo is, however, not satisfied with this statement, or with the definition comprised in it, and he therefore advances and endeavours to establish another in its stead, as follows:—"Rent," he says, "is that portion of the produce of the earth which is paid to the landlord for the use of the original and indestructible powers of the soil."†

Nothing can be more futile and absurd than this definition, or more vain and useless than the attempt to distinguish what is paid for the land independent of any clearing, draining, or any other improvements or meliorations made upon it by human labour and capital, from what is paid on

* Wealth of Nations, book i. chap. 11.

† Principles of Political Economy, chap. 2.

the distinct consideration of such improvements, or for the land as it actually is in its improved state. For what is it, I should like to be informed, that Mr Ricardo means by "the original and indestructible powers of the soil?"—Or how much rent is ever paid for these powers where they have not been in any degree improved, or where no labour or capital has ever been bestowed on the land which claims them?—A field, we shall suppose, is cleared of wood, enclosed, drained, and by a few years' judicious cropping, is brought to a high degree of fertility, and lets accordingly for a proportionably high rent. What, I should beg leave to inquire, is to be considered as the rent of this land according to Mr Ricardo's definition?—Or what part of its present fertility is to be ascribed to its "original and indestructible powers," and what to the factitious improvements made upon it?—The improvements made upon this field (or upon any other field or farm, or upon the whole land of the country) are none of them "indestructible." By neglect alone they will most of them go to decay and ruin, and the land will fall back to its antecedent waste and unprofitable state.

The best of it, however, is, that even if the most correct answers could be given to the questions just put, it would be of no earthly use in the adjustment of this matter. Suppose it were possible to distinguish and exactly to ascertain what part of the value and fertility of the land were owing to its "original and indestructible powers," and what to those that have been added to it by the art and industry of man, it would not be of the smallest advantage or utility in the settlement of this question. And why?—Because, when capital is once sunk upon the land, and rendered inseparable from it, it is identified with the land, and the revenue arising from it becomes subject to all the laws which influence or regulate rent, and it is therefore as properly rent as any other portion of the revenue of land.

One reason why, in treating of the distribution of wealth, it is necessary to distinguish land from other sorts of capital, and rent from profit, is because they are subject to quite different laws in regard to variations in their values, laws which impel those variations in a directly contrary direction in the progress of society,—the value of land and the amount of rent being found uniformly to increase in consequence of the increase of population and wealth; whereas under the same circumstances, and after a certain progress has been made, the value of capital and the amount or rate of profit is found as uniformly to decrease.

When, therefore, capital is sunk upon the land in such a manner as that it cannot be removed from it, it is then perfectly identified with the land, and the revenue arising from it is properly rent, as partaking of the same nature, and being subject to precisely the same laws and vicissitudes with rent. But the capital which is employed in the ordinary cultivation of the land, and which can be removed from it either annually or in the course of a few years' rotation of crops, retains all the character of ordinary mercantile capital, and its revenue is profit.*

---

* From the following note, inserted at the end of his chapter on "Poor-Rates," it plainly appears that Mr Ricardo had himself discovered the faultiness of his definition of rent at that period of his work. "In a former part of this work," Mr Ricardo here says, "I have noticed the difference between rent, properly so called, and the remuneration paid to the landlord under that name, for the advantages which the expenditure of his capital has procured to his tenant; but I did not perhaps sufficiently distinguish the difference which would arise from the different modes in which this capital might be applied. As a part of this capital, when once expended in the improvement of a farm, is inseparably amalgamated with the land, and tends to increase its productive powers, the remuneration paid to the landlord for its use is strictly of the nature of rent, and is subject to all the laws of rent. Whether the improvement be made at the expense of the landlord or the tenant, it will not be undertaken in the first in-

And, in like manner, a capital reserved in money,—as, for example, a mortgage over an estate—produces interest; but a capital invested absolutely in land produces rent; as may be seen when the mortgagee has foreclosed, and the estate is given up to him; his revenue is then converted into rent, and becomes subject to all the laws and accidents which regulate and influence the value of the land and the amount of its revenue.

I conclude this section then with affirming, as I think I may be fully warranted to do, that rent is the price paid, *not* merely "for the use of the original and indestructible powers of the soil," but for the use of the land as it is, in its actual condition and circumstances.

---

stance, unless there is a strong probability that the return will at least be equal to the profit that can be made by the disposition of any other equal capital; but when once made, the return obtained will ever after be wholly of the nature of rent, and will be subject to all the variations of rent. Some of these expenses, however, only give advantages to the land for a limited period, and do not add permanently to its productive powers; being bestowed on buildings, and other perishable improvements, they require to be constantly renewed, and therefore do not obtain for the landlord any permanent addition to his real rent."—*Principles of Pol. Econ. p.* 326; *second edition.*

Here we see that Mr Ricardo had, at the advanced part of his work, where we find the above note, *studied himself fairly out of his theory;* but why then did he not return back and cancel what he found to be erroneous and insufficient? The concessions made in this note constitute a complete renunciation *in substance* of the definition of rent he had previously given. As, however, that renunciation was not made in express terms, and as the definition itself continues still to be adhered to by Mr Ricardo's followers, even in the face of the above renunciation, it was necessary to expose its fallacy and insufficiency somewhat more at large than had previously been done, and at the same time to vindicate the soundness of Dr Smith's definition, both of which objects have, I trust, been sufficiently accomplished in the present section.

SECTION II.

OF THE CIRCUMSTANCES WHICH REGULATE THE AMOUNT OF RENT AT ANY PARTICULAR TIME OR PLACE.

WE come now to inquire into the circumstances which regulate the amount of rent at any particular time or place, or which cause it to be higher or lower at any one time or in any one place than another.

And here, in approaching this question, it is most obvious to remark, (though the circumstance has been the least noticed or attended to of any,) that the highness or lowness of the rent of any portion of land will depend chiefly on the populousness or otherwise of the place, country, or neighbourhood, where it is situated; that is to say, the rent of land will be high where it is thickly-peopled, and low where it is thinly-peopled, and the contrary.

The riches or poverty of the population, and the fertility or barrenness of the land, are also circumstances which add necessarily to the highness or lowness of rent.

High rent is owing therefore to three circumstances:—(1.) To the populousness of the neighbourhood where it is situated; (2.) To the riches and industry of the population; and (3.) To the natural fertility of the land itself. Low rent, again, is owing to the three opposite circumstances,—namely, (1.) To the smallness of the number of inhabitants in proportion to the extent of ground they occupy; (2.) To their poverty; and (3.) To the comparative barrenness of the land itself.

"The rent of land," says Dr Smith, "not only varies with its fertility, whatever be its produce, but with its situation, whatever be its fertility. Land in the neighbourhood of a town gives a greater rent than land equally fertile in a distant part of the country. Though it may cost no more labour to cultivate the one than the other, it must always cost more to bring the produce of the distant land to market. A greater quantity of labour, therefore, must be maintained out of it; and the surplus, from which are drawn both the profit of the farmer and the rent of the landlord, must be diminished. But in remote parts of the country the rate of profits, as has already been shown, is generally higher than in the neighbourhood of a large town. A smaller proportion of this diminished surplus, therefore, must belong to the landlord."*

Local position therefore, in regard to nearness to or distance from the towns or masses of the population, is a circumstance of the very first consideration in the question of rent; insomuch that a piece of land perfectly barren,—even a bare rock in the centre of those masses,—will give a high rent, whilst the most fertile field, if removed very far from them, will give none at all.

And yet the rent of land has been described by the Ricardo economists as depending *entirely* on the *difference* of its qualities, or fertility, in different fields or parts, to the exclusion of every other consideration. But if this were so, why is it that the rent of land of the same quality is higher in the neighbourhood of London, and Manchester, and Edinburgh, and Glasgow, and the other great towns of England and Scotland, than it is at a distance from them? —Or why is the rent of land of the same, or even of inferior quality, higher in Great Britain than in America, and in America than in New Holland or Van Diemen's Land?—Nevertheless the Ricardo economists must have a new and great discovery, and a theory quite simple, whether dame Nature will or no.

In the discussion of this question indeed some slight notice is commonly taken, and some transient reference made, even by the Ricardo economists, to local position as affecting rent; but the consideration is only stated to be at once

* Wealth of Nations, book i. chap. 11.

thrown aside and neglected; every thing being immediately and constantly afterwards ascribed to difference of fertility exclusively.

Thus, in his chapter on rent, Mr Ricardo takes a slight notice in the outset of the former circumstance; but he immediately dismisses from his thoughts all farther consideration of it, and leaves it wholly behind him, dwelling constantly afterwards on the latter circumstance, and ascribing to it exclusively the entire influence in regulating rent throughout his whole subsequent reasonings.

In the chapter just mentioned, Mr Ricardo observes, "If all land had the same properties, if it were boundless in quantity and uniform in quality, no charge could be made for its use, unless where it possessed peculiar advantages of situation. It is only, then, because land is not boundless in quantity and uniform in quality, and because, in the progress of population, land of an inferior quality, or less advantageously situated, is called into cultivation, that rent is ever paid for the use of it."*

Here we have the effect of local situation acknowledged for once plainly and distinctly enough. But this is all that is ever done by Mr Ricardo;—he here stops short at once, and, dismissing the consideration for ever from his thoughts, proceeds immediately on the instant, and in the very next succeeding sentence, as if no such acknowledgment had ever escaped his lips!—"When in the progress of society," he immediately continues, "land of the second degree of fertility is taken into cultivation, rent immediately commences on that of the first quality, and *the amount of that rent will depend on the difference in the quality of these two portions of land.*"†

Here we observe the consideration of local position dismissed at once with contempt, and find ourselves called upon

---

* Principles of Political Economy, chap. 2. † Ibid.

immediately and barefacedly to assent to a proposition which is not only essentially and entirely different from that which went before it, but which is absolutely irreconcileable and inconsistent with it. The proposition we are now called upon to assent to is, that "the amount of that rent will depend on the difference of the quality of these two portions of land!"—and not consequently in any degree on the advantages or disadvantages of situation which had been acknowledged the very moment before!—And so absolutely and entirely do Mr Ricardo and his followers exclude the consideration of situation from their system and theory of rent, that they proceed to *number* the different soils or qualities of land, as 1, 2, 3, 4, 5, &c.,—*with reference to fertility alone*, as intending thereby to indicate the exact difference in the amount of their rents.*

Perhaps the Ricardo economists may think to excuse themselves by saying that they name a part for the whole, (a mode of speech neither unusual nor unallowable in many instances,) and that under the terms fertility or barrenness they mean to include also the advantages and disadvantages of situation, and every thing else which can facilitate or obstruct the improvement of agriculture, as well as access to markets. But, not to mention the absurdity of classing so many different, discordant, and heterogeneous particulars under one appellation,† and to overlook also the endless

* To those readers who would wish to see the Ricardo theory of rent examined more narrowly than I have here thought it necessary to do, I should recommend the perusal of two very able pamphlets on the subject by Mr T. Perronet Thompson of Queen's College, Cambridge; one entitled, "The True Theory of Rent, in Opposition to Mr Ricardo and Others," and the other, "A Catechism on the Corn Laws;" wherein they will find the "fallacies" of the Ricardo theory followed out and exposed in all their details, besides other matters worthy their attention.

† It may perhaps be imagined that the Ricardo economists have a

train of ambiguity and of error which such a lax use of terms must necessarily draw after it; even this poor apology will not serve their purpose; for they uniformly urge their doctrine in its literal construction, and even sometimes carry it so far as to maintain, that if all the land were of one quality, and boundless in quantity, no such thing as rent could ever have been known or heard of, however great its fertility might have been.

Now, in contradiction to this insulting and reckless doctrine, it may be positively affirmed,—and a very slight effort of attention will be sufficient to enable us to perceive clearly the truth,—that if all the land in the world were of one quality, and formed one continuous and uninterrupted continent, still rent would arise as soon as the first rude arts of life began to be invented, and the division of labour to take place, provided the quality of the land were only such that it would afford rent at all; that is, provided it were sufficiently fertile to afford sustenance to more persons than those actually employed in its cultivation. This, I say, must inevitably be the case as long as mankind are found to prefer society to solitude; or unless every person were to retire, as soon as he or she were able to walk, to a distance from the centre of population, and to take up a separate abode in the *back-settlements*. To talk indeed of *all the land* being *equally well situated*, is of all imaginations the most absurd;

---

precedent for thus classing a number of different and distinct particulars under one appellation in the instance of the term *land*, which, as used in political economy, includes mines, fisheries, &c., as was explained in a former part of this work; but it is to be recollected, that the possession or the proprietorship of the land gives a right to these, and all the other natural powers of production which are capable of exclusive possession or enjoyment, and that it is absolutely necessary, in treating of that right, to have a single word under which the whole may be included.

for this could never be, unless every individual or every family were placed at an equal distance from each other !—As soon as any number of people draw together, so as to form even but a small village, the lands that are nearest will necessarily be the most advantageously situated, and will, even in that early stage, if they be then appropriated, draw a rent.

As, therefore, it is natural for mankind to unite in society, and to congregate into towns and villages, so it will follow as a necessary consequence that, as soon as they increase to any considerable numbers, rent will immediately arise from the advantages of situation. And for positive and experimental proof of this, we have only to refer to the North American states, where rents are paid in the neighbourhood of New York, Philadelphia, and the other large and smaller towns, for land in no degree superior in quality to millions of acres unoccupied within the boundaries of the Union, and which might be had for almost nothing, if people chose rather to live in solitude and barbarism, than in the more populous and civilized parts of the world.

SECTION III.

COROLLARY FROM THE PRECEDING VIEW OF THE NATURE AND CAUSES OF RENT—THAT THE INTEREST OF THE LAND-PROPRIETORS IS INSEPARABLY CONNECTED WITH THE INTEREST OF THE COMMUNITY.

From the view which has now been given of the nature and causes of rent, it appears that whatever increases the wealth and population of a country must necessarily increase its rent; and it consequently follows undeniably, and in spite of all the sophistry which can be employed to the contrary, that the true and permanent interest of the landlords is, as

Dr Smith long ago showed it to be, strictly and inseparably connected and identified with that of the community at large.

But, says Mr Ricardo, if you import corn, you reduce its price and lower rent, because you take your supplies from the most fertile lands only, on which it is grown at a smaller cost of labour and capital. But then, I answer, by the same means (namely, the importation of corn) you increase the numbers and wealth of your people, and in as little time probably as you can augment your supplies (allowing importation to be ever so free) you enable your people to consume more corn and more cattle than before, and so augment your rent and your price again; and if you withdraw the plough from some of your lands, you acquire a higher price for their produce in pasture. In Holland, for example, a very wealthy and populous country, and a country where a free importation is allowed, does not every person understand how the rent of the lands in that country should be higher than if its wealth and population were stunted and limited to the amount that could be supported by the comparatively small quantity of corn it could itself produce?—Does not every one perceive that by increasing the numbers of people and wealth of a country, until it were almost one vast town, a far higher rent would be obtained, not only for the ground built upon, but for what should remain to be applied to the pasturing of cattle and to be cultivated as garden-grounds, than could be had or afforded if the population were kept down to the numbers which could live upon its own produce?—If the numbers of people in this island were doubled, and every hamlet and every house, and every small and large town were doubled also, and brought proportionally nearer to one another, who does not see that the rent of all our land would be very greatly increased, although perhaps one-third or one-fourth of our supplies of corn might be imported from foreign parts?—The increased and probably more than doubled demand for pastures and garden-grounds would enhance the rent both of the richest and poorest lands; while the increased and probably more than doubled application and command of manures, would augment very greatly the produce also.*

Even Mr Ricardo himself admits, that the fall of price and of rent, which he supposes to be necessarily consequent upon the free admission of corn, would be but temporary:—

"It is undoubtedly true," says he, "that the fall in the relative price of raw produce, in consequence of the improvement in agriculture, or rather in consequence of less labour being bestowed on its production, would naturally lead to increased accumulation; for the profits of stock would be greatly augmented. This accumulation would lead to an increased demand for labour, to higher wages, to an increased popula-

* The Ricardo economists, in their headlong speculations on this subject, overlook altogether the obvious fact of the *increasing fertility of the land* from the application of *manures*, and *the increasing facilities of production* from the increasing facilities of *communication and carriage*, which attend the progress of society and of population in a country till nearly its latest stage,—and always argue as if *the decreasing fertility of the soil*, or, more properly speaking, *the inferior quality of the soils*, which must be *ultimately* had recourse to, and the consequent difficulty of acquiring the additional supplies of raw produce which are ultimately obtained, were an accident that attended the progress of a people from first to last; whereas the real fact is, that it happens only after a country has approached very near to the limits of its resources that such difficulty occurs *naturally or necessarily*; and even then, and in the very highest state of populousness possible, it may be safely affirmed, that *the whole produce* is invariably procured with far less difficulty or expense of labour, (though perhaps with a greater proportional application of *capital*,) than at first, whatever difficulty or expense may attend the procuring of a comparatively *small quantity* of such produce, from the few ungrateful soils that comprise the *outskirts* of cultivation.

tion, to a further demand for raw produce, and to an increased cultivation."*

After this ample concession, it is extraordinary indeed that Mr Ricardo, who has in general, as Mr Malthus observes,† kept his eye so steadily fixed on ultimate and permanent, not immediate or temporary consequences, should yet maintain that the interest of the landlords is opposed to that of the other classes of the community.

Mr Ricardo indeed adds, that "it is only, however, after the increase of the population, that rent would be as high as before; that is to say, after No 3 (referring to quality of soil, and to that quality, namely, which is two degrees inferior to the first quality,) was taken into cultivation. A considerable period would have elapsed, attended with a positive diminution of rent."‡

Now, admitting this to be the case, still it is but a *temporary*, not a permanent interest which the land-proprietors can have in the exclusion of foreign corn, even according to Mr Ricardo's own showing.§ But it is by no means certain, or probable, that even a temporary diminution *of rent* would take place in consequence of the *temporary* fall in *the price of corn*, which might probably follow upon the re-

---

* Principles of Political Economy, chap. ii.

† Ibid. chap. iii. sect. 10. p. 230.

‡ Ibid. chap. ii.

§ No persons ever raised so loud an outcry against restrictions on importation, and yet none perhaps ever contributed so much to prevent their removal, as Mr Ricardo and his disciples. This extraordinary circumstance has arisen from their constantly maintaining, in the broadest and most unqualified manner, that a free trade in corn would be directly adverse to the interests of the land-proprietors, which doctrine, after the above ample concession, is exceedingly remarkable. The unsoundness of this doctrine is, however, now beginning to be seen and acknowledged more generally than formerly, and even some of the most thorough-going partizans of Mr Ricardo are beginning to fall away from it.

moval of restrictions on importation, even in a country where the home price was considerably above the foreign; because the fall which would probably occur for a short while at first, would in process of time increase the consumption not of corn only, but of cattle, and consequently the quantity of land applied to the purpose of rearing and feeding them, and in this manner counteract the effects of importation on price, and sustain rent before it had time to fall; for it is to be borne in mind, that rent does not vibrate with every vibration in the price of corn, or fall immediately upon the reduction of price, or from a temporary reduction at all.

In the case of a country already wealthy and populous, but which had for a long period excluded foreign corn from its markets, it may be thought that, if surrounded with countries rich in land, though in nothing else, and admitting the importation of corn all at once, the demand and population of such country could not keep pace with the supplies of corn. This, however, is by no means certain; but it is certain that in the surrounding poorer countries the art of farming, as well as the means of farming well, would be wanting, or inferior, and it is probable that the price would not, after a very short period, be considerably different in the one and the other; for countries, however rich in land, cannot increase their supplies immediately at will beyond a certain small measure. No supplies indeed are or ever can be acquired so rapidly as to reduce rent in an extensive and populous country, and, in point of fact, *no case can be shown where rent has been permanently reduced but from a decrease of population or of wealth, or both.*

CHAPTER VIII.

OF THE WAGES OF LABOUR.

SECTION I.

OF THE RIGHT TO WAGES—LIMITS OF THAT RIGHT DEFINED—WAGES DEFINED.

WAGES consist of those things which are given or received for labour or personal exertion, either of body or mind, as the recompense or reward of that labour. "The produce of labour," as Dr Smith very justly observes, "constitutes the natural recompense or wages of labour."* But it is only in the very earliest and rudest state of human society that the immediate actual produce of the labourer can constitute his wages. In the advanced state, and in every period after the first establishment of the division of labour, the immediate produce of the labourer, or rather his labour itself, must in general be exchanged for money, which must again be exchanged for a variety of other things, which things it is that really constitute the wages of the labourer.

For in every period of society after that in which the division of labour is introduced, any single individual commonly performs but one particular operation, or set of operations, in the process of production, and but rarely brings to perfection, by his own separate and independent industry, even one single article or commodity. And even if it should happen that he does, his wants are not confined to a single article, but are, on the contrary, innumerable and infinitely

* Wealth of Nations, book i. chap. 8.

various. Besides, it is to be remembered, that, in the great majority of instances, the labour of each individual is commonly bestowed upon some subject-matter, or commodity, which is the property of another; which has been the fruit of other men's labour and saving, and from which the immediate effects or actual produce of the present contributor cannot be separated.

One man tills the ground and gathers the harvest, another grinds the corn, and a third bakes the flour into bread, before a perfect article is produced. Now it is manifest that not one of these labourers can distinctly abstract and carry away his actual produce. For, besides that none of them do the whole of the work, the subject-matter, that is, the corn, belongs not, perhaps, to any one of them, but to a fourth party or individual, to whom consequently a certain share of the finished article must be also assigned. Not one of these persons therefore can abstract or appropriate his particular produce, nor can any one take the whole, without taking what belongs in part to others as well as to himself. The proper share of each therefore, it is evident, can only be practically or fairly settled (as in point of fact universally it is settled) by treaty and agreement amongst the parties, and by determining beforehand, either that an actual division and distribution of the commodity itself shall be made, or (as is the more usual way) that each individual concerned shall receive his share—the equivalent or reward for his contribution, whether of labour or commodities—in some other article, as money, reciprocally agreed upon and stipulated previously to the commencement of their joint undertakings.

And this which has been just stated is a comparatively simple case. In other manufactures there is a still greater variety of parts to be performed by the different labourers employed in production; not one of whom can abstract, or receive, or appropriate his actual produce; not to mention the provinces of unproductive labour, in which, there being no production at all,—that is, no production of wealth or property,—the labourer in that sort could but rarely be rewarded by the actual or immediate effects of his labour. In the very earliest and rudest state of society, the actual produce of the chase may reward the hunter, the skin he dresses may reward the dresser of skins, and the hut he erects may reward the hut-maker. But in the advanced state, we plainly see that even the productive labourers can but rarely be rewarded by the immediate produce of their labour, because they can but rarely carry away or appropriate that produce; and in the provinces of unproductive labour, how should the physician, the lawyer, or the divine, be rewarded by the immediate effects of their peculiar species of labour, except in those few instances only, wherein they might happen themselves to require "a cast" of their own respective offices, viz. medicine, legal advice, and spiritual consolation?

It is not therefore the actual or immediate produce of the labourer which can, in general, in the advanced stages of society, constitute his wages, but those other things rather which he receives for his labour or for its produce in exchange.

Wages are in general paid in money; but neither is it the money itself which the labourer receives that really constitutes his wages, but those things rather which that money can enable him to purchase and appropriate to his use. It is the quantity and quality of the other sorts of wealth, comprising the actual produce and contributions of many different persons, which the money-wages he receives can enable him to purchase, that properly constitute the real reward or wages of the labourer; which real wages are good or bad, large or small, and high or low, not in proportion to the number or weight merely of the metal pieces he receives, but in proportion always to the quantity and quality of those various other articles, or various descriptions of wealth, as of food, clothes, lodging, &c., which that money can enable him to purchase and command, or appropriate to his use.

Those things, however, which his money-wages enable the labourer to purchase, may still be said to be the ultimate produce of his labour, (using the word produce in this instance in a metaphorical sense,) although they be not by any means its immediate or actual produce.

But further, with regard to the produce of labour; that which the labourer produces with the assistance of capital is not the produce of his labour entirely, but of his labour joined to that of those who produced the capital; and if the capital he uses belongs to another, a part of the produce will belong to that other also. The artisan or manufacturer, for example, who works with a steam-engine belonging to another, and by that means produces any sort of wealth or commodities, is not entitled to the whole produce, even although the raw materials of the articles fabricated were wholly his own; some part, it is evident, must belong to the proprietor of the engine, in whatever way his share of the produce might be agreed to be paid.

And such is the case universally in regard to labourers working with or assisted by any other species of capital belonging to other people: a part of the produce is always due to the proprietor of the capital as well as to the workman. The labourer is worthy of his hire; but so also is the capitalist of his profit or interest. In other words, the person who has laboured before, and not consumed but saved the produce of his labour, and which produce is now applied to assist another labourer in the work of production, is entitled to his profit or interest (which is the reward for labour which is past, and for saving and preserving the fruits of that labour) as much as the present labourer is entitled to his wages, which is the reward for his more recent labour:

It being remembered that this principle holds good equally in regard to the remotest heirs as to the original producer and saver of the capital himself. And here we have another view of the true nature and origin of the right to capital, and to its profit, which evidently stands on the same foundation with the right of the labourer to his wages; the capital being always originally worked for and won in the same manner.

Again, the produce which arises in an extensive and well-arranged work or manufactory, under the management of a skilful master or superintendent, is not the produce of the common labourers or subordinate workmen alone, but of all the persons employed, including inferior managers, clerks, and assistants of every description, as well as the master or chief manager himself; and every one of these (and certainly not least the last-mentioned) are entitled to a certain determinate share of the wealth produced, as well as the inferior labourers.

What the shares of every different labourer should be, the highest as well as the lowest, is properly settled by treaty and agreement between the parties; and the share which should belong to the capitalist is also properly settled in the same manner. As thus:

A capitalist,—that is, a person who has either produced and saved wealth himself, or who has inherited or acquired it from those who could only acquire it by production and saving at first,—lends, we shall suppose, his capital to a master undertaker of a work or manufactory, and treats and agrees with him alone for his share, which is, in this case, strictly profit of stock. The master undertaker again treats and agrees with each of his workmen separately, or with his subordinate managers at least (if he employs such) whom he perhaps empowers to treat with the inferior workmen for their shares or wages; and what remains over, after these several claims are discharged, belongs to the master undertaker as *his* share, and is strictly wages, that is, remuneration or reward for *his* labour; unless indeed in businesses where the risk or liability to losses is considerable, and greater than the average risk in other businesses;—in which case some part of the share that comes to the undertaker may be distinguished and set down as compensation for such risk.

When the labourer and capitalist are one and the same person,—in other words, when a person possessing capital employs it himself in trade or production, without requiring the assistance of any other labourer,—the whole produce accrues to himself alone, and it may happen that he takes no account, nor observes any distinction between what he owes to his labour and what to his capital. But, after deducting the ordinary rate of interest, the remainder is wholly wages or reward of labour. And when the labourer and capitalist are different persons, and when consequently part of the produce must belong to one, and part to another, this distinction necessarily takes place, and their different shares must be settled and agreed upon in the first instance, before the one contributes his stock or the other his labour. And so, in point of fact, it happens accordingly (as an appeal to experience will satisfy us) that the shares of every one, whether labourer or capitalist, is in general thus settled beforehand, in the manner which has been stated by treaty and agreement.

Again, if the capitalist superintending the application of his own capital employs other labourers besides himself, he treats and agrees with every one, or with his inferior managers, as in the manner before specified, for their shares or wages; and what is over after paying these consists partly of wages, and partly of profit of stock: And in this case also it may happen that these two different descriptions of revenue shall be confounded with one another; but, after the payment of all his hired labourers, and a due allowance being made for profit of stock, whatever remains behind is wages or reward to this individual for his own labour; unless, as before mentioned, the business should happen to be more than commonly hazardous; in which case a certain portion of what remains might be separated and recognised as compensation for the superior risk, before reckoning the amount of wages.

It should appear then, from what has been now advanced, that all that part of the joint produce of land, capital, and labour, that is over and above what makes good rent and interest, (and, if we choose to reckon it separately, the compensation for *extra* risk, in employments which are more than ordinarily hazardous,) is properly the fund of wages, and must all go either to the masters on the one hand, or to the workmen on the other. And it is self-evident therefore, that the more the one class of persons obtain, the less must fall to the share of the other class; but the masters, it appears, must, in all the more than ordinarily hazardous businesses, have their shares augmented by a quantity greater or less in proportion to the varieties of risk they incur.

Now, in reference to the mode in which this fund of wages comes to be divided between the masters and the workmen, it is true the masters will always endeavour to keep as large a share as possible to themselves as their own wages, and to give as small a one as possible to the inferior labourers as theirs. But, on the other hand, it is true also, that the inferior labourers will generally endeavour to procure as large a share as possible for themselves, without caring whether any thing at all be left to the masters; and provided the law stands neuter, and shows no undue favour or regard to the one side or party more than to the other, neither the one nor the other will be able to prevail entirely in the contest, or to gain any undue or lasting advantage the one over the other.

The masters or employers of the inferior labourers will not be able to gain any undue advantage over them, because, if the latter did not find that they made better wages under a master than they could do working separately and independently on their own account, they would not accept the employment. Nor will it be found any valid objection to this argument to say, that, in the advanced state of society, the great majority of labourers could get no employment, unless they agreed to accept work under a master; for still it happens, under all ordinary circumstances, that the necessity of the masters, and their anxiety to have their work done, is found in general to be sufficiently strong and pressing to subject them equally with the workmen to the effects and control of the principle of competition, provided the law treats both parties with even-handed justice.

On the other hand, the workmen, or subordinate labourers, will be equally unable to gain any undue advantage over their employers; because, the agreements being voluntary, the latter would not require the assistance of subordinate labourers if they did not find their advantage in employing them at the wages stipulated, whatever these may be.

SECTION II.

OF THE CIRCUMSTANCES WHICH GIVE OCCASION TO A DIFFERENCE OF WAGES IN DIFFERENT EMPLOYMENTS.

THE wages of labour (as has been already cursorily noticed, I think, in some of our preceding chapters,) are regulated *partly* by the nature of the work in which it is employed, —that is to say, by the different nature of employments themselves,—and *partly* by the habits and condition of the labourers in every different employment or species of labour. Of these two subjects, or two different species of accidents or circumstances affecting wages, the *latter* have been already adverted to in a preceding part of this work,* and will be yet farther resumed and illustrated in the third and last section of the present chapter; but previously to this it will be necessary to attend a little to the *former*, namely, to the circumstances which occasion a difference of wages in different employments; and as Dr Smith has given a very full, and luminous, and distinct view of these circumstances, I shall here, by observing the rule I have prescribed for myself,† have little more to do than transcribe such parts of what he advances on the subject as appear to be sufficient for my purpose in the present section.

As introductory to the subject Dr Smith observes,—

"The whole of the advantages and disadvantages of the different employments of labour and stock must, in the same neighbourhood, be either perfectly equal, or continually tending to equality. If in the same neighbourhood there was any employment evidently either more or less advantageous than the rest, so many people would crowd into it in the one case, and so many would desert it in the other, that its advantages would soon return to the level of other employments. This at least would be the case in a society where things were left to follow their natural course, where there was perfect liberty, and where every man was perfectly free both to choose what occupation he thought proper, and to change it as often as he thought proper. Every man's interest would prompt him to seek the advantageous and to shun the disadvantageous employment."‡

* Book i. chap. 10.

† See before p. 71, *et seq.*, in notes, where I have stated my reasons in favour of the expediency of observing this rule.

‡ Wealth of Nations, book i. chap. 10.

Dr Smith observes farther, (in the introductory part,) that wages are extremely different in different employments, as arising from "certain circumstances in the employments themselves, which either really, or at least in the imaginations of men, make up for a small pecuniary gain in some, and counterbalance a great one in others."*

These circumstances he then proceeds to describe as follows:—

"The five following are the principal circumstances which, so far as I have been able to observe, make up for a small pecuniary gain in some employments, and counterbalance a great one in others: first, the agreeableness or disagreeableness of the employments themselves; secondly, the easiness and cheapness, or the difficulty and expense of learning them; thirdly, the constancy or inconstancy of employment in them; fourthly, the small or great trust which must be reposed in those who exercise them; and, fifthly, the probability or improbability of success in them.

"First, The wages of labour vary with the ease or hardship, the cleanliness or dirtiness, the honourableness or dishonourableness of the employments. Thus, in most places, take the year round, a journeyman tailor earns less than a journeyman weaver. His work is much easier. A journeyman weaver earns less than a journeyman smith. His work is not always easier, but it is much cleanlier. A journeyman blacksmith, though an artificer, seldom earns so much in twelve hours as a collier, who is only a labourer, does in eight. His work is not quite so dirty, is less dangerous, and is carried on in daylight, and above ground. Honour makes a great part of the reward of all honourable professions. In point of pecuniary gain, all things considered, they are generally under-recompensed, as I shall endeavour to show by and by. Disgrace has the contrary effect. The trade of a butcher is a brutal and an odious business; but it is in most places more profit-

---

* Wealth of Nations, book i. chap. 10.

able than the greater part of common trades. The most detestable of all employments, that of public executioner, is, in proportion to the quantity of work done, better paid than any common trade whatever.

" Hunting and fishing, the most important employments of mankind in the rude state of society, became in its advanced state their most agreeable amusements, and they pursue for pleasure what they once followed from necessity. In the advanced state of society, therefore, they are all very poor people who follow as a trade what other people pursue as a pastime. Fishermen have been so since the time of Theocritus. A poacher is everywhere a poor man in Great Britain. In countries where the rigour of the law suffers no poachers, the licensed hunter is not in a much better condition. The natural taste for those employments makes more people follow them than can live comfortably by them, and the produce of their labour, in proportion to its quantity, comes always too cheap to market to afford any thing but the most scanty subsistence to the labourers.

" Secondly, The wages of labour vary with the easiness and cheapness, or the difficulty and expense of learning the business.

" When any expensive machine is erected, the extraordinary work to be performed by it before it is worn out, it must be expected, will replace the capital laid out upon it, with at least the ordinary profits. A man educated at the expense of much labour and time to any of those employments which require extraordinary dexterity and skill, may be compared to one of those expensive machines. The work which he learns to perform, it must be expected, over and above the usual wages of common labour, will replace to him the whole expense of his education, with at least the ordinary profits of an equally valuable capital. It must do this too in a reasonable time, regard being had to the very uncertain duration of human life, in the same manner as to the more certain duration of the machine.

" The difference between the wages of skilled labour and those of common labour is founded upon this principle.

"The policy of Europe considers the labour of all mechanics, artificers, and manufacturers, as skilled labour; and that of all country labourers as common labour. It seems to suppose that of the former to be of a more nice and delicate nature than that of the latter. It is so perhaps in some cases; but in the greater part it is quite otherwise, as I shall endeavour to show by and by. The laws and customs of Europe, therefore, in order to qualify any person for exercising the one species of labour, impose the necessity of an apprenticeship, though with different degrees of rigour in different places. They leave the other free and open to every body. During the continuance of the apprenticeship, the whole labour of the apprentice belongs to his master. In the meantime he must, in many cases, be maintained by his parents or relations, and in almost all cases must be clothed by them. Some money too is commonly given to the master for teaching him his trade. They who cannot give money, give time, or become bound for more than the usual number of years,—a consideration which, though it is not always advantageous to the master, on account of the usual idleness of apprentices, is always disadvantageous to the apprentice. In country labour, on the contrary, the labourer, while he is employed about the easier, learns the more difficult parts of his business, and his own labour maintains him through all the different stages of his employment. It is reasonable, therefore, that in Europe the wages of mechanics, artificers, and manufacturers, should be somewhat higher than those of common labourers. They are so accordingly, and their superior gains make them in most places be considered as a superior rank of people. This superiority, however, is generally very small; the daily or weekly earnings of journeymen in the more common sorts of manufactures, such as those of plain linen and woollen cloth, computed at an average, are, in most places, very little more than the day-wages of common labourers. Their employment, indeed, is more steady and uniform, and the superiority of their earnings, taking the whole year together, may be somewhat greater. It seems evidently, however, to be no greater than what is sufficient to compensate the superior expense of their education.

" Education in the ingenious arts and in the liberal professions is still more tedious and expensive. The pecuniary recompense, therefore, of painters and sculptors, of lawyers and physicians, ought to be much more liberal; and it is so accordingly.

" Thirdly, The wages of labour in different occupations vary with the constancy or inconstancy of employment.

" Employment is much more constant in some trades than in others. In the greater part of manufactures, a journeyman may be pretty sure of employment almost every day in the year that he is able to work. A mason or bricklayer, on the contrary, can work neither in hard frost nor in foul weather, and his employment at all other times depends upon the occasional calls of his customers. He is liable, in consequence, to be frequently without any. What he earns, therefore, while he is employed, must not only maintain him while he is idle, but make him some compensation for those anxious and desponding moments which the thought of so precarious a situation must sometimes occasion. Where the computed earnings of the greater part of manufacturers, accordingly, are nearly upon a level with the day-wages of common labourers, those of masons and bricklayers are generally from one-half more to double those wages. Where common labourers earn four and five shillings a week, masons and bricklayers frequently earn seven and eight; where the former earn six, the latter often earn nine and ten; and where the former earn nine and ten, as in London, the latter commonly earn fifteen and eighteen. No species of skilled labour, however, seems more easy to learn than that of masons and bricklayers. Chairmen in London, during the summer season, are said sometimes to be employed as bricklayers. The high wages of these workmen, therefore, are not so much the recompense of their skill, as the compensation for the inconstancy of their employment.

" A house-carpenter seems to exercise rather a nicer and a more ingenious trade than a mason. In most places, however, for it is not universally so, his day-wages are somewhat lower. His employment, though it depends much, does not depend so entirely upon the occasional calls of his customers; and it is not liable to be interrupted by the weather.

"When the trades which generally afford constant employment happen in a particular place not to do so, the wages of the workmen always rise a good deal above their ordinary proportion to those of common labour. In London almost all journeymen artificers are liable to be called upon and dismissed by their master from day to day, and from week to week, in the same manner as day-labourers in other places. The lowest order of artificers, journeymen tailors, accordingly, earn there half-a-crown a day, though eighteenpence may be reckoned the wages of common labour. In small towns and country villages the wages of journeymen tailors frequently scarce equal those of common labour; but in London they are often many weeks without employment, particularly during the summer.

"When the inconstancy of employment is combined with the hardship, disagreeableness, and dirtiness of the work, it sometimes raises the wages of the most common labourer above those of the most skilful artificers. A collier working by the piece is supposed, at Newcastle, to earn commonly about double, and in many parts of Scotland about three times the wages of common labour. His high wages arise altogether from the hardship, disagreeableness, and dirtiness of his work. His employment may, upon most occasions, be as constant as he pleases. The coal-heavers in London exercise a trade which in hardship, dirtiness, and disagreeableness, almost equals that of colliers; and, from the unavoidable irregularity in the arrivals of coal-ships, the employment of the greater part of them is necessarily very inconstant. If colliers, therefore, commonly earn double and triple the wages of common labour, it ought not to seem unreasonable that coal-heavers should sometimes earn four and five times those wages. In the inquiry made into their condition a few years ago, it was found that at the rate at which they were then paid, they could earn from six to ten shillings a day. Six shillings are about four times the wages of common labour in London, and in every particular trade the lowest common earnings may always be considered as those of the far greater number. How extravagant soever those earnings may appear, if they were more than sufficient to compensate all the disagreeable circumstances of the business, there would soon be so great a number of competitors as, in a trade which has no exclusive privilege, would quickly reduce them to a lower rate.

"Fourthly, The wages of labour vary according to the small or great trust which must be reposed in the workmen.

"The wages of goldsmiths and jewellers are everywhere superior to those of many other workmen, not only of equal but of much superior ingenuity, on account of the precious materials with which they are intrusted.

"We trust our health to the physician; our fortune, and sometimes our life and reputation, to the lawyer and attorney. Such confidence could not safely be reposed in people of a very mean or low condition. Their reward must be such, therefore, as may give them that rank in the society which so important a trust requires. The long time and the great expense which must be laid out in their education, when combined with this circumstance, necessarily enhance still further the price of their labour.

"Fifthly, The wages of labour in different employments vary according to the probability or improbability of success in them.

"The probability that any particular person shall ever be qualified for the employment to which he is educated is very different in different occupations. In the greater part of mechanic trades success is almost certain, but very uncertain in the liberal professions. Put your son apprentice to a shoemaker, there is little doubt of his learning to make a pair of shoes; but send him to study the law, it is at least twenty to one if ever he makes such proficiency as will enable him to live by the business. In a perfectly fair lottery, those who draw the prizes ought to gain all that is lost by those who draw the blanks. In a profession where twenty fail for one that succeeds, that one ought to gain all that should have been gained by the unsuccessful twenty. The counsellor-at-law, who, perhaps, at near forty years of age, begins to make something by his profession, ought to receive the retribution, not only of his own so tedious and expensive education, but of that of more than twenty others who are never likely to make any thing by it. How extravagant soever the fees of counsellors-at-law may sometimes appear, their real retribution is never equal to this. Compute in any particular place what is likely to be annually gained, and what is likely to be annually spent, by all the different workmen in any common trade, such as that of shoemakers or weavers, and you will find that the former sum will generally exceed the latter. But make the same computation with regard to all the counsellors and students of law, in all the different inns of court, and you will find that their annual gains bear but a very small proportion to their annual expense, even though you rate the former as high and the latter as low as can well be done. The lottery of the law, therefore, is very far from being a perfectly fair lottery; and that, as well as many other liberal and honourable professions, is, in point of pecuniary gain, evidently under-recompensed.

"Those professions keep their level, however, with other occupations, and, notwithstanding these discouragements, all the most generous and liberal spirits are eager to crowd into them. Two different causes contribute to recommend them: first, the desire of the reputation which attends upon superior excellence in any of them; and, secondly, the natural confidence which every man has, more or less, not only in his own abilities, but in his own good fortune.

"To excel in any profession, in which but few arrive at mediocrity, is the most decisive mark of what is called genius or superior talents. The public admiration which attends upon such distinguished abilities makes always a part of their reward; a greater or smaller in proportion as it is higher or lower in degree. It makes a considerable part of that reward in the profession of physic; a still greater, perhaps, in that of law; in poetry and philosophy it makes almost the whole."*

It thus appears that there is, in all the different species or employments of labour, a very great variety and difference of circumstances, or of advantages and disadvantages attending them, which necessarily give occasion to a correspondent variety and difference of pecuniary wages. And when we contemplate the wide extent of this variety, and of this difference of wages, from the highest to the lowest,—*first*, in the provinces of unproductive labour, from the king, the minister of state, and the judge upon the bench, down to the common beadle or sheriff-officer,—from the military chief, or general, down to the common soldier, —and from the divine, the lawyer, and the physician, to the menial servant; and, *secondly*, in the provinces of productive labour, from the general merchant to the common sailors in his ships and porters in his warehouses,—from the master manufacturer to his journeymen or workmen,—and from the extensive farmer to his ploughmen and other common labourers,—it must appear indeed a most monstrous and unaccountable hallucination that could lead any per-

* Wealth of Nations, book i. chap. 10. By looking into the "Wealth of Nations," and into the chapter just mentioned, whence the above extracts are taken, it will be seen that they are there intermingled with others, on the profit of stock, already quoted in the first section of the seventh chapter of this book, on that subject. In that place it was shown that there is an error in supposing, as Dr Smith has done, that *profit* is affected by *any* of the five circumstances which he describes so justly as affecting wages, and that he was led into that error by another, of which it was there shown also he was himself perfectly aware, namely, that he had not perfectly discriminated between profit and wages.

son in his senses to attempt, as one of Mr Ricardo's disciples has done, to demonstrate the "equality of wages!"* or to treat of them, as has been done by Mr Ricardo himself, as if they were limited to what would command but the lowest necessaries of life, and as if they represented a fixed and unvarying quantity!

Yet, however various and different the wages of labour really are in different employments, they are still regulated *in a certain degree* in all of them by the same principles: *immediately*, by the number of applicants or of hands, candidates or competitors in each, compared with the extent of the employment; and more *remotely*, by the habits and modes of life or subsistence common to each; and consequently by those external and other circumstances which determine, control, and generate the general character and habits of every class and order of the people.

What those external circumstances are which chiefly determine, control, and generate the general character, and habits, and condition of the people, I have already indicated pretty largely and unequivocally;† but I must still endeavour somewhat farther to illustrate my position, and to show more fully than has yet been done the connexion between wages and the habits and modes of subsistence of the labourers, and the connexion of those habits and modes of subsistence, especially in reference to the lower classes of labourers, with the character of the laws and government under which they live.

---

* "Equality of Wages" is the running title of one of the chapters of Macculloch's Principles of Political Economy, at the head of which we read at length, "Equality of Wages in all the different Departments of Industry!"

† See chapter 10 of book i.

SECTION III.

OF THE CAUSES WHICH REGULATE THE NATURAL RATE OF WAGES.

As it is the number of individuals who are candidates or competitors for employment, *at any particular time and place*, which determines the market-rate of wages, and as the natural rate is nothing else but the ordinary and average market-rate, so it is the number of *permanent* candidates or competitors which determines the natural rate of wages.

But there can be no permanent competitors in any employment which does not afford wages equivalent to the necessary outgoings or expenses of those employed, or equivalent at least to what may be sufficient to keep the labourers living. Nor are men contented in general, where they are in any degree enlightened or intelligent, with what is barely sufficient to keep them in existence. They commonly require, except in their lowest state of ignorance and degradation, not merely necessaries, but conveniences, and even luxuries; and to attain these they will, under favourable circumstances, cheerfully undergo much labour, and submit *for a time* to many privations, provided they have a reasonably-assured prospect of arriving at the proposed goal, and attaining their object at last.

The mode in which the number of competitors (or population) can alone be increased is obvious enough; and one of the strongest principles of human nature is the desire of sexual enjoyment and of progeny. But there is another principle which is not less strong, nor less universal, nor less necessary to the preservation of the human species and of competitors in all employments, viz. the desire of food, clothes, and lodging, and of provision for a family; and although, under certain circumstances and habits of the people, this principle or desire may be very easily satisfied, because, under those circumstances, the people will be contented with a very poor and miserable subsistence,—with potatoes, and rags, and hovels,—yet it is capable, under other circumstances and other habits, of being improved into an *effectual desire* for better food, and clothes, and lodging, and of restraining the sexual passion, and the propensity to procreation or marriage, until those other wants,—necessaries, conveniences, and luxuries,—be provided for and gratified.

It has, however, been remarked by Dr Smith, that "every species of animals naturally multiplies in proportion to the means of their subsistence, and no species can ever multiply beyond it. But in civilized society," he continues, "it is only among the inferior ranks of people that the scantiness of subsistence can set limits to the further multiplication of the human species; and it can do so in no other way than by destroying a great part of the children which their fruitful marriages produce."*

But it is only where they are ill-governed, oppressed, and ignorant, that the inferior ranks of people multiply beyond the limits of a liberal subsistence. Under other circumstances they must necessarily, as has been shown,† from the principles of human nature, uniformly improve their condition, and habits, and modes of life, and acquire higher and higher wages in proportion as wealth and population increase.

But, says Dr Smith, "Though the wealth of a country should be very great, yet if it has been long stationary, we must not expect to find the wages of labour very high in it. The funds destined for the payment of wages, the revenue and stock of its inhabitants, may be of the greatest extent; but if they have continued for several centuries of the same or very nearly of the same extent, the number of labourers employed every year could easily supply, and even more than

* Wealth of Nations, book i. chap. 8.

† Ibid. book i. chap. 10.

supply, the number wanted the following year. There could seldom be any scarcity of hands, nor could the masters be obliged to bid against one another in order to get them. The hands, on the contrary, would in this case naturally multiply beyond their employment. There would be a constant scarcity of employment, and the labourers would be obliged to bid against one another in order to get it. If in such a country the wages of labour had ever been more than sufficient to maintain the labourer, and to enable him to bring up a family, the competition of the labourers and the interest of the masters would soon reduce them to this lowest rate which is consistent with common humanity."*

On this passage Mr Buchanan makes the following just and important observation :—

"The wages of labour are not necessarily at their lowest rate where wealth and population are stationary. In these circumstances the condition of the labourer depends partly on his own moral habits. If in poverty he is content to propagate his race, poverty will be his lot; but if he will not marry on such hard conditions, the race of labourers will decline, and wages will rise until the labourer agrees, by marrying, to supply the market with labour."†

But Dr Smith says again,—"It deserves to be remarked, perhaps, that it is in the progressive state, while the society is advancing to the further acquisition, rather than when it has acquired its full complement of riches, that the condition of the labouring poor, of the great body of the people, seems to be the happiest and the most comfortable. It is hard in the stationary, and miserable in the declining. The progressive state is in reality the cheerful and the hearty state to all the different orders of the society. The stationary is dull, the declining melancholy."‡

---

* Wealth of Nations, book i. chap. 8.

† Ibid. Buchanan's edition, note, p. 116.

‡ Ibid. book i. chap. 8.

Now, this is a perfectly accurate description of what will happen to a country under bad government; for even under the worst that ever existed, when by any chance an increase of wealth or improvement takes place (as may sometimes happen from a variety of accidents even under the worst), wages will necessarily rise, and all the other effects here described by Dr Smith will exactly follow.

But under good government a country can never decline, nor even become stationary, but wealth and population, and the natural wages of labour, must go on necessarily and indefinitely to increase, though no doubt by slower and slower degrees when a country approaches the limits of its resources. There is no necessity, however, in the nature of things, or in fact, that wealth, or population, or wages, should ever decrease or diminish, or even become stationary upon the earth; for as the produce of the earth (and still more wealth in general) may be continually and indefinitely augmented, it follows incontestably that both population and wages may be continually and indefinitely augmented also; because, let the augmentation of wealth be great or small, it is evidently possible that a part of it may go to support additional numbers, or inhabitants, and another part to augment the wages of labour; and to produce this result, it is only necessary that population should increase in a less degree than wealth, (which, as I have already demonstrated,* is uniformly and invariably the case,) and that the labourer should be placed under circumstances favourable to the development of his prudential habits, *i. e.* in a state of security under good government.

Even Mr Malthus himself admits that the natural rate of wages, or, what is the same thing, the good or bad condition of the inferior ranks of people, has no necessary con-

---

* Chapter 6 of this book.

nexion with any particular stage in the progress of society, of population, or of wealth.

"Strictly speaking," he says in the Essay on Population, "the good or bad condition of the poor is not necessarily connected with any particular stage in the progress of society to its full complement of wealth."*

And again, in his Principles of Political Economy, he observes,—

"The great resource of the labouring classes for their happiness must be in those prudential habits which, if properly exercised, are capable of securing to the labourer a fair proportion of the necessaries and conveniences of life, from the earliest stage of society to the latest."†

But Mr Malthus, while he thus not only freely acknowledges this important truth, but brings it voluntarily forward in his pages as a part of his system, and while he not only admits, but severally maintains and advances as a part of his system also, all the chief facts and principles which serve, when combined, to establish the conclusion that the misery and poverty, and degradation of the lower classes of labourers, are wholly to be ascribed to the imperfection of government, or political institutions, or, which is the same thing, to the want of good government, yet he constantly and pertinaciously eschews this conclusion, and would fain endeavour to escape from the toils and meshes of that irresoluble net, which, in spite of all his efforts to the contrary, he has gradually worked around himself.

The whole indeed of Mr Malthus's Essay on Population, and a great part of his Principles of Political Economy, will be found, when attentively examined, to be one uninterrupted tissue of special pleading against that conclusion to which

* Book iii. chap. 13, vol. iii. p. 25.

† Chap. iv. sec. 5. p. 291.

all the arguments he advances directly tend, and in which they must necessarily terminate when they are fully sifted.

Mr Malthus admits, and advances it even as a part of his system,* that good and bad government constitute "the principal circumstances" which depress or elevate the character of the lower classes of people, and which improve or deteriorate their habits and modes of life. He admits, and takes considerable pains to prove,† that their habits and modes of life determine the degree of comfort or discomfort under which they will continue to marry and procreate; and that this circumstance again determines their numbers and their wages; and yet he would fain deny what follows plainly and unavoidably from these premises, viz. that the whole depends upon good or bad government.

But this attempt of Mr Malthus will never succeed; and all his arts and endeavours to turn the attention of his readers away from the fatal conclusion (fatal to Mr Malthus and to his theory of human misery) will be found unavailing, and will necessarily end in drawing attention more strongly and irresistibly towards it; for a question of such importance, and charged with such tremendous consequences, can never be allowed to remain in all the confusion and uncertainty in which Mr Malthus has left it.

That these strictures, severe as they may seem, are neither unfounded nor uncalled for, I now proceed to show; and in doing this, while it is believed the sophistries and inconsistencies of Mr Malthus will be made glaringly manifest, the truth itself, it is hoped, will be, at the same time, vindicated, and disburdened and drawn forth from that load of clashing and contradictory statement beneath which it lies buried in Mr Malthus's pages.

---

* Essay on Population, book iv. chap. 9. vol. iii. p. 209.

† Principles of Political Economy, chap. iv. sec. 2.

In the work of Mr Malthus last mentioned, his Principles of Political Economy, and in his chapter of that work on the wages of labour, he gravely and deliberately says:

"It would be very desirable to ascertain what are the principal causes which determine the different modes of subsistence among the lower classes of people of different countries; but the question involves so many considerations, that a satisfactory solution of it is hardly to be expected."*

Now this, to be sure, after what has been already advanced and quoted from Mr Malthus himself in a former chapter,† must be confessed to be rather astounding, and, to the reader who recollects the passages, it must appear not a little extraordinary; for he gives in them that very solution which he here declares "is hardly to be expected." But what is stranger, and more astounding still, this new position of Mr Malthus will be found to stand in the place where it appears, a mere unsupported assertion, not only unattempted to be established by argument, but, *mirabile dictu*, immediately and flatly contradicted by what follows from Mr Malthus himself, in the very chapter, and section, and page, in which it is put forth!

In the passages just alluded to, as already quoted from Mr Malthus, he affirms of "the standard of wretchedness," the point below which the lower classes of people "will not continue to marry and propagate their species," that "the *principal circumstances* which contribute to raise it are liberty, security of property, the diffusion of knowledge, and a taste for the conveniences and the comforts of life. Those which contribute principally to lower it are despotism and ignorance."‡ Now this "standard of

---

* Chap. iv. sect. 2. † Chap. x. of book i.

‡ Essay on Population, book iv. chap. 9, p. 209 of vol. iii., fifth edition.

wretchedness" Mr Malthus will not and cannot deny to be but other terms for "the different modes of subsistence among the lower classes,"—the "point below which they will not continue to marry and propagate their species;" and while therefore in the one place this author affirms that a satisfactory solution of the question, "What are the PRINCIPAL CAUSES which determine the different modes of subsistence among the lower classes of people of different countries" is hardly to be expected, he declares, in the other, that "the PRINCIPAL CIRCUMSTANCES which contribute to" produce that difference, or to "raise" and "lower" those different modes of subsistence, are liberty, security of property, &c., and despotism and ignorance!

Nor is this extraordinary mode of treating his subject and his readers confined to one place, or does his conflicting assertions, in the different places where they are found, arise from any professed or actual change in the opinions or sentiments of Mr Malthus in regard to the effects of good and bad government in raising and lowering the "standard of wretchedness," or "the habits and modes of subsistence among the lower classes of people." On the contrary, his opinions on this subject are not only retained and reiterated in the newer publication, but are actually avowed and enlarged upon in the very place, as has been already mentioned, where this new and conflicting one is introduced; and with the intervention only of a saving clause of four lines, (of what force or consequence we shall see presently,) Mr Malthus proceeds as follows:—

"From high wages, or the power of commanding a large portion of the necessaries of life, two very different results may follow; one, that of a rapid increase of the population, in which case the high wages are chiefly spent in the maintenance of large and frequent families; and the other, that of a decided improvement in the modes of subsistence, and the conveniences and comforts enjoyed, without a proportionate acceleration in the rate of increase.

"In looking to these different results, the causes of them will evidently appear to be the different habits existing among the people of different countries and at different times. In an inquiry into the causes of these different habits, we shall generally be able to trace those which produce the first result to all the circumstances which contribute to depress the lower classes of the people, which make them unable or unwilling to reason from the past to the future, and ready to acquiesce, for the sake of present gratification, in a very low standard of comfort and respectability; and those which produce the second result, to all the circumstances which tend to elevate the character of the lower classes of society, which make them approach the nearest to beings who "look before and after," and who consequently cannot acquiesce patiently in the thought of depriving themselves and their children of the means of being respectable, virtuous, and happy.

"Among the circumstances which contribute to the character first described, the most efficient will be found to be despotism, oppression, and ignorance; among those which contribute to the latter character, civil and political liberty, and education.

"Of all the causes which tend to generate prudential habits among the lower classes of society, the most essential is unquestionably civil liberty. No people can be much accustomed to form plans for the future, who do not feel assured that their industrious exertions, while fair and honourable, will be allowed to have free scope; and that the property which they either possess, or may acquire, will be secured to them by a known code of just laws impartially administered. But it has been found by experience, that civil liberty cannot be permanently secured without political liberty. Consequently, political liberty becomes almost equally essential; and in addition to its being necessary in this point of view, its obvious tendency to teach the lower classes of society to respect themselves by obliging the higher classes to respect them, must contribute greatly to aid all the good effects of civil liberty.

"With regard to education, it might certainly be made general under a bad form of government, and might be very deficient under one in other respects good; but it must be allowed, that the chances, both with regard to its quality and its prevalence, are greatly in favour of the latter. Education alone could do little against insecurity of property; but it would powerfully assist all the favourable consequences to be expected from civil and political liberty, which could not indeed be considered as complete without it."*

Now what have we here but that very solution which Mr Malthus commences by declaring "is hardly to be expected!" that very solution which he had once before, and in another work, given in nearly the same terms, and which every person of sound mind who bestows any considerable attention on the subject, must necessarily come to? What, in reality, have we here exhibited to us but a conflict between the natural candour and knowledge of his subject of Mr Malthus, and the awful idea not to be tolerated for an instant—the overwhelming danger above all things to be avoided—that of removing the imputation of "evil" from "the principle of population," and allowing it to rest unequivocally—God save the mark!—upon bad government?

In order to avoid this Scylla, therefore, Mr Malthus thrusts in the saving clause just alluded to—following therein his ordinary and approved method in similar emergencies: he says—and it is all, as was mentioned, that intervenes between the two passages above cited—between the affirmation that the "solution" of the question he is discussing, "is hardly to be expected," and the solution itself! He says, "Much must certainly depend upon the

* Principles of Political Economy, chap. iv. sect. 2, pp. 250, 251, 252.

physical causes of climate and soil; but still more perhaps on moral causes, the formation and action of which are owing to a variety of circumstances."*

It will be perceived that the latter part of this sentence—the "still more perhaps"—belongs not to the *saving clause*, but to the "solution," and refers to what Mr Malthus proceeds immediately to prove,† in the manner which has been seen in the preceding extract; and *it is only the little and naked assertion*, "MUCH MUST CERTAINLY DEPEND UPON THE PHYSICAL CAUSES OF CLIMATE AND SOIL," to which Mr Malthus here clings as the rock of his hope, and on which he relies, to uphold the tottering and shattered fabric of his system.

But if this which Mr Malthus asserts be really the case—if "much certainly depends upon the physical causes of climate and soil"—why does not Mr Malthus go into the subject, and show us that it is so? Why does he, in a case so momentous and vital to his argument, put us off with a poor and meagre assertion, and leave us to be contented with his word alone? For here again, as in the instance before seen, he does nothing but assert; *he neither proves, nor attempts to prove*, any thing in regard to "the physical causes of climate and soil," as he does in regard to the "moral causes" of good and bad government. He chooses rather to avoid explanation and detail on the subject of the former altogether, as being conscious that, should he attempt to exhibit and draw them out into their full shape and dimensions, (if they have any,) he should the more certainly expose their insignificance and weakness.

And this is a temper of mind and purpose from which it is not at all likely that Mr Malthus will allow himself to be

---

* Principles of Political Economy, p. 250.

† *Vide* the work itself, *in loco citato*.

diverted or seduced by any arts or provocation of his assailants, since he perfectly well knows into whose hands he must fall should he quit this stronghold of general assertion, and descend into the arena of unreserved controversy: he perfectly well knows that Mr Hume has long ago completely disposed of this argument;* and although Mr Malthus may fairly consider himself a giant among the dwarfish race of the flattered and favoured authors of "these degenerate days," he is far too cautious and prudent to measure his strength, and to array his feeble and phantom forces, in the face of those hardy and real troops which stand already marshalled against him, by perhaps the greatest of human intellects that have yet appeared on the theatre of the world.

Wisely therefore was it, and well considered on the part of Mr Malthus, that he resolved to observe a discreet and dignified silence upon this topic: still, however, this may not hinder but that there shall be those who will be troublesome enough to demand a *reason*, and who will be so saucy as to think that even the affirmations of Mr Malthus himself should be accompanied with a statement of the grounds on which they rest.

Dismissing then this saving clause—this forlorn hope—of Mr Malthus, as undeserving of further attention or notice, I shall here return again to his "solution" of the question, "What are the principal causes which determine the different modes of subsistence among the lower classes of the people?" for we must still attend on him somewhat farther upon that subject.

When Mr Malthus says, as he does in the passages already quoted, "Among the circumstances which contribute to the character first described, the most efficient will be

---

* In his Essay "Of National Characters."

found to be despotism, oppression, and ignorance,—among those which contribute to the latter character, civil and political liberty and education;" when he says, "Of all the causes which tend to generate prudential habits among the lower classes of society, the most essential is unquestionably civil liberty;" when he says, "We shall generally be able to trace those which produce the first result to all the circumstances which contribute to depress the lower classes of the people, which make them unable or unwilling to reason from the past to the future, and ready to acquiesce, for the sake of present gratification, in a very low standard of comfort and respectability; and those which produce the second result, to all the circumstances which tend to elevate the character of the lower classes of society, which make them approach the nearest to beings who 'look before and after,' and who consequently cannot acquiesce patiently in the thought of depriving themselves and their children of the means of being respectable, virtuous, and happy;" with what face can he say, as he does in the same page, that a satisfactory solution of the question, "What are the principal causes which determine the different modes of subsistence among the lower classes of people, 'is hardly to be expected?'" Yet Mr Malthus says all this. He tells us that such and such are the "principal causes" and "circumstances" which determine "the habits and modes of subsistence among the lower classes of people;" and in the same breath (*proh pudor!*) he coolly and deliberately delivers the following words, for I must again repeat the most marvellous asseveration,—"It would be very desirable to ascertain what are the principal causes which determine the different modes of subsistence among the lower classes of people of different countries; but the question involves so many considerations, that a satisfactory solution of it is hardly to be expected!!!"

Can words be found—can terms be conceived, or propositions stated, more diametrically opposed to each other than these—and they are all contained within the little compass of the single passage before quoted, precisely as it stands in Mr Malthus's book?

But Mr Malthus does not even stop here; he does not even content himself with answering the question generally which he had the moment before pronounced unanswerable; for that is obviously the meaning intended to be conveyed by Mr Malthus, when he says it "involves so many considerations," that an answer to it "is hardly to be expected." He does not stop, I say, or content himself with the general answer and "solution" already cited; he actually goes into detail, and gives an example from the countries of Ireland and England in illustration of his "solution," and of the effects of good and bad government as being "the principal causes which determine the different modes of subsistence among the lower classes of people of different countries." He proceeds:—

"According as the habits of the people had been determined by such unfavourable or favourable circumstances, high wages, or a rapid increase of the funds for the maintenance of labour, would be attended with the first or second results before described; or at least by results which would approach to the one or the other, according to the proportions in which all the causes which influence habits of improvidence or prudence had been efficient.

"Ireland, during the course of the last century, may be produced perhaps as the most marked instance of the first result. On the introduction of the potato into that country, the lower classes of society were in such a state of oppression and ignorance, were so little respected by others, and had consequently so little respect for themselves, that as long as they could get food, and that of the cheapest kind, they were content to marry under the prospect of every other privation. The abundant funds for the support of labour, occasioned by the cultivation of the potato in a favourable soil, which often gave the labourer the command of a quantity of subsistence quite unusual in the other parts of Europe, were spent almost exclusively in the maintenance of large and frequent families; and the result was, a most rapid increase of population, with little or no melioration in the general condition and modes of subsistence of the labouring poor.

"An instance somewhat approaching to the second may be found in England, in the first half of the last century. It is well known, that during this period the price of corn fell considerably, while the wages of labour are stated to have risen. During the last forty years of the 17th century, and the first twenty of the 18th, the average price of corn was such as, compared with the wages of labour, would enable the labourer to purchase, with a day's earnings, two-thirds of a peck of wheat. From 1720 to 1750 the price of wheat had so fallen, while wages had risen, that, instead of two-thirds, the labourer could purchase the whole of a peck of wheat with a day's labour.

"This great increase of command over the necessaries of life did not, however, produce a proportionate increase of population. It found the people of this country living under an excellent government, and enjoying all the advantages of civil and political liberty in an unusual degree. The lower classes of people had been in the habit of being respected, both by the laws and the higher orders of their fellow-citizens, and had learned in consequence to respect themselves. And the result was, that, instead of an increase of population exclusively, a considerable portion of their increased real wages was expended in a marked improvement of the quality of the food consumed, and a decided elevation in the standard of their comforts and conveniences."*

There is nothing said here concerning the effects of "climate and soil," those "physical causes" upon which we had previously been assured that "much must certainly depend." Nor is there a single particular brought forward of the "so many considerations" which we had been also told previously should preclude the "expectation" of

* Principles of Political Economy, book iv. sect. 2.

a satisfactory solution. What these considerations are no cue is given to discover; but instead of this the "solution" itself is given! And when Mr Malthus's readers should have expected to hear a dissertation upon the difficulties attending the question, and upon the impossibility, or improbability, at the least, of a satisfactory solution of it being ever achieved, he is confounded and astonished by the introduction, all at once, of the solution itself; cooked indeed, and garnished with the usual modicum of oils and aromatics wherewith Mr Malthus is accustomed to drown and deaden the taste of such indigestible and unsavoury viands. "The question," he says, "involves so many considerations:"—"Among the circumstances:"—"It would be very desirable to ascertain:"—"We shall generally be able to trace:"—and such other dubious and hesitating expressions as may be calculated to throw distrust and uncertainty upon what is otherwise clear.—And "with regard to education, it might certainly be made general under a bad form of government, and might be very deficient under one in other respects good; but it must be allowed that the chances, both with regard to its quality and its prevalence, are greatly in favour of the latter." How eminently candid is this last admission! And with what admirable precision of logical deduction is the conclusion made out!

Mr Malthus may quibble, if he pleases, about the word "satisfactory," which he has inserted perhaps to serve as another loop-hole; he may aver that the solution which he has given is by no means satisfactory to himself, whatever it may be to other people. And here we may readily believe him. He keeps the word of promise to the ear at least. He cannot well be satisfied with that which reduces to nought all that he has ever written, and wholly takes out the sting of his "principle of population." And this it is which gives us the proper cue to discover the cause of the inconsistences and contradictions which pervade Mr Malthus's writings. He reasons himself out of his main doctrine, and he must get back to it again the best way he can.

If the specimen that has been here exhibited of these contradictions could be considered in the light of a simple inadvertence, glaring as it is, it would have deserved or required no remarks; but this is far from being the case. It is not here only, or in a few instances, that Mr Malthus maintains these contradictory doctrines, and exemplifies the model of reasoning which has been here examined. On the contrary, the same desultory and contradictory mode of treating his subject is copied in a thousand instances, and indeed pervades and disfigures the whole of his Essay on Population, as well as his "Principles of Political Economy," wherever he touches upon this question.

But if we are not afraid of the truth, or of removing the imputation of "evil" from "the principle of population," and of allowing that imputation to rest where it ought, and where, in spite of himself, Mr Malthus's own reasonings demonstrate that it should rest, the solution which he has given will appear satisfactory enough; and that which he regarded as so difficult of accomplishment as to be "hardly to be expected," will have been accomplished by himself, even while he was unconscious of and dissentient from his own success.

After what has now passed under review, then, I think I have still new and additional reason to conclude, as I before have done* on the same subject, that "there are in fact but two ways of improving mankind, and of bettering their condition, and these are by means of education and good government; and all attempts to succeed by any other methods will always be found abortive and unavailing. But as a liberal system of education can never be thoroughly

---

* See book i. chap. 10, at the end.

and securely established where good government is not found, and as the former naturally follows where the latter has place, these two causes are in effect reduced to one; and *good government* may be pronounced to be the one indispensable and only efficient cause of improvement in the condition of mankind in general, and particularly in that of the labouring classes of people."

CHAPTER IX.

OF POOR-LAWS.

SECTION I.

INTRODUCTION TO THE CHAPTER.

WHEN it happens to an able-bodied labourer, and to one who has nothing but his labour to look to for his support, that he is unable to procure employment, and that, having exhausted any little store or savings which he might previously have had accumulated, he has nothing remaining wherewithal to satisfy even the immediate cravings of his hunger, it must be confessed, that he is then placed in a worse condition than that of the savage in the state of nature, since the latter is always free at least to employ his labour and exertions to procure food, whereas the former is, under the circumstances supposed, debarred from this privilege, and is in effect (where there is no legal or certain provision made for his case) commanded to starve in the midst of plenty, without moving a finger to save himself from perishing. Now, it is in the highest degree important and vital to the question we are about to discuss, to remember, that the case just stated *is the only one* in which an individual can be placed within the pale of civilized society, in which he will find himself more unfortunately situated, and in a worse condition, than even the savage in his wilderness.

It has been one of the chief objects of the present work to demonstrate, and I trust it has been demonstrated, that the institutions which are necessary to the existence of civilized society, and particularly the institutions of *property*, and of *the system of the division of labour*, are naturally advantageous to the labourers, as well as to the two other classes of land-proprietors and capitalists, inasmuch as they are the means of enabling every person, including even the lowest labourers, (so long as they have employment,) to acquire a greater share of wealth,—of necessaries, conveniences, and luxuries,—than they could do otherwise; that is, in other words, than they could acquire in the state of nature. It seems equally therefore the duty and the interest of every community to guard against the incidence of the case just described, by providing, if possible, for all who may be in want, and thus to make it the interest of *every individual without exception, and at all times*, to support those institutions and laws which are necessary to its existence and well-being.

That this ought to be done, if it were possible, without introducing a greater evil than that which it would be thereby attempted to obviate is allowed; but this, it is contended, is impossible.

That it is not so however, and that to maintain the indigent and necessitous *of every description* is not that impossible or very difficult thing which it has been represented to be, I shall now proceed and endeavour to demonstrate.

SECTION II.

THE POOR-LAWS OF ENGLAND ILL CONTRIVED AND IMPERFECT, CONSIDERED AS A SYSTEM CALCULATED FOR ALL TIMES AND CIRCUMSTANCES—STILL WORSE ADMINISTERED.—POSSIBILITY OF A LEGAL AND COMPULSORY PROVISION FOR THE POOR, WITHOUT THEREBY INCREASING THEIR NUMBERS.

WHETHER the poor-laws of England were well or ill contrived at first, or whether they were well or ill suited to the purpose they were then intended to serve, I shall not now pretend to determine; but, if we consider them as a system calculated for all times and circumstances, it must be admitted at once that they are exceedingly deficient; and in regard to the manner in which they are now administered, and to the many collateral evils which grow out of them, it will be universally acknowledged that they are still more censurable.

As they are at present administered indeed, and considered in regard to present circumstances, these laws are nearly as ill calculated to serve the purpose required, or that which should be aimed at by every poor-law, namely, the relief of those who are in want, without occasioning thereby an increase of their numbers, as can well be conceived. But it does not thence follow that a better system could not be fallen upon, or that (as has been contended) no legal or compulsory provision can be made, or any regular systematic relief be given to the poor, without increasing the evil it is intended to cure. The aged and infirm, at least, might evidently be provided for, without any very great or obvious danger of extending the evil, or of increasing *their* numbers, by over-propagation, which is the bugbear set up to scare us from every regular mode of charity.

But I will go further, and maintain, that even the able-bodied, who may happen to be reduced accidentally to want, and who may be unable for a time to procure employment, may be safely kept living without any bad consequences following, provided it be done with caution and judgment, and that no more be given to any of this description of persons than may be barely sufficient to keep them from starving. Such persons might be allowed, perhaps, about half the ordinary rate of wages of the lowest labourers, without any bad consequences following; and that moderate allowance, whilst it would relieve them from the most deplorable and most miserable of all conditions, namely, that of being without food, or any means of honestly procuring it, and consequently from an overpowering motive to violence,—to rob or steal,—would at the same time furnish no considerable incentive or encouragement to idleness, or to redundant propagation; nor would it interfere detrimentally with the interests of the regular employers of labour,—the three great mischiefs to be guarded against when any gratuitous assistance is given to the able-bodied poor.

The evil apprehended is from "the principle of population:"—That if a liberal and undistinguishing relief were given to the poor, their numbers would increase in proportion as they were relieved, and would even outgrow and absorb the utmost amount of any possible funds that could be assigned or applied to their support. But the relief given need neither be too liberal nor undistinguishing. It ought to be liberal only in cases where the apprehended danger (of redundant propagation) could not arise, as in those of the aged and infirm, and of children under age.

These only, therefore, namely, the aged and infirm, and infants bereft of their parents, and without other resource, I would support *liberally*, but the able-bodied *as sparingly as possible;* and all this, I will maintain, might be done by a proper and well-contrived system of poor-laws, without increasing the evil or the numbers of the poor. I think it indeed not improbable that a well-contrived system of poor-laws would of itself, by its own proper effect, tend rather to *diminish* the numbers of the poor, by tending to raise "the standard of wretchedness," at which the lower classes of labourers would consent to marry and propagate;* and, from what has been formerly advanced,† it will probably appear to the readers as most likely that such a system of poor-laws would soon become, under good government, almost, if not altogether, *a dead letter*.

Previously to the period when Mr Malthus first wrote and published his "Essay on the Principle of Population, the defects and bad consequences of the English poor-laws had been fully observed and pointed out by many intelligent writers; nor did their tendency to encourage idleness, and to increase the evil they were intended to cure, escape notice. But it has only been since the memorable era of that publication that it has entered into the heads of thinking men, and has been set down by them as the most certain and indisputable of all political axioms,‡ that no legal provision can be made, nor any regular, systematic, and certain relief of any sort, be given to the poor, without increasing their numbers in such proportion and amount as to

---

* Even the English poor-laws, with all their faults and imperfections on their head, have probably had something of the effect alluded to, as it cannot readily be imagined that many persons would be willing to take their stations, and settle themselves in marriage, below the scale, whether of comfort or of "wretchedness," which was allowed to those claiming relief from the parish.

† See the preceding chapter, and also chapter 10 of book i.

‡ See as a specimen Mr Ricardo's Principles of Political Economy, chap. 5. p. 106, second edition.

increase and aggravate the evil of poverty; and that, in short, it has been dogmatically pronounced, that the objects attempted to be attained by poor-laws universally are absolutely and altogether unattainable.

This doctrine is now, however, so generally, I might almost say universally, received by all who pretend to be adepts in the science of political economy, is maintained by them with such unhesitating and such undoubting confidence,* and is withal so favourably entertained and patronised in all high places,—even in the highest of all, namely, in

---

* This was written many years before the late sudden and ample recantations of Mr Malthus's disciples,—very coolly given, after having been engaged all the previous part of their lives in dogmatizing on the contrary side,—when their nostrums had well nigh seared up the heart and closed the hand of charity in these kingdoms, and had caused thousands upon thousands of unfortunate persons to be starved to death, or to perish from the want of that proper nourishment and maintenance which every civilized community is bound in justice to administer to all who may be in want within its well-stored precincts. For it was nothing else but the prevalence of those nostrums which perverted men's minds and steeled their hearts, and prevented *timely and adequate* public relief from being given to those numerous bodies of men who were thrown out of employment, upon several occasions, and at different places, since the conclusion of the late war. And now the very men, who were chiefly instrumental in propagating those dogmas which have produced all this mischief and misery, come forward and declare them to be wholly visionary and unsound!

To acknowledge an error when a person discovers he has fallen into one, is to be but barely honest, even if he could with credit or safety deny the fact,—and when it is seen that an exposure of it will speedily be made and throw discredit upon its defenders, there is not even the merit of candour in the confession; but to take up opinions involving such inhuman and unheard-of consequences, without the most rigid and scrupulous investigation, and thus lightly to set them down as portions of *eternal truth* and *science,* is to incur a responsibility and a guilt which is but ill excused or atoned for by an unceremonious and disingenuous recantation of them.

the high courts of parliament,—that it might truly appear a very bold undertaking to oppose the current, and perilous even so much as "to hint a doubt or hesitate dislike," were it not that Mr Malthus, the great apostle and universally-acknowledged oracle of this creed, has been himself observed to waver, and has indeed latterly (as I shall presently show) abandoned and retracted in effect, though not in express words, or by a formal disclamation, his whole theory on this subject, even in regard to the very imperfect poor-laws of England; yet strange it is that none of Mr Malthus's disciples or followers take the slightest notice of this circumstance, or even for a moment advert to those numerous and large concessions and acknowledgments dispersed throughout the writings of their master, which destroy altogether the very essence of his theory. Mr Malthus admits, that there are other "principles" in man, and peculiar to him as contradistinguished from the brutes, besides the "principle of population," and which limit and control that principle in man though not in brutes. His disciples, however, can see nothing but the one principle, the principle of population. They have no ear or understanding for the controlling principles. It is sufficient for them to have read the first chapter of the Essay on Population, and to have comprehended the arithmetical and geometrical ratios. They desire to know no further, but set down all other knowledge as idle, unprofitable, and nugatory; and universally to a man, in so far as I have observed, argue invariably as if the principle of increase in animals were no otherwise controlled or regulated in man than in the brute creation. They seem not to be acquainted with the fact, or most strangely to overlook it, that their master admits the counteracting and controlling principles peculiar to man almost in their full extent; and that he has in one place or another of his voluminous writings repeatedly stated and taken notice of the whole of these principles, except, I believe, one;* although, it must be confessed, that he seems always very chary and very unwilling to take a full and connected, or distinct view of them, or to admit that their influence extends, as most certainly it does, to the entire demolition of the fabric he had previously raised.

It has been most distinctly and correctly stated by Mr Malthus, that the problem to be solved in planning out and establishing a system of poor-laws is, "How to provide for those who are in want in such a manner as to prevent a continual increase of their numbers, and of the proportion which they bear to the whole society. † Now the only difficulty that can occur in dealing with this problem must be in regard to those claimants who are able-bodied, but cannot find employment;—for in regard to the others, namely, the aged, the infirm, and children under age, it is evident that there could be no sort of difficulty with them,

---

* I allude to the principle of *luxury and refinement* which, without degenerating into *vice*, will be found, I believe, to have a powerful effect in restraining population in the advanced periods of society.

This principle I have elsewhere endeavoured shortly to develop (in a pamphlet published several years ago, and already quoted in this work, note, pp. 55, 56,) and now I find all my most sanguine hopes and anticipations confirmed by the facts stated, and the assurances given of still more particular proofs to follow, in a recent publication, —Sadler's "Ireland, its Evils and their Remedies,"—a work which holds forth a glorious prospect for the world and for humanity, by what is there already given, and still more by what is engaged to be proved in the work which is announced to follow, namely, a complete deliverance from the thraldom of Mr Malthus's "principle of population."

"Fond, impious man!—think'st thou yon sanguine cloud,
Raised by thy breath, has quench'd the orb of day?—
To-morrow he repairs the golden flood,
And warms the nations with redoubled ray."

† Essay on Population, book iv. chap. 12.

or any possible danger whatever of their increasing and multiplying their numbers superabundantly.

But to look a little more closely into this point:—The circumstances under which any of the members of a civilized community may be reduced to the necessity of claiming or receiving the charity and assistance of their more fortunate neighbours, may be classed under four heads, and are eloquently stated as follows, by an admirable writer on this subject:*—"1. Man in his infancy and childhood, whose little hands are yet incapable of the labour that should procure him the necessaries of life:—2. The aged, whom length of years, and the hardships they have endured, have finally rendered as feeble as helpless infancy:—3. The sick, the cripple, the maimed, and those who labour under one or other of those diseases which make the most fearful part of the picture of human life:—4. Those who, being both able and willing to work, are yet, by the ill constitution of the society of which they are members, or by some of those revolutions to which perhaps all societies are liable, unable to procure employment."†

Now, here, I think, I may set it down as self-evident, and as undeserving of any further argument to prove it,

---

* Mr Godwin, in his Inquiry concerning Population,—a work which it is impossible to read without delight and improvement, though I feel compelled to differ from the author on one point, namely, as to the power of increase in mankind; which, in as far as it has reference to thinly-peopled countries, I think is as great as Mr Malthus has represented it to be. Throughout the whole performance, however, there is much to approve and admire, and in the latter part, (book vi.) where he treats "Of the Moral and Political Maxims inculcated in the Essay on Population," the expositions he has given of those maxims, and of the monstrous propositions and extravagancies into which Mr Malthus's "Principles of Population" has driven him, is inimitably felicitous and masterly.

† Book vi. chap. 3. p. 542.

that the three first-described classes of persons, at least, might be very safely relieved, and that too with any degree of liberality, (provided it were done "judiciously"—and why not judiciously ?) without any danger, or even possibility, of any undue increase or multiplication of their numbers; and that the only difficulty which can occur, in so far as the principle of population is concerned, is obviously confined to those claimants who are able-bodied, and who, though both able and willing to work, are unable for the time to procure employment. But the whole difficulty in regard to this class of persons is at once obviated by the simple expedient which has already been hinted at; namely, by taking care to allow them but a very *small assistance*, or such a one only as would procure them but a coarse and sparing, though wholesome subsistence: and, if we attend to what Mr Malthus himself says on this head, or rather to the occasional important concessions and admissions he makes in regard to it, we shall soon be convinced that he was by no means unaware of this most plain and simple solution of his problem, and most easy method of overcoming the difficulty which he would still represent as so insurmountable. He observes:—"In so large a town as London, which must necessarily encourage a prodigious influx of strangers from the country, there must be always a great many persons out of work; and it is probable that some public institution for the relief of the casual poor, upon a plan similar to that proposed by Mr Colquhoun, (c. xiii. p. 371,) would, under very judicious management, produce more good than evil. But for this purpose it would be absolutely necessary that, if work were provided by the institution, the sum that a man could earn by it should be less than the worst-paid common labour; otherwise the claimants would rapidly increase, and the funds would soon be inadequate to their object. In the institution at Hamburgh, which appears to have been the most successful of any yet established, the nature of the work was such, that, though paid above the usual price, a person could not easily earn by it more than eighteen-pence a-week. It was the determined principle of the managers of the institution to reduce the support which they gave lower than what any industrious man or woman in such circumstances could earn. (Account of the Management of the Poor in Hamburgh, by C. Voght, p. 18.) And it is to this principle that they attribute their success. It should be observed, however, that neither the institution at Hamburgh, nor that planned by Count Rumford in Bavaria, has subsisted long enough for us to be able to pronounce on their permanent good effects. It will not admit of a doubt, that institutions for the relief of the poor, on their first establishment, remove a great quantity of distress. The only question is, whether, as succeeding generations arise, the increasing funds necessary for their support, and the increasing numbers that become dependent, are not greater evils than that which was to be remedied; and whether the country will not ultimately be left with as much mendicity as before, besides all the poverty and dependence accumulated in the public institutions? This seems to be nearly the case in England at present. It may be doubted whether we should have more beggars if we had no poor-laws."*

Here we see that Mr Malthus comes the length of admitting that "it is probable that some public institution for the relief of the casual poor, upon a plan similar to that proposed by Mr Colquhoun, would, under very judicious management, produce more good than evil." So far so good:—"But for this purpose," continues Mr Malthus, "it would be absolutely necessary that, if work were provided by the institution, the sum that a man could earn by it should be less than the worst-paid common labour." No doubt it should:—who denies it? And who does not see that, if this precaution were adopted, the whole danger, which has been so much magnified, of encouragement to

* Essay on Population, book iv. chap. 4, note.

idleness, and of an unlimited increase and propagation of paupers, would be removed? Do not the plainest dictates of common sense point out this course? and does not the same common sense assure us, that if this course were pursued, under "judicious management," (and why should it not be under judicious management?*) nothing but the best consequences could follow from it.

But if such institutions would produce good "in London," why should they not do the same in other places, where, in proportion to their extent and populousness, the need for them may be as great?

Mr Malthus indeed, according to his usual practice, endeavours to throw suspicion and doubt upon the probable ultimate success of this plan of providing for the poor, even though pursued in the most judicious way, by saying, "It should be observed, however, that neither the institution at Hamburgh, nor that planned by Count Rumford in Bavaria, has subsisted long enough for us to be able to pronounce on their permanent good effects;"† and so on, to

---

* In the present day, when the general principles on this subject are so well understood, and when so many intelligent individuals are willing and even anxious to lend their assistance in the management of charitable institutions, the desideratum referred to in the text would seem to be not very difficult of attainment.

† I have not been able to procure any further information than what is given by Mr Malthus himself, in the note before quoted, either in regard to the two institutions mentioned above, or concerning the laws and management of the poor in Holland "before the Revolution," which are also taken notice of by Mr Malthus elsewhere; but, from the manner in which the whole, and particularly the latter, are spoken of by him, I am led to suspect that in them will be found a *practical* refutation of Mr Malthus's doctrine of the impossibility of providing for all who are in want. He admits that "she (Holland) was able to employ and support all who applied for relief;" inventing, and thrusting in of course, at the same time, a saving clause to prevent the total wreck of his theory.

the end of the note above cited. This is no more than was naturally to be expected from Mr Malthus. This little note would have overturned his whole book else. But no person will, I think, be much swayed by this insinuation: on the contrary, when we consider on the one hand the pressing nature of the emergency with which Mr Malthus is beset, and on the other the halting and hesitating way in which this surmise is thrown in, it will be impossible to resist the conclusion, that he was himself wellnigh overpowered here with the conviction that all who are in want might be succoured and relieved under the restrictions recommended, without increasing the proportion which they bear to the whole community, and without producing any other of those ill consequences which he so much fears, and which he is so very anxious to persuade us would happen.

But in order to show manifestly that Mr Malthus comes, at last, not only to doubt and distrust the doctrines and opinions which he had originally promulgated on this subject of the poor-laws, but that he has really, as I have before said, retracted and abandoned them in effect, it will be sufficient to adduce the following passages from the Appendix to the fifth edition of the Essay on Population:—"The obvious tendency," says Mr Malthus in the place just mentioned, "of the poor-laws is certainly to encourage marriage; but a closer attention to all their indirect as well as direct effects may make it a matter of doubt to what extent they really do this. They clearly tend, in their general operation, to discourage sobriety and economy, to encourage idleness and the desertion of children, and to put virtue and vice more on a level than they otherwise would be; but I will not presume to say positively that they greatly encourage population. It is certain that the proportion of births in this country, compared with others in similar circumstances, is very small; but this was to be expected from the superiority of the government, the more respectable state of the people, and the more general diffusion of a taste for cleanliness and conveniences. And it will readily occur to the reader, that, owing to these causes, combined with the twofold operation of the poor-laws, it must be extremely difficult to ascertain, with any degree of precision, what has been their effect on population."* And to this passage Mr Malthus adds the following in a note:—" The most favourable light in which the poor-laws can possibly be placed, is to say that, under all the circumstances with which they have been accompanied, they do not much encourage marriage; and undoubtedly the returns of the Population Act seem to warrant the assertion. Should this be true, many of the objections which have been urged in the Essay against the poor-laws will be removed; but I wish to press on the attention of the reader, that they will in that case be removed in strict conformity to the general principles of the work, and in a manner to confirm, not to invalidate, the main positions which it has attempted to establish."†

The assertion contained in the latter clause of this last sentence I deny. " The main positions" which the Essay on Population " has attempted to establish" are, first, that, " under a government constructed upon the best and purest principles, and executed by men of the highest talents and integrity, the most squalid poverty and wretchedness might prevail from an inattention to the prudential check to population:"‡ and, secondly, not only that the poor have no right to support, but that to support them is an utter impossibility. How then, I would beg to ask, can any objections against the poor-laws be removed " in a manner to confirm, not invalidate, the main positions it has attempted to establish?"

Mr Malthus, however, still maintains his original doctrines as broadly and confidently as ever, just as if none

---

* Appendix, vol. iii., p. 373. † Ibid. p. 374.

‡ Essay on Population, book iv., chap. 6.

of those concessions and acknowledgments which have been here exhibited had ever been made by him. In a performance which he has given to the world, some years later than that from which the above passages are taken, he puts forth the following argument, which he seems to think quite decisive against the possibility of any description of legal provision for the poor being made or executed:

"The existence," says he, "of a tendency in mankind to increase, if unchecked, beyond the possibility of an adequate supply of food in a limited territory, must at once determine the question as to the natural right of the poor to *full* support in a state of society where the law of property is recognized. The question, therefore, resolves itself chiefly into a question relating to the necessity of those laws which establish and protect private property:"* and again, in the same place:—"There is no modification of the law of property having still for its object the increase of human happiness, which must not be defeated by the concession of a right of *full* support to all that might be born. It may be safely said, therefore, that the concession of such a right, and a right of property, are absolutely incompatible, and cannot exist together."*

Mr Malthus here, as in other instances (a few of which have been seen) where he knows himself to be touching on the tender points of his theory, is very guarded in his language; and the little word FULL, (which I have put in italics,) carefully repeated in both the above passages, sufficiently demonstrates that Mr Malthus was perfectly well aware how necessary that word was to the truth of the propositions he was advancing, when he inserts it, although it renders those propositions totally useless for his purpose, and utterly powerless and nugatory in any argument against a system of poor-laws, according to which *a limited and regulated support* only should be allowed. How well aware

---

* Supplement to Encyclopaedia Britannica, article Population, (written by Mr Malthus,) vol. vi. p. 331.

Mr Malthus was of the indispensableness of that word to the truth of the propositions in which he places it will also be seen by turning to the passage quoted from him two or three pages back, wherein he states it as a *sine qua non* to the success of a charitable establishment, where work should be supplied to unemployed labourers, that "the sum that a man could earn by it should be less than the worst-paid common labour."*

Now, if by a *full support* Mr Malthus merely means to say that if a poor-law were instituted which should allow *twenty shillings* a-week to every idle person who chose to demand it, without questions asked, such a regulation would be incompatible with a right of property, and would speedily superinduce such a rapid increase and undue multiplication of applicants as must entirely overwhelm and absorb every fund subjected to their claims,—I am as ready as himself to acknowledge and maintain the truth of his doctrine. But how does this subserve his argument? Or what has it to do with the question of the practicability or impracticability of a legal and limited provision for the poor? Still it may be true that even able-bodied labourers may be safely kept alive during such times as they are unable to procure employment, and may be allowed a small and sparing, though not "a full support,"—may be allowed perhaps three or four shillings (though not twenty) a-week, consistently enough with "a right of property:"—and if this be granted, the above formidable-looking assertions turn out to be altogether harmless, and this new argument of Mr Malthus, though so cautiously worded, and brought forward with an air of so much consequence, is found, nevertheless, entirely to fail him at his utmost need.

When Mr Malthus's doctrines were first broached, and

---

* See before, pp. 351, 352.

the bruit of them began to be heard throughout the land, it was thought to have been discovered and placed beyond the possibility of doubt, that the numbers of the poor, under the English laws and management, would necessarily increase in a "geometrical ratio," and that the "rates," if unchecked, must in the end, and in no long time, absorb and "eat up" the whole value and produce of the land. Land proprietors became seriously alarmed for their estates, and almost every body encouraged them in that alarm. It was no great wonder, therefore, that they should have readily listened to every projector, and entertained with favour every proposition which promised to avert so imminent a hazard, however senseless and absurd might be the nature both of the alarm raised and of the proposed remedy. It was no great wonder that *emigration* should have been most gravely attempted as a palliative, and that even the avowed dereliction of universal charity should have been represented and resorted to as the grand and only effectual *panacea*. Seeing, or believing that they saw, a speedy and inevitable destruction impending over them, every other feeling was overpowered and stifled by the stronger claims of self-preservation.

The consequences have been dreadful;—a conspiracy,—an almost universal though tacit combination was formed against the poor,—a combination the object of which was to resist and obstruct the execution of the poor-laws,—clergymen and heritors have participated in it, and even the courts of justice,—the bench and the bar,—have all united to condemn every form of poor-law, and to obstruct and discountenance an appeal to those we have, as far as their power or influence extended. Here in Scotland, at least, I can safely say that this has been the case; and the best proof of it is, that at the present moment the most miserable and inadequate allowances are given, even to the aged and infirm poor throughout Scotland. But I should do injustice to the actors in this memorable crusade of the powerful against the miserable, if I did not here add, that they have all the while believed they were performing a high and meritorious act of virtue!

Happily, however, there are now many symptoms appearing of the breaking up of this confederacy, and of a strong disposition to doubt the soundness of the conclusions previously arrived at, and relied on as unquestionable. The doctrines that have occasioned all this mischief are even renounced and abandoned by some of those who were chiefly instrumental in spreading them; and a poor-law for Ireland has even been proposed with some hope of success. A ray of heavenly light now irradiates the sky, and has penetrated the gloom which rested on the beginning of the nineteenth century, and a more cheering prospect at length opens upon us.

But what plan, perhaps it may be asked, would we recommend for adoption as a general system for the support of the poor of every description?—To this question I should answer, that this is not the proper place (in a work of this description) to enter into the details of such a measure; nor is it the province or the peculiar duty of an inquirer into the general principles of legislation to frame a *bill* or an act of parliament; yet it may not be improper to notice here one or two of the most material alterations which it seems necessary should be made in our present poor-laws, to render them in any degree adequate to their object, or to that which it appears, from what has been advanced, a well-contrived system of poor-laws should accomplish.

In any measure having the object just mentioned in view, it appears to me that the first thing necessary to be done would be to abolish the present regulation, whereby every parish is obliged to maintain its own poor separately, and with it all obstructions to any person *not a criminal* removing from one place or parish to another, or to his settling himself where he pleases in any honest business. The burden of the whole poor would then be borne equally by *the whole people*, and the expense paid out of the public treasury; which expense would be replaced and the treasury again replenished when necessary, by a general tax and contribution levied upon *all classes of persons*, down almost to the very lowest; since none ought to be relieved altogether from the duty and obligation of charity, and almost none can be so poor as to be incapable of contributing their mite.*

Still, however, the clergymen and church-officers of the different parishes might be constituted guardians and overseers of the poor, and the parish-clerk treasurer, within their bounds, nearly as at present; and the whole system should still likewise remain, as before, under the control and protection of the ordinary law-courts; and I would further propose, that upon any emergency, such as might happen in the case of any considerable number of applications being made by labourers in want of employment, or in any other case of more than common urgency, it should be the duty of the Sheriff of the district to inquire into the circumstances of his locality, (the whole county,) and, with such advice

* As, however, there would still be ample room for *voluntary charity* after all that could be accomplished by the most comprehensive and best-contrived system of poor-laws, such a tax, or *poor-rate*, as is proposed, might be *graduated* and diminished on the smaller incomes and properties, so as to leave the contributions of those who are more closely in contact with, and have consequently the better opportunities of discovering the truly-deserving and necessitous,—to be chiefly at their own disposal. Such regulation will appear the more peculiarly proper and expedient, when it is considered how much charity, or assistance in difficult circumstances, is given by the poorer sort of labourers to one another.

and assistance as he should choose to call for, devise such employment for them as might be useful to the public during the time they should receive the public money.

Then I will suppose that all the aged and infirm might be allowed four shillings a-week each to a man, and three shillings to a woman; whilst the able-bodied labourer wanting employment might be allowed three shillings per week to a man, and one shilling and sixpence to a woman, and to either man or woman who had children, during such want of employment, one shilling additional for each child.*

And thus the proper object of a poor-law would be fully accomplished,—a certain provision would be made for all who might happen to be in want,—public begging might be wholly suppressed,—and no person could afterwards have any just reason to arraign the institution of property as injuring him, or find himself placed in a worse condition in consequence of its existence than he would otherwise have experienced.

But, perhaps, it will be said, that to try such a measure would be a great work and a great experiment; and no doubt it would; but is not the object to be accomplished of great importance also?—The reasons for preferring a legal and certain provision for the poor (supposing it practicable, which has, I trust, been fully demonstrated) to a precarious and uncertain one, as any voluntary provision must be, are neither few nor small, and are indeed so plain and obvious

* I have set down these sums, or pittances, not by any means as unalterable, or as the result of any very nice calculation of circumstances, but as the lowest that could be named with any sort of regard to the calls of humanity or of justice, the present value of money of course being taken into account. So far from being unalterable, I think that if the experiment of a well-regulated legal provision for the poor were fairly tried, it would soon be discovered that much more liberal allowances than those stated might be made with safety, or without entailing any considerable burden upon the community.

as scarcely to stand in need of being stated. In concluding the present section, however, I shall recapitulate shortly the three following:—

I. In the first place, to make a legal and compulsory provision for the poor is the only effectual way to put a stop to public begging, which is unseemly in itself and mischievous in its consequences to all who are compelled to witness it, even while they are able to relieve every applicant, but which becomes tenfold more pernicious when it arrives to that height (which it has frequently done in this country of late years) that you are not only unable to relieve, but scarcely even to hearken to the complaints of the numerous unfortunate objects presented to your view. For when men are obliged to look daily upon nakedness, and hunger, and disease, or upon all three combined, and to tell the miserable sufferer that they can administer nothing to his relief or comfort, but, on the contrary, must drive him from their doors and from their sight, every compassionate feeling must be violated and blunted; and the frequent repetition of such sights and scenes must harden the heart and eradicate all sentiments of humanity out of the world.

II. Secondly, the legal and compulsory provision has this great advantage over the precarious and voluntary one, that it equalizes the burden that actually is and must be borne in supporting the poor, by obliging the uncharitable and hard-hearted to contribute exactly and fairly with the charitable and humane in proportion to their means.

III. Thirdly, the feelings and happiness or unhappiness of the poor themselves are surely not to be wholly overlooked in this question. Now, under a voluntary and uncertain provision, they are condemned to a continual despondence,—to live under continual dread of the most distressful calamity which can happen to them—the dread of starvation;—whereas, under a legal and compulsory provision, all this waste of anxiety and despondency is spared and prevented, and their condition converted into one of comparative comfort; and all this, it is believed, at no greater cost, or sacrifice, even in a merely pecuniary view, than is required to be made under the voluntary system.

But, perhaps, it may be thought and urged still farther, that such a certain refuge and provision for all who might be in want as has been here proposed, would make labourers and servants regardless and insolent to their employers, as not caring about being turned out of their places; but let the same law which bestows upon them the boon recommended correct this evil by being more strict and impartial than it is found to be at present* in compelling them to perform articles and agreements.

SECTION III.

RIGHT OF THE POOR TO SUPPORT.

WHAT has now been advanced may be sufficient perhaps to show the possibility and expediency of providing a maintenance for the poor by a legal and compulsory assessment; but before concluding the present chapter, I must revert again to the question of *right*, which was but slightly touched

* In the justice of peace courts here in Scotland, where the greater part of the disputes between "masters and servants" are settled, it is too much the practice of the judges to *make a merit* of *favouring* the poorer sort, particularly against manufacturers and all other "masters," themselves and the farmers, perhaps, excepted. Even the Sheriffs are not entirely free from this fault.

upon in the beginning of it; and I will contend, that, in a civilized country, where the land is all appropriated, and the division of labour established, and where the liberty to engross and accumulate land and every other species of wealth to any extent is allowed, *all who may be in want have a right to support;*—the aged and infirm unconditionally, and the able-bodied labourer to either gratuitous aid, or to wages and employment.

When, in the midst of a civilized society where the land is all appropriated, the division of labour established, and where no legal provision has been made for the poor, it happens to the labourer that he is unable to procure employment, and has nothing to eat, he is in effect commanded to starve without resistance, and without any effort to save himself. But what sanction has the society of which he is a member to offer, which should induce him to comply with so inhuman and so unreasonable a command?—Death is the highest punishment that the society can inflict; but death stares the person so circumstanced already in the face, and he is certain that he must immediately perish if he yields obedience to this mandate.*

In the state of nature the land would still have remained open to him, and he would have been at full liberty to use all his exertions to procure subsistence; and whatever difficulty he might at times have found in acquiring his daily food, he never could have wanted employment. But in the advanced state of society before described the case is totally changed; to the unemployed labourer in that state the

* As to any religious sanction, or any authority from Scripture, for such a command, it cannot be pretended for a moment; for all religions inculcate charity, and Christianity especially inculcates it, even to the extent, upon some occasions, of enjoining the rich man to "sell all that he hath, and give to the poor."

land is entirely locked up, his hands are tied, and he is placed in the cruellest of all situations, being expected and called upon (where no provision is made for his case) to perish for want in the midst of plenty; and all the while he is denied the use of his arms or exertions in any way that should procure him a morsel of food. These, however, are too hard conditions to be either endured or imposed by human nature; and it always happens when such a case occurs that the rigour of the law is relaxed and mitigated. Judges will hardly pronounce sentence of condemnation, and juries will not find a man "guilty" who takes a loaf of bread under such pressing circumstances; while it is uniformly found that the spectators warmly applaud such lenity and mercy. The law itself is thus suspended and permitted in such cases to fall into abeyance. And why is this?—Clearly because, when an individual happens to be reduced to the unhappy condition which has been described—to the condition of being without food and without employment in a society where no legal provision is made for the relief of his case—all conventional laws are dissolved in regard to him. He is then left to his state of nature, and he that moment re-acquires all those rights which that state implies, namely, a right to use all his energies of mind and body, and all the means within his power, to procure the sustenance immediately necessary to the preservation of his life, how he may, but with as little hurt as he can to his more fortunate brethren. If, therefore, the society of which he is a member maintains and acts upon the doctrine that he has no right to support, it is at open war with him; his hand must necessarily be against every man's and every man's against his. Prudence or pusillanimity, or the hopelessness of succeeding against so great odds, may restrain his arm and induce him to submit patiently and without resistance to his fate,—to perish without any attempt to prolong his life otherwise than by the ordinary and allowed means,—but it never can be his duty to perish in this manner. The common right of nature which belongs to all men,—the right to draw their subsistence from the mother earth, either immediately and directly, as in the state of nature, or in a roundabout way, as in the civilized state, never is or can be annulled or abrogated. After the division of labour is established, the earth's produce cannot be taken by every one directly, but subsistence still comes to every one from the earth, whence alone it can come, although to the greater number of individuals in a roundabout way. In this state of things the right enjoyed in the state of nature to take directly of the earth's produce as much as may be required to support life is relinquished in order to enjoy the greater advantages which arise from the division of labour, by means of which a more ample and liberal subsistence is acquired by every body, and especially by the labourer himself. The one right or advantage therefore is obviously given up for the other. But this arrangement necessarily implies the condition that the labourer shall find employment; and when this condition fails and support is denied him, his original right of nature reverts to him, and he is again at liberty to ransack the world for food independent of all human conventions, which, in as far as regards him, are broken and annulled. That the right to derive his subsistence from the earth, and to acquire it how he may, devolves upon the individual the instant he cannot find either employment or support, may appear evident from this circumstance, that it is obviously on the condition of receiving employment and wages for their labour that the great body of labourers,—always the majority in all countries and in all conditions of society,—consent to the alienation of their original right to take directly of the produce of the land. This condition therefore, (I mean employment and wages, or the alternative of support,) must be looked upon as a fundamental and indefeisible law in every society from the moment that the division of labour is introduced. In a society, therefore, which makes no provision for the poor, or for the unemployed labourer wanting support, the individual so circumstanced is at full liberty, in the eye of reason and of justice, to use his whole force and his whole wisdom in any manner he thinks fit short of inflicting death—the evil he would himself avoid—on another, in order to procure a pittance of food, when it becomes the only alternative by which he can save himself from dying of hunger.

And that this is really the feeling of all men when such a case is brought home to them, appears evident from this, that in all such cases the offender is invariably acquitted. In every case that I have observed to happen, (and I have observed many,) where a person has been brought to account for laying hold, under the circumstances described, of the first food that came in his way, although it was not his own property, *the penalty of the law has been uniformly remitted.** Judges have not condemned nor juries convicted; while the lookers-on have gone fully along with both, and have cordially approved of their conduct and lenity on such occasions. Many readers may probably be able to re-

---

* Since this was written, the following case has come under the author's observation, in which, contrary to what is stated in the text, and to what he had before observed, a person has been punished under the circumstance described, namely, for "stealing through hunger." The case I allude to is thus reported in the Scotsman newspaper of January 21st, 1829.—"*Stealing through Hunger.*—Thomas Curtis, a labourer, was indicted at the Surrey Sessions, on Tuesday se'ennight, for stealing a loaf of bread. The trial of this case exhibited the difficulty of the peasantry procuring agricultural labour. The charge was fully proved against the prisoner—namely, that he snatched a loaf of bread from the window of the prosecutor's shop, and ran away with it. The jury having found him guilty, the chairman asked him in what situation in life he was; to which the prisoner, who to all appearance is a strong and healthy young man, replied, that he was an agricultural labourer, and that being unable to obtain employment, he was allowed

collect instances of such acquittals under the circumstances described; to complete, however, this part of my argument, I shall adduce the following:—

The first case I shall notice of the kind described occurred in London a good many years ago; but, having mislaid the paper in which I found it, I can neither give the statement *precisely* as reported, nor the exact date when it took place. I am unwilling, however, to omit the mention of this case altogether, as it is so much to my present purpose, and I shall therefore state the chief circumstances and particulars of it as I recollect them.* The case was that of an American sailor who was brought before the Lord Mayor of London, either at the Mansion-House or Guildhall, I am uncertain which, charged with stealing a loaf. (This happened at a time when there were many hundreds of sailors going about the streets of London idle and unable to pro-

---

4s. a week by the parish for digging in the fields from morning until night. Out of this sum he had to pay 1s. 6d. a-week for his lodging, leaving 2s. 6d. for him to subsist upon. This was not adequate to his support, and he declared that it was while labouring under the cravings of hunger that he took the loaf. The Rev. Mr Onslow, who was on the bench, inquired of the prisoner whether four shillings was all he got in the week for working for the parish? He stated that it was, and said that even this was not paid regularly; for some weeks, when he was only employed two or three days, he only received 2s. 6d. The Court said, that his loss of character must have been the chief cause of his not being employed. They were informed that he was labouring under some bodily infirmity, otherwise a flogging would have been added to the punishment to which the Court was about to sentence him—namely, a month's imprisonment."

It is to be regretted that "the Court" should not have condescended to state any grounds they had for the opinion expressed, "that his loss of character *must* have been the chief cause of his not being employed."

* After much research in different files of newspapers, I have been unable to lay my hands on this case. Nevertheless, I am certain as to the general accuracy of the statement given above.

cure employment, which was, I think, not long after the conclusion of the late war.) On his defence the culprit stated, that he had been unable to find any employment for several months previously, nor could he procure a passage home, although he was willing to have worked it without any wages but his victuals. He stated farther, that he had expended all his previous savings some time past. He was then asked if he had had any thing to eat that day? to which he answered, "No, nor the day before neither;" and the poor lad could suppress his feelings no longer, but burst into tears. The sympathy of the court and of all present was immediately turned in his favour, and money was thrown to him from all quarters of the hall; and the Lord Mayor not only allowed him to accept the money so presented, and to depart without any punishment, but promised farther to see him taken care of, and assisted to find a passage to his native country.

The next case I shall adduce to the same effect occurred more recently in the Edinburgh Police Court, and is reported as follows:—

"POLICE COURT.—Yesterday, a man about 30 years of age was accused of stealing a loaf from a baker's apprentice. He had the appearance of a machine-maker or founder. When the Magistrate inquired what he was, and what had induced him to steal the loaf, he answered, that he belonged to Glasgow, and had come to this town in search of employment, but could find none. He denied that he *stole* the loaf; he "took it," and was "obliged to do it by necessity." His downcast looks and dejected appearance fully corroborated his melancholy statement, and the Magistrate humanely allowed him to depart, on his promising to set out immediately on his return to Glasgow."*

The third and last case I shall mention is perhaps still stronger to our purpose than even the foregoing, inasmuch as it is not *food* but other property, less immediately neces-

* Scotsman newspaper, June 6, 1827.

sary to existence, which is taken by the accused. It is thus represented in the newspaper report:—

"UNION HALL.—Yesterday, Mary Saunders, a young creature, about 23 years of age, whose emaciated countenance presented a miserable personification of poverty and distress, was charged, a little before the close of the office, before Mr Chambers, the sitting Magistrate, under the following circumstances:—

"Mr Dennett, foreman to Mr Kirkham, pawnbroker, Newington-causeway, stated, that, about half an hour before, the prisoner seized a pair of black trowsers, exposed at the shop for sale, and attempted to make off with them. She was seen to take them, and pursued. When overtaken, she made no resistance, but surrendered herself at once to the officer.

"Mr Chambers—Are you a married woman?—I am.

"Mr Chambers—Where is your husband?—I don't know.

"Mr Chambers—Does he know you are here?—Oh no, he knows nothing of it.

"Mr Chambers—Why did you attempt this felony?—I was starving. I had nothing to eat, nor was my husband able to assist me; he was equally distressed with myself.

"The constable asked her what sort of a man her husband was; on which she evinced a considerable degree of alarm, and, after hesitating for some time, replied, that he was a tall man, dressed in a short jacket of a light colour.

"The constable then stated that his reason for asking the prisoner this question was, that he observed a man outside the office crying very bitterly, and whom he suspected to be her husband, but he did not by any means answer the description given of him.

"Mr Chambers ordered him to be brought in. His appearance was equally miserable with that of the female. The moment the prisoner saw him enter, she uttered a most piercing shriek, and, clasping her hands together and sinking upon her knees, exclaimed, 'Oh, that is not my husband; indeed it is not!'

"Mr Chambers asked him did he know her? to which he replied in the affirmative; when she again exclaimed, 'O, yes! he does know me; he's my brother.'

"Mr Chambers—What relation are you to her?

"Saunders—I am her husband, Sir.

"Prisoner—Oh no, he is not my husband; nor was he with me when I took the property.

"Saunders—I was with her, and am equally guilty; but we were starving. I am a watch-cap manufacturer, and have been out of employment several months. I did all I could to earn what would support us, but failed. I applied to the officers of Cripplegate and elsewhere, but they told us we were young and strong, and treated us like dogs, and at last we have been driven to this. We had not even a place to lie down at night, but were forced to walk the streets.

"Mr Chambers—You seem to have a lodging, for a key of a room door was found upon your wife.

"Saunders—This morning her sister gave her that key, belonging to *an empty room in a house at Clerkenwell belonging to her*, that we might shelter ourselves there at night; also a ticket for a sheet to cover us, to release which I expected to get a shilling from my uncle; but being disappointed, she attempted to take the trowsers to obtain the money.

"The husband wept bitterly during his examination; and so melancholy a case of distress on the part of both, and so singular an instance of affection on that of the prisoner, as displayed in her anxiety to screen her husband from any implication in her guilt, excited the sympathy of every one present; and Mr Dennett, the prosecutor, expressed himself unwilling to press the charge.

"Mr Chambers readily assented to this humane proceeding, and directing Saunders to occupy the empty room in Clerkenwell to-night, and apply for parochial relief to-morrow, discharged the prisoners, a sum of six shillings being given them, half-a-crown of which was advanced by Mr Dennett, the prosecutor."*

In the cases now detailed, (and others of the same kind

---

* The Dumfries and Galloway Courier of November 11, 1828.

might be added and multiplied without number,) the real sentiments of mankind are clearly seen, and it is found that, when a case of such misery comes actually before them, men can no longer adhere to those resolutions, or enforce, in all their rigour, those laws which they framed perhaps in their closets and at their ease, when all such objects were removed far from their sight, and but faintly and inadequately conceived by them.

The real sentiments of mankind universally on the point here discussed, whenever it is brought home to their bosoms and business, may be farther illustrated by the conduct which is pursued and allowed to be justifiable in a city besieged, or in a ship at sea, where, when the stores and provisions run short, bread and other articles of food are taken without scruple, and divided equally amongst all, no matter to whom they may have belonged previously. In such emergencies it is allowable to remember that the stores of food which a man calls his own, and which, being collected by him, are said, in the language of political economy, and in the sense before explained,* to be produced by his labour, are in reality in their matter and essence produced by nature and nature's God;† and that although it may be unquestionably true that it is for the interest of mankind, and indeed necessary, as I have repeatedly shown, to the improvement, and even to the existence of civilized society, that men should be allowed to engross and accumulate, under all ordinary circumstances, as much as they please of food, as well as of any other sort of wealth, yet still, whenever the emergency becomes such that the strict observance of this arrangement appears evidently inconsistent with the end for which it was instituted, the obligation it implied previously can no longer remain in force, but must now

* See chap. ii. sec. 1, of book i. † *Vide ibid.*

give way to the stronger law of necessity and of self-preservation. And hence it is that Mr Hume speaks in the following manner of an equal partition of bread in a famine as a thing allowable and justifiable:—"Suppose," says he, "a society to fall into such a want of all common necessaries, that the utmost frugality and industry cannot preserve the greater number from perishing, and the whole from extreme misery; it will readily, I believe, be admitted, that the strict laws of justice are suspended in such a pressing emergence, and give place to the stronger motives of necessity and self-preservation. Is it any crime, after a shipwreck, to seize whatever means or instrument of safety one can lay hold of, without regard to former limitations of property? Or if a city besieged were perishing with hunger, can we imagine that men will see any means of preservation before them, and lose their lives, from a scrupulous regard to what, in other situations, would be the rules of equity and justice? The USE and TENDENCY of that virtue is to procure happiness and security by preserving order in society; but where the society is ready to perish from extreme necessity, no greater evil can be dreaded from violence and injustice, and every man may now provide for himself by all the means which prudence can dictate, or humanity permit. The public, even in less urgent necessities, opens granaries without the consent of proprietors, as justly supposing, that the authority of magistracy may, consistent with equity, extend so far; but were any number of men to assemble, without the tie of laws or civil jurisdiction, would an equal partition of bread in a famine, though effected by power and even violence, be regarded as criminal or injurious?*"

But what is allowable to a whole people, or to a large body of men, must be equally allowable to one man under the same circumstances; the only difference being, that the latter is not in so good a condition, or, in other words, so

* Inquiry concerning the Principles of Morals, sec. iii. part 2.

able to keep himself or to assert and enforce his right as the former.

I am happy in being able still farther to confirm the doctrine here maintained of the right of the poor to support, by the authority of a no less approved and popular writer than Dr Paley; whose opinion and reasonings will be perhaps more willingly listened to in some quarters than those of the author last quoted:—

"Another right," says this author, "which may be called a general right, as it is incidental to every man who is in a situation to claim it, is the right of extreme necessity; by which is meant, a right to use or destroy another's property, when it is necessary for our own preservation to do so; as a right to take, without or against the owner's leave, the first food, clothes, or shelter we meet with, when we are in danger of perishing through want of them; a right to throw goods overboard to save the ship; or to pull down a house, in order to stop the progress of a fire, and a few other instances of the same kind. Of which right the foundation seems to be this, that when property was first instituted, the institution was not intended to operate to the destruction of any; therefore, when such consequences would follow, all regard to it is superseded. Or rather, perhaps, these are the few cases, where the particular consequence exceeds the general consequence; where the mischief resulting from the violation of the general rule is overbalanced by the immediate advantage."*

And again:—"The poor have a claim founded in the law of nature, which may be thus explained:—All things were originally common. No one being able to produce a charter from Heaven, had any better title to a particular possession than his next neighbour. There were reasons for mankind's agreeing upon a separation of this common fund, and God for these reasons is presumed to have ratified it. But this separation was made and consented to upon the expectation

* Moral Philosophy, book ii. part 1, chap. 2.

and condition that every one should have left a sufficiency for his subsistence, or the means of procuring it; and as no fixed laws for the regulation of property can be so contrived as to provide for the relief of every case and distress which may arise, these cases and distresses, when their right and share in the common stock was given up or taken from them, were supposed to be left to the voluntary bounty of those who might be acquainted with the exigencies of their situation, and in the way of affording assistance. And, therefore, when the partition of property is rigidly maintained against the claims of indigence and distress, it is maintained in opposition to the intention of those who made it, and to *his*, who is the Supreme Proprietor of every thing, and who has filled the world with plenteousness for the sustentation and comfort of all whom he sends into it."*

Indeed the only ground (as has been before observed) on which the right of the poor to support has been or can be denied, is the alleged one of the impossibility of maintaining all who may be in want under a legal provision, and under a full knowledge on their part of their right, and a full acknowledgment of it on the part of those who are to support them. This ground being removed, however, and the allegation by which it is attempted to be maintained being shown (as I trust it has been) to rest on no solid arguments, and to have been already, in effect, abandoned by its ablest and most anxious defenders, the other consequence naturally and necessarily follows, namely, that the poor ought to be provided for by a legal assessment.

I shall conclude this chapter, therefore, by stating it as a theorem which has been demonstrated, that the right of the poor to support, and the right of the rich to engross and accumulate, are correlative and reciprocal privileges, the former being the condition on which the latter is enjoyed.

---

* Moral Philosophy, book iii. part 2, chap. 5.

CHAPTER X.

OF TAXES AND PUBLIC DEBTS.

SECTION I.

TAXES DEFINED—THAT ALL THREE DISTINCT SORTS OF REVENUE AFFORD TAXES, WAGES AS WELL AS PROFIT AND RENT

TAXES are general contributions of wealth, taken compulsatively, or by authority of law, (commonly in money, though sometimes in other sorts of goods,) for the purpose of being applied to pay expenses of a public nature; in particular to pay the expenses of government, that is, the expenses of justice and of defence, &c., as well as every other charge which governments or societies may be called upon or may deem it expedient to incur for the general good.

Taxes, therefore, are the items which make up the public revenue, and must all be paid out of the private revenue of individuals, namely, out of rent, profit, and wages.*

The old French Economists, who still have a few followers, maintain, that all taxes fall wholly upon the land, or upon rent, denying that either profit or wages afford any;—the Ricardo economists again contend that taxes fall entirely upon rent and profit, denying in like manner that wages afford any. It is hoped, however, that what has been advanced in some of the former chapters of this inquiry will have been sufficient to demonstrate the fallacy of both these opinions, and to establish the

* Taxes may indeed be paid out of *capital* as well as out of *revenue*; but they can only be paid *permanently* out of the latter.

soundness of that which is laid down by Mr Hume and Dr Smith on this subject; namely, that all three distinct sorts of revenue afford taxes, *wages* as well as profit and rent.

It will be sufficient in this place, therefore, simply to reassert the doctrines maintained by the two authors just mentioned in regard to taxes, under the three different heads or denominations of revenue, and to refer to the fifth book of the Wealth of Nations for the fullest and most perfect account of the incidence and effect of particular imposts that has ever yet been given to the public.

I. *Taxes on Rent.*—Every land tax ought to be laid on the *rent* of land; that is, it ought to be constituted a proportion, *not of the gross*, but of what is sometimes called the *neat produce;* or of that free surplus above the ordinary charges of production which has been already defined as forming the rent. A land-tax which, like *tithes*, is made a proportion of the gross produce of the land, forms an obstacle to its improvement and to the extension of cultivation,—it prevents the whole produce from increasing to that extent which it otherwise would do, and limits the wealth and population and resources of a country to a less ample development than they would otherwise attain to; whereas a tax proportioned to the *rent*, if confined within any moderate bounds, would be free from these or any other ill effects.

A direct tax upon rent falls wholly upon that particular description of revenue, and presents, as was before explained,* an expedient whereby a part at least of the produce of the land may be conveniently enjoyed in common, although the land itself cannot. Such a tax, if it were confined within moderate bounds, and never allowed to exceed one-eighth,

* See book i. chap. 9, sec. 2, p. 108, *et seq.*

or twelve and a half per cent. would not diminish the desirableness of land-property, or operate in any sensible degree as an obstacle to improvement; and as it cannot be denied that that portion of the value of the land, (namely, rent,) which arises from the mere progress of society, should be applied and enjoyed as a *common good*, in as far as such a thing may be practicable, without too much diminishing the desirableness of the land, such a tax upon rent ought to be made a fundamental law in all countries, and in highly-improved ones would go a great way towards defraying the whole expense of government under all ordinary circumstances, and consequently towards preventing the necessity of all other taxes, if it did not do so altogether.

It must be admitted, however, that if such a tax were allowed to rise much higher than an eighth, it would diminish too sensibly the value and desirableness of properties in land, and, by rendering the proprietors less interested, even operate as an obstruction to improvement of another sort; but kept at or under the rate just mentioned it could not possibly do either.

II. *Taxes on Profit.*—A direct tax on profit* falls wholly on profit, as one on rent falls wholly on rent; but yet profit is not so proper a subject of direct taxation as rent is;—*first*, because the amount or value of the capital from which the former arises is not like that of the land from which the latter arises, so open to inspection, or so easily ascertained; and to ascertain it with any degree of exactness would require too rigorous and vexatious an inquisition into men's private affairs;—and, *secondly*, because capital can be removed from one country to another, and if it were directly

* It will probably be superfluous to remind the reader here that the term *profit* is used as synonymous with *interest*.

and heavily taxed, it would be very likely to be removed to the great detriment and disadvantage of the whole community.

"The interest of money," says Dr Smith, "seems at first sight a subject equally capable of being taxed directly as the rent of land. Like the rent of land, it is a neat produce which remains after completely compensating the whole risk and trouble of employing the stock. As a tax upon the rent of land cannot raise rents, because the neat produce which remains after replacing the stock of the farmer, together with his reasonable profit, cannot be greater after the tax than before it; so, for the same reason, a tax upon the interest of money could not raise the rate of interest; the quantity of stock or money in the country, like the quantity of land, being supposed to remain the same after the tax as before it. The ordinary rate of profit, it has been shown in the first book, is everywhere regulated by the quantity of stock to be employed in proportion to the quantity of the employment, or of the business which must be done by it. But the quantity of the employment, or of the business to be done by stock, could neither be increased nor diminished by any tax upon the interest of money. If the quantity of the stock to be employed, therefore, was neither increased nor diminished by it, the ordinary rate of profit would necessarily remain the same. But the portion of this profit necessary for compensating the risk and trouble of the employer would likewise remain the same, that risk and trouble being in no respect altered. The residue, therefore, that portion which belongs to the owner of the stock, and which pays the interest of money, would necessarily remain the same too. At first sight, therefore, the interest of money seems to be a subject as fit to be taxed directly as the rent of land.

"There are, however, two different circumstances which render the interest of money a much less proper subject of direct taxation than the rent of land.

"First, the quantity and value of the land which any man possesses can never be a secret, and can always be ascertained with great exactness; but the whole amount of the capital stock which he possesses is almost always a secret, and can scarce ever be ascertained with tolerable exactness. It is liable, besides, to almost continual variations. A year seldom passes away, frequently not a month, sometimes scarce a single day, in which it does not rise or fall more or less. An inquisition into every man's private circumstances, and an inquisition which, in order to accommodate the tax to them, watched over all the fluctuations of his fortune, would be a source of such continual and endless vexation as no people could support.

"Secondly, land is a subject which cannot be removed, whereas stock easily may. The proprietor of land is necessarily a citizen of the particular country in which his estate lies. The proprietor of stock is properly a citizen of the world, and is not necessarily attached to any particular country. He would be apt to abandon the country in which he was exposed to a vexatious inquisition, in order to be assessed to a burdensome tax, and would remove his stock to some other country where he could either carry on his business, or enjoy his fortune more at his ease. By removing his stock he would put an end to all the industry which it had maintained in the country which he left. Stock cultivates land; stock employs labour. A tax which tended to drive away stock from any particular country, would so far tend to dry up every source of revenue both to the sovereign and to the society. Not only the profits of stock, but the rent of land and the wages of labour, would necessarily be more or less diminished by its removal."*

Another circumstance which makes the rent of land a much more just and proper subject of direct taxation than the profit of stock is, that the former increases in value without any care, or attention, or labour, on the part of the proprietors, simply in consequence of the increase of popu-

---

* Wealth of Nations, book v. chap. 2.

lation and wealth; whereas profit diminishes under the same circumstances, and the capital whence it arises can only be acquired or increased by saving and privation; the existence and increase of capital being uniformly owing to the industry and frugality or parsimony of the individuals who originally acquire it, or to the care and parsimony of those who continue to preserve it undiminished and unconsumed; but the increase of the value of the land *which cannot be consumed* is owing to the general industry and prosperity of the people, and good government of the country.

III. *Taxes on Wages.*—A direct tax on wages may fall either wholly or in part upon that description of revenue. If such a tax be but moderate in amount, and laid on in a country but moderately taxed, it may be paid wholly by the labourer, who may either "retrench something from his way of living," or "increase his industry, perform more work, and live as well as before, without demanding more for his labour." In a country indeed which is taxed to the highest pitch, where the labourer has increased his industry as far as he can, and has reduced his way of living to the lowest sort of necessaries on which he can subsist, any farther retrenchment, or farther increase of industry, being by the supposition impossible, every direct tax would necessarily, under such circumstances, either raise wages or starve the labourer out of existence. It is denied, however, that the labouring classes ever were or could be reduced generally, or in any considerable numbers, to this condition; and it would be only those individuals who were so reduced that would be unable to pay any taxes, or on whom no portion of them could fall.

Taxes upon commodities may and generally do fall upon every sort of revenue indifferently, and ought indeed to be considered as falling on that particular sort by which they are purchased for consumption.

"When a tax is laid upon commodities," says Mr Hume, "which are consumed by the common people, the necessary consequence may seem to be, either that the poor must retrench something from their way of living, or raise their wages so as to make the burden of the tax fall entirely upon the rich. But there is a third consequence which often follows upon taxes, namely, that the poor increase their industry, perform more work, and live as well as before, without demanding more for their labour. Where taxes are moderate, are laid on gradually, and affect not the necessaries of life, this consequence naturally follows; and it is certain, that such difficulties often serve to excite the industry of a people, and render them more opulent and laborious than others who enjoy the greatest advantages."*

And further, he says,—"If a duty be laid upon any commodity consumed by an artisan, he has two obvious expedients for paying it; he may retrench somewhat of his expense, or he may increase his labour. Both these resources are more easy and natural than that of heightening his wages. We see, that, in years of scarcity, the weaver either consumes less or labours more, or employs both these expedients of frugality and industry, by which he is enabled to reach the end of the year. It is but just that he should subject himself to the same hardships, if they deserve the name, for the sake of the public which gives him protection. By what contrivance can he raise the price of his labour? The manufacturer who employs him will not give him more; neither can he, because the merchant who exports the cloth cannot raise its price, being limited by the price which it yields in foreign markets. Every man, to be sure, is desirous of pushing off from himself the burden of any tax which is imposed, and of laying it upon others; but, as every man has the same inclination, and

---

* Essays, part ii. essay 8. Of Taxes.

is upon the defensive, no set of men can be supposed to prevail altogether in this contest."*

Taxes, therefore, upon commodities, are to be considered as paid in part by all classes of people; and all taxes, except direct ones on rent and profit, have a certain tendency, more or less, to equalize and spread themselves (when continued for a length of time) over the whole expanse and surface of society.

SECTION II.

OF TAXES AND PUBLIC DEBTS, AS THEY AFFECT THE CONDITION OF THE LABOURING CLASSES OF PEOPLE.

As all taxes are necessarily paid either out of the capital or the revenue of the individuals from whom they are taken, their effect must evidently be, to diminish the wealth of those who pay them, in at least as great a measure as they increase that of those to whom they are ultimately paid over; it follows, therefore, that in proportion as the numbers of those who draw their incomes from the public treasury are increased, *under any given circumstances*,† the salaries of each not being diminished, or as their salaries are increased their numbers not being diminished, the greater must be either the industry or the privation of those who pay the taxes; or, to be as exact as possible, the greater must be the *privation* of those who pay their shares of the taxes out of their *land* or *capital*, or out of their *revenue arising*

* Essays, part ii. essay 8. Of Taxes.

† Circumstances which must be given are,—the proportion of capital to population, and of population to the extent of territory; also the fertility or barrenness of the territory, and the degree of skill or improvement which the people have attained in the arts of production.

from land or capital, and the greater *either the privation or the industry* of those who pay their shares out of their revenue arising from labour.

Plain and obvious, however, as the doctrine just stated may appear, and frequently as it may have been set in a clear light by preceding writers, it is still denied. It is still maintained, as it was in Mr Hume's time, that "the public is no weaker on account of its debts, since they are mostly due among ourselves, and bring as much property to one as they take from another."* We are told that taxes can never be burdensome to a country when they are expended within it, because the money comes all back again into the hands of the people; the extraordinary doctrine is advanced, that "a body of unproductive labourers," exclusive of and additional to those which are required both for the private convenience of individuals and for the purposes of government, is not only harmless but absolutely beneficial, as being conducive to a more proper distribution and consumption of wealth than would take place without them; and it is accordingly maintained, that, although it were in our power greatly to reduce our expenditure on account of government, and at once to annihilate the national debt, and all the taxes which are necessary to pay the interest of it; and suppose all this could be done without in the least hurting the public creditors,—yet still it would be nowise advantageous to the public to do so, but, on the contrary, exceedingly detrimental, inasmuch as it would diminish consumption, destroy the demand for labour, and throw great numbers of labourers out of employment.†

---

* See Hume's Essays, essay 9. Of Public Credit.

† "I feel perfectly convinced," says Mr Malthus, speaking of the national debt, (*Principles of Political Economy, chap. 8, sect. 9, p. 486*,) "that if a sponge could be applied to it to-morrow, and we could put out of our consideration the poverty and misery of the pub-

As the fallacies contained in the above paradoxes have been most completely exposed long since, first in a general way by Mr Hume, and afterwards more particularly by Dr Smith, it may well appear unnecessary here to say any thing more about them. I shall only therefore offer a very few observations addressed to the new aspect which one or two of them have been made to assume, before I attempt to delineate the progressive effects of an indefinite increase of taxes and public debts, as they affect the condition of the labouring classes of people.

It is true, as has been already admitted, that taxes, when they are moderate, and laid on judiciously and slowly, may at first, by exciting a spirit of industry where it was before wanting, be for a time rather useful and advantageous than the contrary; but to say that they must be harmless because "the money comes all back again into the hands of the people," is the most extravagant of all absurdities. It is true, the money comes back: this is indeed the very pur-

---

lic creditors, by supposing them to be supported comfortably in another country, the rest of the country, as a nation, instead of being enriched, would be impoverished."

It is singular that Mr Malthus, who maintains that "a body of unproductive labourers tend to push the wealth of a country farther than it would go without them," (Principles of Political Economy, chap. vii. sec. 9, p. 477, *et seq.*) should still continue to be as great an enemy as ever to any form of legal provision for the poor; for what are the poor, when so supported, but "a body of unproductive labourers?" Or are we to suppose that poor-laws would be not only innoxious but beneficial, provided the allowances under them were hundreds or tens instead of units? Are we to suppose that a law which costs the country about *four* millions (I leave out of consideration what is paid as wages) annually, and which Mr Malthus denounces as "an evil in comparison with which the national debt, with all its magnitude of terror, is of little moment," might be converted into a blessing by the simple expedient of increasing the payments till they should amount to *forty* millions?

pose for which it was taken, that by coming back it might transfer the goods of those who receive it the second time into the hands of the persons whom it is meant the taxes should support. True, the money comes back, but it comes for a new value; it does not come back again for nothing. If it comes back, it comes *by purchase* for a new equivalent. If it comes back to the labourer it comes for the sweat of his brow; it comes for the fruits of a new and additional labour. By the sweat of his body he must twice earn it, and by a twofold exertion of his labour produce first the means of living for himself, and then for another. Comes back indeed!—So does the money taken by the highwayman, and by all the cheats, and thieves, and robbers in the country. It comes all back in the same manner that the money taken by the tax-gatherer comes back, viz. for the goods of the lieges. After the money is taken in any of these ways, or when money is parted with in any manner whatever, every one is at liberty to draw it back again, if he has an equivalent to give for it; and to the labourer it will come all back if he can work hard enough for it,—if he can undergo the double toil of again accumulating wherewithal to purchase it a second time.

It is true also, that the expenditure of large sums of money quickens industry, and that any particular mode of laying it out will draw the labourers of the country to work in the corresponding channels. It is true, therefore, that if the money which comes at present from the hands of the stockholders was suddenly stopt, such stoppage would occasion a temporary depression and stagnation in some departments of industry, and great immediate inconvenience to the labourers in these departments; but they would speedily get relief from other sorts of industry being called into existence; for as the whole of the money formerly paid to the national creditors would now be left in the pockets of the people, the same amount would come from thence, and be all expended, though for a different sort of articles; and the channels of industry, though changed, would not be dried up; on the contrary, its streams, though not so large, would be more numerous and more salutary. Instead of one impetuous torrent sweeping rudely across the land, and drawing every thing within the circle of its narrow vortex, there would be innumerable small springs rising up all over the country, fertilizing their native fields, and giving freshness and vigour to the most desert places.

But farther, it may be observed, that these arguments (if they deserve the name,) which we have been here shortly considering, evidently prove too much; for if they were true,—if the doctrines were true which represent a large public debt and expensive government-establishments, and numerous taxes to support them, as not only harmless but positively beneficial, because the money comes all back and circulates through the country,—parliament could not be better employed than in multiplying the one and increasing the other, until every man in the country was pensioned and provided for. There would be no need in this case to confine the grants to those who gave money or service in return. If you are settled that the money coming back makes it not only not hurtful but beneficial to take it, why be at all scrupulous or backward in doing so? If the money coming back could work the wonders ascribed to it, and equally support those who pay and those who receive it, why not pension *every individual*, and make them all rich together? Such are the conclusions and absurdities to which these doctrines and paradoxes directly and legitimately conduct us.

Leaving these doctrines, therefore, without farther comment, I shall here set down what appears to me to be the real effect of taxes and public debts, in their natural progress from first to last, and it will thence appear that a large public debt, and the heavy weight of taxation necessary to support it, is simply *an engine* calculated and adapted to screw up the labour and exertion of a country to the highest pitch.

The real effects of taxation, when increased indefinitely, may be supposed to proceed from the first to the last stage in somewhat like the following manner:—

Every man endeavours as long as he can to keep up his station in society, and to live in his old and ordinary way, or rather to better it if he can. In a country where the taxes are inconsiderable, and only beginning to be felt, therefore, when a new one is imposed, the labourers work a little longer, or a little harder, and continue to live as well *or perhaps better* than before. In working a little harder or a little longer in order to make up the tax, they probably do a little more than make it up; not being in this early stage oppressed or overburdened, every one perhaps does a little more than is necessary, and, after paying the tax, finds he has something over to add to his enjoyments, and to be some small recompense for his augmented labour. Every person in his particular sphere and station augments his industry, and, in this early stage of taxation, instead of being burdened or oppressed by new and moderate impositions, he is only excited to more lively exertions. The merchant, the farmer, and the manufacturer, accustomed to drink their wine, will not relinquish it for a small tax; they will rather increase their exertion, their industry, or their ingenuity; and the result will probably be, that, after making up the tax, something will remain over, which they may either add to their capital or to their enjoyments. They cannot so measure their increased industry as that it should cover the tax exactly and no more. Set agoing with a new impulse, they overshoot the mark, and by their new and additional exertions they produce something more than the tax takes away; and in this manner add more to their income than they are obliged to add to their expenditure. And thus it may happen, that a nation sunk in indolence and lethargy, may be roused and really benefited by the first imposition of new and moderate taxes.* And in this easy manner the first stage of taxation passes over.

The second comes apace. The taxes are gradually increased, and industry, proceeding in the manner just described, increases in the same degree. Year after year adds a new series of imposts, and every man's exertions are pushed to the utmost limits, until, when industry can do no more, economy, retrenchment, and privation begin. The income of every individual, greatly increased by his increased exertions, is yet so reduced and cut down by the numerous taxes as to leave him in much the same state in regard to what he can allow himself to consume as when he began his new career of exertion and industry; and all he has reaped by the additional toil he is now obliged to undergo, —and which toil he cannot for a moment intermit without sinking down into an inferior condition,—is the pleasure of beholding the whole produce of his increased industry going to support a daily-increasing number of persons to live in luxurious ease and idleness throughout the country, without any addition being made by them to the capital, or to any other instrument of production within it; and so concludes the second stage of taxation.

It is easy to see how it happens, therefore, that a country appears to flourish and improve after the first imposition of taxes. It arises from the increased exertions and industry of the whole labouring population, which are at first generally carried much farther than is barely necessary to make good the demands which call them forth.

---

* I do not say, that taxation is necessary or indispensable to rouse a nation to industry. Education and good government will serve the purpose. The United States of North America exhibit an experimental proof of this.

But taxation, we shall suppose, does not stop at this point. It still goes on,—the last stage approaches. It is perceived in the grinding labour which men undergo; it is read in the very countenances of the people.* New taxes are added, and the resources of the individual, from increased industry, being now exhausted, he must retrench from his enjoyments whatever continues to be added to the sums taken from him. He is now placed between two opposing and irresistible forces, pressing and constraining him on either side, and urging and forcing him, at one and the same time, to curtail his expenditure, and to exert all his industry and all his faculties to maintain his wonted ground and station in society. In this situation, every new impost urges and compresses him. Year after year he feels the encroachment, yet still he struggles on with all his might to overcome it, until, after resorting to every expedient, and no longer able to sustain the pressure, he sinks into poverty, (perhaps through "the horn gate of bankruptcy,") with his mind and body probably both exhausted by his long-continued and overstrained exertions.†

---

* Those who are old enough to remember the state of the country and of the labouring classes before the commencement of the late war, can bear ample testimony to the fact, that their hours of labour were not so long, nor their exertions so arduous, as they became towards the conclusion of it, and that they gradually increased with the increase of the taxes.

† A strong confirmation of the doctrine here stated of the effects of a large public debt, in screwing up the exertion of the country to an unnatural pitch, may be drawn from a survey and observation of its actual condition compared with other countries, and with itself before the debt was contracted, or when it was comparatively insignificant or moderate.

As to the state of the country before the debt was contracted, or when it was more moderate, I shall add nothing to what I have said in the preceding note; but, in respect to the comparison with other coun-

Such appears to me to be the manner in which taxation, when carried to the highest pitch, might be expected, *a priori*, to affect the labouring classes of people; and facts *a posteriori* confirm the deduction: for, during the latter part of the late war, when taxation was carried to the highest, such precisely were the phenomena observed; the poor-rates increased *pari passu* with the taxes, and both rose to their *acmé*, and declined together.

---

tries, I cannot avoid adding the following observations of a person writing without any intention, apparently, of establishing this or any other theory or opinion on the subject:—

"The To-day of England," says a writer in the New Monthly Magazine (as quoted in the Cabinet, or Selected Beauties of Literature. pp. 312, 313,) "nationally considered, cannot be reckoned happy. It is too bustling, laborious, and excessive. In France, pleasure is almost the only business; in England, business is almost the only pleasure; and this is pushed to an extremity that surrounds it with hazard and anxiety. By devoting all its energies and faculties, physical and intellectual, to this one object, for a series of years, the nation has attained an eminence so fearfully beyond its natural claims and position, that nothing but a continuance of convulsive efforts, even in the midst of distress and exhaustion, can enable it to uphold the rank it has assumed. Hence every thing is artificial, and in all directions we contemplate tension, excitement, force. Her navy exceeds that of the collected world, so does her debt,—a co-existence that cannot be very durable. Her establishments of all sorts are proportioned to what she owes rather than to what she has; her grandeur can only be equalled by her embarrassments. In one colony she has sixty millions of subjects, while a great proportion of her native population are paupers; and in her sister island famine has lately stalked hand in hand with rebellion * * * * *. No social system was ever pushed to such an energetic extremity, or afforded so envious and glorious a spectacle; but it has not sufficient repose for enjoyment."

APPENDIX

TO

THE LAST CHAPTER.

SUCH (as has been described in the last chapter) being the effect of public debts, and of the taxes necessary to support them, it becomes obviously a matter of the very first consideration, in a country like this, where they have grown to such a magnitude, to inquire if any means could be fallen upon for liquidating the debt, and rendering, consequently, more than a half of our present taxes unnecessary; and for this purpose a plan has been repeatedly brought forward by Mr Richard Heathfield, which, if carried into execution, would, I have no doubt, be attended with, or followed by, all the beneficial consequences which that gentleman anticipates.

Mr Heathfield's proposal is, in his own words, as follows:—

"That the legislative repeal of annual duties to the amount of 31 millions be declared, viz.

" In respect of the interest on part of the debt,........	25 millions.
Sinking fund to be discontinued,...........................	3
Reduction of government pay and pensions, and lower prices of stores for the public service,.........	3
	31 millions.

"That, at the same time, every description of property in the United Kingdom be assessed in the proportion of one-fifth part of its value.

"That all government-stock, not held by foreigners residing out of the kingdom, be reduced in the same proportion.

"That all home-appointments in and under the government, and government pay and pensions generally, be reduced in the same proportion."*

Then, founding on Dr Colquhoun's computation, and other data, Mr Heathfield estimates the private property in the United Kingdom at 2800 millions, and continues,—

"Taking the public debt at 800 millions,† and deducting one-fifth, or 160 millions, for the proposed assessment of one-fifth, 640 millions remain. The assessment of one-fifth to be charged on the private property of 2800 millions would amount to 560 millions, which assessment would be applicable either in principal or interest, according to circumstances, to the debt of 640 millions remaining as above mentioned, leaving the sum of 80 millions for the annuities for terms of years, or to be liquidated by other and gradual means."‡

Some *honest* and "erudite" admirers and panegyrists of the late Mr Ricardo would fain claim the merit of this plan as belonging to him, notwithstanding the fact, that it was proposed and published to the world before Mr Ricardo was born, and that this fact stands recorded in so conspicuous a place as Mr Hume's Essay "Of Public Credit."

"There was, indeed, a scheme," says Mr Hume, in the essay just named, (published in 1742,) "for the payment of our debts, which was proposed by an excellent citizen, Mr Hutchinson, above thirty years ago, and which was much approved of by some men of sense, but never was likely to take effect. He asserted that there was a fallacy in imagining that the public owed this debt; for that really every individual owed a proportional share of it, and paid in his taxes a proportional share of the interest, beside the expense of levying these taxes. Had we not better, then, says he, make a distribution of the debt among ourselves, and each of us contribute a sum suitable to his property, and by that means discharge at once all our funds and public mortgages?"§

---

* Thoughts on the Liquidation of the Public Debt, pp. 8, 9.

† "Strict accuracy in the amount of the debt is not required for the immediate purpose of this outline."

‡ Thoughts on the Liquidation of the Public Debt, pp. 9, 10.

§ Essays, part ii. essay 9.

Here we have the distinct outline and substance of the "plan" or "scheme," comprehensively indeed, but clearly stated; and yet we are told that "It is essentially the scheme of Mr Ricardo;"* just as if nobody had any prior claim to it; as if Mr Hutchinson had never existed and Mr Hume never written; and as if the scheme were not at least as much Mr Heathfield's as Mr Ricardo's.

Mr Ricardo did indeed recommend the proposition *in a very general way*, first in his book, and afterwards in his place in parliament; but Mr Heathfield has accompanied his recommendation of it with all the explanations and details which are required to demonstrate its practicability, as well as the mode in which it might be expected to operate.

The following are a few of Mr Heathfield's explanatory statements:—

"Should a plan so bold in its outline," says this writer, "be received with feelings of undefined apprehension, the reader may be safely assured, that reflection on the subject has hitherto, even with the most discerning, seldom failed to substitute confidence for fear.

"Let it be considered in its application to the several classes of proprietors, living upon and expending their income, or the greater part thereof, at home.

"And, *first*, What is commonly called the funded proprietor, or government annuitant. This proprietor receives L.500 per annum, or any greater or less sum. To redeem himself from the effect of a high scale of duties, he foregoes the receipt of 20 per cent. per annum. Can it be doubted, that the proposed sweeping repeal of 31 millions of duties would leave him in command of more of the comforts of life than he at present enjoys?—In this instance, the operation of the measure is simple and without difficulty. He was, in truth, at once both a creditor and debtor in account with the country. He has paid his debt, and is released from the expensive and cumbrous machinery, brought into action by the previous complexity of his situation, and working with much friction.

---

* *Vide* Scotsman newspaper, 1st July, 1829.

" *Second*, The landed proprietor, who must be considered in several positions, namely,

" The landed proprietor, being also a government annuitant, or possessing other property readily and conveniently convertible into money.

" Or not possessing such facility, but free from mortgage.

" Or being under mortgage.

" In the first case, the assessment would be paid with facility, by cancelling the annuity, if of sufficient value, after the deduction of one-fifth, or by applying other available funds to the same purpose; still, however, retaining the option to pay an annual interest on the assessment, or any part of it, if preferred.

" In the second case, the proprietor would pay the annual interest on the assessment, until convenient to pay the principal, by instalments; or at once, by means of a private mortgage for the purpose.

" In the third case, the mortgagee would pay the annual interest on the assessment, in the proportion of the mortgage to the whole property; but the benefit to the property, from the increase of value which it would acquire from the remission of duties, would result to the proprietor or mortgager; and provided the mortgagee expend the mortgage-interest at home, he also would be benefited in the same manner as the government annuitant; a diminished income in pounds sterling would give more command over the comforts of life. Both mortgager and mortgagee are benefited.

" *Third*, The farmer, in respect of his capital, would be relieved by the remission of duties to such an extent as to be enabled to meet the demand for the assessment, by payments to be made by such instalments as should be considered proper, in reference generally to the circumstances of this class. The assessment would bear only on his actual or net capital, after allowing for the payment of every debt.

" *Fourth*, Merchants, manufacturers, and dealers, would also be relieved from the employment of a large proportion of their capital, now employed in respect of the duties to be repealed, and, consequently, great facility would be afforded to the payment of the assessment by instalments. The four-fifths of capital remaining could not but be adequate to the purchase and sale of more wares and merchandize than the whole of the capital under present circumstances. In this case, also, the assessment would only bear on the actual or net capital, after allowing for the payment of every debt.

" And then all these classes, including the farmer, would be relieved, in their domestic expenses, from the operation of the high scale of duties."*

"It is certain that taxes on consumption do, in fact, fall with accumulated force on most descriptions of property; and that, provided the income derived from property be expended within the United Kingdom, the effect, to the proprietor of such taxes, is aggravated to an extreme degree.

"*Firstly*, The amount of any given tax, levied through the medium of the importer or manufacturer, must be paid by the consumer, together with a considerable addition to each of the successive dealers, through whose hands the commodity passes, for the advance of capital and the risks incident to trade.

"*Secondly*, And by far more important is the consideration that prices reciprocate. If any one article of general consumption be high-priced, every other article of consumption must partake of that high price, and as nearly every article consumed in the United Kingdom, excepting provisions, is directly taxed, so the effect of the tax on each acts upon all, inclusive of provisions; the increased price of which latter re-acts upon prices generally. High prices on the supplies to the landlord and tenant create a necessity for high prices on farm-produce, and the high prices of farm-produce render necessary still higher prices for articles of general supply. In this manner an annual tax of L.1 imposed on any article of consumption will be found to require at least L.6 in the general prices, to effect a distribution of the burden of the L.1 paid to the Treasury. Or, to exhibit the principle in its more extensive application, 23 millions paid by the importer and manufacturer annually, in duties of customs and excise, must operate to effect a distribution of the burden over the mass of consumers, by an augmentation, in the aggregate of prices, of all the commodities annually sold in the United Kingdom, to the amount of upwards of 160 millions."†

"The objects of the measure now proposed are, to cancel forthwith, or as soon as considerations due to the merchants and other holders of goods, whereon duties may have been paid would admit, duties of excise and customs, to the amount of 31 millions. To reduce the

---

* Thoughts on the Liquidation of the Public Debt, pp. 10, 11, 12.

† Ibid. pp. 5, 6.

public debt from 800 to 640 millions, by cancelling one-fifth of the principal, and to provide for 560, part of the remaining 640 millions, by an assessment on private property to that amount, payable either in principal, or by an equivalent in annual interest, according to the circumstances of the several classes of proprietors and capitalists, or the convenience of individuals; leaving 80 millions, or thereabouts, to expire by effluxion of time, or to be disposed of otherwise. To reduce the appointments of government home-pay and pensions in the proportion of one-fifth, and consequently to lead to and justify the reduction of salaries and other pay on private establishments in a corresponding degree.

"Such are the views on these important subjects now submitted to the British public. The author, in his former tracts, has treated the question of the national debt more in detail, and to those tracts he refers, should they be considered deserving attention. It appeared to him, when they were published, (1819, 1820, 1822,) and his opinion is unchanged, that, by the means which he has suggested, the wretched may be relieved; the decline of others to the same condition be prevented; sustenance, at least, be rendered back in return for labour; an adequate return be obtained by the prudent capitalist; and the higher orders of society be enabled to reap the ample returns from property, to which the industry and energy of the British people, and their own conduct as legislators, magistrates, and landlords, give them a claim; unaccompanied by the reflection, that the suffering and degradation of a large portion of the people stand in severe and direct contrast to the means of diffusing ease and comfort, and of raising the moral character of the population, possessed by the country.

"It must, however, be considered, that a measure so comprehensive and searching as the proposed liquidation of the public debt, whatever may be its simplicity of principle or facility of execution, cannot be expected to be proposed by any minister, even the most powerful, without a previous manifestation of public opinion in its favour, and that the measure can have little chance of being brought into operation, unless the great proprietors themselves, who have a principal interest in its adoption, become its avowed and zealous advocates."*

* Thoughts on the Liquidation of the Public Debt, pp. 16, 17, 18.

"The objectors, and the only objectors in the various classes of the proprietory, who could, with a sagacious but selfish regard to their own immediate interest, maintain an opposition to this measure, are the absentee and the accumulator;—proprietors who are protected in their property, but who do not contribute to the wants of the state in common with those who, by a liberal expense, give employment to the anvil and the loom, and bring up the families who are in succession to fill the middle and upper ranks of society.

"Were argument wanting to convince the expending and resident proprietor of the beneficial effect of this measure upon his own affairs, the consideration of its effect on the non-expending and non-resident classes must be conclusive."*

In regard to this scheme, as proposed by Mr Hutchinson, Mr Hume observes, that "he (Mr Hutchinson) seems not to have considered that the laborious poor pay a considerable part of the taxes by their annual consumptions, though they could not advance at once a proportional part of the sum required."†

In this I fully agree with Mr Hume; but if it is desired to confer a boon and a benefit on the labouring classes, and to free the two others, and the whole community, from the turmoil of eternal agitation and alarm, there is no other measure which could be so effectual for the purpose.

---

* Ibid. p. 13.

† Essays, part ii. essay 9. Of Public Credit.

THE END.

GENERAL STATEMENT

OF AN

ARGUMENT

ON THE

Subject of Population,

IN

ANSWER TO MR MALTHUS'S THEORY.

BY

SAMUEL READ.

Edinburgh:

PRINTED FOR MACREDIE, SKELLY, & CO. 34. PRINCE'S STREET,

AND T. & G. UNDERWOOD, LONDON.

1821.

PREFACE.

THE Author of the following sheets has long been convinced, that there are several fundamental errors in Mr Malthus's "Essay on the "Principle of Population," and is at present engaged in a close examination of that production, with a view to demonstrate those errors. But as this will necessarily be a work of time and labour, and as the general outline of the argument which he means to urge against it, and which was sketched to stand as the introduction to the work intended, appears, on reviewing it, to be sufficient of itself to point out the insufficiency of Mr Malthus's tenets,—he has been induced to publish it in its present form, without waiting for that full and particular exposure of them which he purposes, and which a work so voluminous as that of Mr Malthus requires; the author of which, having gained the *ear* and indulgent attention of the Public to all he thinks proper to advance, has made no very sparing use of his privilege, but has taken the opportunity to present his doctrines, in all that variety of forms which are best calculated to hide their defects.

In the following pages, there are some small additions made to what was originally intended to stand as introduction merely, and some amplification of a few of the passages on which the strength of this argument rests ; but the form (of introduction) remains the same, as it was found difficult to alter it ; and it is hoped the reader will accept this apology for the allusions which will sometimes occur to the work intended to follow.

EDINBURGH,
January 9. 1821.

GENERAL STATEMENT,

&c.

THE obstacles which prevent the full and equal population of the globe, and which hinder mankind from dwelling and increasing in its different parts, in numbers proportioned to the various advantages of climate, situation, and soil, are all referable to the deficiency and imperfection of political institutions, laws, and government.

Had the human race, from a remote period, lived under one universal and unvariable system of wise and uniform administration of justice, it cannot be doubted, that long before the present age, the whole world would have been stocked with inhabitants. Every region and corner of the earth, and every isle of the sea, would have been overspread with people, and, according to their various capacities of maintaining human beings, filled with enjoyment, wealth, and industry.

In countries which are but thinly peopled, it is the difficulty of procuring the means of subsistence in abundance and security, which forms the immediate obstacle to the increase of numbers; but in such countries, this difficulty can only have place in the absence of good government. The earth refuses not abundance to the industry of man, but industry cannot exist without government, and cannot flourish or continue for any length of time, but through the steady and uniform administration of law and justice. The total privation of government is the cause of desolation upon the earth: its imperfection is the cause of every political evil.

The foregoing doctrine appears to admit of little dispute, and has been acknowledged, heretofore, by the profoundest writers on political science. On the subject of population, Mr Hume, in whose writings alone is to be found all useful and necessary political information, has sketched with fidelity and truth, in one short and comprehensive paragraph, the only doctrine which is solid and irrefutable, and will be found to withstand the ordeal cf the closest examination. In the essay on the population of ancient nations, he says, "In general, we may observe, that the "question with regard to the comparative popu-"lousness of ages or kingdoms, implies important "consequences, and commonly determines concerning the preference of their whole police, their manners, and the constitution of their government. For as there is in all men, both male and female, a desire and power of generation, more active than is ever universally exerted, the restraints which they lie under must proceed from some difficulties in their situation, which it belongs to a wise legislature carefully to observe and remove. Almost every man who thinks he can maintain a family, will have one; and the human species, at this rate of propagation, would more than double every generation. How fast do mankind multiply in every colony or new settlement, where it is an easy matter to provide for a family, and where men are nowise straitened or confined as in long-established governments? History tells us frequently of plagues which have swept away the third or fourth part of a people, yet in a generation or two, the destruction was not perceived, and the society had again acquired their former number. The lands which were cultivated, the houses built, the commodities raised, the riches acquired, enabled the people who escaped, immediately to marry and to rear families, which supplied the place of those who had perished. And for a like reason, every wise, just, and mild government, by rendering the condition of its subject easy and secure, will always abound most in people, as well as

" in commodities and riches. A country, indeed, " whose climate and soil are fitted for vines, will " naturally be more populous than one which " produces corn only, and that more populous " than one which is only fitted for pasturage. In " general, warm climates, as the necessities of the " inhabitants are there fewer, and vegetation more " powerful, are likely to be most populous: But " if every thing else be equal, it seems natural " to expect, that, wherever there are most happi- " ness and virtue, and the wisest institutions, " there will also be most people *.

On the same subject Smith observes, " Every " species of animals naturally multiplies in pro- " portion to the means of their subsistence, and " no species can ever multiply beyond it. But " in civilized society it is only among the inferior " ranks of people that the scantiness of subsist- " ence can set limits to the further multiplication " of the human species; and it can do so in no " other way than by destroying a great part of " the children which their fruitful marriages pro- " duce †."

It was not deemed necessary by these writers to proceed in consideration of the subject farther, and to display to view those minuter and secondary causes which prevent the powers of generation in

* Essays, Part ii. Essay 11.

† Wealth of Nations, Book I. Chap. viii.

all mankind, and in all countries, from being fully exerted. This task was left for Mr Malthus to perform. To Hume and Smith it must at once have been evident, the moment the inquiry was proposed, that those obstacles to the increase of numbers, which Mr Malthus calls the "immediate checks," depend altogether upon causes of a different and more general nature,—upon causes which equally prevent the complete cultivation of the earth, and the full developement of human industry. It was left for Mr Malthus to fix his attention exclusively on those secondary causes, and on the "immediate checks," and peremptorily shutting out from his mind every other idea, to deny the effectual influence of those primary and more important ones, in which his "immediate "checks" originate, and to which alone they owe their existence.

It was plain to see that it was good or bad government, which elevated or depressed the popular character, and gave effect to, or destroyed the operation and influence of voluntary and prudential restraint, which, under the former, is always sufficient to repress the redundant powers of increase, and to confine population within those boundaries which is necessary to allow of a liberal subsistence, or to the limits which the institutions of every different country, and the nature of its government, prescribe to its industry and wealth.

The effect of good government in elevating the

popular character, and causing the prevalence of what Mr Malthus calls "the preventive check," will be fully explained in the following work, and will be shewn to arise from the protection it affords, and the encouragement which it gives, to individual exertion and good conduct. The effects of good and bad government, the one in elevating, the other in depressing, the popular character, is sufficiently acknowledged by Mr Malthus in numberless passages of his book, although he never chooses to extract, from his own observations, the plain and undeniable inferences which follow from them. He never treats distinctly of the effects of good and bad government on the popular character, although it be the most important question connected with his subject, and one which is constantly presenting itself, and pressing upon his attention, almost in every page of his book.

In his "Essay on the Principle of Population," Mr Malthus maintains the following positions:— First, in his "statement of the subject," in the first chapter of that performance, and in his *most equivocal* discussion concerning "the ratios of in-" crease of population and food," he says, "A " thousand millions are just as easily doubled, " every twenty-five years, by the power of popu- " lation, as a thousand *;" and "population, could " it be supplied with food, would go on with un-

* Vol. i. p. 9.

" exhausted vigour *:" And he contends, that the means of subsistence, taking in the whole earth, and considering its present average state, could not possibly be made to double in less than twenty-five years; and from these premises, which he thinks sufficiently established by their simple statement, he infers a very great disproportion between the powers of increase of population and food, even in the present state of the world, and maintains that the same disproportion would continue undiminished, and " at every period during " the progress of cultivation, from the present " moment to the time when the whole earth was " become like a garden, the distress for want of " food would be constantly pressing on man- " kind †."

Had this position of Mr Malthus been confined to the most populous and highly cultivated countries, such as China, France, and Britain, there might have been some show of plausibility in it; although, if it be true, as he supposes, that the produce even of these countries could be doubled in twenty-five years, it does not appear very evident why the same effect could not be produced in a much shorter period, if population could be increased, and their labours directed to the same object. It does not appear very evident why this doubling of subsistence could not be made to

* Vol. i. p. 10. fifth edition.

† Vol. ii. p. 220.

take place in ten or five years, if population could be doubled in so short a time. But when Mr Malthus extends his observation to the whole habitable world, and maintains that the productions of the earth could not be doubled in a shorter period than twenty-five years *, and that " under " circumstances the most favourable to human in- " dustry," subsistence could not be made to keep pace with the increase of people, even till " the " whole earth was become like a garden," he evidently maintains a palpable absurdity.

In the second chapter of the Essay on Population, where he treats of what he calls " the gene- " ral checks to population,"—those *only* regulations which keep the jarring and unequal forces of population and food somewhat on a balance, Mr Malthus maintains that " these checks are all re- " solvable into moral restraint, vice, and mise- " ry † ;" and this last is one of the three " propo- " sitions" which, he formally announces, " are in- " tended to be proved ‡."

" 3. These checks, and the checks which re- " press the superior power of population, and " keep its effects on a level with the means of

---

* See Note A, at the end.

† Vol. i. p. 22.

‡ Vol. I. p. 33.

"subsistence, are all resolvable into moral restraint, vice, and misery *."

Now, in contradiction to this proposition, so dogmatically put forth, and so confidently maintained by Mr Malthus, I venture to affirm, that there is another principle which arises uniformly, invariably, and necessarily, in the progress of society, and in every advanced and populous state, weakens and diminishes the powers of increase, and this principle is neither moral restraint, nor vice, nor misery. It is a principle which never has place in the early stages of society, when the numbers of people are few, and thinly scattered over the surface of the earth, but has its commencement with the first aggregation of men into towns and populous communities, and gathers new and additional force as they advance in numbers and wealth. It is a principle which acts with the greatest vigour in the most improved societies, but never can produce its full effect, and arrive at its *acme*, till the whole earth be cultivated, the industry and ingenuity of man excited to the utmost, and the powers of production of every sort of riches carried to the highest pitch. This principle is—LUXURY AND REFINEMENT.

This palpable and important principle Mr Malthus entirely overlooks, and proceeds to settle his theory, and sum up his conclusions, without

* Vol. I. p. 34. Fifth Edition.

taking any account of its effects,—effects, which, when conjoined, as they necessarily must be in the higher stages of civilization, and in the most improved and best governed states, with that voluntary and prudential restraint which is the natural and necessary result of good government, and of that elevation of the popular character, which good government, continued for a length of time, always produces, will be found sufficient fully to prevent all undue increase of numbers, and to "keep down population to the level of sub-" sistence," without leaving any room, (so far as "the principle of population" is concerned), for the operation and agency of "those terrible cor-" rectors of the redundancy of mankind," the only acknowledged operators of Mr Malthus' "vice and misery."

On the subject we are now upon, there is an observation in the first book of Smith's Wealth of Nations, chap. 8. "On the Wages of Labour," from which Mr Malthus might have deduced the principle here advanced, and might have been led to observe its effects in weakening and diminishing the powers of population. This observation is as follows:—"A half starved Highland wo-" man frequently bears more than twenty chil-" dren, while a pampered fine lady is often in-" capable of bearing any, and is generally ex-" hausted by two or three. Barrenness, so fre-" quent among women of fashion, is very rare" among those of inferior station. Luxury, in

"the fair sex, while it inflames, perhaps, the pas-
"sion for enjoyment, seems always to weaken,
"and frequently to destroy altogether, the powers
"of generation *."

Here is the plain and distinct foundation of the precise doctrine I am now contending for; and it cannot but appear extraordinary, that a passage so remarkable, and a hint so plain, standing as it does in so conspicuous a place, should have altogether escaped the notice of Mr Malthus, or failed to draw his thoughts to its most evident and important consequences.

It will not be denied, that all great cities, and in all wealthy and populous countries and places, there are always a limited number of females born under those circumstances of affluence, and reared and educated in that careful, delicate, and refined manner, which, while it softens and embellishes their physical frame, at the same time temperates and extenuates, although it does not destroy their prolific powers.

The number of females so reared, and so educated, is always increased with increasing riches and populousness; and as the fecundity of the human species depends upon the power of women in bearing children †, the aggregate power of increase in every community must diminish in proportion as it advances in the career of improve-

* Vol. I. p. 129. Buchanan's Edition.

† "The fecundity of the human species, is, in some re-
"spects, a distinct consideration from the passion between the

ment and wealth. Even in the present uncultivated and unimproved state of the world, there are many places upon its surface, where this principle already exists in considerable force, although, even in the most improved, it has not arrived at its height, nor produces as yet that full effect, which ultimately it may be expected to bring to pass in every country.

How, and in what manner the utmost degree of luxury might prevail, and be enjoyed by a well governed people, without trenching in the smallest degree upon justice, or the rights of individuals, or occasioning any the least oppression or injury to any part of the public, will be fully explained in the following work.

This might be the case among a people deriving their *private* revenues, *immediately* and *chiefly* from land, capital, and labour, or from the exercise of professions, however lucrative, which are *voluntarily* paid and encouraged, and not from taxation. When *private* revenues are derived chiefly, or in a great and undue measure, from taxation, which can only be the case when a great deal more is taken than can ever be required for the just and necessary support of government, an injustice is committed, and an inroad is made upon private rights, transferring the means and

---

" sexes, as it evidently depends more upon the power of wo-
" men in bearing children, than upon the strength or weak-
" ness of this passion."—Malthus' Essay on Population, vol. iii. p. 78, 79, Fifth Edition.

power of luxury from one to another,—from him who has a just title, by inheriting or accumulating those means, to him who has none, and whose only recommendation to favour is probably no other than political subserviency. All public exaction and expenditure, therefore, which is over and above what is fairly required for the just and necessary support of government, is so much power of luxury taken from the possessors of land, or capital, or from the earnings of labour, those only original sources of revenue, and unjustly and forcibly transferred from the proprietors, to those who can have no valid claim to receive it for nothing, and still less to be remunerated for a base and pernicious compliance, and corrupt confederacy, to maintain and continue a system so revolting,—a system which occasions a severe oppression of the industrious classes, and must always inevitably produce a feverish, irritable, and undesirable state of the public mind.

It is perfectly different from this, when luxury arises to its *acme*, by the natural and necessary accumulation of wealth, under a long continued course of justice and good government, and when the resources which support it are derived immediately and chiefly from land, capital, and labour *.

* We say *immediately*, because all revenue must be derived *ultimately* from those sources; and we say *chiefly*, because there must always be *some* private revenue derived immediately from taxation.

Capital extenuates labour to the full amount of the revenues drawn from it; nay, it always does so, in a considerably greater degree, and the poor and unendowed man's lot, as well as the inheritor of those revenues, is improved by it, and always made better by every extension and investment of capital, excepting when that investment is in public funds or securities, the interest of which must be paid from taxation.

Capital extenuates labour in a greater degree than the amount of the revenues drawn directly from it, by the proprietors of that capital, because, if the works or properties in which it must always be invested, (if not in public funds), did not operate such an advantage to the public, those revenues could not be paid. Thus the collections drawn from canals, roads, harbours, docks, ships, &c. and which go to keep up those properties, and to pay the proprietors their shares of revenue, do not exhaust the whole of their benefits. Every one who pays or contributes any part, however small, of those revenues, does previously derive a positive advantage and benefit to himself, either by the immediate use and occupation of that canal, road, harbour, dock, ship, &c. or from the cheaper purchase of the goods he has occasion for, and which are, by means of those and other investments of capital, brought to market at an easier rate, and in greater abundance, and placed more within the reach and ability of every one to procure. And this advantage is independent of, and over and above, that which is derived in the shape of revenue, by the proprietors of those capitals.

If the merchant could have got any cheaper, more convenient, and easier mode of transport, he would not have employed that canal, road, harbour, dock, ship, &c.; and if the smallest purchaser of goods could have got them cheaper borne by any other conveyance, he would not have preferred those, or contributed any part to support and keep up those capitals, and to pay the revenues of their owners. And thus it is that the poorest man shares naturally in every accumulation of wealth, and investment of capital. His command over the luxuries, conveniencies, or necessaries of life, is increased. And so it is with all capitals,—they extenuate labour in a greater degree than the amount of the revenues drawn from them, to which no one is *compelled* to contribute, but does it *voluntarily*, and solely for his own advantage; and thus it is that the owners of those capitals live and enjoy their revenues, not only without being burdensome to the rest of the community, but conferring, at the same time, a boon and a benefit upon it.

It is not so with those living upon revenues derived from taxation. Those revenues are all compulsory, and, excepting in so far as they are paid to support useful and necessary public functionaries, there is no previous or ultimate advantage derivable from them. In so far as they are paid to support government, and the necessary administrators and functionaries thereof, they are the most necessary, useful, and honourable part of all expenditure, and that part of every man's outgoings, without which no man could have any thing either to spend or to enjoy. But for this indispensable purpose, taxes can never become either burdensome or oppressive, however liberally government may be supported. And, considering the talents necessary, and the cares of government, as well as the necessity of its ministers and functionaries having their thoughts freed from every harassing attention but that which arises out of the public interest, they ought certainly never to be rewarded with a niggardly hand. But all other expenditure connected with the public treasury is extraneous, and almost always unjust and impolitic; and it is by such expenditure alone that a country can be oppressed, the best institutions shaken, and the foundations and security of all property endangered by that feverish state of the public mind and passions which such advenient and superadded expenditure must always necessarily produce.

It is here that the vast difference lies, in a country of great wealth, between that state in which the luxuries arising from it are enjoyed by the producers and inheritors of wealth or capital,—the necessary functionaries of government,—and such other administrators and incumbents of every liberal profession and art as are *voluntarily* supported; and that opposite one where those luxuries are given either openly and barefacedly, or in a more concealed manner, to those who have done nothing to deserve them, bringing a cruel oppression upon the industrious community; and by the simple process of passing them through the public treasury, converting the earnings of labour, and the property of all, into the wages of servility and political prostitution.

It is in the manner I have hinted that capital eases and extenuates labour; and that in those countries in which there is great wealth and many capitals applied to all the different departments of industry and labour to facilitate the work of man, and abridge and shorten the processes of production, the humblest and most unendowed individual, as well as the most opulent, ought always to be better off, and more liberally provided with every necessary, than in countries where such wealth does not exist. The whole people ought to be better "clothed, lodged, "and fed," and luxury ought to be more diffused among the different ranks, and stretch itself farther down towards the very lowest, with every accession of new capital; and nothing can prevent this effect from universally taking place, but bad and mistaken administration of government.

It is upon this ground, it will be shewn, that under old established governments, conducted upon the best principles, the people of every class must always be better supplied with the luxuries, "conveniences, and, *a fortiori*, the necessaries of "life *," than in "newly settled countries," even such "as America, where millions and millions of "acres of fine land are yet to be had for a trifle †;" and that whatever *real* wages the American labourer earns, the English labourer must have earned more, if it were not for the effect of taxes, and ignorant or profligate administration of government. And it is thus that shall be turned against himself with tenfold force, that most unfounded and unjust apostrophe which occurs in the second volume of Mr Malthus' book ‡, and with which he concludes and winds up a climax of declamation, as extraordinary and extravagant as ever held a place in any treatise pretending to honest and impartial reasoning,—a climax equally remarkable for unsupported assertion, and unwarranted inference; and in reference to which, it will be far more just and appropriate to apply the exclamation of Malthus, "O monstrous absurdity || !" to his own composition, or with exacter truth reply to it, O monstrous misrepresentation! or, still more monstrous perversion of the reasoning faculty,—ignorance or injustice!

It is true the exactions of government may be carried to such a height, as to take away from that portion of the community who pay those exac-

---

* Godwin on Population, p. 299.

† Malthus' Essay on Population, vol. ii. p. 374.

‡ P. 374. || Vol. ii. p. 374.

tions, or on whom their weight and pressure principally falls, all the advantages of being born in a country of great capital, and stored and accumulated wealth; but there is nothing else which can prevent the natives of such a country from enjoying more of the luxuries, "conveniencies, "and, *a fortiori*, the necessaries of life," than the inhabitants of the best "newly settled countries." And in old countries, with governments well administered, I should expect to see a degree of affluence, and of elevation in the popular character *, and the enjoyments of luxury diffused among the people, and extending even to the very lowest ranks, in a degree "of which we can at present "scarcely form a conception †."

But a question will perhaps arise here, as to how far luxury and refinement may be indulged by different persons. This question, every one

---

* This would arise from the prevalence of voluntary and prudential restraint, produced by good government, in the degree necessary to keep up this elevation, if any such restraint remained necessary for that purpose, after the important effects which would now be produced by the prevalence of luxury and refinement. In this state of improvement, the poorer soils could never be cultivated, but the superior mode of living in the great body of the people, would heighten the value of their produce in pasturage. On this subject, however, we cannot here be particular.

† M. Condorcet, as given by Malthus, vol. ii. p. 227.

will, of course, decide according to his prevailing sentiments; but there are few, it is presumed, who will absolutely condemn every degree of luxury, and still fewer who will be found to practice the abstinence they teach. Luxury and refinement, however they may be decried by some, are nevertheless continually sought after, in one shape or other; and it will generally be found, that they are approved or disapproved by every one according to the measure of his own particular and confined capacity, either of enjoyment or attainment; and that those pleasures which men affect most to depreciate and despise, they either cannot relish or procure. An unshapely gentleman will despise a dandy, as the latter, if he has no pretensions himself to learning or science, will make no scruple to designate the one and the other as pedantry and impertinence. It belongs to the philosopher alone to discard every prejudice, and to make allowance for all the diversities of human inclination and capacity, mental and corporeal, when they are innocent.

It is the *degree* of luxury alone, when it is greater than the power of innocently enjoying it, which can be justly disapproved. Asbtractly from this consideration, luxury cannot be vice, as pleasure cannot be pain, or good evil; and however men, through ignorance or superstition, may preach against it, the most clamorous and austere have always a salvo in favour of their own leading propensities. More or less of luxury is enjoyed by all men in civilized countries; and it often happens, that it is sought after, *in their own way*, not the least strenuously by those who, without argument, condemn it the most.

The antiquated notions of mortification and suffering for suffering's sake, and of merit in self-denial without a purpose, are now pretty generally exploded; and those gloomy and degrading prejudices, which, in the darker times of human intellect, were esteemed serious points of religion and articles of faith, retain but a slender hold upon the minds of men. The reign of spiritual terror, and ascendency of the "horrible imaginings" of fanatic men, who could allow themselves to suppose, that the Almighty Creator of this fair world cast an envious regard upon the happiness of his creatures, is now swiftly verging to its close; and the days, it is to be hoped, are well nigh past, when it could be believed, that delicate fare, and sumptuous apparel, or, as John Knox termed it, "gay gear," were insurmountable barriers in the path which leads to heaven.

"Refinement is better than ignorance. It is "better to be a man than a brute. Those attri-"butes, therefore, which separate the man from "the brute, are most worthy of our affection and "cultivation. Elegance of taste, refinement of "sentiment, depth of penetration and largeness "of science, are among the noblest ornaments of

"man. But all these are the growth of lux-
"ury *."

Whether it be wise to encourage in any that delicate care of themselves or others, which allows them "to be reared as that precious thing that no wind "may blow, and no sun may scorch †," I shall not take upon me to decide. Much, of course, ought to depend on the circumstances of fortune of the individual; the frailness or stability of the system of society under which he lives, does also undoubtedly demand consideration. Under wise and virtuous government, the utmost conceivable degree of luxury might be safely indulged and enjoyed by those who could afford it.

The habitude of luxury in the fair sex, and the highest degree of cultivation and refinement in all matters of elegance, politeness, and taste, cannot well, in them at least, be the object of disapprobation. "A cultivated taste," according to Mr Hume, "improves our sensibility for all the ten-
"der and agreeable passions; at the same time
"that it renders the mind incapable of the
"rougher and more boisterous emotions.

"Ingenuas didicisse fideliter artes,
"Emollit mores, nec sinit esse feros ‡."

---

* Inquiry concerning Political Justice, by William Godwin, book 8. chap. 7. p. 483, 484. 2d Edition. Mr Godwin, although he puts this doctrine into the mouth of his opponents, does not dispute with them its truth.

† Inquirer, Part I. Essay 15. ‡ Essays, Part I. Essay 1.

Luxury and refinement, then, in females, and cultivation and accomplishment in all elegant arts, while it improves their qualities both of body and mind, and diminishes in a degree their prolific powers, increases their susceptibility, and enlarges their capacities of receiving and communicating happiness; and that which takes away from the robustness of their corporeal frame, and which tempers and attenuates their physical powers, carries all their other qualities to a higher pitch of excellence, and produces, perhaps, and constitutes, the true perfection of the female character.

I do not pretend, and it is not my purpose here to interpose any decision of my own, between the simple enjoyments of uninstructed and unsophisticated nature, and those so much more eagerly coveted of luxury and refinement. Perhaps for a short season in the spring and virginity of our days, and at that period of life, and of our ripening years, when " a new existence seems " to descend upon us, and to double all that was " before *," when " the man descends upon the " child, till his whole bosom swells with the gene- " rous freight †,"—the former may be preferable, and more to be prized, than all the pleasures and refinements which luxury has to boast. But this question I wish to leave as I found it; and per-

* Inquirer, Part I. Essay 14.

† Ibid. Part I. Essay 15.

haps it is one which no man can, or ever will be able to decide, even though he had passed through and experienced the extremes of both those states of existence;—so difficult is it, and perhaps impossible, to compare and balance two perfectly different states of feeling. All I mean in this place is, to vindicate the innocence of refined and artificial enjoyments, and to prove that they are not "vice and misery." This will not, probably, be thought by many a very hard task to perform, and perhaps I may appear to have laboured the point too much. I shall only, therefore, add a passage from Hume, who, in his own inimitable manner, and in short space, says all that appears necessary to settle the question.

"Luxury is a word of an uncertain significa-"tion, and may be taken in a good as well as in a "bad sense. In general, it means great refinement "in the gratification of the senses; and any degree "of it may be innocent or blameable, according to "the age, or country, or condition of the person. "The bounds between the virtue and the vice, "cannot here be exactly fixed, more than in other "moral subjects. To imagine that the gratifying "of any sense, or the indulging of any delicacy in "meat, drink, or apparel, is of itself a vice, can "never enter a head that is not disordered by the "frenzies of enthusiasm. I have, indeed, heard of "a monk abroad, who, because the windows of his "cell opened upon a noble prospect, made a *cove-*"*nant with his eyes* never to turn that way, or "receive so sensual a gratification. And such is "the crime of drinking Champagne or Burgundy, "preferable to small beer or porter. These indul-"gences are only vices, when they are pursued at "the expence of some virtue, as liberality or cha-"rity; in like manner as they are follies, when "for them a man ruins his fortune, and reduces "himself to want and beggary. Where they en-"trench upon no virtue, but leave ample subject "whence to provide for friends, family, and every "proper object of generosity and compassion, they "are entirely innocent, and have in every age "been acknowledged such by almost all moralists. "To be entirely occupied with the luxury of the "table, for instance, without any relish for the "pleasures of ambition, study, or conversation, is "a mark of stupidity, and is incompatible with "any vigour of temper or genius. To confine "one's expence entirely to such a gratification, "without regard to friends or family, is an indi-"cation of a heart destitute of humanity or bene-"volence. But if a man reserve time sufficient "for all laudable pursuits, and money sufficient "for all generous purposes, he is free from every "shadow of blame or reproach *."

It will be apparent, that this principle of luxury and refinement, under the best practicable systems of government, may be carried much farther

* Essays, Part II. Essay 2. Of Refinement in the Arts.

than it has been heretofore. This will arise from the great accumulation of wealth, the farther improvement of art, and the application of capital to the work of production, to a much greater extent than has yet been done, or can possibly be, except under a steady and long continued system of justice and liberty.

Under such a system, property being protected as completely as possible, and that not only from private rapine, or individual injustice and injury, but also from too unsparing a seizure of it on the part of government itself, greater powers of accumulation would remain to the individual, as well as greater encouragement to exertion and industry. And where the utmost freedom was allowed in the application of capital, it would increase to a prodigious extent, and, together with industry, (which would be so encouraged, and so wholly redound to the advantage of the industrious), would naturally and necessarily, in process of time, take the best direction; and the powers of production assuming their most effective form, would carry the wealth of the country, and every sort of improvement in all the arts and accommodations of life, to a height "of which we can at present scarcely "form a conception."

The towns would be greatly increased both in size and number, and yet most probably rendered more healthy, from improvements in their construction, which the high state of art, and intelligence, and freedom, would naturally give rise to.

In the country, on the other hand, the number of inhabitants would not by any means be increased in an equal proportion with those in the towns. Under such a prosperous state of affairs, large capitals would exist, invested in every department of industry, art, and manufacture, and large capitals would be laid out on land, and applied to agriculture; estates and farms would be large. The greatest improvements in the modes of cultivation, particularly as respects the abridgement and economical use of labour, can only be practised in farms of considerable extent; and as the price of labour would necessarily be high under a long continued and steady system of liberty and justice, from its effect of elevating the popular character, we may be certain that it would be economized as much as possible, and that husbandry would not be managed with the spade, but the plough. It will follow, that the population of the country would be exceedingly moderate, when compared with the vast extent, and number, and populousness of the towns; and luxury and refinement prevailing in a great degree in the towns, and even to a considerable extent in the country, the aggregate prolific power of the females would necessarily be diminished in a very great degree. If, then, we duly consider the state of high cultivation and improvement that would now be attained,—the number and magnitude of the towns, and the moderate population of the country,—the large influx of new people which the towns would constantly require, in addition to their own increase, and the comparatively small supplies which could be afforded by the country, it will perhaps appear, that under such circumstances, this principle alone might be sufficient to equalize the powers of population, and the powers of production of food; and that, to keep up the great and united population of town and country, would require the full exertion of the whole power of increase which would then exist.

But besides this principle of luxury and refinement which Mr Malthus has so completely overlooked, and independent of it altogether, there yet remains behind another still more important, the principle of voluntary and prudential restraint, which of itself is always sufficient, under good government, to prevent any undue increase of numbers, even in countries the farthest removed from their full complement of wealth and populousness.

This principle is acknowledged by Mr Malthus to be the most powerful and efficient of all the prevailing causes, or "preventive checks," which repress the redundant power of increase under the best governments, and "which, in modern Europe, keep down the population to the level of "the means of subsistence *."

* Essay on Population, vol. ii. p. 218.

But Mr Malthus always touches this topic slightly and very cautiously. The instances are innumerable, wherein he admits, in the most unqualified terms, the effect of good government, and of education, its necessary attendant, in elevating the popular character and circumstances, and of bad government in degrading and depressing them, but he never entertains the question, or pursues it to its consequences.

This he takes care assiduously to avoid, and it is wonderful with what address he flies from the subject, and endeavours never to suffer the attention of his reader to rest upon it, or the very idea to remain one moment under discussion. He never treats this question distinctly in the whole course of his voluminous work, though it be the most important of all that is connected with his subject; and he is continually maintaining doctrines, and forming conclusions, which are utterly at variance with his concessions respecting it. This point will not be forgotten in our more detailed examination of Mr Malthus's book, which the reader can hardly open without observing the proofs of this ingenuity of Mr Malthus.

How, and in what manner, good government gives rise to the prevalence of voluntary restraint, so far as the exercise of that virtue is required by the circumstances of every individual, will be fully explained in the following work, and will be shewn to proceed from the encouragement and energy which it gives to the primary principle of all political and social improvement,—the desire inherent in all mankind of bettering their condition,—a principle which gives rise to every prudential habit, but which can only exist, and be effectual for its purpose, under a steady system of law and government; and it is only when that system is the best, and liberty and justice are entirely predominant, that the principle of voluntary and prudential restraint can acquire its full vigour, and be more than sufficient for all its purposes.

If, then, there be any soundness or truth in what I have now advanced, what becomes of the "propositions" of Mr Malthus, "intended to "be proved?" Immediately they vanish into thin air.

When this subject, then, of population, is fully understood and explained, it will appear, that when a single country or the world at large is completely or highly cultivated, and the powers of industry, of wealth, and of population, have attained, under a steady, liberal, and just system of law and administration of government, to nearly their natural limits, and when the powers of the earth to afford additional subsistence shall be materially exhausted, luxury and refinement will have arrived at their greatest height, and exert their most powerful influence in diminishing the prolific powers of mankind; and that, from this cause alone, it is probable the powers of population will be decreased in a "ratio" nowise inferior, or different, to that of the powers of the earth to yield food.

Little will then remain to be done by the principle of voluntary and prudential restraint, and no more, it is probable, than what may be necessary for the improvement of human character and happiness; for I agree with Mr Malthus, that *some* restraint has a utility, and is probably necessary to the full improvement and perfection of individual character as well as of society, though I cannot go the length with him of supposing, that " the passion between the sexes has often the " greatest influence in the formation and improve- " ment of character, where it is the least grati- " fied *" But it will be apparent, that, under the circumstances which would now exist, and at the period of society to which we are here brought, all might marry at no very advanced period of life.

It will happen also at this time, that the principle of voluntary and prudential restraint will be very powerful, and exist in its greatest strength and vigour; and the only danger and probability seems to be, that, under the steady system of justice here supposed, the force of this principle would bring population to a stand † too soon, and before the cultivation of the earth were pushed far enough.

---

* Essay on Population, vol. iii. p. 75. 76.

† See Note B. at the end.

Mr Malthus argues as if the powers of population were equally powerful and vigorous in every state and period of society, and always equally disproportioned to the powers of production of food. No doctrine can be more wide of the truth. "Population," he says, "could it be supplied "with food, would go on with unexhausted vi-"gour," and "a thousand millions are just as "easily doubled, by the power of population, as "a thousand;" as if the prolific powers of mankind, or of females, were equally vigorous and robust in the most wealthy and populous countries, where luxury prevails, and those the poorest and most thinly peopled, excepting always in so far as they differ in quantity of "vice and mi-"sery."

If this were the case, and the powers of increase in the human species remained as great when the earth was fully peopled and "cultivated "like a garden," and when it could no more yield additional food, as they are in thinly peopled countries, where the means of subsistence may be increased as fast as people can arise to till the ground, it would certainly be exceedingly unlike that admirable adaptation of the general laws of nature to their purposes, which we always observe in the order and economy of the universe *.

It will be the object of the following work to

---

* See Note C. at the end.

shew at large,—that this is not the case,—that "a thousand millions are [not] as easily doubled, "by the power of population, as a thousand,"—and "that population, [although] it could be sup-"plied with food, would [not] go on with unex-"hausted vigour."

All this, I believe, my readers begin to suspect already, but it shall be my object to shew it at large, and still more plainly. If I succeed in my purpose, it will then perhaps appear on what foundation Mr Malthus ascribes "evil" to "the "principle of population," and arraigns (though he disclaims the imputation, and the inevitable effect of the inferences he draws, and the conclusions he arrives at) the order of nature, and the justice of its Author.

NOTES.

Note A.—*See page 12.*

Although Mr Malthus *equivocates* between the assertion of "twenty-five years," and that of "an arithmetical ratio," the position, as stated in the text, is precisely what he maintains. This is plainly his ground through the whole of his reasoning, and it is indeed necessary to support his conclusions throughout. That he does equivocate on this point, will be evident to every one who will examine carefully his first chapter, and the following extract will shew the use he makes of convertible terms.

"If this supposition be applied to the whole earth, and if "it be allowed that the subsistence for man which the earth "affords, might be increased every *twenty-five years*, by a "quantity equal to what it at present produces, this will be "supposing a rate of increase much greater than we can ima-"gine that any possible exertions of mankind could make it.

"It may be fairly pronounced, therefore, that, considering "the present average state of the earth, the means of subsis-"tence, under circumstances the most favourable to human "industry, could not possibly be made to increase faster than "*in an arithmetical ratio.*"—Vol. I. p. 13, 14.

It is here to be observed, with what dexterity the term "twenty-five years," in the first paragraph, is all at once changed into "arithmetical ratio," in the second. The assertion would have been too bold, even for Mr Malthus, had he retained his first term. Yet it is undeniable he maintains the doctrine, that the subsistence which the earth affords could not be doubled in less than twenty-five years, even at the outset, or in the first period of his assumptive progressions, and "twenty-five years," and "arithmetical ratio," are with him convertible terms throughout his book. It is in this manner that Mr Malthus uses his terms, and substitutes one for another, as it suits his purpose, and is necessary to his argument, and it is thus that he lays down his theory. In the first chapter, where this occurs, he introduces the frightful word "exterminate," several times, (vol. I. p. 10, 11.) without the least necessity; and with much art and labour, and with one or two evident truths in his statement, he contrives to involve in obscurity a multitude of errors, and to give an air of demonstration to his doctrines, which, when thoroughly examined, will be found to be utterly fallacious, —to have no solid foundation in themselves,—and to be altogether deceitful with regard to the inferences and conclusions endeavoured to be rested upon them.

Note B.—*See page 35.*

It may perhaps occur to the reader as an objection, that population sometimes increases too fast, and becomes redundant, under the best governments at present subsisting; but this will always be found to proceed from certain false steps they have taken, or unsteady measures they have pursued, giving a stimulus and temporary briskness to trade, and of course improving for a time the condition and prospects of the labourer, who is not called upon or expected to fathom the depths of political science, and to know which appearance and improvement of his condition is specious and alluring merely, and which is steady and secure. Any undue and remarkable increase or redundance of population, never proceeds from an alteration or unsteadiness in the principles of human nature, or of common prudence, which influence in general the conduct of mankind, and which always improve, rather than fall back, under good and steady government. "Though the "principles of common prudence do not always govern the "conduct of every individual, they always influence that of "the majority of every class or order *."

Mr Malthus allows, that, "from a combination of external "and internal causes, a very great stimulus" was given to population in this country, "for ten or twelve years together †." Now, I wish to ask Mr Malthus what those "external and internal causes" were, and why he does not state them? I wish to ask Mr Malthus, if a lavish expenditure of the public money, and the sustentation and support of that expenditure, by an unjust system of favour and protection to the Bank of England, and of excitement to the country, by an extension of paper credit, and unlimited issue of inconvertible notes, was not one and the chief of those causes? And I wish to ask, If this, and other causes which I could mention, were likely to have occurred, with an incorrupt House of Commons to controul the executive?—Let Mr Malthus answer these questions.

Mr Godwin states it as a discouragement which he felt in proceeding with his work in answer to Malthus, that Mr Brougham had conceded, in his place in Parliament, that "an "excess of population was one of the great causes of the distress which at present afflicted the country." In considering this as any discouragement, I think that Mr Godwin has mistaken the true point of controversy, which is not whether an excess of population can by possibility be made to exist, but whether it can arise without false measures on the part of government, giving a counterfeit briskness to trade at one time, which brings round an extreme depression at another;

---

* Smith. † Essay on Population, vol. II. p. 304. 305.

and, at the distance of a few years, converts the situation of the lower classes from one of hope and encouragement, into one of misery and despair. I perfectly agree in the statement of Mr Brougham, so far as it goes; but the question recurs, —*What caused the excess?* Was it a deficiency or falling off of prudence and foresight on the part of the people? or was it their being betrayed by the circumstances and appearances which surrounded them? Was it, in short, the fault of the government or the people?—Let Mr Malthus, if he pleases, answer this question too.

Mr Brougham never said that this excess was the fault of the people, or that the weavers of Manchester and Glasgow were to blame for marrying twenty years ago, or from 1798 to 1808, when they were making twenty and thirty shillings a-week, and prospects were flattering. Nor did he say that in those periods, when an unsound system of paper credit gave a dangerous and unstable excitement to trade, the manufacturer and the labourer ought to have known, that their present prosperous state was but a forced shoot, which must wither whenever the artificial heat was withdrawn from it, and convert their happy situation, and fair prospects, into poverty, despondence, and gloom. No: Mr Brougham never maintained any thing like this; yet this is what Mr Malthus must maintain, in order to fasten the imputation of "evil" on "the "principle of population."

But Mr Godwin may perhaps say, that any increase of people which can take place at present in any country of the world, can only be excessive in reference to the political situation of that country, or to that developement of its resources, which the laws and institutions of such country allows. But it must be recollected, that the habits and pursuits of the people, which are suited to those laws and institutions, cannot all at once be changed, and that no sudden measure could correct the evil, when once it takes place.

In reference to those circumstances, population may be excessive, although it be not so to the possible or conceivable resources of the country. The expression, therefore, and statement of Mr Brougham, appears to me to be perfectly correct.

Note C.—*See page 36.*

It often happens, we observe, in the general laws of nature, that, unlike those which man can establish, they accommodate themselves in a wonderful and apparently miraculous manner to the *particular circumstance*, as well as to the *general state*, of their objects;—that is to say, they embrace the *exception*, at the same time that they are suitable to the *rule*. This is remarkably the case with regard to the freezing of water, which gradually increases in density, till it comes near the point of congelation, when it suddenly enlarges its volume, and of course diminishes its specific gravity, before it turns into ice, and floats upon the surface. Were it not for this truly wonderful circumstance, water would have frozen first at the bottom, and the fishes could not have lived.

If the doctrine which I have attempted to establish in this short Essay, be founded in truth, the great law of the multiplication of mankind, will be found an instance no less remarkable of the bending of the general law to the particular circumstance, and of its admirable adaptation to the varying state of its object. For, when the world is thinly inhabited, the power of multiplication is exceedingly great, so that the earth might be peopled by it in a very short space; and the power of increase continues undiminished, till a country (or the world) be stocked with inhabitants, when immediately it begins to be less powerful, and without any care of man, or any effect to his disadvantage, accommodates itself to his altered circumstances, and to the precise degree of force and intensity to which it is necessary and useful that it should be reduced.

What, then, are we to say to those wonderful dispensations and decrees of infinite power, wisdom, and goodness, but that the more we are enabled to scrutinize the ways, and comprehend the "handy-work" of the Almighty, the more we observe that HE never slumbers, and is never imperfect in his works. We see that ignorant and presumptuous man often thinks he knows *the whole,* when he sees but a *part,* while the Author of providence remembers, and cares for the humblest of his creatures, and prepares for their well-being, in a manner which the noblest of them on earth must behold with humble astonishment, and with commingled sentiments of adoration and gratitude.

FINIS.